Gurus, Hired Guns,
and Warm Bodies

Gurus, Hired Guns, and Warm Bodies

ITINERANT EXPERTS IN A KNOWLEDGE ECONOMY

*Stephen R. Barley and
Gideon Kunda*

PRINCETON UNIVERSITY PRESS

PRINCETON AND OXFORD

Second printing, and first paperback printing, 2006
Paperback ISBN-13: 978-0-691-12795-8
Paperback ISBN-10: 0-691-12795-6

*The Library of Congress has cataloged the cloth edition
of this book as follows*

Barley, Stephen R.
Gurus, hired guns, and warm bodies : itinerant experts in a knowledge
economy / Stephen R. Barley and Gideon Kunda.
p.   cm.
Includes bibliographical references and index.
ISBN 0-691-11943-0 (cl : alk. paper)
1. Information services industry—Employees—United States—Case studies.
2. Information technology—Employees—United States—Case studies.
3. Electronic data processing consultants—United States—Case studies.
4. Independent contractors—United States—Case studies.
5. Self-employed—United States—Case studies. 6. Temporary
employees—United States—Case studies. 7. Part-time employment—
United States—Case studies. I. Kunda, Gideon, 1952– II. Title.

HD8039.I372U63 2004
331.2—dc22   2003068993

British Library Cataloging-in-Publication Data is available

This book has been composed in Sabon

Printed on acid-free paper. ∞

pup.princeton.edu

Printed in the United States of America

3 5 7 9 10 8 6 4 2

CONTENTS

PART III: *Life on the Job*

PART IV: *Living the Cycle*

PREFACE

AS ETHNOGRAPHERS, our agenda is to depict the world of technical contracting from the perspective of those who live it. We are also obligated by the ethics of our craft to shield the people who have so generously opened their worlds to us from unwanted intrusions. For this reason, we have used pseudonyms for the organizations we studied and for the individuals whom we observed and interviewed. This precludes us from publicly thanking the people who took us into their world, gave of their time, and shared their perspectives and knowledge with us. But those whose lives are depicted on the pages of this book know who they are, and to them we are deeply indebted. We hope they find we did justice to the complexity of their world and that we contributed in a small way to making it more manageable.

There are others without whose assistance and forbearance the book would not have been possible. Peter Yessne, chairman of Staffing Industry Analysts, Inc., kindly took the time, early and late in our study, to orient us to the staffing industry. His insights into the industry's structure and practices were invaluable. Our colleagues Galit Ailon, Diane Bailey, Yinon Cohen, Noah Lewin-Epstein, Bob Sutton, and Ely Weitz offered valuable comments on various versions of this book.

Over the course of the two years that we were in the field, a number of graduate students assisted in collecting data. James Evans and Siobhan O'Mahony worked with us over the entire period, doing numerous interviews and field observations and contributing their insights and interpretations. In the process, both became accomplished ethnographers. Fabrizio Ferraro and Ozgecan Kocak did fieldwork at Systems Professionals. Mark Mortenson, Jeff Martin, Joan Ubeda, Greta Hsu, and Filippe Santos interviewed contractors as part of a class on ethnographic field methods taught in Stanford's School of Engineering. Laura Casteneda worked with us for a summer helping interview contractors. We thank them all.

The Stanford University/General Motors Collaborative Work Systems Laboratory and the Department of Labor Studies at Tel Aviv University provided partial support for the preparation of the manuscript. The Network Society Project, under the direction of Rolf Wolff at Gothenburg University and Ingalill Holmberg at the Stockholm School of Economics, funded some of the travel necessary for our collaboration, and its participants offered support and helpful comments along the way.

We dedicate the book to our wives and lifelong partners, Debbi Barley and Lezli Rubin-Kunda, who give a sense of permanence in a world of temporary affiliations and contingent commitments.

Chapter 1

UNLIKELY REBELS

Clothed in a light blue T-shirt and chinos, Kent Cox revealed nothing to suggest that he was in the vanguard of an employment revolt that was spreading quietly across America's industrial landscape.[1] Kent had no obvious tattoos or piercings. He carried no union card. He was not out to change the world. His passions were for code, ballroom dancing, and science fiction, not for politics—especially not for politics of the organizational sort. His short, dusty blond hair was only slightly rumpled, and his wire-rims suggested nothing more than intelligence. Had you seen him that day sitting across from us in a Chinese restaurant in downtown Mountain View in the heart of Silicon Valley, you might not have given him a second glance, so well did he blend in with the other techies who frequent the establishment in search of noonday egg rolls and sweet-and-sour soup. If you had noticed a difference between Kent and the rest, it would have been in the minutiae: he entered the restaurant alone, not as a member of a pack, and his T-shirt bore no company logo.

On the other hand, if you were a programmer who had been in the Silicon Valley long enough, you might have recognized Kent, at least by name, as a guru of sorts. Firms on the cutting edge of high technology eagerly sought Kent's expertise as a software developer. At thirty-six, he had already worked for a "who's who" of companies, some of which are household names across America; others are famous only among the technogensia. Kent's six-figure income was testimony to his talent. Yet, by some people's measure, he had not been gainfully employed in nearly a decade, if being gainfully employed means being permanently employed. Since 1989 Kent had worked only as an independent contractor, a "hired gun" as they are sometimes called, moving from firm to firm every six to eight months in search of another challenge.

---

[1] Because a number of people appear repeatedly over the course of our narrative, we provide a "Cast of Characters" in the appendix, to which readers may turn if they need a reminder of the individual's affiliation, role, occupation, and involvement with contracting. In this way we avoid the awkwardness of introducing our informants more than once in the course of our telling.

At sixteen, when most of his peers were still entranced by the dancing phosphorescence of Space Invaders, Kent began programming. He enrolled in Cal Poly a year later, where he majored in computer science. Hearing no scholarly calling, Kent took several years off to write code. "I was an indifferent student," he admitted. "I was only motivated to program." After eventually graduating in the mid-1980s, he programmed for his father's start-up for several years, and in 1989 he went to work as a full-time developer for Sun Microsystems. After a year of eighty-hour weeks, Kent "burned out," left Sun, and took an eight-month vacation to, as he put it, "put my head back together." He realized he didn't want another full-time job. Indeed, he was ambivalent about work in general. But in 1990 a friend convinced him to join a software project as a contractor. From then on Kent was never permanently employed, yet he had worked continuously on a stream of projects that ranged from building device drivers for printers and digital cameras to developing applications for the Web. He attributed his success not only to his skills but also to his reputation in the technical community. "My career," he explained, "has been not so much getting hired to do the same thing, but getting hired by people I know who can't find someone they need to fill a particular niche, so they hire someone they think can learn to do it."

Like many experienced contractors, Kent found work through colleagues, friends, and acquaintances. "When you want to get work," he explained, "the key is to make sure everybody you know knows you're looking. Just call all of your friends and say, 'Hey, I'm looking and one of 'em will say, 'Oh we need somebody to do IO [input-output].' NEC came through somebody I danced with.[2] Her husband was doing contracting for them. You get contracts anywhere. Anyone you know is a potential contract. One of my friends gets a lot of his jobs through church." Kent was currently charging $90 an hour for his services and working thirty hours a week. He could have worked more, but he preferred to use the rest of his time to surf, read, and write his own software.

At the time we met Kent, he had just run up against one of the catch-22s of being a hired gun. He had contracted to provide guidance to a project team supposedly composed of "crack engineers." But, he explained, "I have not meshed well with this team. Most of them are on their first or second project. I'm more like on my twenty-fifth, and that gives you a very different perspective. I did some egregious political blundering in the beginning when I pointed out things that were going to be problems in three months. They did become problems, but I was asking for trouble because they couldn't see what was coming. I've gotten back into everybody's good graces, but it's been a strain. This is the first time

---

[2] NEC was a company for whom Kent had contracted.

I've really had this problem because I'd been working for a long time with people who have a similar level of experience as me."

Kent's only regret about having worked so long as a contractor was the proverbial Silicon Valley story of opportunity lost: "One of the hardest things is watching people regularly get rich. I turned down a job at Netscape because I wanted to contract.[3] I mean, I turned down a job offer from Netscape the month before they went public! I decided not to apply when they moved to Mountain View even though I was doing Web development at the time. That's the one that hurts. Of course, I had no idea at the time that Netscape was going to do that. I keep reminding myself of that when I start feeling really stupid."

Earlier in the year, Kent had founded the first Java users' group in the Valley, which he described as a platform for advancing as a contractor. "I've decided that I should probably think about moving to the next level," he confided, "where people are hiring you as a name rather than just hiring you as a warm body or a coder. Stenogram has the guy that wrote the book on Microsoft mail's API [application program interface] on retainer. We tried to get the guy that wrote the book on programming for Microsoft on retainer as well. That sort of public recognition was one of the reasons I started the users' group and that also means that people contact me. Java people send me mail. Microsoft invites me up to Redmond to look at things. I just figured it was a way of putting myself in the way of job opportunities." In fact, we were introduced to Kent precisely because our contacts told us that he was central in the emerging network of Java programmers.

If Kent Cox was an unlikely foot soldier in an employment revolt, Yolanda Turner, a well-dressed, fifty-two-year-old African-American woman with three grown children and an infectious laugh, was even less likely. Yolanda had lived her entire life in and around Los Angeles. In 1982, at the age of thirty-six, Yolanda decided to pursue a bachelor's degree in film at Pomona College after raising her children as a single mother. Four years later, she graduated and worked a number of temporary clerical jobs before landing a full-time job, first at UCLA and then at Rockdyne, as an administrative assistant. Had Yolanda's story ended here, she might have served as a classic example of how difficult it is for older African-American women to rise above socioeconomic and racial barriers, even with a degree from a prestigious college. But Yolanda's supervisor at Rockdyne noticed her interest in PCs and paid for her to take courses in hardware and software. Before long, she became an in-house expert who informally assisted and coached her coworkers when their

[3] From today's perspective, Kent's decision not to go to work for Netscape does not appear as bad as it did at the time.

computers went out of whack. Gradually, Yolanda began to spend most of her time fixing workstations and tweaking software, even though she was still employed as a secretary. Six years later in 1995, and still employed as an administrative assistant, Yolanda submitted her résumé to an online job board and landed a contract as a workstation technician at an IBM subsidiary. Since then Yolanda had worked exclusively as a contractor, moving over time from workstation maintenance to systems administration and then on to quality assurance and testing.

Unlike Kent Cox, who relied on his extensive network, Yolanda secured her positions solely through staffing agencies that served as brokers between her and the clients who bought her services. These agencies had sprung up in the 1980s and 1990s to take advantage of firms' lack of information about contractors and contractors' lack of information about job openings. Most, but not all, modeled themselves after temporary help agencies. In return for locating positions, deducting payroll taxes, and occasionally offering access to health insurance, agencies added a markup of approximately 30 percent to 40 percent to Yolanda's hourly pay of $35 per hour. Yolanda didn't much like the markup, which she considered excessive, but she accepted it as the way the game was played. When we met Yolanda in 1998, she was working forty- to fifty-hour weeks for an annual income of about $87,000. Being a morning person, Yolanda typically arrived at work at 6:00 A.M. and left at 2:30 in the afternoon. Often, she worked part of Saturday or Sunday as well. Yolanda's contracts typically lasted between three and six months, and since 1995 her total "downtime"—the time in between contracts—amounted to less than two weeks. When asked why she had forsaken permanent employment, Yolanda left no doubt about her motives: "Significantly more pay! Significantly more independence! And, you don't get immersed in the political environment that goes on in companies. I like the independence. I like being able to move around and see how different companies do things. In most cases you make a significantly higher salary than you do as a full-timer." Yolanda estimated that she typically made $10 to $15 more an hour than permanent employees doing the same work. When she first started contracting, however, this was not the case: "I used to do work on the side fixing people's computers and I was charging $15 an hour and I thought, 'I'm doing pretty good.' Then, I met a girl who was charging $65 an hour and I said, 'Wait a minute. What's wrong with this picture?' So, I started charging more and getting it. To make it as a contractor," she advised, "you need to know what the market is and what your skills are worth." Yolanda did this, in part, by talking with other contractors and, in part, by subscribing to *Contract Professional*, a monthly magazine targeted at contractors.

Yolanda had mastered the art of staying current. At the time we spoke with her, she was learning SAP with the goal of becoming an SAP consultant within three years.[4] She had chosen SAP because "it's very lucrative, and that's what I'm focusing on: money." In addition to buying and reading technical books and surfing the Web for more up-to-date information, Yolanda maintained her own home computer lab. "I have a full system at home. I've got two computer systems and two different types of modems. I've got a scanner and two printers and a little digital camera. So, I have all the equipment I need to learn something, if I need to know it." Yolanda chose her contracts for their learning potential. "I don't have a lot of time to read," she reported, "so while I'm working on this product—and it's a product that's in SAP—I'm learning as I go along. I'm pretty familiar with about three of the modules right now. And in some cases," she added, laughing, "more familiar than some of the people who are the SAP consultants there."

At first glance Julian Stoke could not have been more different from Yolanda Turner. Julian was a corpulent white man with thinning hair and horn-rims. To call him disheveled would have been an understatement. He wore wrinkled chinos, running shoes, and a short-sleeved plaid shirt whose tails had sneaked out on both sides of his pants, revealing twin triangles of pale white skin. A devout Mormon, Julian was the father of seven children ranging from seven to twenty-four years of age. Although Julian was part of the same movement in which Kent and Yolanda had enlisted, his story was different.

After graduating from Brigham Young University in 1974 with a self-designed bachelor's degree in computational linguistics, Julian moved with his wife and first child to the Silicon Valley to be near his parents. Within a year he was working full-time for The Gap, where he climbed the ladder over the next five years from programmer to third-level technical manager. He was working fifty- to sixty-hour weeks and like Kent Cox finally reached the point where he burned out. But rather than take time off, Julian wended his way through three more permanent positions in rapid succession until he finally landed at Citicorp in 1981 as a systems programmer. Before his probationary period ended, however, he was fired.

"They quit me!" Julian explained as if still reeling from incredulity twenty years later. "The irony was that the manager of the group was a contractor. He came to me one day and said, 'You don't fit in with our

---

[4] SAP is the most widely used inter-enterprise software program developed and marketed by the German firm of the same name. Inter-enterprise software is a class of programs that integrate data across a variety of application areas including finance, human resources, customer relationships, supply chain management, forecasting, and so on. It is a kind of one-stop software platform for firms.

group.' I said, 'Right, I agree with you. You are not the same kind of people that I am.' He said, 'We will have to let you go.' I said, 'Well, have I done something wrong? You don't like my work?' and he said, 'No, you just don't fit in.' "

After looking for work unsuccessfully for "quite a while," Julian cast his lot in with a friend, an independent contractor with whom he had worked at The Gap. Like Yolanda and Kent, Julian found the lure of money and autonomy hard to resist. "I am not ordinarily a 'live-on-the-edge' sort of guy, but I was really intrigued by several aspects of contracting: the money, the mobility, and the professionalism." For most of the 1980s, Julian sold his services as a VM system programmer to an array of clients in the Bay Area through his friend's business.[5] But in 1988 the business collapsed and his friend absconded with three thousand of Julian's dollars. Julian then took his first contract through a broker and had since worked exclusively through staffing agencies. "Once burned, twice shy," he explained.

Over the years, Julian had become savvy about dealing with agencies. "Every broker tells you, 'You have a career with us, and when we are done with this assignment, we'll find you another. You're a valued member of our team.' But what it really comes down to is that if they have no openings, there is no commitment to you." To cope with uncertainty and the lack of commitment, and to increase his chances of finding work when he needed it, Julian had learned to work with many agencies simultaneously. Although he did not like it, he accepted their markup—usually around 40 percent, he told us—as an unavoidable fact of the contracting life. Several years earlier, Julian had gone through a trying period without health insurance. At one point he was even forced to fall back on the charity of the Mormon Church to help cover steep medical bills incurred after his son was injured in a road accident. Julian subsequently took a permanent job for a year, largely to qualify for the HMO, which he was able to retain at his own expense once he returned to contracting.

Unlike Kent and Yolanda, Julian's career as a "warm body" had been rocky. Since 1988, he had moved between contracting and permanent employment on four occasions. Although he had seen little downtime, he had been fired on three occasions, once from two separate contracts simultaneously. When we met Julian, he was making $55 an hour, working over sixty hours a week (not including the time he spent keeping his skills up-to-date), and having difficulty making ends meet. He blamed his financial difficulties on old debts, on a wife who was unable to work, and on being "bad with money," especially credit cards. Julian had not taken

[5] VM (virtual machine) is an operating system for IBM mainframes.

a vacation in years. With such wages, "It's a huge temptation to work every hour of the day," he admitted.

Julian, like Kent, was involved in a professional community. But whereas Kent's was formally organized, Julian's existed loosely on the Web. "Do you know about the IRC?" Julian asked in response to our question about professional relationships. "That's one of the major types of chat rooms, where you get online to talk and make friends. I have one group of professional people I get on with every once in a while. That is one of the tools of problem solving. When you can't find the answer to a technical problem in the manuals, the next best thing is use a bulletin board. I subscribe to about ten of them. I go on and put out my question, 'Why is this happening? How do I get around this?' I get answers all the time. Chat has changed the face of contracting in recent years, because when people in a company have problems they ask the contractor, whom they see as a guru, their mentor."

Although Julian's wife had misgivings about contracting and periodically urged him to "get a real job," Julian was reluctant to do so. His last few contracts had gone well, and he had doubts about his ability to hold down a permanent job. The opportunities to learn new technologies were plentiful. And, like Kent, Julian saw himself as an expert, a systems programmer who saved his clients from themselves. "We contractors have a superiority, a superciliousness," he confided. "We sometimes get the impression that we are doing the real work, that we are going the distance. These other guys go home at five and we stay until eight. But we always know that there will come a day when we sign our project over to somebody and it is no longer our problem. It's theirs."

Despite their many differences, Julian, Yolanda, and Kent had one thing in common: all had made a conscious decision to step outside the mainstream of employment. They had questioned and then jettisoned, at least for the time being, the vision to which their parents and society had taught them to aspire: the safe haven of a permanent job. Like most of us, they had been told that with a college education they could get a "good job," a code word for going to work full-time for a reputable employer. In the absence of a major recession and in return for loyalty and hard work, employers would reward them with a good salary, health insurance, promotions, and perhaps most important, reasonable expectations for long-term security. In the end, they'd retire at sixty-five with a pension, a gold watch, and some savings.

At least initially, like most Americans their age, all three had reason to believe in the bargain. They were, after all, technical professionals whom employers historically valued more highly than most other kinds of employees. But for reasons ranging from being laid off to longing for a less hectic lifestyle, each had decided to bet on his or her skills and forgo full-time work, even though all believed they could have secured a permanent job had they so desired. Each knowingly entered a world of work that demanded they change employers two to three times a year and adopt a notion of security based on their continued ability to market their expertise to a portfolio of buyers. In short, they had left behind the familiarity of traditional employment for the uncertainty of a more fluid labor market. None seemed to regret their choice.

Kent, Yolanda, and Julian are what we call technical contractors. They sometimes even called themselves contractors (or consultants), although they usually introduced themselves by their occupation: software developer, technical writer, multimedia developer, systems programmer, and so on. As contractors, they possessed skills and knowledge similar to those of the full-time engineers, software developers, and technical writers with whom they worked. They performed similar tasks and worked in the same firms as the full-timers. Yet, even though they worked at the cutting edge of the postindustrial revolution, the mode of their employment resembled that of craftsmen in the Middle Ages, especially the stonemasons who built the great cathedrals of Europe.[6]

Stonemasonry was, and still is, the queen of the crafts. Although we don't think of stonemasons as high-tech workers, in medieval Europe they were. Shaping artful and well-engineered Gothic cathedrals from hand-hewn stone was a significant technical achievement requiring expertise that took years to master. For this reason, stonemasons were in short supply and great demand. Building a cathedral was an expensive, multiyear project commissioned by the clergy and royalty of a city. Since most medieval cities were small, they needed and could only afford one cathedral. Accordingly, masons could expect to be gainfully employed in one place for no more than a few years. Because of this constraint, stonemasons worked as itinerant craftsmen, traveling from city to city throughout Europe, joining projects and leaving cathedrals in their wake. Like these artisans of old, technical contractors also ply their trade as "itinerant experts." Some, known in contracting circles as "nomads" or "road warriors," even move from city to city in search of projects, just as stonemasons did five centuries ago. Firms substitute for cities and projects for cathedrals.

In late 1997 when we set out to study technical contracting, we didn't think of ourselves as entering a world of itinerant experts. We certainly didn't think of contractors as social pioneers. Our goal was simply to understand how employment relations were changing at the dawn of the

---

[6] Knoop and Jones (1967), Gimpel (1980), and Applebaum (1992) describe the work of medieval stonemasons and the organization of cathedral building in medieval Europe.

twenty-first century. We hoped to document the social dynamics of skilled "contingent labor," a term economists and sociologists now use for an array of short-term arrangements including part-time work, temporary employment, self-employment, contracting, outsourcing, and home-based work. To be honest, if anything, we saw contingent work, in general, and possibly even contracting, as social problems indicative of corporate America's willingness to abdicate its responsibility to employees in return for greater profits. Contingent employment seemed to bear a troubling resemblance to the laissez-faire capitalism of the late nineteenth century, which, in the name of individualism and the free market, spawned a plethora of exploitative practices.[7] In our concern we were hardly alone.

THE UNRAVELING OF PERMANENT EMPLOYMENT

The foundations of the American system of employment were laid after the Great Depression. The system was conceptualized under the New Deal and then institutionalized in labor law and collective bargaining. Permanent employment was the system's cornerstone. It hinged, in large measure, on a bargain struck between employers and employees. According to this bargain, as generations of workers grew to understand it, employers would fulfill legally and culturally prescribed obligations to employees. These included offering reasonable expectations for job security and benefits, such as health insurance and pension plans. In return, employees were expected to offer their loyalty and their best efforts.

By the end of the 1990s, many Americans feared that this bargain and the job security it brought were unraveling before their eyes.[8] A number of interrelated developments contributed to the apprehension. The first, and most troubling, was "downsizing," a bit of forked-tongue corporate-speak that came to replace the older and less Orwellian vocabulary of "layoffs." Until the mid-1980s, everyone thought they understood layoffs. Layoffs were the bad luck that happened to blue-collar and clerical workers

---

[7] Laissez-faire capitalism refers to the doctrine that economic systems function best when they are free of governmental interference. Having first been articulated by French scholars, John Stuart Mill, Adam Smith, and Jeremy Bentham took the doctrine of laissez-faire as the central tenet of classical economics and fused it with a doctrine of radical individualism. In the early twentieth century, laissez-faire practices were associated with the rise of monopolies and cycles of boom and bust. Laissez-faire principles still underwrite conservative economic doctrine in the United States and Great Britain. For a superb discussion of laissez-faire capitalism in the United States and Great Britain, see Bendix (1956).

[8] Peter Cappelli, Paul Osterman, and Thomas Kochan have written extensively about the unraveling of the New Deal and its institutions (Kochan, Katz, and McKersie 1986; Cappelli et al. 1997; Cappelli 1999; Osterman 1996, 1999; Osterman et al. 2001).

whenever the economy headed south or a firm experienced financial trouble for other reasons. But no matter how bad things got for men and women with blue, pink, or no collars, most white-collared professionals and managers could assume that their jobs were relatively safe, even in hard times. It was partially for this reason that the Ozzie and Harriet generation of American parents exhorted their children to get a "good education."

During the 1980s, the rules of the game seemed to change. For the first time in history, firms began to shed professional, technical, and managerial workers in large numbers. In fact, by the mid-1990s corporate downsizings were more likely to target managers and professionals than they were blue- and lower, white-collar workers.[9] Even more perplexing to Middle America was that downsizings, unlike layoffs of the past, seemed independent of economic cycles. The top management of some firms publicly admitted to resorting to downsizing as a way of boosting their firms' stock price.[10] By the late 1990s, the consequences of the new rules of employment finally showed up in aggregate labor statistics: job tenure among white males had begun to fall for the first time since World War II.[11] Furthermore, despite a vibrant economy, people's levels of trust in their employers sank as feelings of insecurity rose.[12] Even managers and professionals who had not yet been hit by downsizing were apprehensive.[13] The business press and career coun-

---

[9] Moore (1996), the American Management Association (1996), the *New York Times* (1996), and Farber (1997) provide discussions of and data on downsizing in the mid-1990s and its effects on workers. Academic research on downsizing has mushroomed over the last decade. Rousseau's work (Rousseau 1995; Rousseau and Anton 1991) is particularly enlightening with respect to employees' perceptions and expectations.

[10] The most vocal and notorious champion of downsizing was Jack Welsh, the CEO of General Electric. He was known among employees at GE as "Neutron Jack": like the neutron bomb, Welch eliminated people and left the buildings intact.

[11] Until recently most economists found little evidence of a general decline in job security when measured as average job tenure (Diebold, Neumark, and Polsky 1997), but this may simply have reflected the fact that analyzable data lagged reality. In 1998, new data compiled by the Bureau of Labor Statistics (BLS) indicated for the first time that job tenure had declined among American men for all but the youngest and oldest age cohorts (Bureau of Labor Statistics 1998).

[12] For data on increasing feelings of insecurity and distrust of management during the 1990s despite stable levels of job satisfaction, see table 2.3 of the National Research Council's (1999) *The Changing Nature of Work*.

[13] Katherine Newman (1989) and Charles Heckscher (1995) insightfully document the stigma and fear felt by managerial and professional workers who were downsized in the 1980s and 1990s. Comparing the lot of blue-collar workers who had been laid off by the Singer company with the experiences of downsized managers led Newman to the conclusion that white-collar workers are more likely to experience depression, alcohol abuse and other personal problems. She argues that managers fare worse because their friends and family see being laid off as a personal failure. The friends and family of blue-collar workers understand that being downsized is simply something that firms do to people for economic gain.

selors began advising managers to treat security as an outdated pipe dream and to focus, instead, on "employability"—the attitudes, behaviors, experiences, and skills that would help them land the next job.[14] The message was clear: in the future, a lot fewer people were going to be earning gold watches. Loyalty was passé and self-reliance was in vogue.

As if downsizing was not enough of a change, during the 1980s employers increasingly began moving jobs offshore to countries where labor was cheaper. In the name of economic agility, firms also began to outsource goods and services that they formerly provided for themselves. The logic of outsourcing dictated that it was often cheaper to buy goods and services from suppliers than it was to provide them internally. Finally, and for our purposes most important, employers began to make greater use of contingent workers—individuals hired, often through staffing agencies, for a limited period of time to perform a specific job. Although firms had long employed temporary workers for seasonal and short-term needs (for example, to staff retail stores at Christmas or to stand in for absent full-timers), during the late 1980s corporations began to view temporary labor as an extension of the broader strategy of outsourcing. Outsourcing labor made it easier for firms to shift their employment mix because contracted services were easier to terminate on short notice. Moreover, hiring contingent workers relieved managers of some of their more difficult tasks, such as worrying about thorny "people issues" or catering to the motivations and feelings of employees. Business strategists, such as Charles Handy, argued that flexibility was key to survival in a global economy. One way to enhance flexibility was to surround the firm's core employees with a buffer of contingent workers who could be hired and fired at will.[15] Business leaders were apparently convinced. How they went about accomplishing this vision, depended, to a great extent, on the laws that governed and regulated employment. The fact that Yolanda and Julian, like most technical contractors, found their jobs through staffing agencies was one upshot of the legal wrangling that ensued.

---

[14] For a sense of the rhetoric of employability, see Bridges (1994), Carlin (1997), and Caulkin (1997).

[15] Handy's (1989) book, *The Age of Unreason,* was a best-seller. The academic literature indicates that firms frequently hire contractors for the reasons Handy promoted. For empirical evidence on firms' motives for hiring contractors, see Mangum, Mayall, and Nelson (1985), Abraham (1988), Pfeffer and Baron (1988), Hakim (1990), Davis-Blake and Uzzi (1993), Abraham and Taylor (1996), Matusik and Hill (1998), and Kalleberg and Reynolds (1998).

The Legal Context of Contingent Work

American tax and employment law has long rested on two assumptions. The first is that people are either self-employed and, hence, work for themselves, or else they are employed by the organization for which they perform tasks. The second assumption is that people traditionally have one employer at a time, and even when they have more than one employer, as in the case of moonlighters, their relationship with each revolves around a separate and distinct task.[16] Lawmakers have drawn on these notions to assign tax liabilities and responsibilities, to distribute and enforce workplace rights, and to secure the American system of social welfare.

U.S. law requires that employers pay employment taxes on every employee and that they also withhold the workers' employment taxes from the workers' paychecks. In short, employers serve as the government's tax collectors. Employment taxes include federal, state, and local income taxes, social security contributions, and federal unemployment tax. Under the Fair Labor Standards Act, employers must pay their workers at least the minimum wage and meet overtime obligations. Title VII of the Civil Rights Act forbids employers from discriminating against employees on the basis of race, gender, or creed. The Age Discrimination in Employment Act adds age to the list of forbidden discriminations, while the Americans with Disabilities Act extends protection to otherwise qualified employees with physical disabilities. The Family and Medical Leave Act guarantees people that they will have time for handling family and medical emergencies by requiring employers to grant employees up to twelve weeks of unpaid leave per year when such events occur. The Employment Retirement Security Act sets parameters for employee pension plans, including how much service is needed before an employee is vested. Finally, the National Labor Relations Act grants employees the right to organize and governs aspects of labor-management relations.

In short, employers have significant obligations to and for their employees under U.S. law. But employers incur none of these obligations when they use the services of an independent contractor. Independent contractors are considered self-employed persons, even if they are not incorporated as a business. Therefore, employers who wanted to outsource labor originally had significant incentives to make use of independent

---

[16] Our discussion in this section draws heavily on Muhl's (2002) useful paper, "What Is an Employee?" Other useful sources on contracting's legal environment include Jenero and Spognardi (1995), Everett, Spindle, and Turman (1995), Fox (1997), Carnevale, Jennings, and Eisenmann (1998), and Zeigler (2001).

contractors, because doing so absolved them from a series of costs and obligations. From the perspective of the federal government, however, any shift from traditional employment to the use of independent contractors represented a potential loss of taxes. It also undermined the law's primary mechanism for redressing discrimination and ensuring the welfare of the labor force.[17] For this reason, the law allows the government, especially the Internal Revenue Service (IRS), to prosecute and seek damages from employers who try to avoid their legal duties. The law also allows workers to seek compensation and additional damages when they believe that a firm has classed them as an independent con tractor to avoid paying appropriate wages and benefits.

During the 1980s, employing technical contractors became popular as firms discovered that they could reduce labor costs by substituting independent contractors for employees. In some cases, firms actually dismissed former employees and then rehired them as independent contractors. In other instances, firms hired people who were clearly independent contractors, but then treated them as permanent employees. For instance, firms might deny contractors' rights to the intellectual property they created (which is illegal) or demand that they work exclusively for the firm as a condition of employment. Microsoft became legendary for employing "permatemps," although substituting independent contractors for employees was widespread among high-technology firms.

Prior to 1990, Microsoft routinely hired a large number of independent contractors, many of whom were former employees. Microsoft required the freelancers to sign agreements stating that they were independent contractors, not employees, and that nothing about the agreement could be construed as implying an employee-employer relationship. Despite the agreement, Microsoft made no distinction between contractors and full-time employees, except that the former were hired for specific projects. Contractors worked the same hours as full-timers at the same locations and were supervised by the same managers in the same way. Yet, Microsoft did not pay the contractors' employment taxes and refused to allow the contractors to participate in the company's pension and stock plans.

Concerned that firms like Microsoft were using independent contractors as a way to avoid taxes, in 1987 the IRS announced a new test by which it would decide whether a worker qualified as an independent contractor.[18] The test, based on a common-law definition of employment,

---

[17] Because independent contractors are required to pay both the employer's and the employee's portion of all employment taxes, replacing an employee with an independent contractor should not reduce the government's total tax income. However, it is more difficult to monitor the compliance of independent contractors than it is to monitor employers.

[18] Revenue Ruling [87-41, 1987-1 CB 296].

rapidly became known in contracting circles as the IRS's "twenty-question rule."[19] Table 1.1 displays the twenty questions and the responses that the IRS expected of an independent contractor.[20] Although the IRS held that the answer to no single question was sufficient to grant or deny the status of independent contractor, long-term contractors like Julian Stoke agreed that after 1987, it became increasingly risky to proclaim oneself an independent without being incorporated.

In 1989, the IRS used the twenty-question rule to go after Microsoft. In a highly publicized ruling, the IRS found that Microsoft had illegally misclassified workers as independent contractors to avoid payroll taxes. Microsoft accepted the IRS's ruling, paid a stiff penalty, and subsequently converted some of its contractors to employees while dismissing many others. Feeling cheated, those whom Microsoft dismissed filed a class action suit (*Vizcaino v. Microsoft*) claiming that they were entitled to participate in Microsoft's pension and stock plans because Microsoft had treated them as employees, not as contractors. The case moved quickly from state to federal court, where Microsoft initially won the case, but the plaintiffs appealed. In 1995, the U.S. Court of Appeals for the Ninth Circuit reversed the lower court's decision, finding in favor of the plaintiffs. The court held that because Microsoft had treated the contractors as employees, they were entitled to pension funds and stock options. Microsoft managed to delay final settlement until 1999, when the Ninth Circuit Court brought the case to a close by ordering Microsoft to distribute nearly $9.7 million among eight thousand to twelve thousand people.[21]

The IRS's decision to prosecute Microsoft and the Ninth Circuit Court's ruling sent a shock wave throughout the high-technology industry. Firms suddenly became wary of hiring independent contractors. To avoid the possibility of finding themselves in conflict with the IRS or in violation of employment law, lawyers advised firms to insist that even incorporated contractors work through staffing agencies, which would serve as the contractors' "employer-of-record." The changes in how firms approached contracting benefited the staffing industry, which grew in leaps and bounds along with the demand for contractors.

---

[19] A common-law definition of employee pivots on the notion of agency, "which, in an employment context, consists of a relationship wherein one person (the employee) acts for or represents another (the employer) by the employer's authority" (Muhl 2002, 5).

[20] It is important to understand that circumstances dictate whether any question is applicable. The IRS treats no question as sufficient for identifying an independent contractor. Nor does the IRS demand that an individual be able to answer all questions in the expected way before granting the status of an independent contractor. Instead, the IRS uses the twenty questions as a general guideline for classifying the facts of a case.

[21] The text of the Ninth Circuit Court's final ruling can be found at www.techlawjournal. com/courts/vizcaino/19990512.htm.

TABLE 1.1
The IRS's "Twenty Questions" for Distinguishing between Employees and
Independent Contractors

Question	Response Indicating an Independent Contractor
Must the worker follow the company's instructions about when, where, and how to work?	No
Does the company provide the worker with training?	No
Are the worker's services integral to the business?	No
Can the worker subcontract the work to someone else?	Yes
Does the company hire, supervise, and pay the worker's assistants?	No
Is the worker employed for an extended, continuous period?	No
Does the company set the worker's hours?	No
Must the worker work full-time for the company?	No
Does the worker perform his or her services on the company's premises?	No
Must the worker perform services in an order or sequence set by the company?	No
Must the worker submit oral or written reports to the company as part of his or her evaluation?	No
Is the worker paid by the hour, week, or month?	No
Does the company pay the worker's business or traveling expenses?	No
Does the company furnish significant tools, materials, and equipment?	No
Does the company have the right to fire the worker?	No
Can the worker quit without incurring a liability to the company?	No
Does the worker have a significant investment in tools or facilities?	Yes
Can the worker realize a profit or loss as a result of his or her services?	Yes
Does the worker provide substantial services to multiple companies at one time?	Yes
Does the worker regularly advertise or make his or her services available to the general public?	Yes

ESTIMATING THE SIZE OF THE CONTINGENT WORKFORCE

By 1997, when we began our study, contractors like Kent, Yolanda, and Julian made up a significant proportion of the technical workforce. The exact percentage, however, was hard to establish because data were scarce. Then, as now, most analysts lumped technical contractors together with other contingent workers, and estimates of the contingent labor force varied widely. The most liberal suggested that up to 30 percent of Americans were contingently employed.[22] The Bureau of Labor Statistics (BLS) offered a potentially more reliable and certainly more conservative estimate. According to their calculations, the percentage of Americans who worked contingently between 1995 and 1999 stood at 13.3 percent.[23]

But even the BLS tabulated data in ways that made it difficult to estimate the number of technical contractors. Technical contractors were spread over several of the BLS's categories of contingent workers. People like Kent Cox, who worked for themselves and who might or might not be incorporated, were counted as "independent contractors." Yolanda Turner and Julian Stoke, who found work through staffing agencies, would have appeared as "employees of temporary service firms." Still other contractors, who were assigned to clients by consulting and outsourcing firms, would have been labeled "workers provided by contract firms." To muddy the waters even further, incorporated contractors who

---

[22] To arrive at such a high percentage, analysts count part-time work and all self-employed people as contingent workers, an assumption that seems difficult to justify (Dillon 1987; Belous 1989; Kalleberg et al. 1997). Most part-time workers, for example, are permanently employed; they simply work less than forty hours a week.

[23] See Polivka (1996a, 1996b) and Cohany (1996). Under its least restricted definition, the BLS defined the contingent workforce as the sum of (a) all wage and salary workers who "do not expect their employment to last," except for those who planned to leave their jobs for personal reasons; (b) all "self employed (both the incorporated and the unincorporated) and independent contractors who expect to be and had been in their present assignment for less than 1 year"; and (c) temporary help and contract workers who "expected to work for the customers to whom they were assigned for one year or less" (Cohany et al. 1998, 43–44). The BLS repeated its assessment of the contingent workforce in the February 1997 and February 1999 supplements to the Current Population Survey. The number of workers in the BLS's broadest definition of contingent labor declined by 0.5 percent between 1995 and 1997 and then stayed the same between 1997 and 1999. The percentage of Americans in each of the four alternative employment relations (independent contracting, on-call workers, temporary help agency workers, and workers provided by contract firms) largely remained constant except for a slight fall of 0.4 percent in independent contractors (Hipple 2001). Since three data points do not make a trend, it is difficult to determine whether the decline represents random variation or an actual shift away from contingent labor. The BLS's data also cannot tell us whether contingent labor increased prior to 1995, even though most commentators contend that it did.

identified themselves as self-employed individuals escaped being categorized as contingent workers entirely. Nevertheless, the BLS data provide a sense of technical contracting's scope.

In 1997, roughly 20 percent of all independent contractors were professional or technical workers, the two occupational categories into which most technical contractors fell.[24] Professional and technical occupations accounted for 12 percent of all temporary help placements and 27 percent of the workers provided by contract firms. In fact, 23 percent of all contingent workers held professional and technical occupations in 1997. Drawing on the 1995 BLS data, Roberta Spalter-Roth and her colleagues estimated that 13.5 percent of all professionals in the United States either worked through staffing agencies, were independent contractors, or were self-employed.[25] Depending on whom one believes, in the late 1990s contractors may have accounted for 15 to 30 percent of the technical workforce in the Silicon Valley.[26] Technical contractors were also common in other cities. In fact, they comprised the majority of some occupations—for instance, multimedia designers in New York City.[27]

Although most commentators believed that contingent work and technical contracting had grown exponentially during the 1980s and 1990s, lack of data also hampered estimates of growth. Before 1995 even the Bureau of Labor Statistics did not collect information on the size of the contingent workforce. In the absence of data on trends in contingent employment, most analysts used data on the growth of the temporary service industry as a proxy for the spread of contingent employment. These data show two indisputable trends. First, the temporary service industry has grown spectacularly over the last two decades. Between 1986 and 1996, employment in temporary services grew 10.3 percent, while total employment grew only 1.7 percent.[28] Second, the distribution of contingent work changed. Between 1991 and 1996, the percentage of the temporary service industry's payroll represented by office, clerical, and medical work fell, while the industrial, technical, and professional segments expanded.[29] Clinton reported that between 1983 and 1995, the percentage of programmers who found work through the business services industry grew from 24 percent to 40 percent.[30] The percentage of

---

[24] Cohany (1998).

[25] Spalter-Roth et al. (1997).

[26] Benner (1996).

[27] Batt et al. (2001).

[28] U.S. Department of Commerce (1997).

[29] Staffing Industry Report (1997).

[30] See Clinton (1997). The business services industry is broader than the temporary services industry. It includes not only the temporary services industry but also firms that specialize in providing outsourced services.

similarly employed computer engineers, computer scientists, and systems analysts increased from 18 percent to 29 percent.

Thus, three conclusions seem reasonable on the basis of available data. By the end of the century, a significant proportion of Americans were contingently employed, the proportion had increased during the 1980s and 1990s, and technical professionals comprised a larger portion of the contingent labor force than in the past. The trend seemed clear. Like Kent, Yolanda, and Julian, more and more technical professionals were leaving the ranks of the permanently employed to work as itinerant experts. The question was how to make sense of the trend. There were two ready-made alternatives.

MAKING SENSE OF CONTINGENT WORK

In the early 1990s, contingent work began to attract the attention of sociologists, labor economists, and journalists. Most commentators focused on the reasons firms employed contingent workers and on the costs and benefits of doing so.[31] Analysts who took the workers' perspective were fewer in number and fell into two opposing camps: the "institutionalists" and the advocates of "free agency."

The Institutional Perspective

The institutionalists were economists or sociologists who interpreted contingent work through a historical and social lens.[32] They told a cautionary tale. From an institutional perspective, contingent work's expansion threatened the security of the workforce and the American system of social welfare, which was based on full-time employment. The institutionalists framed the threat from the perspective of dual labor market

---

[31] We shall address why firms employ contractors in chapter 2. The research literature on firms' strategic reasons for employing contractors includes Abraham (1988), Abraham and Taylor (1996), Davis-Blake and Uzzi (1993), Harrison and Kelley (1993), Kalleberg and Schmidt (1996), Matusik and Hill (1998), Nollen and Axel (1998), Pfeffer and Baron (1988), and Rubin (1996).

[32] "Institutional" and "institutionalist" are words with rich and thick meaning in the social sciences. We use the term "institutionalist" to refer to analysts who view markets as "socially embedded" and who ask how institutions shape labor markets. By "institutions" they typically mean not only laws and established organizations but also cultural norms and practices. Economists who study how social structures affect markets have historically been called "institutional economists." Osterman (1988), Parker (1994), Barker and Christiansen (1998), Cappelli et al. (1997), Carre and Joshi (1997), Kalleberg et al. (1997), and Smith (1998) are institutionalists who have written about contingent labor.

theory, the notion that industrial economies are composed of two sectors: "primary" and "secondary."[33]

Primary labor markets provide stable employment, career ladders, job security, high wages, and attractive benefit plans. Secondary labor markets are, by comparison, less stable and offer lower wages. Classic examples of secondary labor markets include farm labor, food service, and hospitality work. Research has shown that participants in secondary markets are more likely to be members of minority groups and to work for employers who provide meager benefits. Because scholars saw secondary markets as peripheral, they had historically treated them as a social problem to be addressed using existing institutions (for example, minimum wage laws), rather than as a fundamental threat to the system of employment.

Institutionalists warned that the growth of contingent work represented the spread of secondary labor into the economy's core. Many feared that this development would undermine the well-being of American workers and their families.[34] Others warned that contingent work's spread would increase demand for government assistance in a downturn and facilitate the oppression of minorities. Indeed, demographic studies consistently showed that most contingent workers made less money than full-time employees in the same occupation, that they were less likely to have access to health insurance and pension plans, and that in comparison to the full-time workers, women, African-Americans, and Hispanics comprised a larger percentage of the contingent work force.[35] Finally, some critics charged that the shift to contingent labor signaled an attempt to undermine unions.[36] In short, institutionalists saw the spread of contingent labor as an unraveling of the New Deal, and they urged policy makers to bolster existing institutions or search for new ones that would enhance security.

Anthropologists and sociologists who had done ethnographies of contingent work generally confirmed the institutionalists' fears.[37] Their

---

[33] For extended discussions of dual labor market theory, see Berger and Piore (1980), Piore and Sable (1984), Osterman (1984), and Baron and Bielby (1984).

[34] For discussions of the negative social consequences of an expanding contingent workforce, see Dillon (1987), Osterman (1988), Martella (1991), Cohen and Haberfeld (1993), Hipple and Stewart (1996), Polivka (1996b), Christensen (1998), Barker (1998), Spalter-Roth and Hartmann (1998), Banigin (1998), and Houseman and Polivka (1999).

[35] See Spalter-Roth et al. (1997), Kalleberg et al. (1997), and Kalleberg, Reskin, and Hudson (2000) for demographic data on the contingent workforce.

[36] Aronowitz and DeFazio (1994) and Rifkin (1995) level charges of union busting.

[37] An ethnography is a study of a group of people in which the data are collected by some combination of participant observation and interviews. The ethnographer's objective is usually to describe and depict the "native's point of view," the perspective of the people studied. Parker (1994), McAllister (1998), Rogers (1995, 2000), Henson (1996), and Smith (1998) have written important ethnographies of contingent work in clerical and industrial settings.

studies depicted the difficulties that clerical and light industrial "temps" encountered in a world geared to full-time employment. Informants in these studies reported being forced into temporary employment by downsizing and other circumstances that made it difficult to find full-time jobs.[38] Most complained of poor working conditions, low wages, and high work-related expenses. They spoke of disputes with clients and agencies over payment and hours, antagonism with permanent employees, continual insecurity and uncertainty, and a sense of exclusion, estrangement, and dissatisfaction with work.

The ethnographies reported few compensating advantages. Some temps claimed to enjoy the flexibility of scheduling their own work and the freedom to reject particularly unpleasant jobs. Others said they preferred to receive their compensation as "fast cash" rather than wait for a monthly paycheck. Still others reported obtaining satisfaction from knowing that their services were "really needed" by companies in crisis. But, in general, the ethnographic evidence indicated that at least among low-skilled workers, the disadvantages of "temping" outweighed its advantages.[39] It is significant that the institutionalists built their interpretation of contingent work without examining highly skilled workers.[40] In sharp contrast, commentators who wrote for the popular press largely built their interpretations by ignoring the low end. Unsurprisingly, they painted a considerably different picture of contracting.

The Free Agent Perspective

At the height of dot-com mania, "new economy" magazines like *Fast Company* and *Wired* began to lionize highly skilled contractors as "free agents," the heroes and heroines of postindustrialism. Most of free agency's advocates were (and continue to be) futurists, human resource consultants, and staffing industry experts who wrote for the general public.[41] The "free agenteers" agreed with the institutionalists on one point:

---

[38] Jurik (1998) is a notable exception in that only 20 percent of her self-employed home workers felt forced into their home businesses. Nevertheless, Jurik fixes on the perceptions of those 20 percent in assessing how home workers feel about their work arrangements.

[39] For exceptions, see Barker and Christensen (1998), Jurik (1998), Smith (2001), and Rogers (2000).

[40] Some institutionalists have suggested that the situation may be different for highly skilled contractors, but their data do not allow much exploration. This is largely because economists and industrial relations researchers have relied on aggregate data and random samples that are heavily weighted toward the responses of traditional temporary employees.

[41] Free agency's spokespersons include Bridges (1994, 1995), Pink (1998, 2001), Beck (1992), Caulkin (1997), Darby (1997), Reinhold (2001), and McGovern and Russell (2001). Although Bridges was the first to market with the idea, Pink coined the name and gained notoriety. Pink runs a Web page called "Free Agent Nation" (http://www.freeagent nation.com).

employment security and its supporting institutions were unraveling and their demise represented a breach of faith. Corporations had reneged on their part of a culturally well-understood bargain. But, unlike the institutionalists, free agency's spokespersons sang contracting's praises while advocating a kind of libertarian, anticorporate rebellion.

Authors of this ilk portrayed corporate life as stifling and petty. The corporate world, they claimed, forced people to play "politics" and subject themselves to the whims of incompetent managers for inadequate pay. Besides, they added, "jobs" and "careers" were outmoded inventions of the industrial revolution, designed for the benefit of employers. Daniel Pink, a former speechwriter for Secretary of Labor Robert Reich and the best-known advocate of free agency, wrote:

> The old social contract didn't have a clause for introspection. It was much simpler than that. You gave loyalty. You got security. But now that the old contract has been repealed, people are examining both its basic terms and its implicit conditions. Free agents quickly realized that in the traditional world, they were silently accepting an architecture of work customs and social mores that should have crumbled long ago under the weight of its own absurdity. From infighting and office politics to bosses pitting employees against one another to colleagues who don't pull their weight, most workplaces are in dysfunction. Most people do want to work; they don't want to put up with brain-dead distractions.[42]

Sometimes bordering on demagoguery, free agency's antiorganizational rhetoric reframed employment history. Firms had not simply broken the contract; the contract was terrible in the first place because it lulled employees into dependency. Traditional employment and the careers it offered were relics of corporate "paternalism" that encouraged employees to play the role of children and firms, the role of parent. Simon Caulkin, a journalist writing for the *San Francisco Examiner*, explained:

> At the bottom, the trade of loyalty for security was unsustainable and exploitative. By tying their career and skills to one employer, employees sacrificed mobility and market value in return for a promise that couldn't be kept. By contrast, in the emerging new deal, the very mobility of career-independent employees provides a powerful incentive to companies to keep their promises—the most important of which . . . is to provide interesting, motivating work. Otherwise, those valuable staff members will leave. So the death of the security-loyalty contract has made room for a more durable and

---

[42] Pink (1998, 132).

satisfying employment relationship—this time based on independence rather than the employer paternalism of the past.[43]

Faced with the demise of traditional employment and the potential for
firms to renege on their part of the bargain, advocates of free agency recommended that people turn the tables on companies by refusing to give
loyalty and by embracing the shift to a skills-for-hire economy. The trick,
they proposed, was to use the demise of traditional employment as an
opportunity to set oneself free. They encouraged people to view themselves as free agents, to develop and market their own skills to the highest bidder, and to view themselves as a business, even when in a full-time
job. Free agenteers, in short, promoted a postindustrial vision of economic individualism in which entrepreneurial workers would regain independence and recapture a portion of their surplus value.

To support their claims, free agenteers offered readers stories of contractors who vacationed when and where they chose, who telecommuted
to work from exotic places, and who successfully integrated the demands
of work and family. Although the heroes and heroines of these tales were
usually professional and technical workers, proponents contended that
all people could benefit by adopting a similar attitude to work. The central icon of the movement was the hero of the movie *Jerry Maguire*, who
rejected a world of greed and unethical behavior for independence,
wealth, and self-respect. Caught up in the revolutionary spirit, Pink and
Warsaw even penned what they called a "Free Agent Declaration of Independence."[44]

The vehicle of the free agent's independence was the market. In *Job
Shift*, William Bridges promised, "In a market . . . people don't have
bosses. . . . There are no orders, no translation of signals from on high,
no one sorting out the work into parcels. In a market one has customers,
and the relationship between a supplier and a customer is fundamentally
non-organizational. . . . One's boss is really a major customer rather than
an authority in the old sense."[45] Of course, the irony that Bridges and
others had trouble seeing was that freeing oneself from the chains of traditional employment meant catering to the same employers against
whom one was rebelling.

Despite such inconsistencies, the advocates of free agency sketched an

---

[43] Caulkin (1997, 2).

[44] The "truths" that Pink and Warsaw (1997) claim to be "self-evident" are: "Who we
are and what we do should not stand on opposite sides of a psychological divide. . . . Nothing is permanent. Security is an illusion. . . . The power to choose is the power to say no.
. . . Fear has no place in Free Agent Nation. . . . The fun in work is the reason for work. . . .
We're on our own, but we're not alone."

[45] Bridges (1994, 64–65).

optimistic picture of contingent labor based on a rhetoric of free markets that challenged the institutionalists point by point. Free agenteers argued that contingency was a choice rather than a constraint; that it represented liberation rather than isolation; that it minimized uncertainty about employment while enhancing flexibility and personal control; that contractors made more money than permanent employees because they were paid at rates that reflected the real value of their skills; and that relying on one's skills led to self-actualization rather than estrangement.

Who to Believe?

As sociologists with a background in industrial relations and a taste for left-of-center politics, our initial response was to side with the institutionalists and to treat the rhetoric of market freedom with a healthy dose of disbelief, if not suspicion.[46] But as ethnographers, we believed that data should be allowed to speak for itself. No a priori formulations, no matter how elegant or consistent with their proponents' worldview, should be exempt from the requirement that they rest on solid empirical evidence. For us, evidence meant an empathetic and rich description of the perspectives and practices of the people about whose lives social scientists made claims.[47] From this perspective we found both sides of the debate wanting.

How could anyone tell whether the institutionalists or the free agenteers offered a more viable image of contracting when neither had systematically examined the lives of technical contractors? With the exception of the ethnographers of temporary work and Daniel Pink's book, *Free Agent Nation*, analysts on both sides of the debate had given no voice to contingent workers themselves. Most advocates of free agency based their claims, at best, on well-chosen anecdotes. The institutionalists were much better empiricists, but their data were heavily weighted toward the experiences of low-skilled temps. This bias was especially

---

[46] In fact, we had already written a critical historical analysis of how American managerial rhetorics have repeatedly vacillated since the 1870s between rhetorics of rational and normative control (Barley and Kunda 1992).

[47] The ethnographer's creed is that all interpretations of a social system must rest on "the native point of view," or what anthropologists have called an "emic" perspective. The distinction between *emic* and *etic* is the anthropologist's way of distinguishing concepts used by the people being studied and those used by the people doing the studying. The terms comes from linguistic anthropology. "Etic" is a term derived from the word "phonetic." It contrasts with "emic," which comes from "phonemic." "Phonetics" is the study of the sounds that people can physically produce. "Phonemics" is the study of the sounds that people distinguish as meaningful. Others have used the terms *first–order* and *second–order* or *experience near* and *experience far* to make the same distinction.

troubling because students of work have long known that the worlds of low- and high-skilled occupations substantially differ. Permanent professional, technical, and managerial jobs are usually more secure, more remunerative, more varied, and more involving than clerical and industrial jobs. It stands to reason that low- and high-skilled contingent work should vary in similar ways. By ignoring highly skilled contingent work, institutionalists conflated the effects of contingent employment with correlates of low-skilled work. Conversely, advocates of free agency peddled images of contracting built solely on the experiences of an elite. In the absence of adequate data, the institutionalists' and the free agenteers' claims about the everyday realities of contracting and the theoretical edifices they erected on these claims, rang hollow.

We had substantive concerns as well. These rested on our reading of the existing literature, on our experience as researchers of technical work, and on our anecdotal familiarity with technical contracting. Meeting contractors like Kent, Yolanda, and Julian reinforced our concerns. Three issues, in particular, troubled us.

First the discourse on contracting seemed too rigid, too black and white, to be believable. For institutionalists, contingent work was a clear and unambiguous social problem. Temps and contractors were victims of systemic changes promulgated by exploitative employers acting entirely in their self-interest without regard for the common good in the face of a government that was unable or unwilling to protect them. For the advocates of free agency, contingent employment represented no less than a path for escaping a decaying system that had subjugated the many to the whims of the few. If ethnographers have learned anything about social life it is that reality rarely comes so neatly packaged.

Which camp's box, for instance, could comfortably hold Kent Cox, Yolanda Turner, and Julian Stoke? The institutionalists could easily argue that Julian's experience supported their contentions. He became a contractor after being laid off. He had clearly lived on the edge of financial solvency. He had difficulty making ends meet, he had trouble keeping a job, his wife was anxious about their future, and he vacillated between contracting and permanent employment. Even protecting his family's health had been a serious problem. But, to the institutionalist's consternation, Julian didn't seem to mind his troubles! Worse yet, he considered himself to be a success, at least in his own terms, and he planned to continue contracting.

Kent Cox would give the institutionalists an even bigger headache. Other than missing the opportunity to cash in on the fantasy of becoming rich through stock options, Kent seemed in no way disadvantaged. In fact, by all indications, and certainly in his own view, contracting had been good to him. But it would be Yolanda Turner who most violated the institutionalist's worldview. Here was an African-American woman who, despite her efforts, had been unable to flourish until she took her career, her skills, and her wages into her own hands as a contractor.

On the face of it, Yolanda's and Kent's tales should have brought great cheer to free agency's camp. Either could have easily been a sidebar in one of the slick "new economy" manifestos on free agency. Yet, on closer scrutiny, their stories posed problems. At least in Yolanda's case, free agency's promise of freedom, flexibility, and leisure seemed elusive. In fact, Yolanda worked long and hard, at least as much and maybe more than she had as a full-timer. Her employability depended uncomfortably on staffing agencies, and her potential earnings were hijacked by their markups.

But Julian would have been free agency's real embarrassment. Even *Wired* would have had to struggle to find glamour in an overweight, balding middle-aged man with credit card problems and a penchant for being fired. Moreover, Julian lived hand to mouth and suffered seriously from the lack of health care benefits. From an ethnographer's perspective, a satisfying analysis of contracting has to account for all three stories.

Second, except for the ethnographers of clerical work, most analysts on both sides of the debate spoke as if contingent labor markets were dyadic: composed simply of employing organizations and contingent workers. Although this is sometimes the case when a contractor is incorporated or works as an independent, in most instances, contingent labor markets are triadic. In addition to buyers and sellers there are brokers, the staffing agencies that mediate between the two to arrange and close deals. Contractors, like Yolanda and Julian, regularly rely on staffing agencies to find work. An accurate analysis of contracting must, therefore, take the agency's role into account regardless of whether the goal is to portray the structure of the market or describe contractor's experience more fully. Leaving out such an important group of actors guarantees misrepresentation.

Finally, the debate on contingent work was framed as if it were an argument between proponents of organizations and advocates of free markets. Institutionalists set their vision of employment against the backdrop of an organizational society, its laws, and its regulations. When institutionalists recommended reform, they inevitably turned to legal and bureaucratic remedies for the social costs of unfettered markets. They believed that full permanent employment was the foundation of an equitable system. Conversely, advocates of free agency preferred the market as a model for organizing the world of employment. For them releasing the forces of a free market would remedy the ills of an overly bureaucratic society. While organizations and markets are clearly important for framing an understanding of and prescriptions for the world of employment, they do not exhaust the possibilities. Occupations, which both institutionalists and advocates of free agency ignore, are just as important.

Sociologists of work have repeatedly shown that lawyers, scientists, police, carpenters, machinists, accountants, and members of other skilled occupations construct their identities and organize their practice not only around their employer or the market for their services, but also around their occupational affiliations.[48] Ask a doctor what she does for a living and she'll first tell you her specialty, not that she works for Kaiser Permanente. This was precisely what Kent, Yolanda, and Julian appeared to be saying when they highlighted the importance of their networks and their involvement in professional communities, regardless of whether they found those communities at a users' group, through a professional organization, or in a chat room.

Professionals' closest contacts are usually other practitioners of their craft. Professional associations, occupational unions, and communities of practice provide experts with critical support, knowledge, and information. In fact, the more esoterically skilled the practitioner, the more an occupational community is likely to be important. Since technical contractors were highly skilled, it seemed to us that their occupational affiliations had to be at least as relevant as markets and organizations for understanding contracting and interpreting its significance.

The Study

It was to address our methodological and substantive concerns that we entered the world of contracting in the fall of 1997 and remained there until the fall of 1999. But getting inside was a little more complicated than is usual for ethnography. Doing fieldwork in an organization, a subculture, or a tribe requires entering a single, relatively well-delineated social setting, which, as most ethnographers discover, is difficult enough. Getting inside the market for technical contractors meant understanding the story from three perspectives: the contractor's, the client's, and the staffing agency's. It also meant studying a sprawling, emergent, loosely coupled, and at least partly virtual social system.

---

[48] We offer an extensive argument to support the importance of an occupational perspective in organizational analysis in Barley and Kunda (2001).

Staffing Agencies

We turned first to staffing agencies, in part, because their role in contingent labor markets is poorly documented and, in part, because as brokers they continually peer into the other two worlds. By making friends with agents we hoped to make the contacts necessary for branching out into the other two worlds.

In November 1997 we began six months of participant observation in Progressive Staffing, a medium-sized staffing agency that specialized in placing technical contractors ranging from workstation technicians and technical writers to programmers and hardware engineers. Headquartered in Santa Clara County, Progressive Staffing maintained a number of field offices throughout the Silicon Valley as well as offices in eight other American and European cities. Founded in 1993 by Anne Parish, an energetic entrepreneur whose vision included a commitment to running a humanistic corporation that treated contractors well, Progressive Staffing had gone public shortly before our arrival. During our six months there, we observed close-up for several days each week the tribulations and jubilations of matching contractors to jobs. We observed interviews, eavesdropped on telephone conversations, accompanied managers to client sites, read materials, studied computer screens, attended meetings, took part in training programs, and struggled to remain sober at corporate celebrations.

After completing our work at Progressive Staffing, we began similar three-month stints at two other staffing agencies, chosen because their business models differed significantly from Progressive Staffing's. Information Technology Specialists (ITS) was much smaller than Progressive Staffing and specialized in placing independent IT contractors who were incorporated as businesses. ITS had one office, located in San Mateo County, California. Marc Sunberg, a former systems analyst, had founded the firm in 1980. The firm had evolved through a number of name changes as well as changes in strategic direction. The contractors who worked through Progressive Staffing became Progressive Staffing's employees for the duration of their contract, and that was the modal pattern for most other agencies. But ITS was different. It preferred to have a corporation-to-corporation relationship with its contractors.

Systems Professionals, the third agency, was also smaller than Progressive Staffing and even more specialized than ITS. Systems Professionals concentrated exclusively on providing UNIX and Windows systems administrators to firms in the Silicon Valley. It differed from Progressive Staffing and ITS in that it operated as an outsourcer. All but a handful of

Systems Professionals' contractors were full-time employees who re-mained employees even between contracts. Most were young and fresh out of college where they had been responsible for running computer clusters. Because they were outsourced employees, Systems Professionals' contractors could work for clients for long periods of time and they often did, even though they could request and receive a new assignment when-ever they desired. Technical personnel tended to remain with Systems Professionals for two to three years before leaving for another permanent job. Just before we arrived, Systems Professionals had opened a branch office in New York City.

Contractors

During 1998 and 1999 we interviewed seventy-one contractors about their careers and experiences. Kent, Yolanda, and Julian were among them. Because there were no truly representative lists of technical con-tractors from which to draw a random sample, we identified our inform-ants in three ways.[49] Half (thirty-six) were selected from a list of nearly five hundred contractors who indicated their willingness to take part in our study when registering for a seminar on contracting business issues that was broadcast live over the World Wide Web in December 1997. The seminar was sponsored by Progressive Staffing and was widely advertised throughout the nation in contracting circles via a number of channels in-cluding magazines written for technical contractors. To ensure that our conclusions were not regionally biased, we actively sought to talk to con-tractors from outside the Silicon Valley who had registered for the semi-nar. We also made a particular effort to interview women. These original informants referred us to five other contractors whom they thought we would be interested in interviewing for one reason or another—usually because an informant thought a friend's experience of contracting was different from their own. We met another fourteen contractors while we were doing participant observation in the staffing agencies. The remain-ing sixteen contractors were members of the project teams we encoun-tered when studying client organizations. Although our informants were not representative in a statistical sense, they spanned numerous regions, occupations, and age cohorts as well as both genders. For this reason, we are reasonably confident that our data identify key themes, issues, and dilemmas that are of widespread concern to technical contractors.

[49] As we saw it, our alternatives were to convince a staffing firm to make available the names of the people in their databases, to sample from one of several résumé data banks found on the Internet, or to seek subscription records from magazines targeted at contrac-tors. All of these approaches are biased in different ways and seemed no better or worse than the approach we took.

When possible we met our informants in restaurants, cafés, offices, and even their own homes.[50] When it was impossible to do face-to-face interviews, usually because a contractor lived in another state or because he or she did not wish to meet, we conducted telephone interviews. Our interviews covered the contractors' employment history, the circumstances that led them to become contractors, their rates, their experience with staffing firms, how they found jobs and remained up-to-date, their experiences with clients, the impact of contracting on the rest of their lives, and their perceptions of the costs and benefits of being a contractor. With the exception of two contractors who did not wish to be recorded, we taped and transcribed all interviews. Most of the interviews lasted from one and a half to three hours.

Client Firms

The final phase of our study took us to the clients' world: firms in the Silicon Valley that routinely employed technical contractors. Three of the firms were among the largest and best known in the computer industry. In each of these firms we identified two project teams staffed by a combination of contractors and full-time employees. All of the teams were involved in software development or information technology projects. We interviewed the permanent employees and contractors on each team as well as the managers who ran the projects and who had hired the contractors. In one firm, we interviewed all the way up the hierarchy to the chief information officer (CIO).

Our interviews with permanent employees concentrated on their work, their experience with contractors, and their view of the role that contractors played in their firm. When talking to managers we focused on the firm's policies and procedures for hiring and terminating contractors, the costs and benefits of using contractors, the manager's experiences working with agencies, and the challenges of managing a mixed workforce.

We extended our study of clients by interviewing managers at seven other firms. Two were large firms in the telecommunications industry. The rest were entrepreneurial start-ups that employed no more than one hundred people, including contractors. Because these organizations were smaller, the managers tended to have broader responsibilities than the

[50] Anthropologists use the term "informants" to describe the people whose perspectives they study. They prefer the term because it underscores the idea that the ethnographer's job is to learn to see through the insider's eyes. "Informant" contrasts with the idea of a "subject" or a "respondent," terms that are favored by survey researchers and experimentalists, respectively. We use the term "informant" throughout the book to remind the reader that the people we studied taught us everything we know about contracting.

managers that we interviewed in the project team studies. All but three interviews were conducted face-to-face at the client's site where we could observe working conditions.

Collecting and analyzing these data consumed the better part of four years. By the time we were done, it was clear that the world of technical contracting was more complex than the institutionalists or the advocates of free agency suggested. Both perspectives capture a piece of reality, but neither adequately portrays contracting as those who do it experience it. This limits their ability to offer more comprehensive images of how contracting fits into the larger world of employment. Our goal is to provide a window into the day-to-day realities of contracting as a basis for developing a wider interpretation of contracting's relevance in a knowledge economy.

History, however, does not wait for ethnographers to complete their work. About a year after we left the field, as we were pondering the significance our data, the economic conditions of high-tech employment changed dramatically. The Internet boom and the tight labor market it spawned collapsed, ushering in a recession whose effects are still being felt at the time of our writing. Along with the rest of the economy, the world of contracting shifted as well. In short, our tale portrays contracting at a peak of demand. Whether it speaks only to a specific historical period, and the extent to which it continues to be relevant, ultimately remains to be seen. This, of course, is the fate of all social science. But we believe that the dynamics we discuss over the course of this book lie beyond the short cycles of the economy: they define the essence of contracting as an employment relationship. In the book's epilogue, we discuss what has occurred since the recession began and how it affected our informants' world. The data show that like full-time employees, contractors have suffered, but they have not disappeared. On the contrary, their presence remains a significant feature of contemporary labor markets even in times of recession. Thus, with appropriate modifications for changing levels of demand, our analysis of the dynamics in the labor market of the 1990s still holds.

ORGANIZATION OF THE BOOK

What follows is the story of contracting told from the participants' perspectives, especially the perspectives of contractors themselves. In telling the contractor's story, we shall also have much to say about the agencies that place contractors, the clients for whom contractors work, the networks in which contractors move, and the supports on which contractors rely, ranging from magazines to the Web sites and users' groups that lubricate the systems' operation.

Like all ethnographies, ours rests on the details of what we saw and heard, the patterns we found in our data, and the sense we have made of those patterns. To evaluate our claims, readers also need to have familiarity with the data. Accordingly, we tell our tale from the bottom up. Our telling, therefore, differs from the storyline of most academic and business books, which hammer home their main points in the first chapter, often with rhetorical certainty and the desire to relieve the reader of reading any further. The remaining chapters then unpack the conclusion point by point, providing further justification and sometimes supporting evidence. Rather than starting with conclusions, we shall take you on a guided journey through the world of contracting to give you an appreciation for how contracting appears to those on the ground and in the trenches. By presenting a series of grounded portraits, we help you to assemble your own collage as we go along. By the time we are ready to draw together our interpretations of the social world of contracting, you should be in a position to evaluate the adequacy of both our analysis and our conclusions. For readers eager for the security of maps before entering the terrain, we offer the following overview.

The book unfolds in four parts. Part 1 sets the stage. In it we define key terms, introduce the main characters, and examine their motivations. In chapter 2 we explore why firms hire contractors and how they organize themselves to do so. In chapter 3 we explain why technical professionals become contractors and discuss the various ways contractors organize their practice. In chapter 4 we present a typology of staffing agencies and explain how they operate.

Together, parts 2 and 3 depict a turn in the "contracting cycle," which is composed of a period of searching for a job followed by a limited engagement with a client. Repetitions of the contracting cycle provide the rhythm against which contractors' lives unfold. Part 2 immerses the reader in the market. In chapter 5 we tag along as contractors, clients, and agencies try to find deals. We look over their shoulders as they scour the market for potential deals and disseminate information about their own interests. In chapter 6, we see how deals, once found, are consummated. We examine how clients evaluate candidates, how terms of employment are negotiated, and how contracts are signed. By the end of part 2, the contractors have acquired a contract.

In part 3 we follow the contractors onto the job. Chapter 7 shows how managers and staffing firms attempt to create a system for managing contractors that is consistent with corporate policies designed to minimize legal risks. Chapter 8 points to the inherent tensions between corporate policies and the realities of technical work. Chapter 9 shows how contractors navigate between the respect and the resentment that their role engenders among managers and permanent employees to carve out a coherent identity from their experiences.

Part 4 turns to how contractors adapt their lives to the requirements of the contracting cycle. It focuses on the way they develop, organize, maintain, and use three resources crucial for successfully riding the cycle: time, skills, and social relations. Chapter 10 examines the temporal rhythms of contracting, how contractors treat time as an asset, and how they allocate their time to the various requirements of a contracting life. Chapter 11 explores how contractors think about skills and how they keep themselves up-to-date and marketable. Chapter 12 focuses on how contractors build their social networks and how they use them to repeatedly find work.

The book ends with chapter 13. Here we summarize our sojourn through the world of contracting and draw together what we have learned. We then use our findings, in the manner of ethnographers, to build a theoretical interpretation from the bottom up. Not straying too far from the data, we first develop the claim that contractors pursue a form of professional practice that we call "itinerant professionalism." We discuss the attributes of this form of practice by contrasting it to other forms of professional practice, and explore its significance for contractors, clients, and agencies. Then, in a somewhat riskier fashion, we invite our readers to join us in pushing our conclusions even further by speculating on the significance of itinerant professionalism for a knowledge economy. We explicate and critique the institutionalists' and free agency's views of the economy in light of our data, highlighting the cost of neglecting occupational forms of organizing. This critique leads us to argue that the social organization of work in a knowledge economy is usefully viewed as a matrix, which incorporates not only markets and organizations, but occupations as well. We conclude by speculating briefly on the relevance of this perspective for policy makers and practitioners.

PART I

Setting the Stage

In ACT 2, SCENE 7 of *As You Like It*, Shakespeare observed, "All the world's a stage / And all the men and women merely players." Most sociologists would argue that Shakespeare generally had the right idea, but he took too much poetic license to be sociologically accurate. The world is not one stage, nor is it even one world. Instead, social life is a collection of stages, or social worlds, each with its own cast of characters who repeatedly retell a loose but identifiable story by improvising around a set of motives, props, backdrops and stage directions.[1]

Social life is, therefore, best viewed as a set of interconnected stages. People are the accomplished actors who tread across them, momentarily assuming and discarding the various roles appropriate to each stage— father, mother, shopper, lover, employee, driver, manager, engineer, and so on. To participate in the drama of social life means knowing when, where, and how to play what roles and follow what scripts. A dramaturgical sensitivity instructs us to attend to what is "typical" about the experiences, actions, and perceptions of the "actors" who populate "scenes." To the sociological eye, it is precisely these situated "typicalities" that make a social world unique and distinct.[2]

Contracting is one such world. As ethnographers, our job is to depict the world of contracting, with its roles, plots, and scripts, in a way that makes sense to insiders, while offering outsiders a sufficiently well-drawn map so that they can find their way around, should they care to visit.[3] But delving into the intricacies of the world of contracting requires first setting the scene.

---

[1] Theatrical imagery is so central to the sociological perspective that an entire school of research called its approach "dramaturgical analysis." The empirical agenda of the dramaturgical school was identifying the roles and scripts that defined a social scene. The argument was that if you understood these, you would understand the scene's interaction order. Erving Goffman (1959, 1961, 1967, 1983) was a dramatist extraordinaire. His work influenced an entire generation of sociologically oriented social psychologists. Other useful references are Messinger, Sampson, and Towne (1962) and Wilshire (1982).

[2] Theatrical imagery does not imply that sociologists believe that people have no agency or that they participate in systems (i.e., plays) that preordain their fate. Rather, sociologists are interested in understanding how social structures constrain choice and guide action, and theatrical imagery enables them to uncover and display the regularities, the rhetorics, and the interests that structure a social world and that lend its actors their identity.

[3] It is this concern with the typical, the plotted, or the structured that separates sociologists from psychologists and economists. When psychologists and economists contemplate

As would any good playwright, we begin by introducing the dramatis personae, the three groups of characters whom we will repeatedly encounter on our sojourn through the world of contracting: the clients who use the contractors' services, the agents who place them into jobs, and the contractors themselves. Our main objective in part 1 is to offer you background information on the actors and their roles so that you can focus more knowledgeably on the plots and scripts that unfold in parts 2 and 3.

---

social life, both see a seething ocean of interacting individuals rather than the patterned actions of types of social actors. Psychologists focus on how individuals think, perceive, and feel. For them, social life is an entangled web of personal relationships that reflect the complex interplay of people's emotions, needs, beliefs, and perceptions. Psychologically speaking, social life is a story about love and hate, jealousy and empathy, cooperation and conflict, and so on. Economists subscribe to a much simpler but equally individualistic perspective. They assume from the start that people are generally rational, always self-interested and, hence, motivated to optimize their well-being. The world can, therefore, be treated as a collection of markets that emerge as self-interested individuals who adjust to each other's unique preferences to reach a mutually beneficial equilibrium. Every aspect of social life—whether it is marriage, friendship, work, or war—is about one thing: exchange.

Chapter 2

CLIENTS

ALTHOUGH RESEARCHERS have yet to reliably estimate the number of firms that employ technical contractors, we know that between 70 percent and 80 percent of companies in the United States use some type of contingent labor, including part-time workers.[1] In 1996, the Upjohn Institute estimated that 45 percent of American firms made some use of staffing agencies and that 44 percent employed independent contractors.[2] Using a different data set, Kalleberg and Reynolds (1998) estimated that in the same year, 57 percent of American firms used an "employment intermediary" and that 34 percent hired independent contractors.[3] Most relevant for our purposes, a survey conducted in 2000 by the American Management Association found that 45 percent of U.S. employers used contingent information technology (IT) workers.[4] Thus, even though we lack precise estimates of how many firms currently employ technical contractors, it seems reasonable to assume that a large minority does.

The firms or "clients" that engaged the agencies we observed and that employed the contractors we interviewed were highly diverse. High-technology and engineering firms undoubtedly hired the largest percentage of technical contractors. But firms in other industries also employed technical contractors, especially to maintain computer equipment, develop software, provide IT services, and design Web pages. The contractors we interviewed had worked in a variety of settings. This was especially true for programmers and IT specialists. We encountered contractors who had worked for banks, retailers, shippers, railroads, universities, automobile manufacturers, aerospace firms, hospitals, biotechnology firms, defense contractors, nonprofit organizations, and manufacturers of household goods, as well as state, local, and federal governments. Although large firms employed most technical contractors, small firms also made considerable use of their services. Our data suggest that high-tech start-ups were particularly prone to hiring contractors, and that small businesses also turned to contractors, especially for IT

---

[1] Kalleberg and Schmidt (1996).
[2] Houseman (1997).
[3] Kalleberg and Reynolds (1988).
[4] American Management Association (2000).

services. In fact, several of the contractors we interviewed specialized in serving the small business IT market.

WHY DO CLIENTS HIRE CONTRACTORS?

Organizational scholars have recently had much to say about why organizations hire contingent workers.[5] The consensus is that firms have turned to contingent labor in response to an increasingly competitive economy marked by shorter product cycles, rapidly changing technologies, shifting competencies, fluctuating demand, and rising labor costs. At least implicitly, most writers suggest that like any other "make or buy" decision, the decision to hire contractors rests on a calculus of minimizing transaction costs.[6] Analysts have, therefore, focused on enumerating the relative costs and benefits of employing temporary labor and on identifying the conditions under which firms should augment their permanent labor force with a cadre of contingent employees.

Researchers suggest that clients hire contingent workers for three reasons. The first is to reduce the indirect costs of labor. Analysts argue that under certain conditions, employers can reduce total labor costs by replacing permanent with contingent workers, even though they may actually pay the latter higher hourly wages. Savings accrue, in part, because the law does not require employers to pay employment taxes on temporary employees or to provide temporary workers with fringe benefits, like health insurance and pension funds. By hiring contractors through agencies, clients also escape the costs of recruiting, training, and terminating employees. Firms may even reduce the infrastructural costs of employment (providing offices, heat, and equipment) when they hire contractors who work from home.[7]

[5] See Mangum, Mayall, and Nelson (1985), Pfeffer and Baron (1988), Abraham (1988), Abraham and Taylor (1996), Handy (1989), Bradach (1997), Harrison and Kelley (1993), and Davis-Blake and Uzzi (1993).

[6] Transaction costs analysis, as first articulated by Coase (1937) and more recently revived by Williamson (1975), has become the central tenet of the economic literature on organizational strategy. The general idea is that firms will provide a good or service for themselves if the asset is specific to their operation, if information is asymmetrically distributed, if suppliers can be opportunistic, or if there are moral hazards associated with the transaction. Otherwise, they will purchase goods and services on the market.

[7] Empirical studies lend mixed support to the claim that firms hire contingent workers to reduce labor costs. Mangum, Mayall, and Nelson (1985) found that firms that typically offer more benefits to their permanent employees also make greater use of temporary employees. Harrison and Kelley (1993) report that subcontracting is more common among manufacturing firms that pay their machinists higher salaries. Davis-Blake and Uzzi (1993), however, found that the level of benefits provided by a firm did not influence its tendency to hire temporary workers after controlling for the firm's size.

Achieving flexibility in the face of uncertainty is a second widely discussed reason for using contingent employees. Bennett Harrison and Mary Ellen Kelley have argued that flexibility has three interpretations.[8] In addition to providing firms with more control over the wages they pay (*wage flexibility*), employing contingent labor also allows firms to adjust the size of their labor force (*numerical flexibility*) and alter their mix of human capital (*functional flexibility*) in response to economic, strategic, and technological developments. The retail and construction industries have long employed temporary labor to manage seasonal fluctuations in demand. The same logic motivates managers of technical projects to use contractors. Because projects have phases (as well as clear beginnings and ends), they tend to require specific kinds of expertise at particular times during their trajectories. Contractors are attractive when the demand for expertise is so time limited.

Finally, researchers claim that contingent workers enable firms to manage the flow of knowledge more effectively. Contingent workers affect a firm's stock of knowledge in two conflicting ways. On one hand, they can disseminate what the firm knows to its competitors—which, of course, most firms would like to avoid. But at the same time, they can bring valuable knowledge and skills into the firm. Sharon Matusik and Charles Hill, therefore, counsel firms to think contingently about contingent workers.[9] They advise firms in relatively stable markets to minimize their use of contingent workers or to use them only in peripheral tasks to preclude the loss of proprietary knowledge. Conversely, they urge firms in environments where technologies are changing rapidly to seek out contingent workers to acquire technical expertise that is often difficult to develop in-house in a short period of time.

Our conversations with managers and permanent employees in client firms suggest that the research literature offers only a partial explanation for firms' use of contractors. To be sure, managers and permanent employees told us that they used contractors for reasons that resembled those that researchers discuss. But they often put a spin on these reasons that sounded different to our ears from the spin one finds in the business press or in academic journals. Moreover, managers and permanent employees talked about motives that rarely appear in print, even though these motives were fairly common across the firms we studied. Finally, what we learned when we asked clients why they hired contractors depended on whom we asked.

As table 2.1 shows, senior and mid-level managers emphasized reasons for hiring contractors that were less salient to hiring managers and

[8] Harrison and Kelley (1993).
[9] Matusik and Hill (1998).

TABLE 2.1
Percentage of Employees, Hiring Managers, and Mid- to Upper Managers
Citing Various Reasons for Hiring Contractors

Reason	Mid- and Upper Managers (N = 12)	Hiring Managers (N = 7)	Employees (N = 10)	All Informants (N = 29)
Acquiring skills	100%	100%	50%	83%
Budgets and headcounts	67	43	20	45
Screening	25	29	0	21
Unfilled positions	50	29	70	52
Undesirable work	317	14	30	21

employees. Moreover, hiring managers appealed to motives that employees never mentioned, and employees emphasized reasons that were considerably less important to managers. It was as if each level of the organization viewed the use of contractors through a slightly different lens. These lenses were constructed by drawing in different measure on the reasons listed in the first column of table 2.1: acquiring skills, managing budgets and headcounts, screening, staffing unfilled positions, and using contractors to do undesirable work.

Acquiring Skills

Among the firms that we studied, acquiring skills was the most important reason for hiring contractors. Every manager with whom we spoke mentioned this motive, as did half of the permanent employees (see table 2.1). There were two important variants of this rationale, which, in turn, implied different roles for contractors. The first portrayed contractors as purveyors of just-in-time expertise—skills and knowledge that were needed immediately, but only for a limited time. In this case, contractors were thought of as "hired guns" or "warm bodies." Permanent employees might or might not possess similar skills. The second variant held that firms turned to contractors as a way of importing skills that permanent employees lacked but needed to learn. In this case contractors were hired as teachers or "gurus," or in the language currently popular in business, to promote "knowledge transfer." While the first perspective was articulated at all levels of the organization, only managers voiced the second.

Immediate needs for expertise arose routinely in technical work and were tied to the technical and social dynamics of projects. Hiring managers turned to contractors for a quick infusion of skill when they encountered one of three situations. The first was the need to complete a crucial task that the manager thought would be a waste of time to assign to permanent employees, either because they lacked the expertise or because their time was better spent elsewhere. Representative tasks included upgrading software and hardware, writing assembly code, resolving a specific problem in a network, developing a Web site, or porting data from a legacy system to a new database.[10] Such tasks typically required specialized skills for which the client had no ongoing need, which would take permanent employees too long to learn, or which full-timers had no desire to learn. Aron Murphy, a software manager at UNIX Hardware, put it this way:

> Suppose all of our work for the next eighteen months was based on getting this one piece of work done in the next six months. Now six months isn't urgent, but it might be that it's too soon to get one of the existing engineers up the learning curve or [it's] a skill that nobody wants to do. It's very specialized—maybe assembly language programming or some sort of device driver—something that is very specific and not very many people want to do. In that case, the first thing I'm going to do is look for a full-time engineer who has the skill set and the chances are low that I'll find one. So I go out and look for a contractor.

Other limited and immediate needs were tied to phases of a project's life cycle. Quality assurance and technical writing, both of which typically occur in the final phases of a development project, were good examples. Because engineering teams have no need for technical writers or quality assurance (QA) experts until there is something to document or debug, it makes little sense to assign writers and testers to projects until their services are required. Some firms employed their own pool of writers and testers, whom they assigned to projects as needed. But even these firms turned to contractors when their internal pool of writers and testers was stretched thin. "In a product cycle," explained Anthony Greener, who had managed software development at IBM and Lockheed and was currently working for a small start-up, "you have a period of time where you need someone to do graphics or technical writing. So you go out and hire someone who has that specific skill. It's not a skill that you need all the time, but you need it for a three- or four-month period, so you go bring someone in to help you."

---

[10] Legacy systems are older hardware and software that are still in use. "Orphaned technology" is a synonym that draws attention to a legacy technology's abandonment by its maker.

Finally, hiring managers confronted immediate needs for expertise when their projects fell behind schedule. Engineers, developers, and project managers are acutely aware that in the life of most projects there comes a time when work is backlogged and deadlines loom. In fact, accumulations of work that threaten the team's ability to "come in on time and under budget" are so common that technical professionals have a well-developed slang for bemoaning the predicament. During these "crises" or "crunch times," tensions rise, people "freak," and managers ask experts to put in even longer hours than usual, to engage in "heroics" as they scramble to "put out fires." Managers at all levels acknowledged that they employed contractors to manage "bulges," "spikes," and "bubbles" in the workload—times when they just "needed bodies" to "throw at the problem."

Using contractors as "hired guns" or "warm bodies" to satisfy limited requirements for expertise is consistent with the notion that firms use temporary labor for numerical and functional flexibility. But employing contractors to acquire skills that are central to a firm's mission moves beyond what most analysts mean by flexibility. In this case, clients bring contractors into the core of their operation, which most analysts say is unwise. Yet among the clients we studied, importing core skills that the permanent workforce lacked by hiring gurus was widespread.

Clients routinely found that new projects demanded expertise that no one possessed in-house. Although, in principle, firms could acquire this expertise by hiring new employees, in practice, reconfiguring the permanent workforce was difficult. Pressures to ramp up quickly favored contractors because managers found that it took less time to hire a contractor than to hire a permanent employee.[11] Furthermore, as we discuss later, most firms limited the number of full-time employees they were willing to carry: hiring new employees was often forbidden, or "frozen," or it required letting current employees go to make room for newcomers, which most managers were hesitant to do. Finally, when firms needed "bleeding edge" skills, they often discovered that contractors were their only option, simply because the supply of people who had such skills and who were also looking for permanent jobs had not yet caught up to demand.[12] Nancy Cato, a project manager at Advanced Computers in Cali-

[11] Hiring contractors was often "easier" than hiring full-timers because the procedures were less cumbersome and the decision typically required involving fewer people. In general, when hiring a contractor, managers and peers were less concerned about getting just the right person, since hiring a contractor was, by definition, a short-term commitment. As managers repeatedly said, "You can always get rid of a contractor."

[12] In technical circles, being on the "bleeding edge" signifies being so far beyond the leading edge that mistakes are common, failures are frequent, and the consequences of both are serious for everyone involved.

fornia, had recently hired several contractors from the East Coast precisely because she had been unable to find CORBA programmers locally.[13] She explained her decision:

> I've hired a lot of contractors for specific expertise. Maybe we need something quickly or maybe my team hasn't had the time to come up to speed. Contractors have the chance to move from assignment to assignment. They pick up a lot as they go. Our people don't have as much opportunity to delve into things. They have assignments that they have to stay with and carry through for a long time. Recently I had specific requirements that were *more than* extremely hard to find. Two of my current guys [contractors] were imported from the East Coast. They [the staffing agencies] didn't even have Bay Area people, which was surprising. I mean even at any price we were willing to pay! So it wasn't about money, it was about skills.

Hiring managers did not always know that they would need outside expertise at the outset of a project. Permanent employees sometimes initially overestimated what they could do, especially when they saw a task as a challenge.[14] At other times, the need for more sophisticated knowledge only became clear as the team hit unanticipated roadblocks. In either case, a manager might not realize that the team lacked sufficient experience until the project was well under way. At that point, hiring a contractor became a way of salvaging a project. For example, Neal Smith, the chief technology officer at Vision Software, told us that the firm didn't use contractors for "mission critical" work. Joseph Litkin, the CEO, who was also present, immediately contradicted him:

> I've been considering contracting out for a control algorithm [a mission critical tool], and I think we need to do it. One of my biggest worries is the whole measurement control technology. I'm not comfortable that we have what we need to meet the specs. They're not making progress. They have a model and they have a packet guy and he did a good job, but they don't have a control algorithm, and I don't feel comfortable that they have a nice road map or that we have the right resources on it. I don't think we're going to have it in time at the rate we're going. So I would definitely consider contracting.

---

[13] CORBA stands for "Common Object Request Broker Architecture." CORBA-based programs allow programs and databases written in different languages and hosted on different platforms and networks to communicate with each other.

[14] Engineers and software developers are notoriously willing to commit to taking on difficult but challenging tasks, in part, for the opportunity to learn and have fun. In computer firms studied by Kidder (1981) and Kunda (1992), this was known as "signing up," a military term used widely in the computer industry.

Clients sought core skills from contractors for other reasons as well. Several managers noted that customers often encouraged suppliers to move in new technical directions, but that customers were notorious for changing their minds.[15] Thus, before committing permanent employees to new technologies, a client might ramp up with contractors. Not only could the contractors train the permanent employees, but if the customer reneged, contractors could easily be terminated, thereby minimizing the firm's long-term investment. "Say a client comes in and says, 'I need to try this new technology,'" Matt Schmidt of Videonet told us. "We don't want to invest in paying someone $150,000 a year only to find out that the client changes his mind and says, 'I really like what you were doing three months ago better.' Then we're stuck with a full-time person and we don't need that skill. That's when a contractor is ideal."

Managers also turned to contractors when the firm decided to switch technical directions. Anthony Greener claimed that during his days at IBM, the company used contractors in just this way: "You might hire contractors for a particular skill for a short period of time to train some of your own internal people. If you've been moving down this particular path and you're taking a ninety-degree turn—going in a different direction—all your skills are on your old path. So you might have to go out and get a bunch of contract people to come in and help you make the transition." In fact, most mid- and upper-level managers at least mentioned hiring contractors as a way of bringing their organizations up to speed on new technologies. Shirley Daner, the chief information officer at Chipco, spoke for most:

> We'll turn to contractors if we need a new skill. We needed to do some e-commerce stuff, interfacing with Intershop. I was given an "It's-got-to-be-done-yesterday" time frame. I didn't have anybody that knew this stuff. So, we hired some contractors to do the work. The goal was to have them turn over the knowledge so that we could do the next project with maybe one contractor until we built up the skill level in-house. Oracle Order Management was the same thing. We didn't have people in-house that knew Oracle Order Management. So we hired a bunch of contractors who had this expertise to teach us and transition it. So that's a huge reason that we use contractors. The technology is changing a lot and it's hard to keep up.

Finally, start-ups and small businesses used contractors in key technical roles. Employing contractors enabled entrepreneurs to conserve start-

---

[15] This observation is consistent with Eric Von Hippel's (1978, 1989, 1994) long stream of research that shows that customers are the driving force behind most innovations.

up funds and, at the same time, meet unanticipated surges in demand.[16] Micky Cummings, the vice president of engineering for a new start-up, explained:

> It's harder for us, morally and ethically, to make long-term commitments to that many people. If we did, gee, we wouldn't have enough money for eight more months. So we use contractors. For start-ups it works a lot better. We're an outsourcer to other companies. We'll sign a big contract, then we have this huge amount of work that needs to be done in the next three months. When that's in place and it's running, there's less to do. Once there's a little more regularity to these big deals and signing of contracts, we can actually build a group of permanent people.

Small businesses employed IT contractors for much the same reason. Most could not afford to maintain their own information systems, so they outsourced the task to a contractor who provided services as needed.

Budgets and Headcount

As table 2.1 shows, next to acquiring skill, managing the politics of "headcount" was the most common reason managers gave for using contractors. Many firms set hard limits on the number of permanent employees that they would carry during a fiscal year. When commissioning projects, upper management typically set two constraints within which they expected hiring managers to work. The first was the number of full-time employees who would be allocated to a project or area, commonly known as "headcount." Most firms set the headcount ceiling lower than the full complement of people needed to do the firm's work. The second was "budget," the total number of dollars allotted to the project. Because upper management knew headcount would be inadequate for completing the project, they expected project managers to assemble additional human resources by spending a portion of their budget on contractors. In fact, the practice was so common that in the negotiations we observed, hiring managers and agents used the term "budget" to refer specifically to funds available for contractors.

Managers explained that restrictions on headcount varied with the ebb and flow of a firm's performance and the ups and downs of the economy,

---

[16] Start-ups, struggling to survive until their product is ready, try to minimize their "burn rate"—the speed at which a firm spends its venture capital. Because they are so focused on the success of one product, they are more attuned to limiting labor costs and less concerned with building a viable long-term technical community than are more established companies.

but all agreed that headcount restrictions existed even in the best of economic times. The research literature suggests that firms hire contractors not just to reduce total personnel costs, but also to downsize more graciously in hard times. The managers we interviewed agreed that contracting offered these advantages. They sometimes also added that managing headcount and hiring contractors helped protect permanent employees during a downturn. But these were not the only (nor even the most frequently mentioned) reasons for managing headcount with contractors. In fact, some of our informants reported that permanent employees were laid off before contractors were terminated.

Full-time employees counted as fixed costs, whereas contractors were a variable cost. In an uncertain market, variable costs are always preferable to fixed costs and in this sense, hiring contractors made real economic sense. Shifting employment from a fixed to a variable cost would allow firms to respond more quickly to changing demand. When demand increased, firms could quickly augment their labor force with contractors. When demand declined, they could adjust just as quickly by shedding contractors. But there were several other economic and financial reasons for turning to contactors that are less widely appreciated.

As Susan Chen, a former human resources executive at Compaq who now works for a staffing firm, explained, using contractors not only enabled a firm to transform fixed into variable costs, it allowed the employer, in her words, to "manipulate the system." By "burying" personnel costs in the "budget," firms could make it appear that their labor costs were lower than would have been the case had permanent employees done the job. Neal Smith explained how one could use contractors to "adjust" gross margins:

> Our goal with contracting is driven by gross margins. If we think that our gross margin on a product is 30 percent because manufacturing cost is so huge and our development cost is building up to where it's affecting our bottom line, then we turn to contracting. Contracting is cheaper because you can limit your expenses at any time. And we have better control because then we don't have to go in-house struggling to try to bring the gross margins up to, say, 40 percent to 60 percent. Cutting and hiding contract services is easier.

Another reason for preferring the variable cost of contracting to the fixed cost of permanent employment was its effect on a firm's valuation. Informants told us that financial analysts calculate a firm's productivity, in part, by examining the ratio of revenues (or sales) to full-time employees. Because contractors are "buried in the budget," they do not contribute to the ratio's denominator, which is determined entirely by headcount. In other words, hiring contractors was one way to inflate a firm's stock price.[17]

The burden of the politics of headcount fell largely on hiring managers. Their charge was to assemble the personnel necessary to staff projects, which meant filling the gaps that headcount restrictions created. On one hand, hiring managers preferred to use permanent employees whenever possible: increasing one's headcount meant having more predictable resources. On the other hand, having the "budget" to hire contractors was also desirable, because "budget" meant slack that managers could use for immediate and unanticipated needs. Hiring managers told us they often needed assistance from other groups who were stretched thin. With budget, they could hire contractors for these other groups. Contractors, therefore, also served as a kind of currency in an internal system of reciprocity and exchange.

Project managers had an additional incentive to burn budget on contractors. In a partial or full matrix structure, project managers had little formal authority over the permanent employees who staffed their projects. These firms assigned permanent employees to a functional area, like electrical or mechanical engineering. A manager responsible for the functional area then allocated the employees to projects. Technical professionals often served on several projects simultaneously, which meant that the project manager had to compete for their attention. In contrast, when a project manager hired a contractor, the contractor worked solely for the project manager. Thus, by hiring contractors, project managers could gain direct control over people working on their projects, which they otherwise lacked. As Don Perle, a seasoned project manager, succinctly put it, "I love contractors. They work for me! I can hire them and I can fire them."

Screening

As table 2.1 indicates, about a quarter of the managers we interviewed told us that they turned to contractors as a way of screening workers for full-time positions. After hiring a permanent employee, firms legally have a ninety-day probation period to judge the employee's suitability and to terminate employment without building a case for termination. Beyond ninety days, terminations must be documented and employees who believe they have been treated unfairly have a right to contest their

---

[17] Several commentators have noted that contingent labor may also enable a firm to skirt hiring freezes and to increase headcount without affecting productivity, since the contributions of contingent workers are rarely included when analysts calculate productivity figures (Pfeffer and Baron 1988; Christensen 1998).

termination. Hiring a contractor essentially allows a firm to extend the probation period and eliminate disputes. Managers have up to eighteen months to decide whether to offer the contractor a permanent position. Most hiring managers used contracting as a screening device intermittently when they encountered a technical professional about whose fit they were unsure. But some firms, including The Gap and Videonet, were well-known in contracting circles for regularly using a "temp-to-perm" hiring strategy, especially for information technology positions.

Unfilled Positions and Undesirable Work

Table 2.1 shows that permanent employees saw the use of contractors somewhat differently than managers did. Although permanent employees realized that contractors were hired to acquire skills and manage headcount, they were more likely to claim that contractors were brought in for undesirable work or to fill full-time positions that had gone unfilled. Undesirable work was not necessarily viewed as low-skilled work; it was simply work that permanent employees preferred not to do. For example, working on legacy systems was a form of highly skilled but undesirable work. Permanent employees saw no value in learning legacy software because, by definition, the future lay elsewhere. Undesirable work frequently involved maintaining software and hardware or developing reports for clients.

Permanent positions in an organization might go unfilled for a variety of reasons. Sometimes the client simply couldn't find people with the requisite skills who also desired full-time employment. This occurred not only when clients needed someone to work on an orphaned technology, but also when clients demanded cutting-edge skills that were not yet widely diffused. At other times, hiring managers concluded that a contractor was simply more knowledgeable than the people currently on the market for permanent positions. A number of hiring managers and employees noted that UNIX skills were particularly hard to find. Furthermore, at the time of our study, the economy was expanding at such a pace that the number of job openings outstripped supply.

While managers also mentioned an inability to fill positions and the need to do undesirable work, these reasons were far less prominent. The difference may have reflected a difference in interpretation. When managers turned to contractors for expertise they could not find among the permanent workforce, they were implicitly acknowledging that they could not fill a position with a permanent employee. But rather than tell the employees that they were inadequately skilled, they more commonly claimed that they could not find candidates with the requisite skills. Understandably, permanent employees may have interpreted this situation as an inadequacy in the labor market, rather than an inadequacy in their own abilities. The difference in interpretation allowed employees to retain a sense of status and save face, while it enabled managers to avoid disgruntling employees. More important, it allowed managers and employees to sidestep the issue of whether permanent employees needed to be replaced.

How Do Clients Hire Contractors?

When firms hired permanent employees, the human resource department was almost always directly involved. Human resource personnel published position announcements, received and screened résumés, arranged interviews, and managed the paperwork associated with payroll, taxes, and benefits. In most cases we studied, when firms hired contractors, the human resource department was not involved. Instead, managers engaged contractors through the purchasing department. Purchasing wrote requisitions for contractors, engaged staffing agencies as vendors, and administered the contract that the firm signed with the agency. As we shall see, this procedure was designed to protect the firm from the charge that contractors were employees.

The firms that we studied used both decentralized and centralized systems for hiring contractors. In decentralized systems, the manager for whom the contractor would eventually work took responsibility for finding and hiring the contractor. Staffing agencies and contractors referred to these individuals as "hiring managers," regardless of their formal title or position in the firm. A hiring manager who needed a contractor searched his or her professional networks for information on who might be available, contacted staffing firms, negotiated directly with agents and contractors, committed to an hourly rate and an overall budget, and initiated the paperwork necessary to bring the contractor on board.

The advantage of a decentralized system was that hiring managers could choose the contractors and staffing firms with whom they preferred to work. Managers claimed that decentralization increased the odds that they would find a contractor with the proper skills. From top management's perspective, however, decentralized hiring was costly and difficult to control, especially for firms that employed many contractors. Allowing hiring managers to negotiate with contractors and with agencies increased the range of rates that a firm paid for contractors with similar skills. Decentralized systems also made it difficult for firms to monitor the quality of the services that staffing agencies provided, to control the total number of contractors the firm employed, and to ensure that correct legal procedures were followed when hiring contractors.[18]

To avoid these problems, larger firms usually instituted a more centralized system for hiring contractors. Staff managers from the purchasing, human resource, and legal departments typically designed, monitored, and supervised a centralized system that ensured the firm's hiring procedures and practices met financial targets and legal requirements. Firms with centralized systems usually tried to limit the number of agencies with whom a hiring manager could do business. In the world of contracting, staffing agencies that enjoyed a privileged, contractual relationship with a client were known as "approved" or "preferred" vendors. Client organizations that continually hired large numbers of contractors often went a step further and used an "on-site" vendor as well. A staffing agency became an on-site vendor when the client granted the agency an exclusive franchise to procure all of the client's contractors, an arrangement clients often referred to as "single point of contact." In return, the staffing agency agreed to charge less than it would normally charge for its services and to commit to following hiring procedures that would ensure the quality of the contractors (a process known as "prescreening" or "qualification").

Clients with on-site vendors required hiring managers to go through the on-site when requisitioning contractors and adopted policies to dissuade other staffing agencies from dealing directly with hiring managers. In many cases, firms with on-site agencies also maintained a list of approved vendors that were authorized to provide contractors. Approved agencies operated as "third parties." They negotiated with and provided contractors to the on-site agency instead of negotiating directly with hiring managers. The on-site vendor negotiated a deal, took legal responsibility for the contractor (as the "employer of record"), and split the profit on the deal—known as the "margin," or the "markup"—with the third-party.

There were, of course, ways around centralized systems so that decentralized hiring occurred in every firm that we studied. In centralized firms, hiring managers could still search for and attempt to hire individual contractors of their choice, much as they would in a decentralized system. The difference was that in these cases, the hiring manager sent

---

[18] Hiring managers who were anxious to acquire the expertise they needed often agreed to terms that made the firm vulnerable to legal and tax problems. For example, managers might unwittingly agree to an original contract or extend a contract, which would result in keeping the contractor longer than eighteen months. The official policy in many large companies was that contractors were to be dismissed after eighteen months and that some period of time had to elapse between stints of employment so that the contractor could not be misconstrued as an employee by the IRS or the courts.

the contractor to a staffing agency on the company's approved list or to the on-site company, who then arranged the contact. These arrangements were known as "pass-throughs" because the contractor had to pass through the agency in order to be hired, even if the contractor was incorporated and could work independently. Because some managers preferred to work with agencies they had come to trust, they also occasionally tried to skirt the system so that they could hire contractors through a particular agency. To do so they might arrange "approved vendor" status for the agency or set the agency up as a "third party" with an already approved agency.

CONCLUSION

Academic and business writers often make it seem as if firms act with one mind or purpose. This is certainly true of most students of corporate strategy who speak to why firms hire contractors. In reality, however, client organizations do not speak with one voice; organizations are single actors only on paper. We have identified three groups of people inside firms whose interests and viewpoints on hiring contractors often clashed and the clash shaped how clients used contractors. First, senior managers—and the staff who represented their point of view—were generally attuned to long-term strategic issues and to considerations of cost, the proverbial "bottom line." Most discussions of why firms hire contractors reflect top management's perspective. Their perspective also underwrote the policies and procedures that firms adopted to guide the everyday use of contractors. Hiring managers were the second type of actor. Although the way hiring managers used contractors was subject to corporate control, their decisions were driven by the everyday tribulations of managing technical projects, and they had considerable discretion in their interpretation of and adherence to corporate guidelines. A third role was that of the permanent employee. Although employees had no explicit voice in the decision to hire contractors, they had to interact with contractors daily. The permanent employees' view of and reactions to the contractors' temporary presence in their world shaped not only the contractors' experience on the job, but also posed hiring managers with the additional challenge of managing a sometimes conflicted workforce.

Hiring managers play leading roles in the mini-dramas of contracting that unfold in parts 2 and 3 of the book, since it was they who actively sought, evaluated, negotiated with, managed, and terminated contractors. Senior and staff managers will appear in secondary roles as the voice of corporate interest, sometimes supporting and sometimes obstructing hiring managers' efforts to find and use contractors. Permanent employees will emerge from the background when we review contractors' everyday life on the job.

Our data also indicated that firms hired contractors for reasons that are rarely mentioned in the business press, and despite what one finds in either institutional or free agent treatises, these reasons were often the most important. First, firms often turned to contractors for skills that they could not find among their permanent employees. To the degree that this was true, contractors served as more than a source of labor, they served as an important source of expertise. Second, firms hired contractors to manage the politics and finances of headcount. Contractors allowed firms to appear more productive on paper than they actually were.

Chapter 3

CONTRACTORS

THE CENTRAL CHARACTERS around which the social world of contracting revolved were the contractors themselves. As table 3.1 reports, the contractors we interviewed worked in a variety of engineering or information technology–oriented occupations, although 41 percent were software developers or programmers. Most of our informants were men and women who had previously worked as permanent employees. Although a few entered contracting after working in permanent positions for only a year or two, the majority had worked full-time for at least five years, and many had been employees for over fifteen years before becoming contractors. The exceptions were the UNIX and NT systems administrators who came to work for Systems Professionals directly from college, and even they were only partial exceptions. All had previously worked as network administrators for a college or university.

Because experience was part of what made contractors valuable, contracting was not a young person's game. As table 3.1 indicates, our informants ranged from twenty-six to sixty-eight years of age with an average age of forty-two. Only 10 percent of our informants were under thirty. Nearly 30 percent were in their thirties and almost 40 percent were in their forties. The remainder (22 percent) were fifty years old or older.[1]

Choosing to contract was a clear shift in career strategy for most informants. After initially working as a contractor, only 22 percent of our informants had returned to permanent employment at least once. Six (8 percent) were so new to contracting that it was impossible to determine whether they would really adopt a contracting lifestyle. The remainder (70 percent) appeared to have become converts. These contractors never took another permanent job after their first contract, although many claimed that clients had tried to convince them to "go perm."

Most of our informants became contractors during the 1990s, and they had contracted on average for six and a half years. Forty-five percent had been contracting for less than five years, and another 33 percent entered contracting six to ten years earlier. Nevertheless, over a fifth (22

---

[1] Black and Andreini (1997) found roughly the same distribution in their survey of contractors in the Silicon Valley.

TABLE 3.1
Descriptive Statistics for Informants[a]

Characteristic	Mean (N)[b]	Standard Deviation	Minimum	Maximum
Demographic				
Age (in years)[c]	42	11	26	68
Education (in post–high school years)[c]	4.2	1.6	0	8
Pay rate (in $/hour)[d]	65	28	20	125
Male	.77 (55)			
Married[h e]	.60 (36)			
Have children[h f]	.51 (28)			
Caucasian[h]	.75 (53)			
U.S. citizen[h]	.80 (40)			
California resident[h]	.76 (53)			
Bay Area resident[h]	.60 (42)			
Technical Specialty				
Software	.41 (29)			
Hardware	.10 (7)			
IT specialist	.10 (7)			
System administrator	.10 (7)			
Technical writer	.10 (7)			
Database designer	.04 (3)			
Multimedia developer	.03 (2)			
Program manager	.03 (2)			
Quality assurance technician	.07 (5)			
Marketing (Web)	.01 (1)			
Machine tool programmer	.01 (1)			
Career Structure				
Years contracted[c]	6.6	4.9	0.5	21
Years worked[g]	17.1	9.0	2	44
Years contracted/years worked[g]	.43	.27	0	1
Independent contractors or corps[h]	.30 (21)			

[a] N = Seventy-one individuals. Numbers are drawn from semi-structured interview data and so all of the information is not available on all cases.

[b] Parentheses indicate actual number of cases for dummy variable tabulation.

[c] Only includes data on sixty-nine cases.

[d] Only includes data on forty-four cases.

[e] Only includes data on sixty cases.

[f] Only includes data on fifty-five cases.

[g] Only includes data on sixty-eight cases.

[h] Dummy variable and so only frequencies are given.

percent) had been contractors for at least a decade. In fact, one informant had been a contractor for twenty-one years. Sixty percent (thirty-six) of the contractors were married and nearly a quarter (sixteen) were women. Sixty percent (forty-two) lived and worked in the Silicon Valley. The remainder worked in the following cities: Austin, Houston, Baltimore, Seattle, Toronto, Los Angeles, Atlanta, Billings, and Norwalk, Connecticut. Thirty percent (twenty-one) were either independent contractors or incorporated as a business.[2] The rest worked solely through staffing agencies.

Statistics such as these give us a picture of technical contractors as a group, but they tell us almost nothing about who contractors were as people, what they valued, or how they differed from other technical professionals. To learn these things one must listen to the stories that contractors told about why they become contractors.

WHY DO CONTRACTORS BECOME CONTRACTORS?

When asked to reflect on their career paths, our informants told tales of becoming—stories of identity and self-discovery that focused on what set them apart from their permanently employed colleagues. Although our informants' tales differed in their details, they revolved collectively around three themes, which, when arrayed sequentially, traced an underlying narrative of transformation.

The narrative usually began with the lament of a permanently employed technical professional for whom the tension between an ideal of technical rationality and the realities of organizational life had become a source of simmering discontent. Eventually, an employer's action or an unanticipated calamity goaded the discontented professional into realizing that he or she had to act. Aided by serendipitous encounters with the world of contracting, the expert finally decided to escape the world of full-time employment into the world of contracting, which promised a way of life more consistent with the expert's worldview.

---

[2] The distinction between an independent contractor, a contractor who works as an employee of a staffing firm, and a contractor who is incorporated as a business is based on the contractors' tax status, not whether they use staffing firms to find jobs. Independent contractors are individuals who satisfy a number of criteria set by the IRS, who are paid directly for their work, and who pay their own taxes and social security on a quarterly basis. Contractors who are incorporated have registered themselves as a business and bill for their services via an invoice from their corporation. All other contractors are "W-2s"; they work as employees of a staffing firm that withholds taxes and social security. Like W-2s, independent and incorporated contractors sometimes use staffing firms to find jobs, but unlike W-2s they are not obligated to do so.

Expertise and Discontent

Contractors wove their tales of discontent around three motifs: "politics," "incompetence," and "inequity," which together depicted organizational life as irrational and capricious. Of the three motifs, politics was the most common. "Politics," as contractors use the word, is best understood as a cover term for the myriad ways in which personal agendas and interests undermine technical rationality as a criterion for action. Contractors' complaints about politics often targeted managers. The perception that managers acted to further their own interests was so widespread that contractors frequently portrayed technical professionals and projects as pawns in management's political games. Donald Knight, a board designer without a college degree who had risen through the ranks at Motorola from technician to engineer, began his story this way: "I used to have written on my grease board, 'Politics Is Our Most Important Project.' The boss came around and saw it. It went away real quick. But it's true: we were just tools in their project." Bill Smith, an electrical engineer who once shared the same employer, offered a similar, albeit less humorous, view:

> I worked a lot of long hours. It was for politics. It wasn't for getting the project done. It was like I was doing this for somebody else's ego, or somebody else's personal or career goals. They could check off, they got this or that done based on my work. I was getting the project done not for the goals of the project but for the goals of the people above.

Although managers were the most common target of complaint, contractors did not spare their peers from the charge of political gamesmanship. According to our informants, organizational life was rife with conflicting agendas, which they saw as a waste of time and a source of tension. They understood meetings, in particular, as venues for political grandstanding. "You have to listen to a lot of people's agendas," explained Anil Rao, a mechanical engineer and CAD designer. "You spend time in a lot of unnecessary meetings, trying to keep everybody happy, trying to play their game. It's not strictly work-related, it's very unproductive, and it can be very tense. I've seen people in meetings who don't talk to each other there's so much tension going on."[3]

---

[3] This sentiment, which was common among our informants, brings to mind Leslie Perlow's (1997) observation that engineers waste significant time "statusing" upper-level managers in meetings. Perlow showed that limiting the number of interruptions to which engineers are subjected makes it more likely that projects will be finished on time.

Incompetence was a second source of discontent for our informants. Whereas they viewed politics as endemic to organizational life, they saw incompetence as an attribute of specific individuals. Top managers were sometimes targets of critique. Doug Hill, a software designer with over fifteen years of experience as a contractor, offered a scathing indictment of entrepreneurial management in the Silicon Valley, which he claimed was full of "egomaniacs who just happened to stumble into a bunch of money." He continued: "There's plenty of people out there who've made money in spite of themselves. It's the Beverly Hillbillies story. They were shootin' at a rabbit, struck oil, and now they think they're a genius." Brian Willingham, an IT consultant to small firms, said he turned to contracting after encountering a series of senior managers whose incompetence shaded into dishonesty:

> I was at the naval shipyard for a couple of years, and they were going nowhere. I theoretically reported to the chief financial officer [CFO]. They brought in a couple, how do we say, "yo-yos." We caught one of the CFOs funneling stuff into his condo in Florida. We had a series of CFOs and each one had a different idea of what needed to be done and how to do it, and I'm going, "No, I'm not playing anymore." You know? There was no real strategy or anything.

However, it was middle management—and project managers, in particular—for whom contractors reserved their most sustained accusations of incompetence. The comic strip *Dilbert*, which captures the travails of technical professionals, was a popular source of imagery. Yolanda Turner was one of many who drew the parallel: "I don't know if you read *Dilbert*, but it's almost prophetic. I mean, they hire people to be managers that you'd say, 'Why in the world is this person leading?' They just don't have the skills." Often underlying such complaints was the contractors' belief that they were more rational and capable than the managers for whom they had worked. Victor Post, a database administrator who had returned briefly to permanent employment, was particularly articulate on this point:

> I think I am a little bit smarter than a lot of people out there. If there were really good project managers, there wouldn't be any contractors. The reason contractors are hired is because they [companies] are in deep shit. And the reason they are in so deep is because they have been poorly managed or poorly planned. Like when I was working at Astrotech, the project manager was bordering on schizophrenic; things changed every day: the project plan, the features of the software product. When that happens, people cannot get work done. And then the team would be berated for not getting enough

work done. They hire people as project managers who have not done the work that the people they are managing are doing. They have no clue as to what is required to get things done. They don't know what is reasonable and what is not.

Contractors believed that managerial incompetence spelled trouble for the organization as well as its employees. Living with incompetence bred a sense of indignity and injustice. Brenda O'Boyle, a quality assurance technician who had been laid off several years earlier by a manager whom she perceived as incompetent, was still angry: "To have a person like that say, 'You have been tagged and you don't have a job anymore,' was just too much. This bozo is telling me I don't have a job anymore and he's still working?" Incompetent management also stifled the expert's voice, a situation that informants saw as detrimental to organizational performance. Tony Rodriguez, who specialized in project management, underscored the costs of suppressing expert opinions: "In the corporate world you may have an opinion, but you are not allowed to say it. When I worked on the project in Missouri, I said: 'We are going to lose our rear ends on this project!' They recognize that now. But then they said: 'You are not a team player. You are giving up before the battle starts.' Fifteen million dollars later, they will come back and say: 'Why didn't you tell us?' "

The inequity of permanent employment was the third motif that permeated contractors' tales of why they entered contracting. Many felt that employers exploited technical experts by requiring long hours without commensurate pay. Bill Smith's complaint was typical: "There's no compensation for engineers. I had to take a lower salary, I didn't get to take any vacation, and I worked a lot longer hours. When I worked at Motorola the last time as a permanent employee, I was required to work twelve-hour shifts with no extra pay. And it just went on like that for months and months and months." Inequity was not, however, just a matter of money. Contractors claimed that the new fashion of demanding loyalty without offering security was fundamentally unfair. Like most contractors, Julian Stoke saw the irony and rebelled:

> As time went on I saw that companies want loyalty, but they will not—and in some sense cannot—give loyalty to their employees. You know, if the company is falling apart, if it's going bankrupt—they're going to lay off employees. They're going to try and remain a viable entity. But they want loyalty from me as an employee! Now, why should I do that? What do I get out of this relationship? I have to subject myself to reviews, to whatever the latest reviewing technique is out there. Peer reviews this week, something else next week.

I have to subject myself to all of this stuff, company politics, for what? What is it that I'm going to get out of that?

Ultimately, politics, incompetence, and inequity exacerbated insecurity, engendered unpleasantness, and undermined a climate of trust. Judy King, an experienced programmer, spoke of the pettiness and competitiveness she had observed among full-time employees who felt they were improperly compensated:

> I was working a contract at TRW just around Christmas. People were very upset because the bonus was $1,000 and to get your $1,000 bonus you had to walk on water. Bonuses were graded, and they were arguing and complaining and yelling in the halls. And I'm thinking, "What is the matter with you people? Why are you doing this for a thousand dollar bonus? You're highly paid people. Why are you standing here screaming about a mere $1,000? It's *nothing* in the grand scheme of things!" But everybody's involved in all the politics of stuff—who should be getting what, and why.

Paula Ritter, a technical writer, described the fear of layoffs she had observed among full-time employees in firms in the Silicon Valley: "You can smell the fear in the halls when you walk into some of those buildings. People are so tense, so afraid that they are going to screw up. They wonder about the next layoff."

Triggers for Change

Although discontent with the exigencies of permanent employment was widespread, by itself it was insufficient to motivate most contractors to turn to contracting. Our informants did not generally decide to become contractors until they encountered layoffs, acquisitions, financially troubled employers, deteriorating work conditions, and other events that made changing jobs suddenly seem inevitable or desirable. These were events that informants could neither anticipate nor control.

The most common triggers for taking action were downsizings and other events that signaled that the contractor was about to lose his or her job. Twenty-one percent of our informants were laid off from their last permanent job. Most went directly into contracting, although a few (three informants) initially looked for permanent work after being laid off, but could not find it. Steve Louthan, a forty-five-year-old technical writer, was one:

> I didn't realize that when I quit DEC, I was changing my life forever. I went to Apollo. Four months later I got caught in the first wave of

layoffs that decimated the entire tech writing department. Four months after that, another 20 to 30 percent were laid off. Shortly after that Apollo was bought by Hewlett-Packard. Apollo went right down, it was absolutely amazing. When I got laid off at Apollo, that was it. I could not find a permanent job anywhere in Massachusetts. So I started to go contract instead.

Another 20 percent of our informants didn't wait for the pink slip. Observing that their employer was having financial difficulties, like Stu Davis, an embedded systems engineer, they decided to leave before the firm collapsed around them:

Hayes filed for Chapter 11 protection. They successfully reorganized but in the midst of all this, I said, "Look, they're not being very innovative technology-wise. And they're not putting any money into new products." People were bailing out left and right. My former boss, who had already quit, said, "Look, call up this company, MRJ, Inc. [a staffing agency]. They need somebody like you and they're paying really good money." MRJ made me an offer. I said, "Man, this is just too good to turn down." So I left Hayes.

For another set of contractors, deteriorating working conditions were sufficient to trigger the shift to contracting, even though these events did not explicitly threaten their job security. Ray Gregory, a multimedia developer, felt unappreciated and saw the acquisition of his company and his subsequent demotion as a sign: "It was like the universe was giving me a hint: Maybe you should move on." Still others claimed they turned to contracting because they had become bored or because their employer had asked them to relocate and they did not want to move.

Escape into Contracting

Triggering events were crucial because they led informants to consider their options. But by themselves, triggers were not enough. Even the experience of being laid off was insufficient to tip the balance in favor of becoming a contractor, since most could have easily secured permanent employment at another firm. Over half of our informants reported that the decision to enter contracting required exposure to people or opportunities that made contracting seem more viable than taking another full-time job. Exposure could occur through encounters with contractors, staffing agencies, or potential clients.

Most of our informants had worked beside contractors in previous jobs where they had opportunities to observe the practicalities of contracting. Informants were particularly taken with the idea that contractors made more money for doing the same work. Twenty-one percent of our informants noted that when they finally made their decision, other contractors served as role models. Herman Jay, who had been contracting since 1963, was one:

> There were several contractors also working at General Electric, and I found out that they were making a lot more money than I was even though they didn't have the benefits I did. So at one point I had a disagreement with the people I was working for and I said, "The heck with you," and I quit General Electric and I went to the job shop that was employing the guys that were working at GE and I said, "Do you guys have a call for anybody?" And they said, "Oh yeah, we do, and we will even give you your job back." So they gave me my job [at GE] back at about a third increase in salary.

Encounters with staffing agencies were another stimulus for considering contracting as a realistic possibility. Technical professionals, especially those in managerial roles, routinely encountered representatives of staffing agencies seeking new recruits and job openings. Eleven of our informants (15 percent) reported being lured into contracting after encountering agents just at a point in time when they were ready to consider change.

Another 12 percent said they entered contracting because they wanted to work for a specific firm, but found that the firm would only hire them on a contingent basis. A final type of encounter that pulled informants into contracting was a direct offer of contingent employment from a potential client. In some cases, offers came from personal friends and acquaintances. "A friend of mine, a diving buddy actually, who was the assistant dean of UCLA, needed someone with my skill set to do a major project," recalled Charles Eaton, an applications programmer who specialized in migrating from mainframes to personal computers. "She said, 'Gee it would be *great* if you were available!' and I was like, 'Well, maybe I *could* be available.' So I decided that it was time to get out of the corporation, go off on my own and start making some money for myself and be my own boss. All of a sudden I had a one-year contract full-time with UCLA to do this project."

Opportunities also came from customers of former employers who believed that an informant had valuable skills for which they were willing to pay high rates on a contingent basis. Teresa Dolan, a software developer who worked with financial applications, explained how she was hired to develop and maintain software sold by her former employer:

> The customers were very easy to find. They wanted custom development. They were existing customers of the software house that I was

working for. The company did not offer custom development services. In the last two years, in fact, it became obvious that the president didn't really want to take the company anywhere and was actually looking to sell it. More and more customers were getting
antsy. They still wanted modifications. So that's when I went into
contracting. And it was by word of mouth. I had to turn down
work; there was so much work.

Anticipated Rewards

Encounters with contractors were crucial for informants because they
modeled contracting as a way to escape while also gaining benefits
that seemed more attractive than those of full-time work. Of contracting's various advantages, the most important was money. Forty-four
percent of our informants said they were drawn to contracting primarily because they thought they would make more. Les Cousteau, a numerical control programmer, was explicit about contracting's economic lure:

> A little less than a year ago, my family and I were living in Seattle
> and we were getting a little tight on money—getting behind, getting
> in debt, too—because Boeing did not pay enough for me to support
> my family without my wife working. She doesn't work and I don't
> believe she should have to. We have four children. I actually worked
> two or three jobs at one time for about a year. I was even delivering
> newspapers and doing other odd jobs. At Boeing I was making
> about $40,000 to $44,000 a year plus overtime, which maybe aver-
> aged out to be another $5,000 a year. Here, in eight months I've
> made about $115,000.

Our data indicate that technical contractors were indeed making
more than their permanently employed peers. We systematically asked
our informants to estimate how much more they made by becoming a
contractor. After taking into account the cost of providing one's own
benefits (approximately 26 percent of an annual salary), most contractors estimated that by becoming contractors their income increased by
50 percent to 300 percent. Enhanced income, however, was not the
only attractive feature of contracting. A number of informants (14
percent) anticipated more autonomy in their work. Others (15 percent) hoped to develop new skills. Still others (12 percent) sought
more control over their time. A few were drawn to contracting not because they wanted money, flexibility, or control, but because they liked
the excitement of stringing together a series of challenges (6 percent)

or because they sought the variety that contracting inevitably brought (8 percent).

Other scholars have emphasized the motives about which our informants spoke. As the institutionalists would predict, downsizing, outsourcing, and related practices triggered movement into contracting, at least for a significant minority. The majority of our informants also mentioned the desire for flexibility and greater income that figure so prominently in free agency's rhetoric of employability. But none of these structural and economic factors seemed to capture fully the contractors' own interpretation of their transition. The decision to become a contractor also involved a set of motives rooted in a professional ideology of work. These motives are usually overlooked in the literature on contingent employment.

Most of our informants viewed themselves as technical professionals. They believed that decisions about work should be governed primarily by an ethic of technical rationality based on logic, reason, and practicality. They discovered, to their chagrin, that organizational life deviated from the way they believed the world should operate. More important, they were not always given the respect that they thought a technical professional deserved. In this sense, the contractors' dissatisfaction was reminiscent of the difficulties that sociologists of work have repeatedly discovered among professionals in bureaucratic settings.[4] Our informants were, after all, engineers and software developers who had entered their fields because they were attracted to technology and who believed that problems had solutions.

Although some contractors found their discontent sufficient for entering contracting, most required a push. At this point, an encounter with a contractor, a staffing agency, or a potential client made contracting seem like a way of finally aligning their work life with their professional ideology. Contractors not only hoped to make more money, they wanted to be treated as knowledgeable and to enjoy the autonomy, flexibility, and influence they believed they deserved. Our informants initially saw contracting as a way to escape the burdens of organizational life while securing the benefits and respect befitting a professional. After entering the world of contracting, they gradually found that their choices and skills sorted them into different groups or types of contractors by their tax status and level of expertise.

---

[4] There is a large literature dating from the 1960s that examines the difficulties that engineers and especially scientists have in working in a bureaucracy. Engineers are particularly likely to demand a say over techniques and technical issues. See Kornhauser (1962), Peltz and Andrews (1966), Ritti (1971), Raelin (1985), and Bailyn (1982, 1985).

What Kinds of Contractors Are There?

Legal Standing

Contractors and others drew a distinction between "W-2s" and "independent contractors," terms that signaled the contractor's tax status. "W-2s" worked through staffing agencies as an agency's employee for the duration of a contract. As employees, they signed an IRS W-2 form, which authorized the agency to withhold taxes from the contractor's paycheck. As a result, the agency legally became the contractor's employer-of-record.

Independent contractors were individuals who chose not to become temporary employees of a staffing agency, although some still used agencies as brokers. Most of the independent contractors whom we encountered were incorporated as businesses. Whether they negotiated directly with a client or worked through an agency, they carried their own liability insurance and struck contracts that were agreements between two organizations. The client or the staffing agency paid the contractor's corporation and then the contractor paid himself or herself. Some independent contractors, known as "1099s" after another IRS form, remained unincorporated. They rarely made use of staffing agencies, and clients paid them directly as individuals. Clients then reported the payment to the IRS on a "miscellaneous income" form, a "1099."[5] Whether incorporated or unincorporated, independent contractors were responsible for paying their own income, social security, and employment taxes.

Expertise

Although differences in legal standing affected the way contractors did business, far more important for their everyday lives were differences in expertise. Contractors, staffing agencies, and hiring managers routinely classified contractors by perceived skill. When asked, "What kinds of contractors are there?" informants drew lines between "gurus" and "warm bodies," "pros" and "bottom-feeders," "consultants" and "contractors," "specialists" and "generalists," or "seniors" and "juniors." Although each set of terms carried slightly different connotations, all invoked an informal understanding of occupationally specific hierarchies of knowledge and skill. Where contractors stood, or were thought to stand, in an occupation's pecking order influenced the jobs they obtained and, by extension, the roles and relations they enjoyed on the job. A contractor's place in an

---

[5] Twenty-seven of our contractors worked as independents at least part of the time. Of these, only five reported that they worked as 1099s. The rest were incorporated.

occupational hierarchy varied by specialization, reputation, breadth of experience, and type of task. To decide where a contractor stood, one had to know something about the subculture of the contractor's technical community.

Programmers and software developers judged practitioners' expertise by whether they did "design and architecture" or simply "wrote code" and did "maintenance." Although maintenance was difficult and necessary, it was considered to be boring and without glory. The status structure of software development also reflected how "close to the metal" one worked: whether one specialized in writing operating systems, designing applications that sat on top of operating systems, or simply tailoring commercial applications to a customer's needs. Glenn Arthur, an experienced contractor and software developer, put it this way:

> There's a food chain. At the top you have super specialists—UNIX kernel programmers, network programmers, people who do real-time operating systems, people who do optimized object-oriented databases. I mean people who know architecture and performance issues down to the metal. They get $120, $200 an hour for the short-hit kind of thing. At the bottom it starts to overlap with office administration. You know, word processors and that kind of thing. People who do SQL, people who do Visual Basic, people who do things like FoxPro. I mean, just dumb database programs. There has been increasing stratification of skills. There is more of a caste system. So, you have the bottom-feeders. When I first got into contracting it seemed more like a consulting model; if you were contracting you had to know something and it had to be fairly high leverage. Now I think there's a lot of room for, "I know ELIAS QL." "Okay, fine, twenty-two bucks an hour. Thank you very much."

At the pinnacle of the market for contract developers sat acknowledged "gurus," contractors who had written books on languages and systems, who were widely known as experts in a technical community, and who could command large sums of money.

Among technical writers, individuals with reputations for deep knowledge of a function or technology were considered the most skilled. Clients often granted these contractors responsibility for planning and executing entire projects. Experienced writers might also be given more journalistic challenges, such as writing copy for public relations materials. Less experienced writers were hired for copyediting or writing portions of documents, which were thought to be less creative tasks. Katrina Labovski, a technical writer who had done both sorts of work, explained the distinction in terms of "specialists" and "generalists."

There are contractors who are very specialized. Like, they'll only write API documentation—application programming interfaces—the documents that tell you how to write an application that integrates with, you know, a particular set of Java classes or whatever. And then there are contractors who just go from contract to contract, who have a general know-how. They might also be generalists with respect to the tools they use. You know, like RoboHelp, a Windows help–authoring tool. It's a tool for creating help systems that run on Windows. All of some writers' work is RoboHelp work. I think people who are more specialized are more technically savvy. I think that's the main difference. I mean the reason they're specialized is they are generally very, very good in their area and by specializing they become even better at what they do. They develop an even stronger network. And they can command higher rates.

In quality assurance, status and expertise hinged on whether one could design a plan for testing software and hardware or simply modify and execute a method, perhaps using standard tools. Brenda O'Boyle, who had worked twelve years as a contractor, explained the difference between "consultants" and "contractors" by contrasting her own work to that of her husband, who also was a QA contractor:

> My husband works at a salary level higher than mine. He does the $100-an-hour-plus stuff. At that level, you are really getting a consultant as opposed to a contractor. They want them to do testing, but they also want them to set up procedures. They want test plans put in place. They probably wouldn't ask contractors to do that, a least not on a regular basis. If you are paying somebody $100-plus an hour, you are expecting "Pro from Dover" who can do something that someone with less experience and knowledge couldn't do. Generally, he goes into start-ups or organizations that are floundering. They need a pro to tell them what they need, and he may just come in for three to six months. Now as a contractor I certainly write test plans. But often I will test plans that are already there and they need someone to edit the test plans. You know, bring them up-to-date, follow through, and see if they still test for what they want and frequently they don't.

Contractors and hiring managers also distinguished between QA contractors who did "white-box" and "black-box" testing. The former worked directly with source code, which required knowledge of programming languages. The latter tested software using "tools," other programs, written specifically for finding bugs. White-box testing was considered to be more skilled and of higher status than black-box testing.

The Roles Contractors Play for Clients

The client's needs (which we discussed in chapter 2) and the contractor's level of expertise combined to shape the roles that contractors eventually played in the various firms where they worked. By "role" we do not mean the work that a contractor performed, although the nature of the work was involved, but rather the relationship that a contractor had with the firm's managers and employees while on contract. Victor Post, an Oracle database administrator, succinctly summarized the range of possible relationships: "There are two kinds of environments that I have worked in. In one, contractors are running the show. In the other, contractors are brought in more or less as technical janitors to clean up or do the extra work." Most contractors, and the managers who hired them, concurred with Victor's assessment. Four broad roles characterized how our informants described the way contractors fit into client firms. The roles carried different degrees of expertise and autonomy, responsibility, and authority. Although contractors did not have explicit terms for these roles, they recognized the distinctions.

Developer-Consultants

We use the term "developer-consultant" for contractors who were hired to design, implement, modify, or maintain an entire component of a firm's information system or who were responsible for other significant, but bounded, tasks. Developer-consultants, who were sometimes known as "gurus," might configure and implement a local area network, develop an application or database for managing business transactions, customize an existing application to a firm's needs, conceptualize a firm's Web presence, develop protocols for testing a firm's technology, and so on.

Most developer-consultants were independent contractors who worked primarily (but not exclusively) for small firms. They served as the firm's expert on a range of tasks within a specific domain of responsibility. Consequently, developer-consultants often had ongoing relationships with clients, which meant repeat business and opportunities for retainers. Some contractors, like Brian Willingham, only accepted contracts that allowed such a role.

Other contractors might work as developer-consultants only for some clients. Jeff Dorsey was a QA contractor who had begun to design Web pages. He acquired QA contracts through a staffing agency. On these, he worked as a W-2 and performed tasks much like those done by other permanent employees. But as a Web designer, Jeff contracted independently. He acquired his Web contracts by word of mouth and enjoyed an exclusive relationship with his clients. As Brian Willingham explained, developer-consultants enjoyed considerable autonomy and opportunities to tackle a wide array of problems, thereby developing a range of skills:

> I have built inventory systems, customer-tracking systems. I've done the database for Top-5. Now, I'm getting into Web sites and Web site design and databases for Web sites. With some exceptions, I don't think any two customers have been the same thing. Rather than focus on a particular industry, I just say, "Hey, whatever needs to be done, give me a phone call and we'll see if we can work something out." And so, the jobs have been kind of scatterbrained, but on the other hand, I've had a lot of fun. You know, I've built multimedia CD-ROMs, and all the issues that go along with that. Mac and PC. Take the same CD-ROM and put it on a Mac or on a PC and it'll run. That was a neat trick.

Experienced Experts

Contractors whom we call "experienced experts" resembled developer-consultants in important ways: both tended to be older, had contracted for a significant period of time, had reputations for expertise, and were granted considerable autonomy. But unlike developer-consultants, experienced experts worked for larger firms and played less of an advisory role. Experienced experts were valued primarily as technical authorities, virtuosos, and, when particularly accomplished, "gurus."

Experienced experts had deep knowledge of a technology and were gifted at their craft, whether it was writing technical documents or Java code. Some worked with legacy systems, which were especially important in creating opportunities for experienced experts during the Y2K scare when large firms paid high rates for programmers who knew FORTRAN and COBOL. Other contractors were considered experienced experts because they understood a technology in ways that young engineers were no longer trained to understand. Bill Smith explained how automation had created a market for his knowledge:

> Used to be that circuits were handcrafted. Circuit designers would figure out what the minimum size was. It was very critical to get the smallest transistor, you know, because the die area was [*makes a circle with his hands*]. Or it would use power; that's another consideration. Well, the tools now are such that it's all kind of automated. And everybody runs—what's it called?—Synopsys, a synthesis tool [for designing integrated circuits]. But a lot of people really don't know the details of how that works. And that's where I come in, checking to make sure the real transistors work like what the tool says they're supposed to work like. I actually designed the cells at

one point in time, so I'm fairly familiar with what's underneath the symbol for an N-gate. So one of the things I do is make sure the systems tool is not lying to the designer. The tools are set up so that people who come out as a B.S. Double-E can design and integrate the circuits with very little experience. You know, like go take a class and get to work. But they don't have the experience to understand the design flow and stuff like that. So it's an opportunity for somebody like myself.

Experienced experts frequently called themselves "hired guns," "troubleshooters," "problem solvers," or "analysts." By these terms they conveyed their preference for working on problems that permanent employees were having difficulty resolving. Sam Muller, an experienced technical writer with a degree in electrical engineering, illustrated the way experienced experts worked:

> Here is what I do. It depends on the level. It depends on if someone wants a high-level description of how something works. For example, Toshiba MRI needed me to do just that. They did not want me to go into the bits and bytes of the computer and all that other stuff. They just wanted to know how the system worked and what that system did. That is called high level. High level does not mean "better than low level," it just means that it is more of a bird's-eye view. Low level, in fact, is more difficult than high level in some ways. They say, "Well, we have a problem." One of my assignments right now is to find out what the problem is. I will be specific. They have a simulator that simulates one of these expensive machines. The software people use the simulator to test their software. By doing it on a simulator instead of a real machine, the company saves the cost of owning and maintaining an expensive machine. It seems as if no one is keeping the simulators. They have four or five of them. One is broken, another got burned up in a truck fire, another seems to be over in another building, and the two that the software engineers are using are out of order half the time. There are no technicians assigned specifically to those machines. So the boss usually begs the other department to lend him technicians for a short while. Get the idea? Now he says, "Is there anything you can do about this? Can you pull together some documentation on how this machine works and how we can fix it?"

Hiring managers concurred that the experienced expert was a distinct type of contractor and admitted that they hired such contractors because they needed a troubleshooter. Anthony Greener, director of software development in a small start-up, explained the role by contrasting the breadth of the charge he gave to experienced experts with the charge he gave to most contractors, who were hired for their "particular skills":

If we're looking for a particular skill, we throw them on the job. We
assume that they're coming in with that skill and get immersed very
quickly in what's going on. Now the individual, John Gregory, that
I was telling you about—we basically said, "John, okay. We have a
problem with our database. I want you to take a look at it. Come
back with a recommendation for what we should do. I want you to
take a look at the skills of the people that we have on board, and I
want you to put some training programs in place to bring up their
skills and to work with them to improve the design and clean it up
and get up to a point where we've got a reliable database." So he
was given a lot of discretion.

Like many hiring managers, Russell Brown, a software manager at
UNIX Hardware, expected experienced experts to serve as consultants
and educators: "I have a total of three contractors. One is actually a person who worked on the project in the past, had a great deal of experience
with what we were doing. He was full-time two years ago and left UNIX
Hardware ultimately to do contracting. One of his roles was to be a—I
don't want to say liaison—but an educator, you know because he knew a
lot about the product. So he really helps out a lot just letting people
know how the whole process works, how the product works. That's not
normally what I'd expect from a contractor."

Temporary Full-Timers

What hiring managers did usually expect was an extra hand. Consequently, most contracts entailed assuming a role very much like that of a
permanent employee. From the perspective of the work itself, there were
no significant differences between what contractors and full-timers did.
Temporary full-timers were usually hired because a project team needed
assistance but was not authorized to increase its headcount. Because
these situations were not remarkable, contractors rarely discussed these
experiences in depth. Instead, they would simply remark, "I was treated
like an employee." Contractors did note, however, that in such jobs there
was an initial period of adjustment and that it took time before they were
fully integrated into the work process.[6]

Support Technicians

As we have seen, some clients hired contractors to do important but relatively mundane work that full-time employees didn't want to do. This was

---

[6] The need to integrate contractors into the work flow clashed with the requirement to
keep them at arm's length with respect to the social aspects of work. We explore these con-
flicts and ambiguities in part 4.

the work of Victor Post's "technical janitors," or what others often called a "warm body." Precisely what the work entailed varied from occupation to occupation and site to site, but it usually contributed to the maintenance of a technical infrastructure. Accordingly, on such contracts, the contractor became a kind of support technician. Contractors generally had two broad responses to playing such a role. The first was to complain that the work wasn't challenging, that it offered no chance to learn new skills, and that the client really wasn't making use of the contractor's talents. In short, the contract offered no leverage on the future.

The contractors' second response was usually to offer caveats. Even though working as a support technician lacked challenge, the work was easy and the level of compensation was so high that it didn't matter. This was especially true for those contractors who had a more instrumental orientation to work. Fred Tyler, a sixty-year-old contractor who specialized in data conversions, found technical support roles to be precisely what he wanted at his stage of life. He remarked on his current job: "I'm pretty much following a plan that has already been set up. I'm just dealing with quirks of the data, idiosyncrasies—you know, data problems, that sort of thing. It's not a very creative job; it can get to be very tedious. The only reason for doing it is it's reasonably straightforward, it's easy to do, and it pays well."

Fred's commentary underscores how technical contracting belies the institutionalists' image of contingent work based on temporary employment in lower-skilled jobs. Technical contractors were relatively well paid, even when doing the work of a support technician. It would also be a mistake to equate mundane technical work with low-skilled work. In technical fields, routine work was not thought to be unskilled; it was simply thought to be uninteresting. Sara Munzer, an IT specialist at Chipco, explained the difference:

> These contractors have specific Oracle tool experience, with the Oracle SQL language. We assign them to projects. Like when we went through an upgrade, all the reports needed dates changed or they needed certain changes made over and over and over again through all the reports. And we had to test the reports to make sure they worked right. We used them for that: to make those kinds of changes. It's routine and it's specific too. But nobody here really knows Oracle tools very well. It's complicated. It's hard to learn. And it doesn't always work the way you think it's going to. [So] the routine change wasn't all that easy. But it had to be done. It had to be done over and over and over again. It may be complicated, but it is repetitive. That's the type of thing that contractors can be very effective on.

In sum, working as a developer-consultant or experienced expert brought contractors considerably more autonomy, responsibility, and authority than did working as a temporary full-timer or support technician. Although the roles that contractors played varied from contract to contract, most of our informants seemed to accept contracts that suggested they specialized in playing a particular kind of role. Those who worked regularly as support technicians were a minority among the contractors we interviewed. Although most had done mundane work from time to time, only twelve (17 percent) of our seventy-one informants had careers that fit Victor Post's notion of "technical janitor": individuals who were routinely hired as support technicians to perform tasks that were undesirable to permanent employees. With several notable exceptions, like Fred Tyler, these contractors were younger, had fewer years of experience, and specialized in information technology, quality assurance, or technical writing. Nearly 40 percent of our informants described careers in which they now functioned either as developer-consultants or experienced experts. As one might expect, these individuals were older and had more experience. The rest (43 percent) were neither newcomers nor pros and typically worked in the role of a temporary full-timer.

CONCLUSION

As we have seen, contractors come to contracting from diverse backgrounds with a wide range of technical skills. Yet, despite this diversity, common themes ran through their stories: the desire to avoid the politics of permanent employment, a willingness to take risks, and a readiness to experiment with forging a new type of professionalism based on independence and continual exposure to the market. Although some wound up doing relatively routine work, many found themselves playing a substantial role in client firms. In this respect their motives more closely resembled those celebrated by the discourse on free agency than those feared by the institutionalists. But as we shall see in parts 2 and 3, once our informants became contractors, they encountered the aspirations of other actors, and that began to create tension. In particular, as we saw in chapter 2, clients wanted to hire contractors for instant access to skills at a reasonable cost with no strings attached and without the threat of legal hassles. Crucial for the clients' ability to attain these objectives were the staffing agencies that brokered the market but who remain offstage in the tales told by institutionalists and free agenteers. To understand the world of contracting, agents must be brought center stage where they belong.

Chapter 4

AGENCIES

STAFFING AGENCIES were the third set of actors central to the world of technical contracting. Agencies brokered the market: they compiled information on job openings as well as information on contractors who desired jobs, they negotiated matches, closed deals, and in most cases, acted as the contractors' employer-of-record. In return for their efforts, agencies charged clients a "margin," or a "markup," which they attached to the "pay rate"—the hourly wage that the contractor actually received. Markups worked as follows: if a contractor's pay rate was $80 per hour and the agency's markup was 35 percent ($28), then the "bill rate"—the rate the client paid the agency for the contractor's services—was $108 an hour. In this example, the agency would make $28 in revenue for every hour that the contractor worked.

Out of the markup, agencies deducted payroll taxes (approximately 15 percent of the contractor's income), the costs of recruiting, and the administrative expenses associated with maintaining the contractor on its payroll. Agencies also paid a percentage of their markup as commissions to the agents who placed the contractor. The remainder was the agency's profit. Most agencies considered the size of their markups to be proprietary information and instructed agents to avoid discussing markups with contractors and clients. Some agencies charged a fixed markup, while others tried to negotiate the best markup possible on every deal.

The markup an agency actually charged in any particular case depended on a number of factors. Most agencies had policies about the lowest percentage they would accept. Some also had ceilings, as well, justified by the belief that a reputation for price gouging would only hurt the agency in the long run. Within these usually wide parameters, markups depended on the parties' negotiating skills and on the circumstances of the deal. For example, skilled, experienced contractors who were savvy about how agencies operated could usually bargain down the markup. Agencies complied in these cases because they understood that being able to offer an attractive candidate to a client increased the odds of repeat business. Moreover, because skilled contractors usually demanded higher pay rates, an agency could reduce its markup on an experienced contractor and still make a handsome profit. The markups on pass-throughs were generally lower than markups on deals in which agents had to work to make a placement. Markups were also usually lower on third-party deals because collaborating agencies could not each charge a full markup and still present the client with an acceptable bill rate. Our observations and interviews indicate that markups ranged from a low of 15 percent to highs of 100 percent or more, with an average of 30 to 35 percent.

Two frontline occupations were central to every agency's practice: *account managers* (or *sales managers*) and *recruiters*.[1] Account managers were agents whose job it was to identify client organizations, locate hiring managers, and convince them to open job orders and, eventually, close deals. To do their work, they relied on databases and cold calling, as well as on their network of contacts with hiring managers. Recruiters were agents who specialized in locating the contractors with whom the agency filled its 'job orders.' To do so they also managed and searched databases, made cold calls to candidates, attended events where contractors could be found, and so on.

How to best structure and allocate the work of recruiters and account managers was a matter of debate among staffing agencies. Some, especially the smaller ones, combined the two roles so that agents were responsible for both recruiting and sales. Others delegated portions of the recruiters' or the account managers' work to specialists. Information Technology Specialists (ITS) and Systems Professionals, for example, employed *inside sales* agents, telemarketers responsible for calling potential hiring managers, identifying leads, and cleaning databases. The telemarketers passed potential leads to account managers who then pursued job orders. At the time of our research, Progressive Staffing was experimenting with agents who specialized in searching the Internet for potential contractors and who then passed promising leads to recruiters.

SALES CULTURE AND TECHNICAL CULTURE

The culture of work in most agencies revolved around sales, and most agents, especially account managers, thought of themselves as salespeople. The senior managers at Progressive Staffing and ITS had previously worked in other temporary or permanent placement agencies. At Systems Professionals and ITS, a number of senior managers had also worked as software developers and engineers. But even at Systems Professionals and ITS, where the sales culture was less strong than at Progressive Staffing, the majority of recruiters and account managers had backgrounds in sales in other industries ranging from computer equipment to retail merchandizing.

---

[1] We shall use the term "account manager" throughout the book.

As in all sales organizations, "closing deals" was every agent's overriding concern, in large measure because the agents' compensation was tightly linked to their sales performance. Of course, recruiters and account managers were paid annual salaries, but these were low, especially by Silicon Valley standards (usually between $24,000 and $40,000). Recruiters and account managers whose salary made up the bulk of their earnings quickly left the agency, not only because they could not afford to live on their salary but because they were, by everyone's definition, performing poorly and would sooner or later be fired.

The bulk of an agent's compensation came from bonuses and commissions. Agencies used numerous measures to track an agent's performance. For example, managers at Progressive Staffing tracked "traffic," the number of contractors that recruiters interviewed on-site. They also tracked the number of cold calls that agents made, the number of leads they landed, the number of interviews they scheduled, and the number of on-site visits they made to clients and working contractors. Progressive Staffing promoted, gave raises, and offered sizable bonuses to agents who performed well on these criteria. In addition, managers publicly celebrated high-performing agents at weekly meetings with songs, testimonials, and group cheers. Placing a large number of contractors and generating exceptional levels of revenue brought special awards ranging from gift certificates and dinners at upscale restaurants to vacations in Mexico, Hawaii, and other exotic locales.

Although bonuses and one-time rewards mattered, commissions were the most important element of an agent's compensation. Using one formula or another, every firm we studied allocated a portion of a deal's markup to the agents who closed the deal. This meant that for some portion of every hour on the job, contractors were earning money for the agents who placed them. An agent could increase her commission in four ways: by negotiating higher markups, by concentrating on placing skilled contractors who commanded higher rates, by maximizing a contractor's billable hours, and by placing more contractors. At Progressive Staffing agents posted and updated the number of dollars that "their" contractors were generating per hour on white boards near their desks, a practice encouraged by the company and designed to motivate both the agent and her peers. Most agents claimed that with bonuses and commissions they could double, triple, or even quadruple their base salary depending on the year.

Although many recruiters and account managers made out handsomely, like all sales work, the job of selling contractors was heavy on disappointment. A day in the life of a recruiter or account manager was a string of unreturned phone calls, misleading information, verbal rejections, edgy negotiations, and missed opportunities, balanced by constant hope, unrelenting ambition, and the occasional elation of closing a deal.

Because rejection and disillusionment dogged even the most successful and cheery agents and because the demand for experienced agents was heavy, turnover ran high.[2] For example, during the six months that we were at Progressive Staffing, nearly a third of the agents whom we met left for one reason or another. Nationally, turnover among recruiters and account managers in 1999 stood at 70 percent and 50 percent respectively.[3]

Unlike salespersons in most other settings, agents who brokered technical contractors faced an additional dilemma: the challenge of selling technical people to technical companies with only a dim understanding of technical work. Few recruiters and account managers had training or experience in a technical field. Yet to be successful, or at least to avoid appearing foolish, agents had to be minimally conversant in the technical language of the market segment in which they plied their trade. Conveying competence and building trust with contractors and clients demanded projecting at least a rudimentary awareness of the ins and outs of technical work. Of course, there were some agents who found that they could get by knowing very little about technology, because they could capitalize on their good looks, interpersonal skills, and sexuality. But for the majority these qualities were not enough.

Accordingly, agents tried hard to develop a working knowledge of the technical worlds that provided their livelihood. During our fieldwork, we met recruiters and account managers who routinely read magazines and newsletters on computer technology. Some had even tried their hand at programming and developing Web pages. Most followed the fortunes of high-tech firms and avidly consumed articles in the business press on trends in technology. Most also sought on-the-job training from their more experienced colleagues and from the contractors and managers they encountered. But even with such efforts, few agents developed more than a rudimentary understanding of technical terminology and a passing acquaintance with technologies and technical practice.

Encounters between agents, contractors, and clients were, therefore,

---

[2] Because of the hot labor market and the growth of the staffing industry, at the time of our study, there was considerable demand for agents. Progressive Staffing's managers regularly raided the competition and also tried to recruit people with sales experience in other industries. Successful agents were also faced with the temptation to strike out on their own. Turnover at Systems Professionals was reasonably high as well. Turnover at ITS was lower, in part because ITS's agents were considerably older than those employed by either System Professionals or Progressive Staffing. Although the management of staffing firms recognized and, in fact, capitalized on the lack of loyalty between employers and employees, they were less tolerant when their own employees sought to become free agents.

[3] Data were provided by Tim Brogan, Senior Manager, Public Information, American Staffing Association on the ASA's Web site: http://www.staffingtoday.net/memberserv/1100ss/story15.htm.

almost always encounters between members of very different social worlds. Hiring managers and contractors were acutely aware that most agents had little technical knowledge. As a result, they initially approached agents with suspicion and, in some cases, even hostility. Agents brought biases of their own to the encounter. For instance, recruiters and account managers generally believed that as a group, technical people lacked social skills and graces, which they more than made up for with an excess of arrogance. Agents claimed that the combination was particularly deadly not only because it made contractors unpleasant to deal with, but also because it often undermined the agents' efforts to make contractors presentable to clients.

How agencies handled the disappointments inherent in a sales culture and the trials and tribulations of standing outside the technical worlds that provided them with business varied from firm to firm. Progressive Staffing's approach was to embrace and amplify the sales culture under the assumption that fostering competition within a climate of support and enthusiasm would not only counterbalance disappointment but also neutralize the staff's lack of technical acumen. Judging by the firm's tremendous growth and financial success, the strategy worked.

Upon entering Progressive Staffing, even the most casual observer would have to be blind to miss the sheen of energy and optimism that pervaded everyday life in the firm. In the main vestibule of the firm's headquarters, visitors encountered receptionists seated at a long oak counter greeting every phone call with a clearly scripted, but nonetheless enthusiastic, "Good morning! It's another great day at Progressive Staffing!" On "the floor," as the sales area was called, outsiders would immediately notice well-dressed and attractive young men and women, milling about or sitting at clusters of desks working phones and computers while soft rock played noticeably, yet unobtrusively, over the intercom.[4] The constant murmur of otherwise ordinary conversations was punctuated with a cheery stream of superlatives—"Great!" "Super!" "Outstanding!" "Awesome!"—that gave talk at Progressive Staffing a buoyant tone.[5] From time

[4] Progressive Staffing was organized by technical market: Windows developers, UNIX developers, CAD technicians, network technicians, technical writers, and so on. The recruiters and account managers in these groups sat at desks so close to each other that the desks sometimes touched. The arrangement defined groups in open space and contributed to a consciousness of team effort.

[5] The degree to which enthusiasm could become a linguistic reflex became apparent on those occasions when emotional trouble was met with incongruent optimism. One morning an account manager was telling his peers in the coffee room that his daughter had been diagnosed with cancer. He confided that although the original lesion had disappeared, the doctors had recently found seven more. In response to his revelation, another agent, who must have only been half listening, replied with an cheery, "Great!" "What do you mean, 'Great'? inquired the overwrought father, clearly offended. "It's much worse."

to time, the reverberation of a brass gong parsed the flow of action, signaling "a close." Recruiters and account managers across the floor then
momentarily stopped work and rose from their seats to congratulate the
lucky agent with high fives, slaps on the back, and way-to-go's, suppressing for both themselves and for others whatever envy they might have instinctively felt at the agent's good fortune.

Twice weekly, Progressive Staffing's managers held fifteen- to twenty-
minute "morning meetings," assembling agents from across the floor in
an open space to review business, announce birthdays, and, most important, celebrate the achievements of the past several days, both major and
minor. Agents who had landed new leads, scheduled interviews, brought
in especially promising contractors, found a useful new Web site, or
made other sacrifices or contributions were publicly acknowledged with
applause, hugs, and sometimes even kisses. Managers used these occasions to give "stump speeches," Progressive Staffing's version of a pep
talk that focused on "productivity" and "numbers." Individual agents
stood and testified to being "pumped up" and encouraged others to be
"pumped" as well. Cookies were shared; songs were sung; and occasionally a manager would announce a game or competition that pitted agents
against each other in good spirit, ritualistically acknowledging the real
competition among them for clients, contractors, and placements. The
climate of energy and optimism of Progressive Staffing's morning meetings reached crescendos on holidays and other special occasions, as our
field notes attest:

> We arrived at around 9:15 A.M. to discover today's morning meet-
> ing, a Halloween party, in full blast. The door from the outer lobby
> was propped open under the pressure of the onlookers' bodies. The
> only people at work, sort of, were the receptionists, who asked us to
> close the door so they could continue fielding calls. Anne (the CEO)
> pulled us into the group. Practically everybody was there, standing
> in a circle and dressed in costumes, some quite elaborate. The MC,
> Nathan, was dressed as a greaser straight out of *American Graffiti*.
> He invited competitors for the best costume award to come for-
> ward. Against the far wall stood the judges: Maria, director of R&D
> (all decked out in white), and Anne and Leo, the CEO and vice pres-
> ident, looking as if they had time-traveled from Haight-Ashbury via
> the *Sonny and Cher Show*. One by one, Nathan called competitors
> to come forward to raucous cheers and catcalls: there was Orrin the
> fairy, Karen the box of chocolates, and a host of others. After the in-
> dividual awards, the group awards began. The Windows Group ap-
> peared as the crew of the starship *Enterprise*. The Network Group
> debuted as the Three Blind Mice. Finally, Anne and Leo delivered a
> hootenanny version of "If I Were a Carpenter," with Anne on guitar

and Leo flashing peace signs as if he had once had a bit too much practice. While the judges conferred, John did a convincing interpretation of a male stripper, which brought Julie screaming forward to grope. Awards were administered, costumes removed, and people returned to their desks just as the receptionists once again began forwarding calls to the desks. Another great day at Progressive Staffing had begun.

Progressive Staffing also collectively acknowledged and managed the disappointments of selling. The loss of a lead, a put-down from a rude contractor or an impatient hiring manager, and especially the breakdown of a deal triggered public commiseration. Agents not only offered other agents sympathy, they helped each other attribute failure to external causes: to the personalities of contractors and hiring managers ("He was a twerp"), to the collective shortcomings of technical people ("They can't tie their shoes without help"), or to the cultures of companies ("They work by mushroom management. They're always in the dark standing in shit."). Tasks that guaranteed a stream of rejections were sometime done as a group in an atmosphere of play. Such was the "Big MAC Attack," a collective response to the emotional disincentives for doing "marketing action calls" (MACs). To stage a Big MAC Attack, recruiters and account managers set aside four or more hours during the day or evening, ordered food, and began making call after call after call from a bank of telephones—sometimes to potential hiring managers, at other times to potential contractors. The ritual put agents with various levels of experience simultaneously in the same situation where it was easier to see that everyone failed most of the time and to learn from the more jaded how to discount rejection with humor.

Progressive Staffing openly embraced sales culture in other ways as well. Although no one said so explicitly, Progressive Staffing clearly understood what social psychologists have long known: that most of us are willing to let ourselves be influenced by attractive people.[6] The men and women who worked at Progressive Staffing were, on average, younger, better looking, and definitely better dressed than agents at Information Technology Specialists and Systems Professionals. Most of the women wore makeup and dressed to accentuate their femininity while remaining well within the bounds of good taste. Fashion was a standard topic of conversation among Progressive Staffing's agents, as were nutrition, health, tips on dressing, and critiques of sales at Nordstrom's, Macy's, and Neiman-Marcus. The men all wore ties and many wore two-piece

---

[6] The social psychological literature on liking and attractiveness as determinants of successful influence is both large and convincing. Robert Cialdini's *Influence: The Psychology of Persuasion* (1984) offers a particularly well-written and entertaining introduction to this line of research.

suits, except on Fridays, which were known as "dress-down days."[7] A significant number of the men were bodybuilders and preferred fitted dress shirts. All of the men had short, neatly trimmed hair. Progressive Staffing required account managers to make visits each week to hiring managers even in the absence of job orders. Recruiters were expected to visit contractors in the field every Friday to deliver paychecks. Agents distributed "collateral," ranging from mouse pads and T-shirts to "stress-relieving squeegee balls," to clients and contractors at every opportunity. In dress and behavior then, Progressive Staffing's agents consciously stood out amid the rumpled, jeaned, and T-shirted engineering managers and contractors to whom they hawked opportunities.

At the opposite end of the spectrum lay Systems Professionals' approach. Whereas Progressive Staffing embraced sales, Systems Professionals went to great lengths to distance itself from the typical sales-oriented companies, which Paul Van Leer, Systems Professionals' president, seemed to enjoy characterizing as "thieves and dolts." Systems Professionals wished to avoid being perceived as anything other than technically sophisticated, competent, and appropriately arrogant. For the most part, Systems Professionals had gotten its wish. Among clients and competitors, Systems Professionals was known as one of a handful of staffing agencies that actually understood the technologies its contractors serviced. Systems Professionals was able to build such a reputation, in part, because it specialized almost entirely in providing UNIX and NT (Microsoft Windows) systems administrators. UNIX and NT operating systems were reasonably well-defined bodies of technical knowledge. Widely accepted standards for testing and classifying a "sys admin's" knowledge of UNIX and NT also existed.[8]

---

[7] The social practice of having "dress-down days" had its beginnings in the high-tech industry in the 1960s and 1970s, especially among manufacturers of minicomputers (like DEC and Data General) on the East Coast where suits and ties have always been more de rigueur than in California. Dress-down days were ways of signaling to the rest of the world that computer engineers and software developers are a different breed. That Progressive Staffing had adopted this practice in the Silicon Valley where everyday is usually a dress-down day provides not only a signal of the difference between the staffing industry and the firms it served, but also a measure of the firm's identification with high technology.

[8] For UNIX, Systems Professionals assessed skills using tests and guidelines developed by SAGE, the Systems Administrators' Guild which is a "Special Technical Group" of the USENIX Association. USENIX is the Advanced Computing Systems Association. (Don't expect acronyms to map onto the first letters of English words. We have entered the land of UNIX!) According to SAGE's Web site, SAGE "is organized to advance the status of computer system administration as a profession, establish standards of professional excellence and recognize those who attain them, develop guidelines for improving the technical and managerial capabilities of members of the profession, and promote activities that advance the state of the art or the community" (http://sageweb.sage.org/about/#STARTED). For NT administrators, Systems Professionals was exploring using Microsoft training and certification procedures.

Systems Professionals employed a small staff of technical experts, former UNIX systems administrators, who tested and rated every contractor that Systems Professionals hired. Systems Professionals' technical services staff were widely recognized as experts within the larger UNIX community. Members had published a number of papers in professional journals, and Randy Sorrow, the head of the group, had authored a text on the Windows Domain Name System. When Systems Professionals' testing regime revealed that a contractor lacked sufficient knowledge, he or she was not hired. Systems Professionals' technical staff also ran training programs for the firm's contractors and formally documented the growth of each contractor's technical ability at annual intervals.

Systems Professionals maintained a cutting-edge computer laboratory where contractors could hone existing skills, learn new ones, and practice with new hardware and software in the evenings or when they were "on the bench" (between jobs). Systems Professionals offered seminars for their contractors and for the larger technical community, including one of the Valley's first workshops on Linux, which was well attended. Systems Professionals had also developed a Web-based repository of technical tips, information, workarounds, and documentation, which it called its "Virtual Technical Community," and which its systems administrators could access and post to at any time. Finally, Systems Professionals provided Internet chat rooms and bulletin boards, which its contractors could use to consult directly with each other about technical issues.

Because Systems Professionals could verify its contractors' skills and because the firm understood the work of systems administration in detail, the agency encouraged its account managers to approach sales as a technical negotiation. In fact, Systems Professionals had only recently begun to hire account managers without a technical background. "We vacillate back and forth between whether we want staffing industry experience or we don't," explained Paul Van Leer. "For three years we wouldn't hire anybody who had ever worked in the staffing industry. Then a few years ago, we decided that's too arrogant even for us. So we hired a few and were not unsatisfied with them. We used to think that account managers had to be technical people, but we don't think that anymore. But they have to have sold something pretty technical and they have to have a pretty good grasp of what we do, or it's going to take too long to explain enough so that they can draw up requirements intelligently."

Systems Professionals' approach to filling job orders was also unorthodox among staffing agencies. After explaining the agency's business model, identifying a hiring manager's needs, and assessing a job's requirements, Systems Professionals' account managers insisted that the agency be allowed to pick the consultant for the job without client input. In return, Systems Professionals promised that clients could request that their contractor be replaced, without charge and without question, if the contractor proved technically or interpersonally inept anytime within the first two weeks. Approximately 60 percent of hiring managers assented to Systems Professionals' terms. In the other 40 percent of the cases, Systems Professionals allowed what it called an "interview start." Systems Professionals would send out one (and only one) of its "sys admins" who were on the bench at the time. The client interviewed the contractor and if the hiring manager was satisfied, the contractor went to work immediately. If not, Systems Professionals would send another contractor on an "interview start." What Systems Professionals refused to do was to provide clients with a set of résumés or allow them to hold a series of interviews from which the hiring manager could choose the contractors he wished to pursue further. Systems Professionals' account managers were instructed to walk away from clients who wouldn't do business on these terms. In this way, Systems Professionals framed itself as a provider of technical services, rather than a broker. Such deals usually took on the aura of a negotiation between members of the same technical community, thereby circumventing the clash of cultures that haunted other agencies.

Systems Professionals differed from most other agencies in several other ways, as well. Because 80 percent of Systems Professionals' contractors were full-time employees, its recruiters functioned more like talent scouts. They scoured college campuses and the IT departments of firms in search of working system administrators whom they could lure into Systems Professionals' vision of contracting. Recruiting at Systems Professionals, therefore, more closely resembled traditional personnel work. Systems Professionals also employed "staff managers," individuals who served as human resource liaisons and career advisors to Systems Professionals' contractors. The role was unique among the staffing firms we encountered, and as we shall see in later chapters, staff managers significantly shaped Systems Professionals' involvement with contractors when they were on contract.

Information Technology Specialists' approach to managing the disappointments of sales and the clash of cultures lay somewhere between Progressive Staffing's and Systems Professionals'. Like Systems Professionals, ITS specialized in placing highly skilled contractors for a small range of occupations, primarily IT and software development. Also like Systems Professionals, ITS actively tried to position itself as a technically sophisticated agency. But unlike Systems Professionals, ITS did not immerse itself in the technical culture of its contractors and clients, nor did it concern itself with technical practice. Instead, it sought to develop a reputation for technical savvy through marketing and research.

Marc Sunberg, ITS's founder and CEO, was an experienced and well-educated software developer. He had put considerable energy into building an artificial intelligence tool for processing contractors' résumés found either in ITS's databases or on the Internet. In the early 1990s, Sunberg had financed survey research on clients' needs and on IT contractors in the Silicon Valley. With the help of a survey researcher, Sunberg analyzed the data and wrote a series of research papers on the IT labor market and on staffing strategies as well as a monograph on the demography of highly skilled contractors in IT occupations in the Silicon Valley.

ITS employed a marketing specialist, Lynn Papper, whose job included turning Sunberg's working papers into attractive publications that account managers could send to prospective clients and hiring managers as part of a "nurturing packet" of brochures and information. Lynn explained ITS's strategy:

> As part of the research, Marc surveyed 1,700 consultants and hiring managers. Through these surveys we identified the kinds of publications they read. What we wanted to do was build relationships with the editors of those publications so that they would be writing about us and about the research that we've done and that would help. First of all it would position us with the media as an information resource, a very credible staffing firm. And the more we're in the media, the more it builds awareness with our clients and prospects. We did a book launch, which meant one-on-one meetings with various editors at target publications. We did a press release. We did white papers based on the data that usually give insight into a very specific industry market trend.

As a result of its research and publication strategy, other staffing agencies saw ITS as an intellectual leader and as a source of credible information about contractors and clients. Whether clients also perceived ITS to be intellectually and technologically credible was less clear, although ITS was known among clients for supplying experienced, highly skilled contractors.

Nevertheless, ITS's agents worked like salespersons, even though the firm lacked Progressive Staffing's sales culture.[9] The daily practices of ITS's account managers and recruiters were strikingly similar to those of Progressive Staffing's agents, but its work climate was quieter, more individualistic, and more subdued. Recruiters and account managers rarely held meetings and worked mostly on their own. Recruiters specialized in one or two technical markets, known as "disciplines" or "product lines."

---

[9] In fact, at the time of our study, ITS's managers had identified sales as the area in most need of reorganizing. Management felt that ITS required a stronger sales model.

ITS believed that such specialization reduced the chance that recruiters would compete with each other for the same contractors. Also unlike Progressive Staffing, ITS did not pair recruiters with account managers. Instead, recruiters worked out of private offices in ITS's headquarters, using databases and the Internet to supply candidates for contracting jobs to any account manager who needed experts of the type in which the recruiter specialized. Thus, at ITS, recruiters rarely searched for a contractor until an account manager was reasonably sure of a job order.

ITS granted its account managers geographical monopolies. Within their region, account managers were free to pursue any client or job order so long as the job required the skills in which ITS specialized. Unlike the recruiters, account managers worked from their own homes and rarely visited the agency's offices. Most communication between agents and account managers occurred via e-mail and over the phone. ITS's agents were generally older than Progressive Staffing's and had worked in the industry for many years. Most either had technical backgrounds or had worked as salespeople in a technical industry before coming to ITS.

What Types of Staffing Agencies Are There?

Progressive Staffing, Systems Professionals, and Information Technology Specialists illustrate the range of strategies and cultures that can be found among agencies that broker the market for technical contractors. Because this segment of the staffing industry is so young, the business world has yet to develop a system for classifying agencies by strategy or structure. But for those who live in the world of contracting, distinguishing among agencies is a matter of practical importance. Putting a label on an agency helped contractors and hiring managers decide whether they wanted to work with that agency and cued them about to what to expect. Labels also enabled recruiters and account managers to talk about, set themselves apart from, and if necessary denigrate, competitors. "Folk taxonomies" of agencies, therefore, infused our informants' talk. These taxonomies pointed, at least implicitly, to those attributes of agencies that mattered most to insiders.[10] As one might expect, the attributes that agents and clients considered important differed somewhat from those that concerned contractors. Moreover, even when clients, contractors,

---

[10] As throughout the book, we focus only on agencies that place individual contractors in client locations on an hourly basis. Some agencies also engage in project work, sometimes known as "turnkey projects." They assume full responsibility for a technical project or a part of a project. Although such agencies may do some or all of their work at the client's site, they are compensated on a fee-for-project basis.

and agents agreed on an attribute's importance, they were likely to hold different ideas of why it mattered.[11]

Size

If nothing else, contractors, agents, and hiring managers agreed that when it came to agencies, size mattered. Along this dimension, Progressive Staffing, ITS, and Systems Professionals were somewhere in the middle, although Progressive Staffing bordered on being large. Informants routinely referred to large agencies as "job shops" or "body shops," terms that usually connoted an array of dubious practices that everyone thought were most common among large agencies. But even small agencies merited being called a "body shop" if they played the game like one.

When informants referred to an agency as a "body shop" or a "job shop," they implied, at minimum, that the agency put making a profit ahead of ensuring the quality of the fit between the contractor and the job. From an agent's perspective, body shops "pushed résumés." They did little more than locate jobs and candidates, make quick matches, issue W-2s, and charge their markup. Body shops were not particularly rewarding places for an agent to work. They were agencies where agents were put under extraordinary pressure to produce. Body shops lacked professionalism. Rebecca McGuirk, one of Progressive Staffing's more experienced account managers, explained: "A body shop is like a sweat shop. They're order takers. Take the order. Match the résumé. Boom! Send them out. Not a whole lot of screening, not a whole lot of extra value. They don't go out to the customer and find out what the customer is really looking for. They don't look at the environment and the personality. It's like throwing darts."

Contractors and hiring managers generally concurred: using a "body shop" was like entering a "meat market." Charles Eaton, a highly skilled financial applications programmer, articulated the contractor's perspec-

---

[11] This portion of our analysis draws heavily on the tenets of "linguistic" or "cognitive" anthropology, the study of indigenous terms and their meaning. Linguistic anthropologists argue that the mental schemes that insiders use to chunk the world into manageable segments are the essence of a culture and that a culture's rules for chunking are encoded in its language. As the text indicates, the domain "kind of agency" had a number of mappings, which varied across speaker as well as role (contractor, client). Agents were more consistent in their use of these taxonomies than were contractors and clients. Hiring managers had the least well-developed language for talking about agencies. Anthropologically, this makes sense since agencies are a more important phenomenon in an agent's and a contractor's daily life. Nevertheless, the domain "type of agency" was not nearly as well developed as taxonomies that compose the slang of fully formed subcultures. For further information on linguistic anthropology, see Frake (1969, 1981), Conklin (1955), Barley (1983), and especially Spradley (1979).

tive: "The 'body shops' couldn't care less about who you are. All they want to do is get you billable. It does not matter if you have twenty-seven years of experience. If they have a job that will get $35 an hour, they will try to stick you in there." Contractors and clients quickly learned which firms operated as body shops and, hence, which could not be trusted to offer much beyond a cursory evaluation of résumés and occasional reference checks. In dealing with a body shop, hiring managers remained wary of being given "doctored" résumés and contractors were wary of being "taken advantage of." Nevertheless, hiring managers and contractors routinely worked through large agencies like Manpower and Volt that they otherwise derogated as body shops. They did so either as a matter of convenience or because they had no other choice, since many firms made such agencies their on-site vendors.

Less passionate informants noted that a "job shop" strategy was really nothing more than a "commodity strategy," which was not unreasonable for a large agency that sought economies of scale. Agencies that took this approach sought to minimize operating costs and focused on placing contractors with less esoteric skills while accepting lower markups in return for a higher volume of placements. Because job shops often trafficked in less skilled occupations, contractors sometimes called them "bottom-feeders." "Commodity staffing companies," explained Cynthia Lucha, a recruiter and a cofounder of ITS, "do low-end, high-volume, low rates and low margins. Their margins might be 15 percent, 20 percent, something like that. They don't provide a lot of service. They take résumés and send them out. They don't have strong recruiters because they can't afford them. Most have been involved in clerical placement and they are trying to do IT with the same model." Interestingly enough, although an agency might admit that it subscribed to a high-volume, low-margin strategy, none admitted that they were body shops. "Body shops," it seemed, were always other firms.

At the other end of the spectrum were "Mom and Pops," one- or two-person agencies that placed no more than a handful of contractors, doing what agents called "onesy-twosy" deals. Because barriers to entry into the staffing industry were low, Mom and Pops represented the majority of the agencies that brokered technical contractors, even though together they accounted for a small percentage of the market.[12] Often these tiny agencies were founded by an agent who learned the trade in a larger agency or by technical professionals who decided that they could make

[12] Organizational researchers have repeatedly shown that small firms account for most of the organizations that operate in a given field, market, or locality. They also account for most employment. Said differently, most organizational fields tend to be skewed toward smaller organizations, even when larger organizations that account for the most business attract the most attention. See Kalleberg et al. (1996).

money by brokering their colleagues. In fact, two of the contractors we interviewed were running a small staffing business on the side while working as contractors themselves.

"Fundamentally, this is a business that anyone can get into," admitted Leo Robinson, the president of Progressive Staffing, echoing what the top management of every agency told us. "If you are an ex-VP of engineering, you know something about hiring, you know something about what it takes to employ someone under a W-2. If you were an engineering guy, you probably have three or four buddies who are engineers. That's how a lot of the people get into this business. They were engineering types. They became a contractor. They have three people who are looking for a gig. They go find a gig. They bring their friends along. If they take a little bit of a fee for helping their buddies along, they realize, 'Hmm, I got an extra buck an hour off their payroll.' Next time they get five bucks for their payroll. Voilà! A staffing business is born."

Agents generally considered Mom and Pop agencies to be amateurish, "seat of the pants" operations. Hiring managers and contractors were less judgmental. Agents from Mom and Pop agencies were more likely to establish close personal relationships with their clients and contractors, which the latter generally preferred. Informants implied that Mom and Pop agencies founded by technical experts were more likely to understand the hiring manager's technical requirements and the contractor's skills than were agents at larger firms. But because a Mom and Pop agency's reach was limited and its volume was low, it usually could not deliver quickly when a hiring manager had a job order to fill or when a contractor needed a job. As with most small businesses, the failure rate among Mom and Pops was high. A small agency that was here today could well be gone tomorrow, leaving a contractor with unpaid wages, an experience that was not uncommon among our informants. For the most part, then, hiring managers and contractors generally preferred to work through larger agencies with more solid business credentials.

Specialization

Informants also used the scope of an agency's business to distinguish between staffing agencies. At one end of the continuum, were "generalists," agencies that made placements in a large number of technical occupations. Being a generalist enabled an agency to expand its market and increase its volume of business, but it also increased the range of knowledge and expertise that its agents required to work effectively. Other agencies were known as "specialty shops" or "niche players." These firms concentrated on placing contractors in no more than a handful of technical occupations. Specialization allowed a firm to develop greater familiarity with a market segment and, hence, develop deeper knowledge of technical requirements and skills. In general, specialists, like Systems Professionals and Information Technology Specialists, tended to be smaller firms. Progressive Staffing was an exception, but it simulated niche markets by dividing its staff into groups that focused on specific technologies and occupations, which allowed the groups to operate as if they were specialty shops. Excluding Mom and Pop agencies, generalists were more common than specialists. Paul Van Leer, for example, believed that generalists were common because most agencies found it difficult to turn down the possibility of a placement:

> This is an industry dominated by generalists from the very biggest like Andersen, all the way down to the smallest. Everybody wants to do everything! Their idea of focus is, "We only do IT!" I mean, seventy job categories! How do you do that? We don't know. They'll tell you, "We have six areas of focus and our Sacramento office does this focus and this office does that focus." So you ask the question, "Well if your Sacramento office gets an order for this thing which isn't in their focus, what do you do with it?" They all look at you like you're stupid! Because what they're going to do is take that order. No one can believe that anyone wouldn't.

Sales or Technical Orientation

The final major distinction that informants used to sort agencies was whether an agency had a sales or a technical culture. As we have seen, it was this dimension that distinguished Progressive Staffing from Systems Professionals. From a contractor's or a hiring manager's perspective, the agents of a technically oriented agency were more likely to understand their work and, hence, more effectively match skills to job requirements. Although our data cannot tell us whether the perception was accurate, there is no doubt that the perception existed. Nevertheless, sales-oriented agencies were far more common than technically oriented agencies, if for no other reason than agencies had trouble remaining technical without also specializing, and specializing narrowed the market in which the agency could effectively operate. For this reason, contractors' and hiring managers' stereotypes of agents drew primarily on practices common among sales-oriented agencies.

These stereotypes usually revolved around the practice of cold calling and the agent's ignorance of technology. Noah Swetka's experience with agencies as an IT manager with Western Phone Company was similar to that of most hiring managers: "Somehow [agents] usually get wind of the fact that I have a 'req' out there, and so they start calling. And it's just a personality thing between the agent and me, but they call at inopportune times and pester me about, 'Do you have any openings?'—that kind of thing. They present people that just don't fit. They obviously don't hear when I describe my requirements or I wasn't clear."

But it was the contractors who were least forgiving of a sales orientation. "A lot of the recruiters who call you up on the phone aren't technically knowledgeable," confided Yolanda Turner. "I had one rep ask me, 'Would you rewrite your résumé so I can understand it and explain it?' And, I'm like, 'I don't think I'm going to work with you.' I mean, give me a break! That's his job! He's supposed to know that! And then there's the guys that call me and say, 'Do you know how to do such and such?' And you'll say, 'Well, is it on my résumé?' 'Well, no.' 'Then, why did you think I could do it?'" Stu Davis, an embedded systems engineer with years of experience as a contractor, was even less charitable about agents who lacked technical knowledge:

> You can tell you're in trouble when your recruiter acts like a pimp, and that's what most of them are. You can tell 'cause they'll call you up and say, "Look, do you have any [experience with] Visual Basic?" You say, "Well, no." "Well, have you ever done Basic?" "Yeah, I've done Basic." "Okay, good, we've got somebody who needs Visual Basic, you've done Basic. That's close enough." They are the ones who only want to find someone, no matter how tenuous the connection. Then you have others that really know, but these are the exception. They'll say: "Oh, we want somebody who has Motorola, PowerPC experience in telecommunications doing Sonnet," which is a very specific protocol. Those are the exception. Most are clueless. They're reading the requirements and you can tell when they mispronounce the jargon, that's a real big tip-off. They'll call me and say, "We need somebody to do an 'S.C.S.I. driver.'" What they mean is they want somebody to do a "Scuzzy" driver because everybody calls them Scuzzy. We don't call them S.C.S.I.

In sharp contrast, hiring managers and contractors typically claimed that they had better experiences and preferred to work with agents who understood the technical aspects of the work. Randy Bouchet, a manager in charge of font development at Raster, claimed that working with an agent could be "a good experience when the [account manager] has done a good job of interviewing you to start with. They really understand what the 'req' is, so that after they do the prescreening you will only be given résumés that are good matches. Unfortunately that means that the recruiter actually has to be fairly technical because they need to be able to ask questions, understand the answers, and do a little probing. There are recruiters that meet those requirements."

Good and Bad Agencies

Ultimately, however, what mattered most to contractors and hiring managers was the quality of the experience they had with an agent. These experiences directly affected how they classified agencies, and the classification was simple: agencies were either "good" or "bad." When clients and contractors found an agent acceptable to work with, the agency became a "good" agency. Agencies whose agents proved troublesome or ignorant were known as "bad" agencies. The distinction between "good" and "bad" agencies was so important in the culture of contracting that entire Web sites existed to provide contractors with a venue for sharing information on which agencies to use and which to avoid.

Among contractors, a good agency employed agents who treated contractors fairly, respected their needs, and understood their skills. For Anna Kapoor, an Indian software developer on an H1B visa, Progressive Staffing was such an agency:[13]

> My colleagues tell me about agencies where they had bad experiences. They do not have a good connection. The agency will place them and forget them. I feel Progressive Staffing is really very good in that way. Each week [an agent] will call and ask if I have any problems. Even the person who placed me, the manager, sometimes comes and sees me in the company and he will take me for lunch. He used to send me e-mail, "What do they say about the contract? Do you like the job?" If I am uncomfortable with the job, they say they will place me in another company. They are really good, compared to my colleagues' companies.

For hiring managers, the criteria for a good agent and, hence, a good agency were similar. Noah Swetka explained: "The good agents usually keep in touch. They come in and periodically just sit down and talk with me to find out where I'm going with the business, what projects I have. They'll have people in mind, so when I do need somebody, they are ready. They know exactly who to recommend and who they have available on a very short turnaround. It's that personal touch. I get to trust them, they know what I want, and it kind of works out." James Hambly, who managed the development of Advanced Computer's supply chain software, echoed Noah's assessment:

> You know, there are different types of placement people. A lot of it is the bonding that you end up having with the placement person. I

---

[13] Other contractors, however, said that Progressive Staffing was a "bad" agency to work for. The difference in opinion underscores how important relationships between particular agents and specific contractors (or hiring managers) were for the agency's reputation.

work with Trisha at Lloyd Ridder because I've been very successful in working with her. I like the way she thinks. She works hard and she gets good people. She also works with me over time and understands what kinds of teams and what kinds of environment I tend to build. She factors that in just as importantly as a person's rates or qualifications. Not every agent understands that. And she's not a high-pressure person. She knows that I won't always work exclusively with her, but I will always give her first crack at a placement.

CONCLUSION

In short, our contractors and hiring managers used several attributes to categorize staffing agencies, the most important being the way they treated contractors and clients. Good agencies were those that aspired to what we might call, for lack of a less hackneyed phrase, high-quality service. While most agencies presented themselves in such a light, contractors and hiring managers knew that only some agencies met their standards for quality. These agencies instituted and enforced procedures for selecting contractors and for testing their skills and checking references. They invested in training to enhance the technical sophistication of their agents. They maintained contact with contractors already placed on the job. The very best, as far as contractors were concerned, offered benefits packages, some technical or professional training, and even stock options. For contractors this meant they "were not taken advantage of" and for hiring managers it meant they could reliably get skilled contractors on short notice and a professional response when there were problems with contractors on the job. At the other extreme were cost-oriented agencies, so-called job shops, that skimped on service to cut costs and maximize profits. Thus, even though size mattered, in the sense that size was correlated to other ways in which agencies operated, in the end there appeared to be no clear connection between a staffing agency's size and the way it was perceived by clients and contractors. On this score, what mattered was how agents went about their business, a topic to which we turn in parts 2 and 3.

PART II

LIFE IN THE MARKET

IN CHAPTER 3 we learned that most technical contractors chose to forgo the comforts of permanent employment to avoid the travails of working for an organization. They preferred instead to subject their skills and expertise to the discipline of the market—an institution often said to be objective and fair, but just as often reviled as cruel and exploitative. Regardless of which perspective contractors took (and most voiced both at one time or another), it was to the market that they periodically returned as the contract cycle turned, and it was through the market that they strung together the stints of employment that made up their careers. But what exactly was "the market" and how did it work? How did contractors experience and manage the daily exigencies of market life? What, in short, was life in the market like from the point of view of those who chose to live it?

From a neoclassical economist's perspective, the answer is straightforward, if not simple. The impersonal, abstract, and elegant laws of economic behavior govern the market for contractors, just as they do all other markets. In the market, contractors selling skills, clients trying to fill positions, and agencies hoping to bring the two together for a fee seek each other out to close deals that maximize their returns. So-called exogenous factors, like legislation and government intervention, sometimes constrain their behavior. "Endogenous" variables, such as the availability and cost of information, may even channel their choices. But these complications only make deciding more complex; they don't change the rules. In the end, rational self-interest prevails so that the various parties jointly produce an aggregate level of supply and demand whose equilibrium is a price that clears the market. Everyone goes home happy.

Sociologists, anthropologists, and institutional economists usually find this story a bit too thin.[1] Neoclassical models may accurately describe the bare bones of market behavior, but the devil is in the details—and especially the assumptions. These voices remind us that markets are complex human institutions. As such, they are subject to social rules of individual

---

[1] Smelser and Swedberg (1994b) and Granovetter and Swedberg (2001) offer comprehensive overviews of sociological perspectives on market dynamics. Mark Granovetter's *Getting a Job: A Study of Contacts and Careers* (1974) is especially relevant because it examines how people use social networks to find full-time jobs. Geertz (1963, 1978) offers an anthropological approach to market behavior.

and collective conduct. These rules are much more nuanced than traditional economic analysis allows. For sure, individuals may try to be economically rational, but their behavior is always shaped and constrained by other factors, as well: their access to information, their limited capacity to process that information, their bargaining skills, and, of course, the values, customs, and norms to which they subscribe. Markets, then, are elaborate social institutions where deal making is not only an economic but also a sociocultural game.

The relative merits of the economic and institutional views of markets are grist for a never-ending debate that should keep academics busy for years to come, just as they have for many years past. Our sympathies lie with the institutionalists. But as ethnographers, we also believe that understanding the market for technical contractors requires that we first understand the perspectives of those who repeatedly enter the market to find and close the deals on which their livelihood depends. For them, intellectual questions, no matter how stimulating, pale before the practical problem of how to make deals happen.

As it turns out, this is no simple task. The highly differentiated nature and quality of technical skills, the variety of client requirements, the complexity of technologies and their rates of change, pressures to close deals quickly, and the ubiquity of information technologies and relevant databases make deal making in this market a fast-moving, highly competitive, information-saturated game. To succeed, participants must develop the skills and resources required to play and master the rules of the game.

In part 2 we offer a detailed, ethnographically informed examination of the market for technical contractors. Our quest is for the rules of the game and how it is played. We focus on each of the actors in turn—contractors, clients, and agencies. We describe the motives, skills, and resources that each brought to the game, their view of its rules, and the steps they took to play as well as they could.

In the world of technical contracting there were two significantly different versions of deal making. In *brokered deals* contractors and clients found each other through agencies. The agencies orchestrated the search, the evaluation, the negotiation, and the close. For these services, they took a markup. In *direct deals,* contractors and clients bypassed agencies. Both parties managed their own searches and negotiated directly with each other. Agencies were sometimes invited in at the end of a direct deal to provide pass-through protections at a reduced markup.

Chapter 5 focuses on the "information game." We watch as actors formulate, disseminate, seek, organize, and interpret information about candidates and positions. At this stage, contractors and clients were uncommitted to one type of deal or the other. They often searched for direct and brokered deals simultaneously, while staffing firms actively promoted the latter. Chapter 6 explores how brokered and direct deals were actually made. We describe how the parties evaluated and selected each other, how they negotiated terms of employment, and how they eventually closed deals.

Chapter 5

THE INFORMATION GAME: FINDING DEALS

IN 2001 George Ackerlof, Joseph Stiglitz, and Michael Spence received the Nobel Prize in economics for their groundbreaking work in the 1970s on information asymmetries in markets. Among economists, whose models of behavior often favor elegance and parsimony over realism, the trio's claims were indeed revolutionary. Each argued that economics' tradition of assuming that buyers and sellers have equal access to information was unwarranted. In many markets, either the buyer or the seller has better information than the other. Ackerlof's, Stiglitz's, and Spence's contribution was to show that who knows what—and how and when they learn it—significantly shapes the way a market operates. The Nobel Foundation concluded, and most economists today would concur, that this insight transformed the field of economics.[1]

Most of our informants, however, knew little about "the dismal science" and cared even less. Had they taken the time to ponder it, they would probably have wondered how anyone could win a Nobel Prize for discovering such an obvious fact of life. It should not have taken a genius, some would have smirked, to figure out that information is the lifeblood of a market and that good information is hard to come by. Anyone who ever tried his or her hand at contracting knows—or soon finds out—that to close a deal, you first have to find one and that finding one is no trivial task. Doing so regularly is even harder. Contractors have to sort through a maze of poorly indexed, unevenly distributed, and sometimes intentionally inaccurate data to find the information necessary for locating and closing deals. Consequently, our informants had become, or had at least learned to rely on, skillful creators, disseminators, manipulators, and consumers of market information.

In this chapter we explore how contractors, clients, and agencies went about finding and using information in the course of searching for potential deals. We document and compare the resources and skills that each brought to the market, and we describe the strategies and practices they used as the search unfolded. We begin our story with the contrac-

---

[1] The Noble Foundation has published a useful and concise summary of Ackerlof's, Stiglitz's, and Spence's contribution at http://www.nobel.se/economics/laureates/2001/ecoadv.pdf.

tors at the point where their contract was ending and they once again faced the problem of finding another job.

What Contractors Do

To land contracts, contractors had to locate a hiring manager with an appropriate job and then bring themselves to the manager's attention. Neither task was simple. The supply of jobs changed rapidly and was widely dispersed across a large number of companies and across the managers within those companies. Competition for jobs was intense and the managers who offered them were usually inundated with information from a host of candidates and agencies, all clamoring for attention. Under such conditions, contractors had two options for finding a job. They could manage their own job searches using their own resources to locate direct deals, or they could turn to staffing agencies for help and settle for a brokered deal.

Self-Managed Job Searches

Most informants said that, in principle, they preferred direct deals. The advantage was immediately apparent: a direct deal avoided an agency's markup, which, at least in theory, meant more money in the contractor's pocket.[2] This advantage came at a price, however. Managing your own job search not only meant investing your own time and resources into handling flows of information, it also meant accepting the costs of working as an independent contractor. These costs included the price of incorporating, paying both the employer's and the employee's share of employment taxes, filing estimated taxes quarterly, and either managing one's own books or hiring an accountant. Contractors who chose to bear these costs managed their own searches by marketing themselves directly to clients and by enlisting the help of their professional and personal contacts.

DIRECT MARKETING

At one time or another, most contractors tried to market their services directly. Inexperienced contractors who wanted to avoid sharing the fruits

---

[2] Our data don't allow us to say for sure whether direct deals were actually more lucrative for contractors. Direct deals certainly created an opportunity for contractors to capture some of the agencies' profit for themselves by charging higher hourly rates. But doing so required that the contractor be able to assess the hiring manager's budget as well as the average bill rates of contractors being brokered by agencies for the same position. Our sense is that this kind of calculation required considerable experience and access to fresh data on the labor market.

of their labor with an agency were particularly likely to try their hand at self-promotion. Their strategies inevitably drew on their notions of how to find permanent jobs and on their images of how small businessmen and women market their wares. Newly minted contractors almost always turned first to publicly available sources of information: magazine articles on companies doing the kind of work they desired, word of mouth, the Internet, and even want ads for permanent employees. Once they had identified a pool of potential customers, they usually sent a résumé and cover letter to the hiring managers, called clients directly on the phone, or both.

Sending résumés to a large number of companies was cheap and not particularly time consuming, but contractors quickly discovered that unsolicited résumés rarely produced results. Free information about a company's needs was, at best, partial and inaccurate, and even when the trail of information led to a hiring manager with a job, contractors discovered that most managers preferred contractors who came to their door by other paths. Anil Rao, a CAD designer who tracked companies and regularly sent his résumé to promising leads, had few illusions: "Out of fifty, one or two might call me," he said, "and with one of them I get lucky sometimes."

Given the long odds of landing a job with a standard résumé, a few of our informants had decided to invest in more elaborate ploys. Maria Sanchez, a technical writer, had tried "plain vanilla" résumés when she was starting out: "I was sending out fifty and not getting a single response." Rather than give up, Maria developed a brochure with eye-catching graphics to accompany her cover letters. This, she found, increased clients' response rates. After developing the brochures, Maria added: "I started getting one to two interviews for every five to ten résumés I sent." Carmella Diaz, a graphic artist and Web designer, also decided to take direct marketing seriously. In the process, she discovered the first law of sales: "Persistence pays."

> I would literally knock on doors, not knowing anybody. I was just persistent. I would always try to prove why they needed, let's say, a Web site. And it really takes a very patient person because I kept going back and forth for a year or two with some clients before I got a job. The way I look at it, the worst thing they could say was no. You know, it wouldn't kill me if I embarrassed myself, so I would just go ahead and do it. I just kept sending my résumé, kept calling them. I said, "I'm flying to the Bay Area, I'll be there this week. If you have time to meet with me, na, na, na, na, na, na." I've been lucky. The people I've approached have agreed to hire me. But it took me bugging them.

Maria and Carmella were exceptions. Most of our informants possessed neither the skills nor the inclination for time-intensive direct marketing. Almost all who tried told us that it was rarely as effective as other ways of finding jobs, especially when measured in terms of time, effort, and money. Katrina Labovski, another technical writer, explained why she stopped trying to market herself: "I would call companies that I wanted to work for and tell them about myself. I'd spend a lot of time on the phone, and nothing would happen. People would tell me, 'Oh, you know, in a few weeks we might have something.' But they never did." Katrina, like most contractors who insisted on marketing themselves, eventually turned to another source of information: their networks.

ACTIVATING NETWORKS

Networks, our informants told us, were the most important marketing tool in a contractor's tool kit. Contractors' networks were made up of people that they had encountered from many walks of life over the course of their careers.[3] Kent Cox, the long-term contractor whom we met in chapter 1, put it succinctly: "Anyone you know is a potential contract." Like many informants, Kent did not leave things to chance. He made a sustained effort to build, extend, and maintain his network, and it was to his network that he invariably turned when he needed a new contract.

Who comprised a contractor's network varied. Most informants had, at one time or another, turned to family, friends, teachers, neighbors, members of religious congregations, and other acquaintances for leads. But as the contractor's career unfolded, three types of professional contacts proved more important: former coworkers, ex-clients, and fellow contractors.

Even poorly connected newcomers eventually realized they had one ready-made network: the fellow workers they had known when they were permanent employees. Donald Knight began contracting after Motorola closed the facility where he worked. Many of Donald's friends had transferred to other Motorola sites. These contacts enabled him to return quickly to Motorola, this time as a contractor:

We'd been together about fifteen years and we were all pretty close friends. I kept in contact with most of them by e-mail. When I was ready to go back to work, I e-mailed the people I knew [at Motorola] telling them, "If anybody knows of any openings or any leads for the things I do, let me know." One of the guys e-mailed

---

[3] In chapter 12 we will discuss how contractors went about building and managing their networks.

back saying, "We're constantly hiring contractors. We can use you anytime if you're interested." So I sent a résumé and said, "Certainly I'm interested." Got back [from traveling] and walked in [to Motorola]. They wanted me to go to work the next morning.

Christopher Laube, an electrical engineer working as a programmer, had a similar experience after layoffs at Tandem. Most of his coworkers were let go at the same time and were now spread throughout the Silicon Valley. Christopher gradually recognized the significance of these ties: his former coworkers became the backbone of his network, a reliable source for a steady stream of contracts:

> Everybody knew everybody very well. They were the focal point of my social and professional life. [They] are all over the Bay Area now, so I have contacts in seventy different companies. Some are in start-ups. There are people at Novell and Cisco, Netscape, Sun, Oracle. There's another one at Bechtel, one at Air Touch, PacBell, and Aspect. It's easy to find work. Just pick up the phone and see who's got a project going on, who knows of any projects. If you keep those contacts alive and keep your friends going, you've always got enough people. If they don't have anything, they usually know somebody who does.

Ex-clients, managers for whom contractors previously worked, were a second important group of contacts in many informants' networks. Calling ex-clients was, in fact, one of the first things experienced contractors did when they needed a job. "Right off the bat," said Donald Knight, "I'll call the people I used to work for and let them know I'm interested in coming back." With luck, a hiring manager for whom he had previously worked might offer a job. More often, however, ex-clients did not themselves have openings, but as Katrina Labovski told us, they "might know of what's available in their companies." In some cases, an ex-client's reach lay even further. Ashish Goshal, an applications developer, found that former clients were occasionally willing to refer him to managers in other companies: "My project managers know about other project managers in other companies who are looking for similar skills. They will sometimes give me a number to contact. Sometimes they will actually refer me and say: 'We had this consultant and he's available. He can do some of that work for you guys.' "

Fellow contractors were the third type of contact that contractors regularly consulted when looking for jobs. As they moved from job to job, contractors met other contractors. Because most contractors were always on the lookout for work opportunities, they were a rich source of information. Like many of our informants, Les Cousteau discovered that it paid to cultivate such ties. As part of his "network maintenance," Les kept a list of the contractors that he had met over the years. He called or e-mailed members of the list when looking for a job. "If they hear of an opening where they are looking for several people," he explained, "they give me a phone number and a name to call."

Although in most cases our informants said that their ties with fellow contractors were fleeting, some had developed long-term alliances that had produced a series of contracts.[4] Brian Willingham described how one such relationship became a source of continuing work:

> I've probably gotten three contracts off one of my friends. First, he was working for a company, then they brought me in. And he ended up going to different companies and bringing me in. I usually come along for the ride and end up with a nice contract out of it. He's on my Christmas card list forever! He gets on projects and then I come and bail him out. That's how I got this contract, and this one will keep me going for the rest of winter into spring. GT Mart was going to build this database, and Francis goes, "Hey, I've got this friend who seems to know what he's doing with the Web. Let me phone him and see if he can help us out."

A small number of our informants relied almost exclusively on their contacts for finding jobs. They prided themselves on the range and responsiveness of their network and on their ability to activate ties on short notice. These contractors usually began canvassing their network some time before their current contract ended. Hernando Galvez, a programmer, found that putting out feelers about three months before he expected to need a job practically guaranteed him a contract: "I go through my little list of forty to fifty people. I start reaching out, finding out who's where, what's going on, what projects are happening where, if there's a need for somebody. You put five or ten things in the fire and one of them is going to pan out. These are just basic stats."

Although most informants said they turned to their network early in the process of finding work, unlike Brian and Hernando, few found their networks sufficient. Some were beginners with limited experience and few acquaintances. Others lacked the type of social skills that networking requires. Some even found cultivating networks distasteful or too time consuming. Still others discovered that because their technical skills were so esoteric, they could not dependably produce jobs no matter how extensive their network. Moreover, many jobs were inaccessible via self-

---

[4] The importance of other contractors as sources of information, coupled with the fleeting nature of the ties between contractors, implies that there was considerable turnover among the contractors who were members of an informant's network.

managed searches because they were channeled exclusively through staffing agencies. Consequently, most of our informants at least supplemented self-managed searches with brokered searches, and for some, brokered searches were the only way to go.

Brokered Job Searches

Contractors did not have to look very far for an agency to broker a search. In fact, many did not have to look at all. Agencies were ever present in the world of high technology. Even when they were still permanent employees, most contractors had seen agencies in action. Agencies specializing in technical talent routinely ran advertising and marketing campaigns in the media and on the Web. Several agencies in the Valley even advertised in the slide shows that movie theaters used to distract audiences as they waited for the movie to begin. Most important, at least in the Silicon Valley, one would be hard-pressed to find a contractor or permanent employee who did not regularly dodge phone calls from agents pitching the services of one agency or another.

Contractors chose to work with agencies for a variety of reasons. As we have already seen, some contractors engaged agencies as a hedge against coming up empty handed on their own. Others used agencies because they had been persuaded to do so by an agent or because they modeled their search strategies on the advice of more experienced contractors. Still others worked through agencies because they had had positive experiences with such firms in the past. But the most widely acknowledged reason for working through an agency was that "going W-2" alleviated the administrative, financial, and legal burdens of working as an independent. "Making it all go away," as one contractor put it, was well worth the cost. Our informants usually found their way to agencies and, then, into brokered deals by two paths: they either used the Web to lure agents to their door or they went directly to an agency for help.

USING THE WEB

By the late 1990s the Internet and the World Wide Web had become a virtual bazaar for buyers and sellers of contract labor. The Internet hosted a growing number of "job boards" or databases, most with browser-friendly front ends that served as clearinghouses for contractors in search of employment and for agencies or clients in search of contractors. On these sites contractors could post their résumés and firms and agencies could post job announcements. In practice, however, contractors and agencies generated most of the traffic; clients rarely participated. The sites allowed contractors to search for openings and agencies to search for contractors using sophisticated search engines that matched the skills listed on résumés to the requirements listed in job postings. Some sites, like those offered by Yahoo and AltaVista, were free, while others like DICE, one of the oldest and most popular job boards, charged a fee for posting jobs and searching résumés, but allowed contractors to post résumés for free.[5]

Many contractors valued the broad exposure that the Web offered. When Stu Davis, an experienced embedded systems engineer, was ready for a new contract, he not only activated his network, he posted his résumé on numerous job boards. His objective was to maximize the odds of being "found." He told us that besides DICE,

> the biggest one is *CE Weekly*. I get a lot of hits off of that. There are a couple smaller ones that I also use. I can't remember the names of all these things, there's just too many [*consults his browser's bookmarks*]. Okay. Ah yes, there's the Résumé Bank, Select Jobs, Tech Job Bank, Computer Jobs, Contractors Direct, E-span, High Tech Jobs in Georgia, Infoworks, Career Shop, Career Mosaic, Career Web, Contractors Employment Exchange, on and on and on. Nation Job. I've got my résumé posted at all these places. But, in reality, there's only about a dozen that regularly contact me.

Steve Louthan went beyond merely posting, he created his own Web site that automated his job search. Steve had wanted to learn both HTML and "submission software." So he developed a Web site to which he could post and from which he could distribute his résumé. Steve explained, "You must have seen spam that promises, 'We can submit your Web page to three hundred directories for $70.' Well, for $70 you can buy the program they're using and do it yourself! It's easy to use and it does a great job!" Steve bought the software, linked it to his Web page, where he posted his résumé, and wrote a program to distribute it to over a hundred job banks every other week. His résumé contained hyperlinks to the Web page of every client for whom he had worked, but he wrote the code so that choosing a link would open another browser window. Thus, Steve's résumé stayed on the searcher's desktop. Steve also made it easy for agents and clients to download his résumé as a Word file. "Everybody contacted me," Steve smiled, clearly proud of his handiwork. "Even when the economy was bad, I was averaging ten calls a week from agencies all over the country."

---

[5] Yahoo and AltaVista were Web portals, search engines that offered the ability to search the entire Web for specific topics. Their job boards were one of several services offered in the hope of attracting users. DICE was exclusively a job board. Contractors posted their résumés by attaching them to a form on which they stated their preferences for types of jobs, rates, and the geographical areas where they would work. See www.dice.com.

Other contractors posted their résumés more selectively. Paula Ritter, for example, posted to only three job boards: DICE, Job Engine, and the Online Career Center. Even such limited postings triggered numerous solicitations. Like Paula, informants who limited their postings almost always included DICE because they knew that most agents frequented DICE daily. Our work in staffing firms confirmed the contractors' claims. Whenever recruiters at ITS or Progressive Staffing required a contractor with specific skills, after searching their agency's own databases their first act was to turn to DICE.

Indeed, contractors with widely sought after skills found that posting a résumé to a job bank brought nearly instantaneous inquiries from agencies. Asaf Weiss, a COBOL programmer, told us how, at the peak of the Y2K craze, he was landing jobs on the day he posted: "I ended up leaving Toyota and I immediately put my name out on the Internet. Let's see, they sent me home by twelve. I was on the Internet by one-thirty, and I had my first offer by four o'clock. It's not hard. Put your name out there. Let 'em know you can do COBOL and you'll have five hundred offers by tomorrow morning!"

Although we heard many such stories, our informants also told us that wide exposure had its downside as well: it could produce too many responses. Once résumés began circulating, they could attract unwanted attention, especially to contractors whose skills were "hot." Skilled contractors sometimes found themselves deluged by e-mail and phone calls from agencies with unsuitable offers. Marty Keely, a systems architect with many years of experience as a contractor, explained:

> Any recruiter who wants to find a person with a certain skill goes to DICE and searches against your talent. If your name shows up, they pull down your résumé and give you a call. For guys at my level that no longer has value. If I put my résumé on the board, I will get five thousand calls a day. I've done so many projects that my name shows up for just about anything anybody is looking for. Many recruiters don't pay attention to the details you give them. If you tell them: "Don't call me unless this is a senior level position," they still call you for a testing position. As long as your name shows up, they don't care. I had to change phone numbers a couple of times [*laughs*] because I was stupid enough to put my name on DICE. But, if you're starting out, that's the way to go.

Some experienced contractors, like Marty, no longer posted their résumés on the Web. Instead, they used the Web solely to search for job postings that they felt matched their skills and personal preferences. When they found a potential match, they contacted the agent who had posted the job. Although this approach significantly reduced nuisance calls, it had its own pitfalls. "You have to remember," Marty cautioned, "that just because a job is posted, it doesn't mean the job is open. It may be that the job is closed, but they haven't removed it from the database. When you send them a résumé, it also doesn't go directly to the recruiter. It typically goes to a résumé processing office because these companies want to build a database of professionals. So there's a time lag. The minimum lag that I've seen is three days. I've seen it be as bad as three weeks. Well, guess what happens in those three days to three weeks! The position closes, so you may find something that was tailor-made for you, but by the time they learn about you, it's closed." Even more troubling was that some of the positions listed in job banks never existed. These jobs were fictional postings placed on the Web by recruiters hoping to flush out highly skilled contractors whom they could include in their agency's files.

INITIATING CONTACTS WITH STAFFING AGENCIES

It was partially to avoid these problems and partially to gain more control over their searches that contractors chose to contact staffing agencies directly. Some contractors, like Judy King, took a scattergun approach: they sent their résumés to a large number of agencies reasoning that one would come up with an offer. Judy sent résumés to nearly fifty of the larger and better-known agencies and waited for offers. "I also give my résumé to friends," she explained, "and they pass it out to the agencies they deal with. It won't take long for something to show up; it just doesn't." Yolanda Turner, who told us that she hadn't been out of work for more than two weeks in two years, also preferred this method. When we spoke with Herman Jay, he was registered with twenty-six agencies that produced a steady stream of offers. When he finished one job, he told us, there are "job shops all over me to go to work somewhere else."

Other contractors limited the number of agencies they contacted. They preferred to work through a small number of agents with whom they developed personal relationships. Contractors who used this strategy believed that agents they befriended would better understand their needs and desires and would feel more obligated to contact the contractor when appropriate jobs crossed their desk. Marty Keely explained: "Once you get to know the recruiters, you cut down on your search time. When you're really good, you don't need five thousand agencies. You need four or five, because with four or five you're bound to hit a job or two that piques your interest. So you start to specialize even in the companies."

A number of informants told us that they had built relationships with recruiters that had lasted after the recruiter switched agencies. Contractors gave these recruiters priority when looking for a job and turned elsewhere only as a second choice. Loyalty, however, only went so far. No informant felt obliged to forego other methods for finding jobs or to avoid working with other staffing agencies, if the opportunity or need arose. In short, contractors knew that even when an agent became their friend, business was still business.

WHAT CLIENTS DO

Once hiring managers decided to hire a contractor, they faced the problem of finding suitable candidates on short notice with minimal investment of time and effort. As was true for contractors, when hiring managers entered the market, they were immediately flooded with information of uncertain validity. The pool of potential candidates for most positions was large. Job banks overflowed with résumés that might or might not accurately reflect a person's skills and experience, and even if they did, résumés might not contain sufficient information for making decisions. Once word of a search leaked out, agents appeared on the manager's doorstep, as if out of nowhere, aggressively hawking candidates, often without a solid understanding of either the client's needs or the contractor's skills. Because managers were pressed for time, they hoped to close deals quickly, but their need for trustworthy information and proven skills counseled caution. The trick was to navigate the market efficiently without being duped.

The managers we encountered generally searched for contractors in one of two ways. Like contractors, they either tried to manage their own searches and negotiate a direct deal or a pass-through, or else they accepted the idea of a brokered deal and enlisted the aid of an agency. But unlike contractors, the hiring managers' choice depended not only on personal preference and available resources, but also on their company's policies and procedures.

Self-Managed Searches for Candidates

Most hiring managers with whom we spoke preferred to manage their own searches. They did not, however, make use of direct advertising or the Web because both consumed too much time. Instead, they relied exclusively on their personal and professional contacts. Experienced managers usually had extensive networks of friends, peers, bosses, subordinates, and professional acquaintances whom they had encountered over the course of their career. Although managers did not build their networks explicitly to find contractors, they used them as a resource when the need arose. Managers also typically activated their subordinates' networks to reach even further into the technical communities from which they hoped to recruit. Managers preferred self-managed searches for four reasons.

First, managers believed that professional networks yielded more trustworthy information about candidates. As Matt Schmidt of Videonet explained, managers thought that friends and colleagues were likely to be more honest than an agent:

> We would prefer to use somebody that knows somebody over an outsider that no one has any idea about. A résumé is only a piece of paper. A person who says, "This is my friend who works at E-Bay or Charles Schwab in their Internet division," carries a lot more weight than, "Let's read this piece of paper and hope this person is not lying or exaggerating." If somebody in our engineering department said, "I have a friend who programs in Java; he can be in here tomorrow; do you guys want him?" We'd say, "Sure!"

Second, because technical professionals tended to know other people with similar expertise and because they could evaluate the quality of each other's work, managers claimed that networks were better than agencies at locating candidates with specific skills. "If one of our clients would come to us and say, 'We have a project. It's going to involve WebObjects Programming,'" Matt continued, "We say, 'Sure, no problem.' Then we would come back and sit in a room and go, 'Does anybody know anybody who knows WebObjects?' We find more people that way than going through our internal groups (approved vendors and the HR department), because everyone, you know, hangs with their fellow types."

Third, managers preferred to work through networks because passthroughs reduced and direct deals completely eliminated an agency's markup, which significantly reduced the cost of hiring a contractor. Monty Kirkman, an IT manager at Chipco, estimated the financial benefit of a self-managed search: "Yeah, [we hire independents] all the time. We're much more likely to hire them, because we don't have to pay the headhunter's fees which are about 25 to 30 percent. We like to skip agencies. If we know the person, we go direct to that person. We pay less *and* we know they're qualified." Finally, some managers said they preferred working through professional networks because they had had a negative experience with a particular agency or because they had a general distaste for brokers.

In practice, the managers we interviewed varied widely in their reliance on self-managed searches. Some, like Micky Cummings, vice president of engineering at Webworm, relied exclusively on his professional network. Micky hired only a few contractors at a time. He disliked working with agencies and found that with "recommendations, word of

mouth, and asking around," he could fill all his hiring needs. Others
turned to agencies only when their professional contacts failed to deliver.
Vic Verma of Savant Technologies told us that he always turned to his
network first: "I get on the phone. I look through my files. I'll ask
around, 'Hey, do you know anybody?' I'll think about who used to work
here that I know is consulting or I'll call some friends and say, 'Who
do you know who's consulting?'" Vic turned to staffing agencies if his
network produced no viable candidates. For still other managers, self-
managed searches were rare and of secondary importance, usually because company policy discouraged managers from conducting their own
searches. Matt Schmidt told us that he almost always used the company's
on-site vendor, but on a few occasions, when the on-site was unable to
deliver, he turned to his network. "If we're really in a pinch and we can't
get the resource in-house then we do it ourselves," he confided. "You just
turn on every source. You start calling all your friends and you ask everyone in your department."

Although hiring managers genuinely believed that networks produced
better information and better candidates, especially when esoteric skills
were required, they ultimately hired relatively few contractors through
self-managed searches. Networks simply could not produce the necessary flow of candidates for managers who hired many contractors.
Moreover, some firms required their managers to use staffing agencies
from the start, especially when the firm had contracted with an on-site
vendor. Consequently, most managers we interviewed turned to staffing
agencies to find contractors, even if they would have preferred to do
otherwise.

Brokered Searches for Candidates

Brokered searches were of two types: *restricted* and *unrestricted*. Restricted searches occurred only in companies with centralized hiring
policies that limited managers to using on-site and approved vendors.
Unrestricted searches occurred in companies with decentralized hiring
policies (or when managers in firms with centralized policies circum-
vented procedures). In an unrestricted search, managers chose the
staffing agency with which they wanted to work; in a restricted search,
no choice was allowed.

RESTRICTED SEARCHES

Companies with centralized hiring policies expected managers to use
only preapproved agencies and to follow a set of rules for hiring contractors. Hiring managers at Western Phone Company, for example, specified the requirements for a job by submitting a form to Alert Staffing,

Western Phone Company's on-site vendor. Alert then distributed the requirements to other approved vendors with an invitation to submit résumés. Approved vendors were warned against communicating directly with hiring managers, lest they lose their approval. Alert collected résumés and sent them to hiring managers for review. Managers at Advanced Computers (AC) enjoyed a slightly less centralized system. Although Advanced Computers encouraged managers to work directly though Volt, its on-site vendor, managers could also communicate directly with other approved vendors or instruct Volt on which staffing agencies to use as third parties.[6] The flexibility was particularly important to managers who believed that many skilled contractors avoided working directly with Volt because of its reputation as a "body shop." All contractors hired by AC, nevertheless, passed through Volt, which served as the contractors' employer-of-record.

Hiring managers varied considerably in their willingness to accept centralized systems and policies that restricted their options. Randy Bouchet, for example, thought Raster's system worked smoothly and used it regularly. "At Raster," he said, "we have a contractors' clearinghouse sort of a place, where I can go to with a job description. They have a ready cache of résumés on hand. I mean, within a day I had a stack of résumés to go through and with one of my coworkers I was able to go through them. In fact, Adecco [the agency] has an office over in the East Tower. So, it's real easy for us to just go over and talk to them."

Other managers complained that centralized systems were too bureaucratic and inflexible and, thus, yielded less suitable candidates. Noah Swetka, for example, described Western Phone Company's system as "rigid" and "irritating." He told us: "The last couple of times [I hired contractors], I actually contacted someone whom I knew had the bodies I needed. I went around the system and the billing was sent directly to me." Shirley Daner told us that at 3-Com, where she previously worked, "we hated the fact that we had to look to Kelly Services and we hated being told, 'You've got to use this source.' I will tell you, we found every way around it." Rather than comply with the policy for centralized searches, managers like Shirley and Noah rebelled. Adopting the philosophy that it was better to ask for forgiveness than to seek permission, they launched unauthorized unrestricted searches—an approach to recruiting that was both commonplace and legitimate in companies with decentralized hiring policies.

---

[6] Volt was the on-site vendor at the AC site we studied. Manpower was the on-site at other AC sites.

When the need for contractors arose, most managers in firms with a decentralized policy told us that they simply began calling agencies, describing their needs, and asking agents for résumés. They typically preferred to work with smaller, local firms that specialized in finding technical professionals than with branch offices of nationally known agencies. If you wanted to hire a specialist, they advised, it was better to work through a specialist. Agents eventually sent these managers a portfolio of résumés from which the managers chose candidates to interview. More often than not, soliciting the help of an agency triggered a wave of sales calls from other agencies that the manager had not contacted, but which had heard about the open position. Donna Lawyer, a manager at Chipco, explained how the grapevine worked:

> If I need someone to start on Monday I'll start calling people today and say: "I need someone to start on Monday with these qualifications." Word gets out on the street very fast—especially in the Oracle world—that Chipco is looking for someone. I'll usually start getting flooded with calls and e-mails at that point. I will start getting résumés on the same day. I probably get about a dozen or so a day. So it can add up pretty quickly. Contracting companies will start calling me every hour: "Can I set up a phone screen for so and so?" I mean, they know how we operate. I'll have firms that I've never worked with before coming out of the woodwork because the contractors hear about it and start telling their friends. I'll have firms call me out of the blue and say: "I hear you're looking for someone and I have the perfect candidate for you."

The grapevine to which Donna alluded was at least a four-step chain. Her agent called contractors (step 1) who then notified friends (step 2). The friends contacted their agents at other agencies (step 3) who then called Donna (step 4). That hiring managers could be so quickly inundated provides an index of how efficient contractors were at circulating information.

To avoid being deluged by calls and swamped by information of questionable quality, many of our informants limited their unrestricted searches by calling only agents whom they knew and whom they considered competent and trustworthy. Informal relationships between agents and managers invariably grew out of earlier encounters in which an agent proved capable of delivering a valued contractor. These market-limiting relationships sometimes survived even when agents moved to other agencies. Anthony Greener, for example, had maintained a long-term relationship with one trusted agent for a number of years. "This is a guy I worked with for three years back at IBM," Anthony told us. "He quit and set up his own agency. If this guy sends us somebody with a good recommendation, you're pretty sure you want that person."

More often, relations between hiring managers and agents were based on loose understandings rather than on close business or personal ties. Sally Hynes, for instance, had developed ongoing relationships with a small number of agencies which she considered contingent on the agents' continued ability to deliver. "We have a group of companies that we've used in the last two years," she remarked. "If we have good luck in getting really good people from them, we continue to use them."

Because hiring managers fielded dozens of cold calls weekly from agencies selling their services, informants found that they did not always need to contact agencies to launch unrestricted searches. All they had to do was wait for an agency to show up. By all accounts, the wait was short. Micky Cummings explained why: "Now I'm not exaggerating, I get, quite literally, two to three calls a day from these contracting shops. 'This is Joe at Pyramid Consulting and we're just calling to see if you have needs.' Some of these guys call me once a week. It's the same person every week. No matter how many times I say no, no matter how many times I don't return their calls, they just call over and over and over. It's brute force. I get hundreds of these little companies calling me." Most managers found cold calls from agents to be disruptive, unpleasant, and time consuming. Shirley Daner was clear on this point. "I hate them," she told us. "They're like used car salespeople, except they're selling people instead of cars. They're out to get as much from you as they can."

Yet, not every manager automatically rejected agents' advances, even though they might be critical of the agencies' practices. Russell Brown, for example, mocked the predictability of the scripts: "Every one of them, the first time they contact you, says, 'We're not a body shop.' I've heard that story a hundred times, if I've heard it once." Yet, Russell did not close the door on future options. "The first question they have is, 'Do you have contracting needs right now?' And invariably my answer is no because I don't make an effort to hire a lot of contractors. For me, it's a last-minute or an emergency kind of approach. The next thing out of their mouth is: 'When can I call back? When do you think you might need something?' And I say, 'Two to three months,' because that's roughly the budgeting time frame. In two or three months our budget may change dramatically and our project assignments may change, and I might actually have to wrap something up quickly. So that's been my approach so far."

Like Russell, Tony Larson of Groove Technology told us that if he happened to have an opening, he often agreed to review the résumés and, on more than one occasion, had hired contractors off cold calls. Thus, as in all sales efforts, no matter how unpleasant to the client, success from the agent's perspective was a matter of persistence, convenience, and luck. "It's the luck of the draw whether they get into a company or not," Shirley Daner explained. "If they make the call at the right time to the right manager who happens to be looking for a person, that manager will say: 'Well, I do need a person that knows Oracle Reports 2.5, do you have anybody?' And, of course, somewhere in their database there must be an Oracle Reports 2.5 person."

WHAT STAFFING AGENCIES DO

Indeed, the staffing agency's job was not only to persuade clients that brokered searches were more fruitful and convenient than self-managed searches, but also to persuade contractors of the same thing. Such convincing required agencies to hunt continually for open positions while simultaneously seeking contractors interested in filling them. Account managers took responsibility for the first type of search, while recruiters handled the second.

Searching for Positions

Among agents, finding positions was known as "sales" or "prospecting," a process that involved three steps: *"finding leads," "following up,"* and *"getting job orders."*[7] During the first step, account managers (and inside salespeople) sifted through leads, information on companies and hiring managers who might need contractors. Upon locating a promising lead, they followed up by making an initial contact, usually by cold calling, but sometimes by visiting the potential client. Whenever possible, account managers tried to bypass corporate gatekeepers and the controls they imposed and to deal directly with hiring managers. The objectives when "following up" were to learn about the hiring manager's needs,

---

[7] In this section we describe the activities of account managers doing unrestricted searches. As we have noted, some agencies tried to restrict the market for job openings by becoming a client's on-site or preferred vendor, an act that essentially created a monopoly franchise on a firm's flow of job orders. The three agencies that we studied sought the status of approved vendors, but none competed for on-site contracts. Progressive Staffing had appointed a vice president for client relations whose job was to negotiate restricted market agreements with large client organizations. Senior managers at Information Technology Specialists and Systems Professionals also occasionally negotiated deals that guaranteed limited sourcing rights in return for lowered markups. By and large, these arrangements accounted for a negligible percentage of each agency's business, and we did not have occasion to observe such negotiations. Consequently, we confine our discussion to unrestricted searches for job openings.

provide information about the agency, and, in some cases, distribute contractors' résumés. The final step in the "sales cycle" was to turn the hiring manager's needs into a "job order," an actual requisition that specified the skills and experience that a contractor should possess and that set the initial terms of the contract. With a job order in hand, the account manager turned to a recruiter whose job was to find candidates to fill the order.[8]

FINDING LEADS

Leads were the lifeblood of an agency. To ensure a continual flow of leads, agencies invested heavily in acquiring information about firms and their operations, their structures and personnel, and especially the names and phone numbers of managers who actually ran projects. Agencies stored such information in databases that account managers regularly used and continually updated. In fact, an agency's databases were its most jealously guarded asset. As Erin Bailey, a trainer at Progressive Staffing, told a classroom of new account managers, "Whoever has the best database wins the war!"

The information that made its way into an agency's database came from a variety of sources. As a start, most agencies purchased commercial compendiums of data on companies and their managers. These included such publications as *Rich's Technology Directory* and *Hoover's Guide to Computer Companies*, which contained background data on companies and their products along with contact information for corporate executives and mid-level technical managers. Some agencies also purchased lists of people who subscribed to technical publications or who belonged to technical and business associations. Data of this sort were always "dirty." Harold Sykes, the vice president of sales at Information Technology Specialists, told us that ITS's database was "more of a phone book than a database. There are twenty-seven thousand contact names in there loaded from the *San Francisco Business Journal*, the *San Jose Business Journal*, and other lists that we bought. When the account managers started calling names," he admitted, "they find that out of a hundred calls they have a 5 percent hit ratio." Most of the time, the contact information was inaccurate and out-of-date. To be useful such data required continual cleaning and updating, a process known as "scrubbing."

The media were a second source of information about clients. Account managers avidly scanned the business sections of local and national

---

[8] If the client required that the agency be an approved vendor before it could fill an order, the account manager also initiated the process necessary for attaining this status. Becoming an approved vendor typically meant showing the client that the agency was financially solvent and otherwise trustworthy.

newspapers for articles on companies in their area. Journalists frequently mentioned events, such as new projects and layoffs, that might speak directly or indirectly to a company's need for contractors. Reporters also usually mentioned the names of managers who might become leads. Account managers also scoured classified ads. Although clients almost never used the classifieds to recruit contractors, account managers read ads for permanent positions to infer trends in the job market and to assess the potential demand for contractors at particular companies.

Work activities and encounters offered a third and more immediate source of leads. When visiting clients, account managers were constantly on the lookout for information on hiring managers. In fact, account managers sometimes visited clients specifically to gather intelligence. An experienced account manager at Progressive Staffing gave the following advice to newcomers: "Always be looking for managers' names. They will use contractors somewhere down the line. This account manager I knew, Dennis, Mr. Oracle, would walk through a client facility with me. I'd be looking ahead and he'd be looking for names on doors. If he got three names from a visit, that was worthwhile."

Contractors on assignment or who were simply interviewing for a position were a fourth and especially rich source of leads. "Essentially, we're dealing with a very closely knit network," Charles Larsen, an account manager at Information Technology Specialists explained. "Every one of these contractors has a whole résumé of companies where they've worked. In conversation with them, I get names of other companies and people." How account managers solicited information from contractors was nicely illustrated in an encounter between Bob Lamp, an account manager at Progressive Staffing, and Bill Lazer, a contractor who had just converted to a permanent employee. Bob had ostensibly called Bill to discuss the money that Progressive Staffing still owed him. After settling the issue, Bob asked if Bill was aware of open positions at the company and the following conversation ensued:

Bob: Oh, so they need someone on your project? Can I make a suggestion? Go to Mike (Bill's project manager), tell him you need another device-driver person down there, so he probably needs a contractor to accelerate the project.

Bill: But Mike says he wants a full-time person.

Bob: Oh . . . okay. I'll go to Mike and say I heard—I won't say from you—that he's looking for a device-driver person. I'll tell Mike—not based on our conversation—that it sounds like he could use someone else. I'll use that route. Someone like you, right, a networking device-driver, not someone who's basically read the book. I'll talk to people here, see if we can market someone out there proactively. I'll say: "This is the person, this is the rate."

Bill then told Bob that he believed that Mike did not actually make decisions about hiring. In response, Bob asked for the name of the manager who did and noted her name and phone number in the database. Such leads, Bob told us, were considered "hot."

Finally, many account managers prospected for leads whenever they found themselves talking to friends, acquaintances, and even strangers. Diana Judd, a longtime account manager who ran Progressive Staffing's training programs, acknowledged how prospecting became a way of life:

> Our job is networking. That's what it's all about! I go out on the weekends and when I go to restaurants and bars I'm passing out my business cards left and right, everywhere. Everyone I meet is a potential source of leads. "Oh I work at Intel" or "I have my E.E." "Here we go!" Everywhere! If they're not in the field they know someone who is, or someone who's looking, or someone who's hiring. It's always something. And I don't mean to—it just happens in the conversation. "Oh, so what do you do for a living?" As soon as I mention that I work in staffing, everyone seems to have someone to tell me about. "Oh, I know someone who is looking, is hiring, is something." I met a gentleman at an airport. He's the VP of sales for his own start-up company and they're going to be needing people.

FOLLOWING UP LEADS

Having found a lead, the next step was to make a cold call. "What you need to do," Miranda Hill, one of the top account managers at Progressive Staffing, told us, "is sit down at your desk and call, call, call." Account managers at the firms we studied usually set aside extended blocks of time for calling. To assist account managers, ITS employed two inside salespeople, telemarketers who specialized in making cold calls and who passed successful "hits" to the account managers. Cold calling had several purposes.

The primary goal was to locate a hiring manager with specific needs, to elicit information about the job's requirements and the project's budget, and to arrange a face-to-face meeting. Account managers considered setting up a meeting with a hiring manager to be a success worthy of celebration. Even better was to be invited to submit candidates' résumés for a position, but cold calls that led to invitations were rare. In fact, few calls led to any discussion at all. Most ended in an encounter with a secretary or a voice mailbox and calls that made it past a manager's first line of defense typically evoked rejections, which, as we have seen, were not always polite.

Consequently, the account manager's secondary goal was simply to "get a foot in the door"—to get the hiring manager to commit to communicating sometime in the future. Whenever the slightest opening presented itself, account managers tried to get the manager's e-mail address and to set a date for a future call. If successful, they recorded the information in their database for future reference and instructed the program to remind them to follow up on the appointed date. Account managers at ITS also mailed the hiring manager a "nurture package" that contained the agency's promotional material.

Finally, if nothing else, account managers used the information they gleaned from calls to scrub the database. Callers always updated the manager's contact information and attempted to gather general information on the company's organization and products as well as specific information on its hiring policies. Account managers were particularly interested in determining the hiring manager's degrees of freedom and whether the firm used a centralized or decentralized system for acquiring contractors. Invariably, account managers used the call as an opportunity to elicit the names of other potential leads.

GETTING JOB ORDERS

If a call lasted long enough for account managers to make a sales pitch, they moved toward generating and specifying a job order. Although hiring managers were occasionally willing to specify job orders over the phone or by e-mail, the most common procedure was to arrange a "client visit," a meeting between the account manager and the hiring manager, usually at the client's location. On a visit, account managers presented the agency and its activities, whetted the manager's appetite with sample résumés, and tried to convince the manager to work with the agency. Successful visits culminated in a job order that established the nature of the task, the skills the task required, the monetary terms of the contract, and the procedure by which the hiring manager would review and evaluate candidates.[9]

The top executives of the agencies we studied regularly admonished account managers to specify the client's requirements and the terms of employment fully before attempting to fill orders. In practice, however, account managers cut corners, in part, because they were evaluated on the number of orders they generated and, in part, because they knew that if they did not land the order, another agency would. But regardless of how well or poorly specified it might be, once an account manager secured an order, recruiters set out to fill it.

[9] How the monetary terms of the contract were negotiated and how evaluation and selection took place are discussed extensively in the next chapter.

Searching for Candidates

Recruiters specialized in finding, enticing, negotiating with, and placing contractors. Locating candidates with the right skills on short notice was just as vital for an agency's success as finding job openings. Accordingly, agencies also invested considerable resources in developing computerized databases to manage information on contractors. At most agencies, recruiters searched for contractors along two paths.[10] *General recruiting* was an ongoing activity focused on continually updating and expanding the agency's database. *Job-specific recruiting* entailed searching for suitable people to fill existing job orders, usually under time pressure and in competition with other agencies. In theory, recruiters should have been able to fill job orders directly from their databases, and sometimes they could. In practice, however, recruiters found that most of the candidates in their databases were either unsuitable or already on contract, so they were forced to "beat the bushes" to fill most new job orders. Continually "generating traffic" or a "flow of fresh blood" through the agency was, therefore, critical to filling job orders and as a result, the two approaches to recruiting blurred. Recruiters often identified contractors for existing job orders while doing general recruiting. Conversely, they added individuals who were not suited for a specific job to the agency's database for future reference. Generally speaking, then, the recruiter's task almost always entailed three steps: "sourcing" candidates, contacting leads, and "qualifying" candidates in preparation for deal making.

SOURCING CANDIDATES

Recruiters used a variety of strategies to "source" contractors, many of which mirrored the account manager's methods for finding positions.[11] Agencies purchased databases that contained information on individuals, a significant percentage of whom they hoped would be interested in contracting jobs. Progressive Staffing bought subscriber lists from magazines like *Contract Professional* that targeted contractors. Marc Sunberg, ITS's founder, compiled the agency's first database by combing voter registration files for people who worked in the computer industry. During the course of our observations, a recruiter at Progressive Staffing convinced the organizer of a professional conference to fax him a list of all the participants. Because these lists and databases were compiled for other purposes, they always contained large numbers of irrelevant and inaccurate records that needed to be verified—a time-consuming process.

---

[10] Systems Professionals was an exception because its contractors were full-time employees. Because Systems Professionals contractors remained with the firm for several years, recruiting at Systems Professionals was never as frantic as it was at other agencies.

[11] Recruiters frequently used the term "prospecting" as well.

Recruiters quickly learned that other sources of information offered better yields.

Online résumé banks were especially popular for sourcing contractors
because just about everyone who posted their résumés were committed
to contracting. Like most recruiters, Linda Cline of ITS searched all over
the Web, but preferred DICE because the contractors who listed themselves on DICE were usually "in play." "The DICE list is hot," Linda
told us. "The people who list themselves are much hotter than those in
our database. They are becoming available. They are interviewing, looking around, ready to move." Benjamin Close, a recruiter at Progressive
Staffing, made use of Career Mosaic and Intellimatch as well. He preferred the former because of its powerful search engine. "You can enter
multiple terms, like skills or applications," he explained, "and it shows
matches and tells you how well each hit fits your terms." Intellimatch, on
the other hand, had "junk you don't need," and the search engine could
not distinguish between applicants and employers, which required Benjamin to spend additional time sorting data.

In addition to searching job boards for résumés, recruiters posted attractive job openings on boards to lure contractors into responding.
Carol Fitler at Progressive Staffing posted all her open positions on
DICE. "I get a lot of responses directly to my e-mail," she told us. "It's a
great way to get résumés." Linda posted to DICE, to Online Career Center, and to Headhunter, and less frequently to HotBot and Yahoo Classifieds. She received between forty and fifty e-mails daily, most with résumés attached. Linda entered all respondents into ITS's database,
converted their résumés into machine searchable files, and contacted
those who seemed promising.

The agencies we studied sank significant sums of money into adver-
tisements and promotional activities to gain exposure in the technical
community and to encourage contractors to contact the agency when
they were searching for jobs. Agencies that specialized in technical contractors regularly advertised in such publications as *Silicon India, Self-
Employed Professional,* and *Contract Professional.* Progressive Staffing
attended national trade shows and local job fairs. Diana Judd explained
how recruiters used job fairs to source contractors:

> The job fairs are the big things. It's in a huge convention center. Pro-
> gressive Staffing goes and sets up a booth and we talk about the op-
> portunities that we can provide for people and we collect résumés
> from people who are looking to make job changes or who are un-
> employed. We set up a computer at our booth. We have people enter
> their name and address. We collect their résumés. The referral net-
> work is incredible. For every résumé we get, we get to eventually

talk to a person. Even if the person isn't available we get to talk to them and find out who they know that might be. You could speak to as many as five hundred people. Job fairs can cost anywhere from $3,000 to $10,000 depending on how big the city is and how big the draw. But you know a newspaper ad can cost you $3,000, too, and you might not get anything.

Because attending job fairs and trade shows was so costly, ITS attended only local events. Because Systems Professionals specialized in systems administrators, its recruiters considered job fairs a waste of time. Instead they regularly visited college campuses across the country, where they arranged career nights for students who ran campus computer clusters.

Agencies were continually experimenting with creative ways of sourcing contractors. Progressive Staffing, for example, produced Web-based seminars, live Internet broadcasts for contractors on topics like the contracting lifestyle, or tax tips for contractors. For each seminar they employed a public relations firm and recruited acknowledged experts to participate. Contractors could listen to the seminar by signing on to the agency's Web site, downloading the appropriate audiovisual software, and accessing the seminar's URL at the appointed time with their browsers. Through the sign-up procedure, Progressive Staffing acquired contact information on hundreds of contractors around the nation, all of whom were added to the agency's database.

Attending professional events that attracted contractors was a popular and considerably less costly way to source contractors face-to-face. One evening we accompanied two of Progressive Staffing's recruiters, Connie Brickert and Lea Bach, to a monthly meeting of a Java users' group in Palo Alto. The organizers allowed them to make their pitch at the beginning of the event:

> Connie and Lea set up a table just outside the meeting room. Before the meeting they stood behind the table with a pile of fliers for the Web seminar and a stack of registration forms for the "contractor fair" [an event to be held at Progressive Staffing in a few months]. Beside the fliers sat a large bowl of chocolates, a few Progressive Staffing T-shirts, a Progressive Staffing squeegee ball, and another bowl with a sign inviting participants to enter a raffle for three Pizza Uno certificates (worth $10 each). To enter the competition all you had to do was put a business card in a bowl. By the time the meeting started, the bowl was half full. During a break between speakers, the organizers invited Lea and Connie down front to give their "spiel." Lea grabbed the bowl and walked to the front of the room. She raised a squeegee ball in her hand. "For a squeegee ball," she challenged the audience, "do you know who we are?" "Progressive

Staffing!" a few shouted. Lea tossed the ball to one of the respondents. Next Connie led the drawing for the pizza. She had someone from the audience draw a card from the bowl. The winner was awarded a certificate. Then attendees were given an opportunity to add their business cards, two more cards were drawn, and the winners announced. Two surprise drawings are held: one for a T-shirt and another for a squeegee ball. When the games ended, Connie briefly described the contractor fair: "If you want to learn about insurance, incorporation, 1099s, we will have people who've worked as contractors answering questions. You can fill out forms telling us what you'd like to learn." Connie then described the Web seminar: the topics and the names of the presenters. She handed out forms and asked for more business cards. A few were offered. Lea walked up the aisle and collected them. Soon afterward, Connie and Lea left the meeting, quite happy with the cards they had collected.

Recruiters routinely tried to persuade contractors to tell them about friends and acquaintances who might be interested in contracting. Carol Fitler told us: "I always ask every contractor I meet, 'Who else are you working with?' 'Oh, Joe Smith. Great! What's Joe's phone number?' I call Joe Smith, introduce myself, and then, hopefully, get him to come in and interview with me and develop a relationship." Benjamin Close also found that contractors were a source of useful leads. For Benjamin, weekly visits to distribute paychecks doubled as reconnaissance missions:

The second contractor we visited worked at LSI Logic in San Jose. Benjamin and I entered the lobby of the two-story building where Qui Bai worked, and he immediately approached the receptionist behind the counter. Benjamin smiled appreciatively at the receptionist, looked her in the eye, and asked if Qui Bai had a phone number. The receptionist immediately recognized Qui Bai as a contractor from Progressive Staffing. The receptionist called the manager for whom Qui Bai worked and, after a brief conversation, hung up the phone saying, "He'll send Qui Bai down." We seated ourselves on a semicircular sofa and awaited Qui Bai. Shortly, he came down the stairwell on the far side of the lobby. Benjamin and I rose and met him in the middle of the lobby where we shook hands. We walked back to the sofa and sat down. After asking how things were going, Benjamin eventually steered the conversation to Yinon, the contractor who had caused Mark (another recruiter) so much trouble last week by terming unexpectedly. Yinon had worked at LSI with Qui Bai. In fact, he and Qui Bai were hired at the same time. Benjamin eventually asked Qui Bai if he knew of any other contractors who might be good for Yinon's job. He said he especially wanted someone with embedded systems experience who knew MPEG2 technology. Qui Bai said that he did and asked us to wait a moment while he went to get his address book. Qui Bai returned to the recesses of the building and soon reappeared carrying a yellow loose-leaf binder that contained several typed sheets of names and addresses. Qui Bai sat down beside us and located three names and addresses. Two of the people he mentioned were contractors. The third ran a consulting company that contracted engineers to other firms. Benjamin and Qui Bai talked about each person's skills. Qui Bai had worked with all three and felt that they would be good for the compression and decoding technology on which he was working.

In fact, tapping a contractor's network was such a fruitful way of sourcing that some recruiters offered contractors cash rewards in return for successful leads. Mary Troxell, a recruiter at Information Technology Specialists, had a sliding scale: "It's $500 if they accept the job for at least three months and earn a minimum of $60 an hour. If I get a longer contract—for six months—then I give them $1,000." Experienced contractors, like Asaf Weiss, were well aware that their contacts were worth cash, and they sometimes banded together to enhance their income through joint referrals: "There is a small network of QA analysts in the city. We kind of keep in touch because a lot of these head-hunting firms offer referral bonuses to the tune of 500 or 1,000 bucks if you refer somebody that they end up using. So, it's beneficial to you and to the person you're referring if it works out. The headhunters make no bones about it. They tell you right up front, 'Hey, if you've got any friends or anybody else who you think can do this, let me know. We pay you $1,000 a pop for each name that we end up using.'"

Finally, like account managers, recruiters learned that friends and acquaintances could offer links to contractors. Carol Fitler explained, "I am constantly recruiting. I work twenty-four hours a day. I always have my recruiter hat on, whether I'm in a restaurant or in an elevator or at happy hour or just out on a personal errand. At social gatherings I will ask people what they do, if they have friends. And if I overhear a conversation in a restaurant, engineers talking, I walk up and say: 'Excuse me, where do you work? Are you contractors?' Or I say: 'I place contractors; are any of you interested?' I've had people give me their business cards or e-mail me because I gave them my cards."

In sum, recruiters' efforts to locate candidates ranged from anonymous encounters on the Web, where information was abundant, cheap, and easily accessible to more personalized sales approaches based on referrals, solicitations, and face-to-face encounters. But sourcing contractors was only the first step in securing a candidate for a specific job order; the next step was to make contact.

Leads usually contained limited information: a name, a business card, a phone number, a colleague's reference, and, at most, a résumé. These bits of data gave a recruiter sufficient warrant to justify a call, but recruiters had to decide whether making a call was worthwhile. Their decision was usually based on an evaluation of the candidate's résumé in light of a job order's requirements and their own notions of what made candidates "placeable." For recruiters résumés were the basic units of information in the market for contractors. In fact, experienced recruiters boasted that their expertise centered on their ability to interpret a résumé's subtleties. As Wayne Davey, a recruiter at ITS, told us, "My job isn't to list on job boards. Yeah, I do it. But that's not 'what I do.' What I do is I read résumés. If you know what you are looking for you can see it all on a résumé, and if you don't know what you're looking for, you end up sending a big stack of résumés to the manager's desk and none of them are the right ones."

When reading résumés, recruiters looked first at the contractor's "skills"—the code word for the technologies they claimed to know.[12] For software developers these included operating systems, programming languages, such as Java and C++, and the specific applications with which they had worked. Next, recruiters examined the contractor's work experience, the specific projects in which she had been involved, for evidence that the contractor had applied the skills she claimed to have and for evidence of involvement in "exciting" projects at reputable companies. After examining the contractor's skills and experience, most seasoned recruiters could decide whether the contractor would fit a job's rudimentary requirements and what rates he or she could probably command.

To establish a contractor's "reliability" and "ability to deliver," recruiters had to read between the lines. Particularly important were patterns of employment. An uninterrupted sequence of contracts reinforced by repeated engagements at the same client suggested a "career contractor," someone truly "committed to contracting." Gaps in the sequence or too many short contracts were "red lights," warning signs that the can-

---

[12] In high technology, "skill" and "skill sets" almost always refer to knowledge of a set of technologies and tools. This way of thinking about skills is much more concrete and specific than the more abstract descriptions of skills favored by human resource specialists and industrial psychologists. The vast array of technologies and their many possible combinations helps explain why technical managers seem to contradict themselves when they say that they have a hard time finding people with the right skills even in a weak economy where many technical professionals are under- or unemployed.

didate might be "unreliable" or "cause problems" on the job. Recruiters were particularly wary of any indication of poor technical performance, the tendency to "jump ship" in the middle of a contract, or an apparent preference for permanent employment. Contractors who "bailed" or who turned out to be poor performers could embarrass the recruiter, jeopardize the recruiter's relationship with the hiring manager, and threaten the recruiter's income.

Candidates who cleared these initial screens warranted a call. Like account managers, recruiters spent considerable time on the phone. Top recruiters knew that one call was never sufficient, given the nature of the contract cycle. "I have stacks of people that I'm constantly calling," Carol Fitler told us. "You never know when they're available because contracts end just like that [*snapping her fingers*], so I'm constantly calling the same people over and over again." Calls typically had several purposes: to determine whether the person was interested in contracting, to interest the person in the recruiter, to learn more about the person's skills and experience, and to begin negotiations over possible terms of employment—rates, working conditions, and time commitments. At the end of a call, recruiters added any information they had gleaned from the conversation to their database.

Most cold calls proved futile. Leads often turned out to be wrong numbers or led to a voice mailbox, where recruiters left well-rehearsed messages, few of which were returned. Contractors who answered their phones were often already on assignment or were no longer interested in contracting. In the latter case, recruiters quickly trashed their résumés. When recruiters managed to get through to a promising candidate, they started a conversation during which they described the agency, elicited additional information, and tried to convince the contractor to work through them. The task was not always easy. Consider the conversation that occurred between Scott Ahl, a recruiter at Progressive Staffing, and Hubert, a longtime contractor whose résumé listed thirty years of experience as a hardware engineer:

> Hubert answered and Scott opened with, "Hi, Hubert. My name is Scott and I'm a recruiter with Progressive Staffing. I found your résumé on DICE and you fit the profile of people I recruit. Are you available? Do you have time to talk?" Hubert curtly agreed to listen, and Scott launched into his standard spiel: "We're one of the largest staffing agencies, rated number one by everybody. We have twenty-three offices. We went public and we're doing well. We bring in contracts continually and fill them within twenty-four to forty-eight hours. I have jobs anywhere in the U.S.—California. Portland. Phoenix. Chicago. Austin. Denver."

But Hubert was suspicious and claimed to have never heard of Progressive Staffing. "Progressive Staffing is known for software," Scott responded. "Maybe that's why you haven't heard of us. I'll send you company material." Scott tried to ask questions about Hubert's skills. "I have an old résumé. It says you were last at Boeing. You've been there awhile, a nice long contract. . . . Tell me what you enjoy working on, what you've been doing, what you want to do." As Hubert talked, Scott began to take notes and ask clarifying questions: "Uh-huh, mostly design. Do you come in at the beginning? In the middle? At the end?" Scott was clearly unfamiliar with the details of the work and Hubert cut his questions short: "Why are you grilling me? I don't like being pigeonholed." To which Scott responded, audibly on guard, "I wasn't grilling you! I'm not pigeonholing you! I just want to know what makes you tick. You can ask me any question you like."

Hubert was silent for a moment and then asked about rates. "What were you making?" Scott immediately returned Hubert's question with a question. Hubert was reluctant to answer without assurance that Scott would not record his answer in a database. When Scott promised, Hubert asked what Scott could offer. Scott replied with practiced evasion: "Well, we try and get you as much as possible." Hubert seemed unimpressed and told Scott that he had had plenty of bad experiences with recruiters: "You guys always make promises and never keep them."

Scott tried to reassure Hubert: "I hear a lot of negativity coming from you. I'm not in the business of lowballing contractors. It's in my interest to get you as much as possible." Scott launched into a litany of the advantages of working with Progressive Staffing: the health insurance, a 401k, stock options, and direct deposits. Sensing that Hubert was not convinced, Scott added: "If you work with me I'll book you, I'll meet with you, we'll always have something for you in the pipeline. We're not a Mom and Pop shop. We do full representation, not pushing paper."

Hubert went silent and Scott asked: "Have any of the recruiters you've worked with been good?" Hubert wanted to know why Scott was asking. "I want to know how to treat you," Scott explained. "For me honesty is a virtue; I shoot from the hip, I don't like bullshit. I can't promise a contract tomorrow." "How long will it take?" Hubert inquired. "Maybe three days," Scott replied. "I'll be very honest every step of the way." Hubert reminded Scott that he was busy and that the conversation was taking too long. "Just send out my résumé and get me a job," Hubert said impatiently. "I want my paycheck. I don't need your benefits, I'll go with whoever gets me a job first."

Hubert hung up, leaving Scott visibly upset. "The guy was so rude and opinionated! He has thirty years of experience. Some of the older ones are like that. I wanted to say: 'Hey dude—settle down!' The guy was loony! He broke my rhythm. That's what we call such conversations. Breaking the rhythm. I don't like to represent such people; they could make problems later, too. But we could still use him." Scott updated the database and got ready for another call.

Fortunately for recruiters, most conversations with prospective contractors were less contentious, especially when contractors had posted résumés on the Web and expected recruiters to call. For example, after a series of dead-end calls to people who had posted résumés on DICE, Julie Cochran, another recruiter at Progressive Staffing, encountered Sam, who was attempting to contract after working for years as a perm. After introducing Progressive Staffing to Sam, Julie asked about his skills, which he explained at length. Julie took notes, interspersing encouraging comments as Sam listed his skills. When he was done she added: "That's a good skill set to have!" Julie asked Sam if he would travel. In response, Sam told her about one son who was in college and about another who was playing minor league hockey in Canada, and was just about to be drafted into the majors. "Really? What team? Wow! A son in the NHL!" Julie responded enthusiastically, adding: "Do you miss him? We can get you a contract in upstate New York to be closer to him."

After a few minutes, Julie got back to business, explaining how she and Sam would work together. "You get paid for every hour you work. A lot of our contractors are incorporated in the U.S., or they work with a W-2 plus per diem. You can maintain residency in California and travel." Sam said he was interested in proceeding. Julie turned to a recruiter sitting at an adjacent desk and gave a thumbs-up. Sam agreed to send Julie an updated copy of his résumé on condition that she not send it out without his permission. Julie emphasized: "We won't send your résumé anywhere, absolutely nowhere, without your agreement! And we'll agree on the rate first." Before saying good-bye she added as an afterthought: "If anybody from Progressive Staffing calls, tell them you're working with me—it will save you a headache."[13] Julie was very pleased with the conversation. "He was very nice and he has attractive skills," she said, adding that she hoped his rate would not turn out to be so high

---

[13] Julie also knew that his saying so would save her a headache as well, because it would serve as a signal to other recruiters that Julie already had "dibs on" Sam.

that it would cut into her markup. Julie would begin to negotiate a rate after receiving his résumé and qualifying his skills, the final step in finding a candidate.

QUALIFYING CANDIDATES

Most agencies promised clients that they would not send candidates to interview until recruiters had verified the contractor's skills and experience, a process known as "qualifying the candidate."[14] Although interpreting the contractor's résumé was actually the first step in qualifying a candidate, staffing agencies typically reserved the term for interviewing contractors and checking their references. Progressive Staffing and ITS guaranteed clients that they would check at least two references for each candidate they submitted. Systems Professionals went even further by requiring that all candidates go through a battery of interviews and pass standard technical tests. Each agency, to some degree, also enforced the requirement that candidates be qualified. Progressive Staffing ran classes to teach new recruiters how to interpret résumés and evaluated their performance, in part, by the number of contractors they were able to bring in for detailed, face-to-face interviews. ITS measured recruiters' performance by calculating "interview to hire ratios," the percentage of submitted candidates who were actually hired. Higher percentages suggested that recruiters were submitting well-qualified candidates.

Recruiters sometimes felt that qualifying candidates slowed down the process of placement, but they also knew that it was to their benefit to do so. Submitting a contractor who proved to be incompetent or dishonest would cause the recruiter to lose face and the agency to lose business. Wayne Davey emphasized the importance of qualifying candidates by recounting what one hiring manager had told him early in his career: "He looked me straight in the eyes and said, 'If you ever send me someone without meeting them first and I find out, I will personally pull all of the contractors that we have through you and never work with your firm again!'" In practice, how thoroughly candidates were qualified varied considerably across recruiters and from candidate to candidate depending on the situation.

Although the agencies' management preferred face-to-face interviews and most recruiters did make efforts to "bring contractors in," many interviews, like Julie's interview with Sam, occurred by phone as an extension of a cold call. Recruiters also had no option but to interview by phone when contractors lived in distant locations. Moreover, recruiters and contractors both preferred the convenience of a phone interview when the contractor had a strong résumé and when there was pressure to

---

[14] Recruiters, contractors, and hiring managers also referred to this process as "prescreening." Many used the terms interchangeably.

make an immediate placement. Linda was typical of most of the recruiters we observed. She told us that despite ITS's policy, the decision about face-to-face interviews was really a "judgment call." "If they're senior," she explained, "if they've had ten or fifteen years out in the Valley, I don't need to bring them in. It depends. But I *always* meet the junior or mid-level people before sending them out for an interview."

The first purpose of an interview was to screen the candidate on technical criteria. Whether interviewing in person or over the phone, recruiters at Progressive Staffing and ITS used computerized forms to compile detailed information on the contractors' technical skills and experience. The forms prompted the recruiter to ask specific questions, and as the contractor replied, the recruiter entered responses directly into the database. Some recruiters, especially those with considerable experience, appeared knowledgeable about the technologies and technical skills they were discussing and were able to probe and challenge interviewees. Sometimes they used the information they compiled to help the contractor prepare a more "professional" or "attractive" résumé. Other recruiters seemed less familiar with the relevant technologies, took the candidate's claims at face value, and sometimes made mistakes that the contractor noticed. Recruiters also modified their questioning based on their assessment of the contractor's experience. Linda, for example, told us that with "junior people—two to three years of experience—I may interrogate them a little more, ask them questions about specific skills and experience." But with most contractors, "it's a gut instinct. You don't have to hear about all of their skills. Where they've been is usually enough."

The second purpose of the interview was a "personality screen." Recruiters used face-to-face encounters to assess candidates' attributes and social skills and to predict their "fit" with the client's environment. Experienced recruiters had strong opinions about the personal attributes that specific clients would tolerate and claimed that they could quickly assess fit, even in a phone conversation. Linda, for example, told us: "It's really easy to tell within a minute whether they'll fit the culture of the client. I don't know all of the Valley, but I am familiar with enough companies to know what fits and what doesn't. Somebody with really mediocre communication skills would fit right in at Oracle. But they wouldn't at Wells Fargo Bank in San Francisco." Yet, despite such claims, recruiters rarely made refined evaluations of a candidate's personal fit, and assessments of social skills were always secondary to assessments of technical skills, especially when a job opening was waiting and the technical fit seemed reasonable.

Even face-to-face interviews served primarily to identify the rare case of "freaks and frauds," candidates with obvious behavioral problems or inconsistencies in their stories. "What you really want to know," Carol told us, "is whether he's a weirdo, if he hasn't taken a bath for a while, if he has green gobs hanging from his nose." Ultimately, the recruiters were interested in protecting themselves. Wayne Davey explained: "You can't go, 'I don't really see those beer cans in the back of the car [*holding his hands on his face like blinders*]. I don't really see them. They're not really there.' They are there! If you submit them anyway, then it'll come back and bite you in the butt. What if the guy's an alcoholic? What if the guy's a slob and you send him in and they call you back and ask, 'Did you meet this contractor?' You better believe you don't want to say, 'No.'"

Nevertheless, the pressures and rewards of quickly placing candidates at attractive markups sometimes led even seasoned agents to discount troubling and inconsistent information. One such incident occurred while we were shadowing Charles Larsen as he was trying to fill a job order for a technical writer and Web developer. Charles was working from home when Linda, who had been sourcing contractors for the position, e-mailed him a résumé. As Charles perused the résumé, "red lights" began to blink. Although Ted, the contractor, claimed to have been a technical writer and Web developer, most of his positions had lasted for no more than a month or two, which suggested to Charles that Ted might be unreliable. Ted's résumé claimed that he had been an attorney in the late 1980s and that in the 1990s he pursued a Ph.D. at Stanford in operations research while simultaneously working on project teams at Sun Microsystems and Hewlett-Packard. Prior to being a lawyer he claimed to have worked at the State Department specializing in Soviet Bloc operations, to have won an exceptional service medal from both the U.S. and the British governments, to have served in the U.S. Army Psychological Operations Division, and to have been a member of the Military Police. The résumé listed a law degree from Notre Dame but claimed that Ted had served as an editor of the *Princeton Law Review*. Charles's response was to say, "It sounds like he's telling us he was a spy," and then he backpedaled adding, "but I've met some exceptional people," apparently not fully appreciating that such a career history was impossible, if for no other reason than students who get law degrees from one university can't edit the law reviews of another. Being uneasy, Charles decided to consult with Linda, who told him that she had discovered the résumé on the Web while searching for people who developed Web sites. Charles told Linda, "If he's on the level, he's pretty high-powered," to which Linda responded, "Yes, he knows Java and Java-Plus."

Because Linda was less skeptical of Ted's honesty and stability than Charles was, they decided to set up a teleconference and interview Ted together. The teleconference lasted fifteen minutes, during which Charles and Linda asked Ted to discuss details of his résumé. In response to their questions about his career history, Ted replied, "My career progress looks invented. I started contracting when my daughter was abducted. When she was returned to me I needed work." Ted went on to say that he had been a very successful lawyer winning "102 out of 107" cases in three years. When Charles asked about his rates, Ted replied that they were "obscene," between $55 and $250 an hour. Charles pointed his finger to his head and made circles in the air while telling Ted that he was unlikely to get such rates.

Near the end of the conversation, Charles told Ted that he had several "concerns." The first was that the company didn't "want someone who was too pushy," to which Ted replied, "Let me put it this way: I'm not going to stand by and watch the manager slide off a cliff, even if I have to grab him by the proverbials." Charles's second concern was that on his last contract Ted left the client because the engineers and managers "apparently didn't have too high of a regard for technical writers." Ted's tone became even more belligerent: "I can hold my own with the top ten scientists in the U.S. If they want to butt heads, I'll butt heads. I like to treat my engineers as artists, but if they want to butt heads, no problem." As the conversation wound down, Charles asked Ted if there was anything else they should know about him. Ted offered that he had been nominated for a Pulitzer Prize but had not received it.

At the end of the conversation Charles and Linda discussed the interview. Although Charles was clearly uncomfortable, he stopped short of saying that the candidate was lying or that he might be mentally unstable. Linda, however, was positive and upbeat. Almost as if she had not taken part in the same interview, she noted that the candidate had the skills that the position required and that she could place him. She discounted Ted's "idiosyncrasies," by reminding Charles, "There are a lot of high-powered people out there and he's just a high-powered contractor." Charles, still uncomfortable but clearly influenced by Linda's optimism, suggested that Linda contact Ted's references. Later in the day, when Ted's references revealed that he was indeed unstable, Linda and Charles went on to other options.

As the story of Charles, Linda, and Ted indicates, reference checking was the core of the qualifying process. It was in checking references that recruiters acquired information that kept them from making mistakes. Recruiters invariably asked candidates for references and contractors were usually happy to comply, although those who were still permanently employed were often reluctant to give out names lest the agent's call expose their intention of leaving. Reference checking usually entailed a short phone conversation with a former boss or coworker. The conversation between John Heathcote, an account manager at Progressive

Staffing, and Jack, the former supervisor of a contractor, Nelsen, whom John was trying to place, was typical.

John called Jack, Nelsen's ex-supervisor, introduced himself, and explained that he was trying to place Nelsen, who had listed Jack as a reference. John quickly focused the conversation: "I'd like to verify his technical skills." Jack explained that it had been several years since he had worked with Nelsen and that he was actually quite busy and didn't have much time to talk, but he agreed to answer questions after John assured him that the conversation would be brief and that his opinions were valuable. John activated a reference checking form on his computer screen, which he completed as they talked. First John verified the information on Nelsen's vita: "Was he doing MVS work for you?" "What other operating systems did he know?" Satisfied with the response, John asked about Nelsen's technical performance. Jack answered in detail while John recorded the following in the reference file:

> *Technical Strengths*: Tenacity. Strong ability to explain things to other people. Great deal of energy. Toured eleven cities in ten days in Europe.
> *Department Functions*: Handled technical problems. Sometimes wrote code. More often worked with problems that companies had trouble solving. Early days of MVS. 60 percent technical, 20 percent hand-holding.
> *Languages*: Assembler VSPC, APL Operating Systems: OS, VS.

John moved next to questions about social skills. "How does he get along with others? What's his work ethic like? Can you tell me about his communications skills?" Jack was noncommittal. To each question he answered, "Fine," and John recorded his answer. The last question was designed to elicit weak points: "What improvements does he need?" John recorded the answer: "Can work with others, but tends to be a loner. Could easily position himself as a holdout. Focused on the best solution, but could have opened up to compromise a bit more. But I couldn't find a problem." At the end of the conversation John thanked Jack for his help and then switched to prospecting: "What are you doing now? Do you use contractors? Can you use additional help?" Jack declined John's offer of assistance, but John had gotten what he wanted: Nelsen's vita appeared to be accurate, and he apparently had no major personality problems.

Many of the calls we observed were less detailed than John's conversation with Jack. Some referees were reluctant to answer, others seemed to give pro forma answers, and in no case did we observe referees offer blatantly negative information about the candidate. Recruiters, however, claimed that they did occasionally uncover negative information. Carol

Fitler listed the types of negative comments she sometimes heard: "Oh, he did not perform. We have a computer missing and we think that he took it with him. Technically doesn't produce. He's all talk. He's very arrogant. He works only by himself. He doesn't communicate. We just couldn't stand him." When she heard such comments, Carol claimed, she would check with another referee, and only if a second referee corroborated the negative information would she consider not placing the candidate.

CONCLUSION

If there is one universally acknowledged rule of market behavior, it is caveat emptor—let the buyer beware. This rule rests on a belief, so widespread and pervasive as to be nearly axiomatic, that valid information is the first casualty of trade. In this view, markets are places where, to further their interests, sellers offer, intentionally or not, partial, biased, distorted, and otherwise misleading information when describing and promoting their wares. Thus, it is incumbent upon those seeking a deal, especially those whose livelihood depends on successful deal making, to always treat market information with suspicion and to take steps to ensure that they get what they want.

The market for contractors was rife with imperfect and potentially misleading information. Firms seeking contractors and contractors seeking jobs found that information about each other was, at best, scattered, difficult to uncover, and frequently stale. Contractors and hiring managers both had incentives to put positive spins on the positions and skills they offered each other while holding negative information close to their chest. Contractors stood to benefit by overestimating their skills and experience. Hiring managers stood to gain by enhancing the technical challenge of their positions while downplaying budgetary and organizational uncertainties. Nor was the quality of market information the only problem that managers and contractors faced. Both confronted issues of quantity: all else being equal, managers and contractors both wanted to choose from an array of alternatives. But finding an array of alternative candidates and positions was difficult. Furthermore, both contractors and hiring managers wrestled with the timeliness of information about jobs and candidates. Learning about a position after it was filled or about the absolutely perfect contractor who was already on a job was of no use.

Managers and contractors had two options for navigating the informational morass they confronted: they could manage their own searches or they could turn to staffing agencies to do the job for them. As we've seen, managers and contractors preferred self-managed searches because they believed that personal and professional networks carried higher quality information. Managers considered recommendations and referrals from peers and colleagues to be trustworthy because they came from people whom they saw as technically sophisticated, experienced, and relatively disinterested. Contractors held similar beliefs: not only would their colleagues provide more accurate and trustworthy information about clients, but they also believed their networks were more likely to carry exclusive information on jobs. Because reputations and friendships were at stake in each case, hiring managers and contractors also felt that their contacts would have their best interests in mind when making recommendations.

The quality of market information gleaned through one's network, however, came at the expense of its quantity and timeliness. Even the networks of the most well-connected contractors and hiring managers had limited reach, compared with the size of the entire market. Moreover, to control costs and protect themselves from lawsuits, many firms channeled their demand for contractors entirely, or almost entirely, through agencies. Contractors had difficulty learning about such jobs. Thus, when networks worked, they carried information that contractors and managers valued and trusted; but in most cases their networks were simply not extensive enough to be able to locate potential deals on a regular basis.

It was this limitation that created a niche for the staffing agencies' services. Agencies profited from their ability to gather, organize, and disseminate large quantities of market information quickly and systematically. By culling data from a variety of sources and then creating and updating databases that tracked jobs and candidates, agencies, in effect, cultivated and sold access to wide-ranging "commercial networks" that extended the reach of hiring managers' and contractors' personal networks. On the other hand, the quantity of the information that agencies provided came at the expense of its quality.

Staffing agencies were able to serve as information brokers precisely because they relied on personnel who were knowledgeable about sales and marketing techniques rather than technology, because they emphasized sweeping, superficial searches in the name of speed, and because they offered commercial rather than professional relationships. Thus, the very factors that allowed agencies to amass quantities of information on jobs and candidates in a timely fashion undermined their ability—and, in some cases, their motivation—to provide accurate information. Moreover, aggressive sales tactics and the competition between agencies quickly created the converse of scarce information. A chief complaint among managers and contractors was that going to agencies generated too much information, much of it of questionable validity.

In short, hiring managers and contractors faced a choice between the quality, the quantity, and the timeliness of information. Firms tried to balance the trade-off by striking alliances with approved and on-site vendors, which placed limits on the hiring managers' degrees of freedom. Hiring managers and contractors tried to skirt the trade-off by developing networks and by establishing relationships of reciprocity with agents whom they trusted. In the end, however, the system left much room for ambiguity, uncertainty, and even deception. Managers, contractors, and agents each played the information game to achieve their own ends, which conflicted along a number of dimensions. Managers wanted the highest quality candidate at the lowest cost. Contractors wanted the right job at the highest wage. Agents hoped to make placements quickly and maximize the agency's cut of the deal. Moreover, what hiring managers actually wanted and what contractors could actually do was often ambiguous, required further clarification and validation, and remained open to negotiation.

Thus, it would be inaccurate to view the information game simply as a process that compiled and filtered scarce and ambiguous information to yield potential matches between those who offered and sought jobs, although matches were certainly what the system produced. Searching was a three-way game in which information was not simply found, it was shaped, negotiated, and tailored to the needs of all parties in ways that were not always explicit. Even when potential matches were produced, the information game left much to be negotiated and resolved before deals could be struck. If nothing else, the terms of employment—the contractor's compensation and working conditions, as well as the staffing firm's markup—were rarely fully specified up front and left considerable scope for bargaining. Thus, participants in the market for technical contractors knew that locating a potential deal was just the first step toward closing it: once found, deals still had to be actively made, and this required considerable investment of time, energy, and skill.

Chapter 6

MAKING THE DEAL

SOONER OR LATER in the course of every foray into the market, all parties shifted from finding to negotiating and closing deals. Although the transition to deal making was gradual, it escalated as hiring managers began to evaluate and interview candidates. It was then that managers and contractors were finally able to assess how well they had fared in the latest round of the information game. Interviews allowed contractors and managers to decide whether they wanted to advance toward signing a contract or retreat back into the market. The tone of the evaluation and the path along which subsequent events unfolded depended on the type of search that brought the manager and contractor together and on the type of deal they would strike.

Generally speaking, managers and contractors were less cautious about deal making when their pairing resulted from a direct search and when they anticipated striking a direct deal. In this case, each party had been referred to the other by someone they trusted. Implicit obligations of reciprocity were also involved. Hiring managers knew that referrers might someday ask them to return the favor, although not necessarily in kind. They believed no referrer would knowingly jeopardize his or her future interests by making a poor recommendation. In direct searches, contractors also relied on professional contacts, who could usually evaluate the firm, if not the specific job. These contacts also realized that they might someday ask the contractor to reciprocate and knew that they would lose credibility if the match were poor.

The situation was altogether different when the search was brokered by an agency. Although managers and contractors felt reasonably comfortable moving toward a deal with agents whom they trusted, as we have seen, it was often impossible to work through an agent they knew. Experienced contractors were wary of matches brokered by unknown agents because they knew that most agents had little technical expertise. Hiring managers also believed that agents lacked the technical knowledge necessary for understanding their needs or for making valid assessments of a candidate's skills. As a result, Randy Bouchet of Raster explained, "You spend the time giving them the information you need and then they just start throwing stuff at you. You get résumé after résumé with people that don't even come close to what you're asking for."[1]

Contractors and managers were also cautious of brokered matches for a darker reason: they suspected that some agents intentionally misled people in the hope of closing deals. Micky Cummings had discovered many cases where "a [candidate's] skills didn't match the résumé." This led him to suspect that agents "tailored résumés to get placements." "You could tell the résumés had been doctored," he explained, "because it said they knew Java, but it turned out that all they'd ever done was write a project in Java when they were in school." Randy believed that agents told candidates "to put buzzwords on their résumé because they know that's what you're looking for and they just want to make the sale." He offered an extreme example:

> I had this one poor woman. She was really honest with me after the fact. But up front, her résumé said she was a C++ programmer. So I started asking her classic C++ questions, and it was clear she had no clue what was going on. So I said: "Your résumé says you know C++ and it's clear that you don't." She said, "Well, I know C. And that's 80 percent of C++, so therefore I know C++." Whap!! [*He waves his hand as if slapping someone.*] Turns out, that's what the recruiter had told her to do. C++ was one of the buzzwords she needed to add, so since she knew C, he told her to do this. I didn't work with him again.

Our data do not allow us to estimate the frequency of such practices. We saw agents helping contractors reformat their résumés, but we never observed an agent fabricate or stretch the truth. Stories of this type of behavior were nevertheless common enough for hiring managers to believe that the line between reformatting and "sprucing up a résumé" was thin and tempting, at least for some agents. As is often the case with salespeople, the shadier practitioners soiled the occupation's reputation and led technical managers to act as if agents were "guilty until proven innocent." What our data do show is that hiring managers had enough doubts about the competence and professionalism of staffing agencies that they almost always insisted on evaluating candidates themselves, and it was this evaluation that marked the transition between finding and making deals.

---

[1] As we noted in chapter 4, we observed a number of experienced recruiters and account managers who made serious and reasonably successful efforts to learn enough about technology to perform their jobs effectively. But because most agencies recruited agents from sales backgrounds and because turnover in the staffing industry was high, inexperienced and technically naïve agents were common.

Hiring Manager Evaluations

A hiring manager's first encounter with a candidate usually came in the form of a résumé accompanied by a preliminary evaluation from a colleague or an agent. When the referral came from a colleague accompanied by a strong recommendation, a résumé was occasionally sufficient for immediately offering the contractor the job. But even then, most managers insisted on meeting the candidate before making a decision. When referrals came from agencies, managers always began the evaluation process by reviewing résumés to compile a "short list" of candidates who seemed to possess the requisite skills and experience.[2] A quick glance at the contractors' list of skills and past projects was usually enough for managers to exclude candidates they deemed unsuitable. Some, like Monty Kirkman, had even learned how to compensate for the biases of inexperienced agents:

> What we've found out is that agencies make the mistake of thinking that if somebody has twenty years [of] experience, they're more senior and need more money. But we've found that some people fresh out of school are more effective in some cases than the so-called senior people. I had somebody fresh out of Stanford [on] his first contract. Did beautifully! Others had twenty years of experience and couldn't get anywhere. You can have a terrible contractor jumping from case to case, working three months here, three months there, never long enough to make a good assessment of their skills. When you see that on the résumé, you can't tell if they did a good job because you don't know if the project was for that long or what. Sometimes you can tell, because they say they finished a project in two months that you know should have taken two years.

Hiring managers generally considered résumés to be inadequate for making more than the first cut, because, as Micky Cummings put it, "it's just too easy to write a résumé that looks good." Consequently, managers almost always insisted on interviewing contractors at least by phone.

Because staffing agencies understood that interviews were watershed events, they actively tried to arrange, influence, and orchestrate the process. At the very least, agents insisted on serving as go-betweens who arranged the interview's time and location. In the process, agents

---

[2] The only regular exceptions were the contractors that System Professionals brokered. As we discussed in chapter 4, System Professionals strove to place the contractor they had chosen into the job without presenting the client with a résumé or allowing an interview. Not all hiring managers accepted this approach. It required considerable persuasion, and in roughly 40 percent of the cases, System Professionals had to compromise.

coached contractors on what to say and primed managers for the contractors they would see. Although most interviews occurred at the client's site, some, as was often the case at Progressive Staffing, took place at the agency's offices. Progressive Staffing believed that bringing contractors and clients together on the agency's turf gave the agent more control. In any case account managers tried to be close at hand during the interview regardless of where it occurred.

Interviews served two purposes: to confirm the contractors' technical abilities and to size up their interpersonal skills. Interviews varied widely in style and depth. At one extreme were extensive face-to-face interviews with several interviewers that focused on both technical and personal issues. At the other extreme were short phone interviews that dealt primarily with technical matters. Most interviews lay somewhere in between. Although most hiring managers said that personal characteristics mattered, in practice, technical assessment consumed most, if not all, of an interview.

Technical Evaluations

Technical evaluation took two forms. Interviewers invariably quizzed candidates with technical questions designed to gauge the candidates' knowledge and skills. Randy Bouchet described this strategy: "You ask a lot of questions about how they would solve a particular problem—test them on their knowledge of the particular [programming] language and the environment that you want them to work in. Test them about platform issues. At Raster, we work across platforms, so we need people that can do Mac, Windows, and UNIX—actually several variants of UNIX. So you poke on each of those operating systems, just find out how much they know. Of course, you have to temper that with how much they really have to know in order to do the job."

Many interviews, however, especially those with experienced contractors, moved beyond simple testing into extended discussions of the tasks and technical problems that the contractor would confront. Tom Adams, an experienced programmer, summarized the plot of such interviews: "They say, 'Here is what we're trying to do, here are the constraints; how would you design it?'" Stu Davis recounted how he closed a direct deal in the course of such a discussion:

> I walked into the interview and they showed me the product. This thing was a good 75 to 80 percent done. "We just need somebody to finish it up." They took me in a room and plopped down a source code listing in front of me, and—you have to almost be a programmer to understand this—what I got was uncommented, undocumented

assembly code. There were three guys in the room. For all I knew, one of them had written it and it was the proudest thing he'd ever done. So they said, "What do you think about this?" I looked at it and it was terrible. I mean it was abysmal! So I go: "Well, this is not very maintainable." And I saw one guy smile real big and the other guy started to chuckle and I knew I was safe. So I told them: "This is garbage. There's no commenting here. I have no idea what's in the guy's mind who's doing this. He doesn't even use any program labels. Things like 'Load R45 at A13.' Well, what does that mean? R45—that's some kind of internal register. Is that for some of the IO functions, like a timer, calendar, or serial port? When is it safe to use R45? Can I use it in this interim routine? Is it a global thing? Is it only used in a certain frame? I don't know! A13? Where is that? Is that a decimal value? Is that a bit-map? Is it an ASCII character? Is it a lube counter? What is it? We're going to start from scratch."

Contractors described several strategies for demonstrating technical acumen in the course of an interview. Those, like Stu Davis, who felt they knew enough to do the job, made efforts to display their skills. Sometimes, however, contractors interviewed for positions for which they believed they were not fully qualified, although they were confident they could learn what they needed to know on the job. In such cases it was necessary to "talk yourself into the job." Our informants reported two ways of doing this. Some tried to hide or disguise their shortcomings. "If you can't dazzle them with brilliance," said Steve Louthan, a technical writer, "you've got to baffle them with bullshit." Contractors who took this approach usually made an effort to learn enough about the specific technology before the interview to appear knowledgeable.

A second approach was to acknowledge that one was unfamiliar with the specific technology, but that one's general skills and ability to learn were more than sufficient. This was Judy King's preferred way of managing interviews:

I say: "I may or may not have experience with it, it doesn't matter. I have thirty years of experience doing software. That's what you're hiring. You're hiring technical management. You're hiring project management. You're hiring a senior engineer. You're hiring somebody who can walk in, figure it out, and do the job. If you don't want that, okay, but you're going to spend more time looking for somebody who can do exactly what you want than you will hiring me and letting me get to work." I may be nice about the way I say that, but essentially that's the line that I give them.

Steve Louthan described how he had convinced a hiring manager to give him a job by being similarly candid:

> I can't remember the question that he asked, but what really turned his key was I looked him in the eye—at that point we were on a first-name basis—and said: "Joe, I promise you that you will not have to teach me a thing. I will come up to speed on VI," which is a very, very basic ASCII text word processor. "I will come up to speed on Tek," which is an embedded command programming language to format documents, "and produce this first manual for you in less than six weeks. And if I can't, fire me. That's it. Just fire me! No hard feelings." He said: "Can I put that on paper?" I said: "Sure, I'll sign it." [*Steve laughs.*] He was pretty impressed. He had no intentions of following through, but he was—I could tell he was—so impressed with how gutsy I was taking such a bold stand. I think he wanted to see if I could actually pull it off.

Because clients were primarily interested in verifying technical skills, some managers, like Nancy Cato at Advanced Computers, were satisfied with interviewing contractors by phone. Nancy preferred phone interviews, even when candidates were local, because she thought they were more efficient than face-to-face meetings and because experience had taught her that they were almost as good for determining a candidate's suitability. "We used to bring [contractors] on-site and send them to be interviewed with two or three people," Nancy told us. "We probably had about the same success rate as when I read the résumé, screen it myself, and call them up." Although Nancy acknowledged that phone interviews probably had a higher margin of error, she was not concerned: the ease of replacing unsuitable contractors justified the effort she saved. "You think to yourself, 'Well, I've hired the guy and if he doesn't work out a month from now, we can find somebody else.'" UNIX Hardware's Russell Brown took a similar view: "I'm maybe willing to take a little higher risk with a contractor, because if there's a real downside, I can terminate the contract early very easily."

Although phone conversations might at first appear more superficial than face-to-face interviews, phone interviews could become quite complex, especially when they centered on technical knowledge. Donna Lawyer, of Chipco, had developed an approach to phone interviewing that allowed her to delve into the candidate's technical skills using both strategies outlined earlier:

> I'll do an initial screening in a phone conversation to see if they can communicate and if they know the basics. I'll ask them some basic

UNIX questions and basic Oracle questions just to see if they can answer them. I can tell right away that some of them don't know anything and the conversation will end right there. If I think it's going to be a good fit, I'll schedule follow-on phone conversations with some technical folks. I'm technical, [but] since I'm in a lead position, I'm sort of removed from the day-to-day report writing and some of the developer tools. I don't have time to do that anymore, so I like to get someone that's current on all of the tools to talk to them and ask them real specific technical issues to make sure they're technically competent. If the technical people okay them, I'll okay them.

Although clients were primarily interested in confirming that contractors had the technical skills they claimed to have, few subjected candidates to formal testing. Those that did were large firms that hired many contractors and that relied on human resource departments to administer tests that ranked candidates, sometimes against nationwide norms. Most managers, however, simply trusted their own abilities and believed that the cost of an occasional mistake did not justify the cost of testing.

Personal Evaluations

Hiring managers who attested to the importance of assessing a contractor's personal traits always insisted on holding face-to-face interviews. But with rare exceptions, evaluation consisted of simply forming an opinion about the individual based on impressions gathered in the course of a technical discussion. The overriding concern was whether the contractor would, as one manager put it, "fit in with the people I've got here." "Fit" was almost always cast as another type of competence, albeit of an interpersonal rather than a technical sort. Discussing technical issues face-to-face offered an opportunity to learn about the candidates' "social" and "communication" skills on the side. Randy Bouchet explained the approach favored by most hiring managers:

> You talk to them, just to get sort of a feel for their personality and make sure that they're going to be a reasonable fit with the team. We're not looking for a perfect fit because they're pretty much going to be in their office and stay there. But they are going to interact with people, so you want to make sure you get someone who has some social skills. They don't need a lot; they need a little. We tend to do interviews in the half hour to forty-five-minute range. The truth of the matter is that the technical probably will fill up most of it and you are going to be picking up the social and personal dy-

namics as part of the process. So it's not like you split it. But at the end of the day when you sit down with your piece of paper, you try to pull it out into the two different areas.

Videonet placed slightly more emphasis on fit than most firms we studied. Matt Schmidt claimed technical skills "get you the interview, but that's not what gets you the job." Matt looked for people that his technical staff could "connect with," and along with Videonet's founder and the technology manager who reported to him, Matt interviewed all contractors. "The three of us will interview the candidate and come to a consensus. We're very informal. We're just like, 'Hey, what's up, dude? How's it going? Do you ride a motorcycle?' We listen to the way they talk, to their ability to carry on a conversation effectively." What Matt and his colleagues hoped to get was a sense of whether they could get along with the contractor and whether the contractor would break norms that they thought were important:

> Someone could go: "I know Java, I know Web Objects, I know C++, I know every programming language on the face of the earth," and we'll go, "Oh, my God! We totally want to interview them." They come in here and they put their feet up on the table and they'll never come back. If they make us feel like, "Oh, you guys are such idiots. I can't believe you're doing it that way," then they're not going to fit in. So then we all get together and go, "Okay, do we want to work with this person?" It's fine to have answers like, "No, I just don't feel that person's right." And that's it. We'll turn the page and go, "Okay, next person." We don't necessarily care about appearance. Don't care about shyness. I mean they have to fit in to a degree. They have to get along with the other engineers. But that's pretty easy because most of the engineers are introverts by nature.

Ultimately, then, interviews served to reassure hiring managers that contractors were not misrepresenting their skills and, in the case of a brokered deal, that the agency was not stretching the truth. The urgency of making such assessments depended on the manager's level of comfort, on whether the manager had previous experience with an agent, and on the degree to which the manager would become dependent on the skills that the contractor brought to the job. The more central the contractor's task to the project, the less willing were managers to take chances. In the end, however, managers realized they could be less thorough in evaluating contractors than when hiring permanent employees because hiring a contractor was less binding. If the manager felt reassured, the parties could proceed toward negotiating the terms of employment, the first step in closing the deal.

Negotiating the Terms of Employment

Contractors, managers, and agents negotiated over two issues: working conditions and the price of the deal. In most cases, working conditions were secondary and rarely discussed. The parties simply assumed that the contractor would work at the client's site and that the client would provide suitable space and access to the equipment, resources, and people that the contractor needed to perform the work. Unless otherwise specified, the parties also assumed a forty-hour week and an eight-hour day for the contract's duration, which the client specified unilaterally in terms of weeks or months.[3] Working conditions became a topic of discussion only when contractors desired to work from home or wanted to be reimbursed for expenses. Hours of work might be discussed if the client or contractor desired more or less time than a standard workweek or if overtime was involved. Agents and managers occasionally put working conditions on the table in later phases of negotiation as a ploy for convincing contractors to accept lower rates.

In contrast, setting a deal's price often occasioned pointed, protracted, and sometimes heated bargaining. Although a few contractors reported closing deals for a fixed price to be paid at a project's completion, most deals were struck by reaching agreement on hourly rates. The price of a deal usually consisted of three components: the *bill rate*, or hourly price the client would pay for the contractor's service; the *pay rate*, or hourly wage the contractor would receive; and the agency's *markup*, or the difference between the bill rate and pay rate, expressed as a percentage of the latter.

Precisely how negotiations unfolded depended, in part, on the type of deal. When the deal was direct, clients and contractors usually delayed bargaining over terms until the interview occurred. In brokered deals that involved unrestricted searches, negotiations typically happened in two stages. *Preliminary bargaining* occurred *before* the interview as account managers and recruiters interacted with hiring managers and contractors to identify job orders and candidates. *Deal-specific bargaining* began once matches were made and then gathered momentum as soon as a manager expressed interest in hiring a particular contractor. Restricted searches made preliminary bargaining moot because preexisting agreements limited the bill rates or the markups (or both) that an on-site or

---

[3] Because employment could be terminated instantly, duration was significant only for computing the total amount of compensation for the period of the contract and to mark a point in time for renegotiation.

preferred vendor could charge.[4] But regardless of the type of deal, each of the parties entered negotiations with an idea of the terms they desired. They differed with respect to how explicitly they formulated their opening positions and how flexible they were willing to be.

The Parties' Opening Positions

CONTRACTORS

Experienced and well-connected contractors usually knew the going rate for their skills and could specify the minimum rate they would accept.[5] In fact, our more experienced informants told us that being a professional contractor meant developing what Marty Keely called "market know-how." Market know-how, according to Marty, involved "staying in touch with the pulse of the industry and knowing what's hot." One way to do so was to talk to other contractors. Another was to consult Web sites such as DICE, Contract Employment Daily, Realrates, Job Smart, and Salary.com, which published data on wage rates by occupation, industry, and region. Contractors were sometimes willing to lower their rate for work they found convenient or interesting and especially to land jobs that promised new skills and, thus, the opportunity to charge higher rates in the long run.

Less experienced contractors were more uncertain about what rates to charge. Often, beginning contractors entered negotiations knowing only that contracting was supposed to be more lucrative than a permanent position. Because they were accustomed to thinking in terms of annual salaries, they typically evaluated job offers and pay rates by translating hourly wages into annual salaries and the reverse. Their objective was to make sure their projected annual income exceeded that which they might make as a permanent employee.[6] We met some inexperienced contractors who tried to negotiate the maximum rate possible. But with a job or two under their belt, most new contractors simply set their rate based on their last contract or relied on the advice of friends. Anna Kapoor, who had been working as an Oracle developer for a year when we met her, set

---

[4] Account managers also skipped preliminary bargaining when they approached a contractor with a fully specified job order in hand or when they could present a prospective hiring manager with the bill rate of a contractor whom they were already authorized to represent.

[5] Among our informants, rates varied from $20 to $125 an hour depending on skills and occupation, with an average of $65 an hour.

[6] The calculation usually assumed a forty-hour week and a fifty-week year. Annual hours of a permanent employee were assumed to be two thousand. Thus, the annual salary equivalent of an hourly rate of $60 was $120,000 a year. Such calculations were used only for an estimate and did not take into account the costs of benefits, overtime, and so forth.

her rates in this way. "My last contract was for $65 an hour. My current rate is like seventy, but don't quote me on that. This is something I have been trying to get off, because I have heard that the current market rate is really better. I have friends that tell me that you should go for ranges like $115 to $125. I am like, 'Wow, where am I? What did I do wrong?' I don't know the real rate. But I hear that from people all the time. I think it is really only here in Silicon Valley. It depends on where. I mean if you move out, your rate suddenly goes down."

Contractors' stances toward an agency's markup also varied. We encountered some contractors, usually the less experienced, who paid little attention to markups and focused solely on the pay rate, leaving agencies to charge whatever margin they could extract. With experience, contractors became more concerned with the size of the markup. Seasoned contractors realized that exorbitant markups narrowed the number of jobs they could consider. They also believed that exorbitant markups signaled that an agency was willing to take advantage of the client as well as the contractor.

Charles Eaton, like many of our informants, resented the idea that agents might use him to become wealthy. "I don't like paying, or having my clients pay, for them to have fancy offices in downtown Bellevue or for the owner of the company to be able to go on trips on his boat," he complained indignantly. Others, like Victor Post, believed that exorbitant markups were more than unfair: they suggested that the agency did not respect the contractor's professionalism. "I consider myself to be a professional and I am a part of the business process," Victor explained. "I am the product that these people are selling. I feel I have a right to know how much they are selling me for. If they are making an inordinate profit on me, it shows me they do not have a lot of respect for me or what I do for them."

Nevertheless, most contractors who worked through agencies accepted the idea that some kind of markup was a legitimate or, at least, an unavoidable cost of doing business. Agencies were, after all, providing both the contractor and the client with a service. The question, then, was how much of a markup was justified. Contractors quickly learned that agencies needed to charge at least a 15 percent markup to offset the employment taxes they absorbed, taxes that the contractors would have had to otherwise pay. Our informants considered markups in the range of 25 to 35 percent to be customary, if not reasonable. Anything above this range they considered exorbitant.

Although most contractors avoided bargaining over working conditions, they became important when the contract involved travel or relocation. Contractors known as "nomads," who specialized in taking jobs that required moving long distances, expected employers to reimburse travel and living expenses, at least at a per diem rate. Julie Cochran, a recruiter at Progressive Staffing whose job was to locate and then negotiate with nomads, described their demands: "The people I'm recruiting are at least $100 an hour and they want the moon and the stars to go anywhere. They want expenses on top of their rate. They want accommodations; they want airline tickets to fly home every two to three weeks; they want a car; they want food. They'll ask for everything because they're inconveniencing themselves by traveling."

A handful of our informants stood at the opposite end of the spectrum: they abhorred long commutes and strongly preferred to work from their homes. These contractors also negotiated for working conditions. For example, one preferred jobs that were either "BARTable [accessible on the Bay Area Rapid Transit system] or below Route 92 [within a one-hour commute from his home]." But even these contractors rarely posed their demands as deal breakers. Like Anna Kapoor, most would accept lower rates for off-site work or a short commute: "When I talk to people I say: 'Okay, tell me what the whole package is.' If someone gives me the flexibility to work from home, I'm not as particular about the rate. But if I have to go to San Francisco five days a week and I'm spending three hours going up and back, I'll be sure to quote something really high to make it worth my time."

HIRING MANAGERS

On the whole, hiring managers seemed less concerned than contractors with the size of an agency's markup. Instead, they entered negotiations with their eye on the overall cost of the contract.[7] Their flexibility depended on the budgetary constraints they faced, on their sense of urgency, on corporate policy, and on their experience. Firms typically gave project managers a fixed pot of money to purchase the various resources that the project would require. Within this limit, managers were free to allocate funds as they saw fit. Based on projected needs, project managers estimated the amount of money they could reasonably allocate to contractors. Given the size of their budget, the rates that managers were willing to pay for a specific contractor reflected the pressure they were under. When a project was in crisis and urgently needed the contractor's skills, concerns about cost became secondary to issues of time and quality. In such cases, managers often adopted an attitude of "just get them in here, whatever it takes." When deadlines were more distant and the

---

[7] Some hiring managers also had preferences concerning on-site work, but expressed them only when contractors raised the issue. Although most managers preferred their contractors to work on-site, some were willing to accept a telecommuting arrangement in return for lower rates.

work was going smoothly, managers were more inclined to keep costs down.

Managers who worked for companies with centralized hiring policies had less discretion over the rates they could pay than did managers in companies with decentralized policies. Managers who faced ceilings on bill rates or markups sometimes found that they could not hire the individuals they desired. A manager's familiarity with the market and the way staffing agencies operated also affected the rates he or she would accept. Generally speaking, managers who were new to the market expected a contractor's compensation package to be much closer to the cost of hiring a permanent employee. Experienced managers knew better and usually accepted the rules of the game, although many found the income gap between permanent employees and contractors to be personally troubling.

AGENTS

In the brokered deals we studied, agents were primarily, if not exclusively, concerned with closing the deal and ensuring their markup. Going into negotiations, they usually had clear targets for the markups they desired. The size of the markup varied for open and restricted market deals and from agency to agency.[8]

In unrestricted deals, agents aimed for the highest markup they could negotiate without alienating either the contractor or the client. Our data suggest that a 25 percent markup above the cost of employment taxes (on average, 15 percent of the pay rate) was the average markup that agents initially targeted. In practice, this meant a 25 percent markup for 1099 and corporation-to-corporation deals in which the contractor paid his or her own taxes and a 40 percent markup (25 percent + 15 percent) when the contractor worked as a W-2. In restricted deals, agents had fewer degrees of freedom, because the master contracts that clients negotiated with on-site and preferred vendors typically set ceilings for bill rates and markups.[9] Margins for restricted deals were, therefore, usually less than what agents could obtain in an unrestricted deal.

Because markups determined an agency's profitability, agencies set guidelines for markups and then pressured agents to adhere to them. Progressive Staffing pegged its agents' compensation to the size of the

[8] In a third-party deal, the agency providing the candidate negotiated with the agency holding the job order over the split of the markup. Because we did not observe such negotiations, we cannot speak to their dynamics.

[9] Agencies were willing to negotiate contracts that set ceilings on their rates and markups because they anticipated that easy access to clients and guaranteed job orders would increase the volume of their business while lowering their costs.

markup they negotiated and periodically published pricing tables that recommended, for each pay rate, three bill rates reflecting "high," "medium," and "low" margins.[10] Within these guidelines, managers urged agents to negotiate as high a rate as possible. Rates that fell below "low" required a manager's approval. Approval was granted only when upper management believed that marketing concerns justified being seen as a "price leader." ITS, on the other hand, was more concerned with sales volume and, therefore, sought a markup of 25 percent on all deals, compensating agents on the basis of the revenue they generated. The reward structure was designed to motivate agents to close a larger number of deals rather than maximize markups.

Direct Negotiations

Negotiating the terms of a direct deal was usually straightforward, in large measure because agencies were not involved. The contractor and the hiring manager bargained informally and often face-to-face with a reasonably clear idea of each other's requirements and constraints. To be sure, contractors and clients sometimes gamed each other, as Doug Hill candidly illustrated:

> I spent about an hour and a half showing them a few tricks. Said, "No, you can't do it that way, you have to do it this way, and so on and so forth." At the end of the hour and a half, they said to me: "Gosh. Thanks. We really appreciate the help, I think we'll take it from here." I said: "Daaa, you're doing fine." They said: "What do we owe you?" I said: "It's not worth billing. I don't bill anybody for an hour and a half." I said: "Thanks for being a Microsoft client," got in my car and drove off. Two days later, they called me on the phone and they said: "Look, it's more complicated than we thought," which I already knew. And they asked: "What would it cost to have you come in here for ten days?" I said: "Well, I charge $800 a day." And they said: "Geez, can we get a deal?" I said: "If you're willing to contract for all ten days, I'll knock 20 percent off of it." And they kind of gulped, and said: "We'll get back to you." Two weeks later, they brought me in.

Most of the time, the logic of striking a two-way direct deal between contractors and clients was uncomplicated. The more skilled the contractor, the stronger the contractor's recommendations and reputation, and the more pressure the hiring manager faced, the higher the rate the

---

[10] These grids were considered sensitive documents and, hence, never carried the company's name.

contractor could command. Direct negotiations sometimes led to a two-party contract between the client and the contractor (a 1099 deal) or the contractor's company (a "corp-to-corp" deal). But as we saw in chapter 1, many clients were wary of being held to the legal responsibilities of an employer and alleviated their anxiety by requiring contractors to do a pass-through with an agency willing to serve as the contractor's employer-of-record. Some hiring managers simply referred the contractor to an approved vendor. Others held the contractor responsible for finding an agency on his or her own. But in either case, the pass-through made negotiating the terms of a direct deal more complicated, because now contractors had to contend with an agency's desire for a cut. How contractors managed the cost of the agency's markup varied by the contractor's circumstances and proclivities.

Some contractors simply demanded that the client absorb the cost of the markup, a strategy that worked best when the contractor spoke from a strong negotiating position and made his or her expectations clear from the start. "My rate," Stu Davis reported telling a hiring manager who was eager to hire him, "is sixty an hour, plus whatever the agency wants." The manager, faced with pressing deadlines and aware of Stu's considerable technical reputation, agreed. In other cases, clients forced contractors with less experience and weaker negotiating positions to absorb all or part of the cost of the pass-through themselves. Having already negotiated a bill rate, the contractor was forced into a second round of bargaining to convince an agency to accept the lowest possible markup.

Katrina Labovski's stories of negotiating pass-throughs were instructive. On one occasion, after setting a rate with a hiring manager who refused to hire independent contractors, Katrina called several agencies with the intent of negotiating a low markup. "Lloyd-Ritter told me they'd take 25 percent of what the client was paying and give me the rest on a W-2 basis. When I asked what their markup would be if they'd found the job for me, they said 25 percent," Katrina complained incredulously, adding, "The gall! Charging the same for a pass-through as for recruiting work, and not being up front about it! I finally settled on a firm that took 18 percent, the lowest I could find among the four or five firms I called. The president of the firm made it clear that he was giving me this special rate almost below cost, and only because my hourly rate was above a certain amount."

After negotiating the pass-through, Katrina tried to convince the client to absorb the markup. "I asked them to pay more to offset the agency's take," she said. "I figured this was reasonable because the client was the one insisting I work through an agency to protect itself, so the extra few dollars would be an insurance premium of sorts." Although "the client wouldn't budge," she decided to accept the contract anyway. "I wasn't thrilled with this arrangement," she said. "I lost a few dollars per hour, but I had to accept it because it was the only way I could get that contract." On a subsequent deal with a different client, Katrina had more success renegotiating her bill rate. "The client ended up meeting me halfway. They paid the agency more than they would have paid me on a 1099 basis, but still less than would have yielded me my regular rate after the agency's cut."

Although, like Katrina, most contractors had only occasional success at getting clients to absorb the cost of a pass-through, they were usually savvy enough to convince agencies to take a markup lower than the going rate for fully brokered deals. Because staffing firms incurred few expenses on pass-throughs, they regarded any markup over the cost of payroll taxes (15 percent) to be "easy money." Experienced agents were often willing to drop their margins rather than lose the pass-through to another agency.

Brokered Negotiations

Negotiating the terms of a brokered deal was even more complex than negotiating a pass-through. Here agencies coordinated, facilitated, and managed the deal from the start and then signed separate contracts with each party. To maximize their markup, agencies tried to conceal their percentage of the take from both the client and the contractor. This meant that agents had to keep the two parties from talking to each other about rates. The dynamics of brokered deals revolved around the agent's attempts to control each party's knowledge of the other's position and around the contractor's and client's tactics for thwarting the agency's efforts to keep information secret and increase its markup.

PRELIMINARY BARGAINING

In brokered deals, agents began negotiating long before the client and the contractor met. In preliminary bargaining, the agent's agenda was to set the contractor's and the hiring manager's expectations about the terms of employment and then secure their authorization to propose deals based on those expectations. For all parties, preliminary negotiations were a mixed motive game. Because contractors and clients could easily take their business to another agency, agents walked a fine line between maximizing their markup and establishing enough credibility so that both parties would authorize the agency to make the deal. Contractors hoped to maximize their pay rate and hiring managers hoped to minimize costs. Yet, both needed the agency's access to the other and wanted to close deals as quickly as possible.

Facing such trade-offs, the agent's primary objective was to secure informal agreements: one with the contractor on a range of acceptable pay rates and one with the hiring manager on the "budget" for hiring contractors or at least on a range of acceptable bill rates. Experienced negotiators were aware (and the inexperienced soon found out) that preliminary commitments were little more than "ballpark figures" that could easily change as the deal unfolded. In fact, as we will see, savvy negotiators often revised their demands once deal-specific bargaining began.

Agents used several tactics to convince contractors and hiring managers to accept lower pay and higher bill rates. One tactic was known as "educating" the manager (or contractor) or "helping them understand the business." "Educating" meant persuading the contractor and the manager that it was actually advantageous for them to accept low pay and high bill rates respectively. Recruiters reminded contractors that interesting work and the opportunity to learn new skills often merited charging a lower rate because doing so would enhance their future earnings. At the same time, account managers reminded hiring managers that authorizing high bill rates gave them access to more experienced contractors, who were more likely to deliver high-quality work on time. For example, after explaining that bill rates covered the cost of taxes and the contractors' willingness to assume the risk of short-term employment, Charles Larsen concluded his sales pitch to hiring managers by asking, "What do you drive, a BMW? How much do you pay your mechanic, ninety bucks an hour? Are you going to take your car to the ten-dollar-an-hour place down on the corner? You'd think twice, wouldn't you? If that's what you pay the person who is working on your car, what do you pay the person working on your system?"

As preliminary negotiations progressed, agents often shifted to the "hard sell." One hard sell tactic that recruiters often used with contractors involved eliciting the contractor's commitment to a rate and then persuading the contractor to retreat to a lower rate by implying the possibility of lost opportunities. We observed Mark, a seasoned recruiter at Progressive Staffing, use this strategy when qualifying Gil, an inexperienced contractor who had recently resigned from a $70,000-a-year permanent position to try his hand at contracting. Halfway into the interview, Mark asked for Gil's "drop-dead rate," his minimal acceptable pay rate, saying, "I won't bother you with jobs where the client wants to pay less." In the ensuing interaction, Mark induced Gil to retreat from his initial commitment by implying that rigidity might lead to loss:

Gil: [*Replying to Mark's question*] I'm not sure. I don't want to put myself out. Around $50 an hour?

Mark: 70K (a year) is 35 an hour. If you had a range of 32 to 50, would you take it?

Gil: I would go no lower than 45 an hour.

Mark: Should we call you, if the *perfect* job came in at 40 an hour?

Gil: [*Thinks for a while before answering.*] Sure you can call me. You won't turn in my résumé until I tell you, will you?

Mark: [*Enters $40 into the computer as "requested rate."*] You might have to start at lower rates until you get a reputation with employers.

Account managers used similar techniques with hiring managers. Andrew Wegman, a veteran account manager at Progressive Staffing, prided himself on his sales skills. In fact, he taught classes on sales techniques to Progressive Staffing's newly hired account managers. As in all salesmanship, Andrew told us, the secret to staffing lay in shaping the contractor's and the client's definition of the situation. As illustrations he told us about two cases that had just occurred. In the first, a hiring manager wanted "three years of management experience," was given a quote, and then countered by saying: "My numbers are lower." Andrew told him, "We'll look at it. Which component are you willing to lose?" The manager finally agreed to forgo the managerial experience. "You don't dicker with dollars," Andrew explained, "You dicker skill sets and if there is a gap in the rate, you pare down the skill set," which allowed the account manager to retain his margin by searching for a contractor who charged lower rates.

As another example of defining the situation, Andrew explained why he always tried to persuade clients to view their cost in terms of rates rather than budgets: "All the negotiation is in terms of dollars per hour. So the difference between 'I'm going to charge you $65' and 'I'm going to charge you $70' is $5, right? Why are we even talking about it? Everybody's got $5! I mean nobody multiplies. One good rule of sales is: 'Clients don't multiply.' Nobody ever says: 'What's $5, times 160, times nine months? Hey, that's a lot of money!' Nobody ever does that. You don't need to worry about them doing it, because they don't need approvals to bring on a contractor. You call a guy up, he's having a bad day, he thinks a contractor could help him, he says, 'Send me one.'"

Ultimately, the agents' most important ploy for managing preliminary expectations was to downplay, divert attention from, and if necessary, avoid discussing, the size of the markup. Agents tried to focus each party on only his or her part of the deal, on pay rates or bill rates. Because hiring managers were generally less interested in markups, most of the agents' efforts to maintain secrecy were directed toward contractors, who, as we have seen, were usually quite concerned about the issue. As did most recruiters that contractors told us about, recruiters at Progressive Staffing refused, as a matter of principle, to reveal markups to contractors.

The refusal was often delivered as if the contractor's asking about the markup was an affront to the agency's dignity. One morning we observed Benjamin interviewing a software developer who was toying with the idea of leaving Hewlett-Packard to become a contractor. After requesting a wage rate of $50, the contractor demanded almost belligerently, "What's your markup?" Benjamin looked her in the eye and spoke firmly: "We don't discuss that. We don't talk about markups. We try to get you the highest rate we can. It's a moral point. You have to remember, we have to be competitive with others. As you can see from looking around you, we have a large overhead. We don't price gouge our clients. We're not looking for one-shot deals. I get a margin from the client, but for you fifty is fifty."

Our informants had encountered such an approach so often that they viewed bans on discussing markups as standard operating procedures for most staffing firms. Julian Stoke succinctly summarized the consensus, "I have never met a staffing firm who would tell me what the magic number is. I heard through the grapevine [at] one of my staffing firms that their magic number is 40 percent. I think most of them are close, I'm guessing, but nobody will say." There were exceptions, however. As we noted, ITS allowed agents to offer a lower than average markup to increase volume and revenues. Although not always the case, ITS's recruiters sometimes revealed their markup to contractors, especially if they believed it was lower than other firms would charge. Linda Cline, for example, claimed that contractors were "really sensitive about the markup" if it was above 25 percent. "If a contractor is making $50 an hour," she explained, "and they find out they are being billed out at a hundred, it's embarrassing. They are not going to want to work with you again. So when I can, I tell them it's under market, which makes them feel good and makes them feel like we're open."[11]

Although some contractors succumbed to the agents' attempts to persuade them to accept lower rates, those with more experience issued ultimatums, tried to defer bargaining, or both. Some contractors insisted on the rates they wanted, adopting a "take it or leave it" attitude. They might even insist that the agency lower its markups to afford their rates. At this point, recruiters had to make a decision. In some instances, recruiters held their ground and told the contractor that she was being unrealistic, even at the cost of losing the deal. Orrin Head, a recruiter at

[11] Some of the contractors in our sample reported having encountered staffing firms that were "open book," that is, they revealed their markup as a matter of policy. These were usually small firms that charged low markups. Victor Post worked for such a firm. He claimed that the agents told him: "We will get the best rate we can, and we will give you 80 percent off the top, and we need to retain 20 percent to cover our cost." Victor was quick to note that there were few such firms around.

Progressive Staffing, rarely minced words, especially with contractors whom he perceived as arrogant about their value. "Most contractors do not ask about the markup," Orrin explained. "But if someone tells me they don't want to work with a company that charges over 30 percent, I tell them I don't want to represent contractors who are constantly asking about markups." In other cases, recruiters yielded to ultimatums, even at the expense of their markup, if they believed that the contractor was marketable enough to command a high bill rate or if they thought that representing the contractor would enhance the agency's reputation for providing gurus. Progressive Staffing granted "senior rates" (lower markups) to contractors who could command high pay rates and, hence, high bill rates. In fact, during our time there, the agency decided to take but a 6 percent markup to retain the business of one highly sought after contractor.

In most cases, however, agents preferred to compromise, rather than acquiesce to or stonewall a contractor's ultimatum. After first trying to defend their position, most agents settled on a range of rates rather than discontinue negotiations. The strategy allowed the deal to proceed while deferring real bargaining until later. Agents usually recorded agreed upon rates in a database and promised to abide by the agreement when marketing the contractor's services. Reaching a preliminary agreement on a range of rates not only set expectations, but also allowed the range to become a bargaining tool for agents and contractors alike. Both hoped that once a specific deal was proposed, they could use the range to drive the rates to their advantage. To avoid contractors trying to renegotiate their rates during deal-specific bargaining, ITS required contractors to sign and date a "résumé release" form, which stated that the contractor agreed to have his or her résumé released to clients at a specific rate. Although not legally binding, ITS's management claimed that the frequency of renegotiations had fallen after instituting the form.

Preliminary bargaining between account managers and hiring managers evinced a similar dynamic. Agencies exhorted account managers to establish clear and agreed upon budgets with hiring managers from the outset. Progressive Staffing rewarded account managers for the number of job orders they produced and defined a legitimate job order as "obtaining a hiring manager's commitment to a budget." Agents discovered, however, that hiring managers were reluctant to commit—sometimes because they were limited by company policy or by funding uncertainties, sometimes because they resisted high rates and markups as a matter of principle, but most often because they were unwilling to agree to a price before seeing "the goods." As a result, preliminary negotiations with hiring managers also moved between ultimatums and compromise. Ultimatums were common when account managers negotiated with large companies that used their market power to squeeze down rates and with managers who faced financial constraints or who were unfamiliar with the market. Because ultimatums could cause deals to fall through at this stage, agents preferred to compromise.

An example of compromise occurred after John Heathcote, an account manager at Progressive Staffing, told a client in Minnesota that a MIPS developer would cost $122 an hour. The next day the manager called John to say the rate "was out of range." He claimed he was accustomed to paying "in the eighties." John tried to explain that while wages "in the eighties" might be common in Minnesota, the manager was now recruiting from the Silicon Valley where wages were higher. The manager replied, "I know, but I won't be able to push it through." After discussing the situation with his manager and concluding that rates in the eighties were "at the bottom of the chart" (the expected markup was too low), John tried a different tactic. He offered to lower the rate to $89 but allow the contractor to work part-time. The hiring manager insisted on a full-time contractor. Believing that the hiring manager was under pressure and that MIPS programmers were rare in Minnesota, John decided to insist on the higher rate but keep "working the deal," hoping that the hiring manager would either choose to pay more or accept a part-time contractor as a compromise. In this particular case, the deal fell through, but in other cases, agents and account managers were able to find middle ground.

In most preliminary negotiations we observed, account managers and hiring managers agreed to "a ballpark budget" (or bill rate) after some posturing designed to "narrow the gap" and postponed further negotiations until the manager could evaluate specific candidates. When the gap between the parties' positions was small, compromise was easily reached. When the gap seemed larger, agents and hiring managers usually agreed to move toward qualifying candidates without agreeing on even a ballpark figure. Thus, during preliminary bargaining the parties used their bargaining skills to specify nonbinding expectations regarding the terms of employment. These expectations were often vague enough to allow the agency to continue its matchmaking effort. If and when a contractor became a candidate for a specific job order, preliminary expectations served as the foundation for a second round of negotiations, deal-specific bargaining.

DEAL-SPECIFIC BARGAINING

Once a hiring manager began to interview candidates, the bargaining situation changed. The encounter gave contractors and managers access to information they had not previously possessed. Hiring managers gained a better sense of the candidates' skills, and contractors could now better gauge the job's attractiveness as well as how eager the hiring manager was to fill the position. Interviews also provided contractors and hiring managers with an opportunity to exchange information on the preliminary terms they had negotiated with the agency, thereby allowing them to calculate the agency's markup. With such information in hand, contractors and hiring managers often revised their demands.

Deal-specific bargaining typically unfolded as a series of dyadic encounters between the agent and one of the parties. The agent served as the parties' go-between, trying to bring them closer together while simultaneously struggling to maximize the agency's markup and resist the parties' efforts to reduce it. Because information about the markup became crucial at this stage of the deal, agents redoubled their efforts to prevent contractors and clients from exchanging information about rates during interviews. Agents were usually blunt about their expectations. Illustrative was John Heathcote's directive to a hiring manager who was scheduled to interview Tim, a UNIX programmer, later that afternoon. "I just want to remind you rates are not to be discussed," John cautioned. "We've prepped him so he's not likely to bring it up. There's an employee-employer relationship between Progressive Staffing and Tim. The relation between you and Tim is different. It probably won't come up. But I just want to remind you, that's just the way we do it."

Hiring managers usually cooperated by withholding information about bill rates, not so much because they had made a promise to the agent, but because they worried that contractors might use the information to make demands that would increase their own costs and jeopardize the deal. Contractors, on the other hand, were almost always motivated to learn the size of the markup. Doing so was not easy, and some contractors, like Julian Stoke, invariably remained in the dark: "I do all my negotiations through the staffing firm. I will dicker a price from them, and what they tell me is they will have to see if the client will go for this. I know that's not what is going on. They have already come to a price, and they are trying to decide how much of a profit they can take. I'm on fifty-five [dollars an hour] at Progressive Staffing. I have no clue what they charge. The clients won't tell you either. It's covered in their contract. They are not allowed to divulge that information to the contractor."[12]

[12] Like many staffing firms, Progressive Staffing included a clause in its contracts that forbade clients from discussing rates with contractors. Such agreements covered not only the bargaining process but also the period of the contract. The practice was designed to prevent contractors from becoming dissatisfied during the contract, to prevent other contractors from learning about the staffing firm's practices, and to prevent contractors from trying to increase their rates if the contract was extended. Such agreements were, of course, very hard enforce.

Other contractors found ways to learn about markups. John Nagley reported he was usually able to glean this information from hiring managers during interviews and to use it during negotiations. More typically, numbers were revealed after the deal was closed. Peyton Nugen discovered that by befriending his clients' administrative assistants, he could easily discover his bill rate. Jose Martinez claimed that after signing a contract, rates were an open secret: "You're not supposed to find out. But— boom! Within three hours of landing in a company, I know everything. You find out what they're billing at, you find out what they pay. We all know. We know!" Of course, learning about rates after closing a deal would not change the terms of the contract, but it was valuable for future negotiations with the agency, especially if the contract was renewed.

Armed with the best information they could get, after one or more rounds of negotiation, the parties usually moved toward closing the deal. In the final stages of deal-specific bargaining, account managers proposed bill and pay rates to hiring managers and contractors respectively, often in the form of contracts to be signed. When waiting for replies, agents sat on pins and needles, hoping that their attempts to limit information, the contractor's inexperience, or both parties' reluctance to bargain would work to their advantage.

As Julie Cochran sat at her desk one afternoon, waiting for a contractor's response to the $90 pay rate she had proposed, she crossed her fingers and told her account manager: "If he's savvy he'll come in at one twenty-five. But if he's not, he'll come in a lot lower." If necessary, Julie intended to accept $125. She knew that if the contractor came in any lower, it would mean serious money for Progressive Staffing as well as a considerable boost to her reputation and her own purse.[13] In fact, closing deals with large markups earned agents bragging rights. When Barbara Pacek, an account manager at Progressive Staffing, learned she just closed a deal at a bill rate of $77, she let go a squeal of delight and told her envious colleagues, "It's a six-month contract and he is cheap, too! Forty an hour! He is worth much more, but he didn't know it."

More often than not, contractors were not as naïve as agents hoped. Experienced contractors were often savvy negotiators. They knew the market, understood the agents' interest in closing the deal, and realized that agencies inflated their markups to make room for further bargaining. When a deal neared closing, these contractors often demanded higher pay rates than they initially indicated they would accept. As

---

[13] Finding inexperienced contractors was not always a matter of luck. Agents knew, for example, that "visa hostages"—foreigners on H1B visas—were in weak bargaining positions and could yield "nice markups." In fact, some agencies chose to specialize in such business, even at a cost to their reputation.

Marty Keely put it, "You have to haggle with your agency." Brenda O'Boyle concurred: "Having been in business for a while, I know you can negotiate with your agency. They have money they can play with. It just depends on how much they can afford." At this point, effective bargaining depended on having accurate data. Marty always estimated the minimum markup an agency would accept and did his best to find out what bill rate the agency had quoted the client. If he couldn't discover the bill rate, he researched the average rate for people with his skills. Armed with such data, arriving at a target pay rate was simply a matter of "doing the math." If the agency's offer was below this target, Marty advised, "you haggle aggressively, hold your ground, and say no!"

Jose Martinez entered last-minute renegotiations with a theory of the recruiter's psychology. "The recruiter will say, 'Okay, we'll pay you fifty-five,' but you know they're going to bill a hundred," Jose smiled slyly.

> So you say, "Okay, I'll go talk to the company." You talk to the company and come back to the recruiter and say, "Okay, they want to hire me." The recruiter says: "Great!" Now they've got a sure thing. They're looking at their bonus! They get around 25 percent of the markup, so if they're billing a hundred and the markup is thirty, the recruiter is looking at $7.50 an hour. A good recruiter has twenty to thirty people on contract. They're like used car people. At the end of the week, they always rank who's got the most people working and who's bringing in the most money. It's mega-competition. They get bonuses for placing people, plus a bigger percentage, even tickets to Hawaii. So the recruiter, he's seeing double dollar signs. He's looking at his bonus. That's when I say: "I want more than the old price." Now, they're willing to pay slippage to get me. Okay, so they won't get $7.50, but they'll get $5.50, and even that's serious money. So, I can leverage another $10 an hour, which is 20K a year. They don't care! They're making $250 an hour.

After evaluating candidates, hiring managers also occasionally tried to lower the ballpark budget or bill rate, sometimes by a considerable sum. They usually justified reductions by appealing to what they had learned about the candidates' skills during the interview or by claiming unanticipated budgetary constraints. Hiring managers assumed that their demands would force the staffing firm to renegotiate a lower pay rate with the contractor, reduce the markup, or some combination of the two.

When facing the squeeze from a hiring manager or contractor, agents had a number of alternatives for salvaging markups and saving the deal. Some, like Wayne Davey, began by trying to stare hiring managers down. In response to a hiring manager who demanded a reduced bill rate of $60, Wayne put on a poker face, told the manager, "My client's worth $90 an hour or it's not worth it," and waited for a response. Later, after the manager agreed to a compromise rate, Wayne explained his stance: "The best thing you can do is leave them with a short answer and then silence. 'You're charging $75 an hour!' 'Yup.' It throws it back in their court. They expect you to keep talking and drop $10 or $15. They hate it when you just leave in silence and they'll come back to you."

As part of formal training, Progressive Staffing taught new agents how to pressure hiring managers to accept the agency's terms. Diana Judd, the firm's star trainer, suggested that account managers approach hiring managers immediately after the interview, "when they are still in love with the candidate," and ask for a quick decision. "Tell them you need it by the end of the day," Diana counseled. "Never lie about other job offers he already has, but create your own urgency. Say he is skilled and will be snapped up. You can say: 'Mr. Manager, by the end of the day I will need to submit him elsewhere. I'm his agent. I need to represent his interests!' "

Recruiters were also willing to reject contractors' demands. Stu Davis described his experience with a large staffing firm notorious for tough bargaining: "You ask them to cut their markup by a nickel, forget it! They'll boot you out so fast it'll make your head spin. You don't do this." During our observations at agencies, we observed several negotiations fail because contractors insisted on their positions. In most cases, however, an accommodation was found. Stu found that he was sometimes able to bargain up his rates at the expense of the markup: "Aerotech had me set up with Siemens and everything clicked real good at the interview. Aerotech said, 'Forty-five dollars an hour, that's our limit.' And I replied, 'I just wrapped up at $55 an hour. There's no way you're going to get me for any less than that. I want 60.' Finally I got them to very grudgingly come up to 50."

Agents were sometimes willing to work to shift the cost of a contractor's demands to the client, if they suspected the contractor would defect to another agency. Anna Kapoor, for example, was able to increase her pay rate from $60 to $70 by claiming she had a higher offer from another agency. After several rounds of telephone negotiations in which the agent insisted on maintaining the markup, the cost was transferred to the client who agreed to a $10 increase in the bill rate. A number of contractors reported that it was easier to extract concessions from agents with whom they had an ongoing relationship. Brenda O'Boyle noted that the odds of a concession were also greater for longer contracts and for contractors who had a reputation for having their contracts renewed: "I find with longer-term contracts it is easier to negotiate a better rate because they know they are going to make a good amount of money. They know me and they know that I like long contracts and that I am often renewed."

CLOSING DEALS

Unless negotiations fell through, the parties eventually settled on the terms of employment and proceeded to close the deal. Deals were closed when all parties assented to a contractual obligation. Written contracts were important for two reasons. As in all commercial agreements, contracts served to specify the terms of the deal unambiguously. Had this been the only issue, however, contractors and clients might have handled their obligations more informally, as is often the case with professional services. The more important reason for signing contracts was to protect clients from contracting's legal ambiguities. As we discussed in chapter 1, clients strove to keep the courts and the Internal Revenue Service from interpreting a contracting relationship as an employment relationship. In the case of direct deals with no pass-through, clients signed contracts directly with contractors. In brokered deals or when a pass-through was involved, clients and contractors did not typically sign agreements with each other. Instead, the staffing agency that brokered the deal executed one with the client and another with the contractor.

Direct Contracts

Although it was once common for firms to employ unincorporated independent contractors by cutting a simple purchase order, by the late 1990s the practice had waned. Most employers believed that hiring contractors as 1099s left the firm too vulnerable to legal action and tax audits. Only small firms or companies that seemed unconcerned about legal ramifications continued to pay unincorporated contractors directly.[14] The majority would sign directly only with independent contractors who were legally incorporated. In this case, the client cut a "corp-to-corp" contract with the contractor's corporation rather than with the individual. Before signing papers, it was common for clients to demand that contractors show proof of incorporation. Acceptable proof included articles of incorporation, a business license, business cards, and other legally acceptable

---

[14] To our surprise, we actually uncovered a few cases in which the firm demanded no formal agreement at all. Judy King described such a case: "When I was working at Ascend there was no contract, no nothing. It was just a purchase order. And I would submit time sheets and an invoice. Ascend was perfectly happy with invoices and time sheets and they would just place it against a purchase order, and after the purchase order ran out, they'd open another purchase order."

documentation. Clients also expected independent contractors to carry liability insurance, usually for a sum of no less than $1 million. In fact, some clients were so concerned about these issues that they asked contractors to endorse a clause stating that they had not misrepresented their status. Vic Verma explained Savant Technology's rationale for doing so: "If there's been any kind of misrepresentation, the onus falls back on the contractor. If we're audited by the IRS, at least we can say: 'We did our due diligence. He signed saying he was telling us the truth.' I know we're responsible, but the consultants are also going to be fined."

Clients and contractors typically closed direct deals by signing standard professional service agreements that specified the rates, hours, per diem expenses, and terms of payment. These contracts usually committed the client to "net plus thirty": making payments thirty days after the contractor submitted an invoice. Large companies often included a nondisclosure clause that protected their proprietary information and granted them ownership over any intellectual property that the contractor might develop in the course of the contract. Some firms inserted additional clauses specifying deliverables, committing contractors to work for a fixed period of time, or requiring notice before quitting. Most agreements allowed the client to terminate the contract immediately, and a few contractors insisted on adding a clause that required notice from the client as well.

Brokered Contracts

The contracts that concluded brokered deals were designed to create a clear legal distinction between the client and contractor and to protect the agency's future interests. To achieve these objectives, agencies executed one agreement with the client and another with the contractor, thereby establishing the agency as the contractor's employer-of-record and the client as the agency's customer. In some instances, clients required contractors to sign additional agreements intended to offer the firm additional legal protection.

AGENCIES' AGREEMENTS WITH CONTRACTORS

Agencies cut two kinds of contracts with contractors. The first acknowledged the contractor as an independent. Like client organizations, agencies preferred to establish a "corp-to-corp" rather than a 1099 relationship with independent contractors, and for the same reasons. Before signing, agencies also took considerable care to ensure that the contractor was incorporated. ITS even assisted contractors in the incorporation process. Contracts with independent contractors typically specified rates, hours, and terms of payment, usually "net plus thirty," subject to the staffing firm being paid by the client organization.[15] They also often included a nondisclosure agreement and specified that the client would own any intellectual property created by the contractor in the course of the contract. Some agencies added "noncompete" clauses designed to protect their future business by preventing contractors from bypassing the agency and marketing themselves directly to the client at a later date.[16] Noncompete clauses usually covered a period of a year or more.

Most agencies preferred contractors to sign on as their employees for the duration of the contract. Doing so was administratively easier and legally less complicated. Although some contractors insisted on working only as independents for tax purposes, in most brokered deals, contractors agreed to work as W-2s.[17] Contracts that structured the obligations of the agency and the contractor as an employment relationship covered three types of issues.

First, like all contracts, W-2 agreements set the pay rate, the number of hours the contractor would work per week, and the duration of the contract. In addition, they specified whether the contractor would be paid overtime or accrue vacation.[18] Agencies usually committed to paying W-2s more quickly than independent contractors. In most cases, the agency agreed to pay within seven days of receiving the contractor's time sheets and regardless of whether the client had paid the agency. Many contractors saw this as an important advantage of working through an agency.

Second, although California (and other "right-to-work" states) allowed either party to terminate employment "at will," many contracts confirmed only the agency's right to do so. Some contracts specified the period of notice that a contractor was required to give the agency before quitting. Most contractors understood that the "at will" clause was in force, even if it was not specified. Nevertheless, we encountered a few contractors who were surprised to find their contracts suddenly terminated, and our informants also told us about staffing firms that had tried to prevent them from quitting.

Finally, W-2 agreements usually included a "noncompete" or "single

---

[15] The fact that agencies need not pay independent contractors until the client had paid them led many contractors to prefer working as a W-2.

[16] ITS actually preferred independents to W-2s because it was possible to write contracts whose clauses were more easily enforceable.

[17] For example, working as an independent allowed the contractor to claim a home office and deduct computer equipment and other business-related expenses.

[18] Clients were usually exempt from paying overtime. Some contracts made this explicit. Our informants told us about cases in which the staffing firm billed the client for overtime but did not pay the contractor overtime. According to California law at the time, only people who make no more than two times minimum wage were eligible for overtime whether calculated on a daily (over eight hours) or weekly (over forty hours) basis unless covered by a union contract that specified otherwise.

source obligation clause," known among contractors as the "fear and loathing clause." This clause forbade contractors from contracting with the same client through another staffing firm (or as an independent) for up to a year. Some agencies mandated that the contractor provide proof of citizenship and pass a drug test before considering the contract valid.

After ensuring that the pay rate and other terms of employment were as expected, the majority of our informants signed "the paperwork" perfunctorily without questioning the contract. Mike Rudolph's casual approach was typical:

> I've been pretty satisfied. I had one sour job, but otherwise it's been pretty good. If you're flexible, you just sign the contract. I mean the contract just says you'll work for this amount of money, and they'll pay you that amount of money. It's not like a professional services contract, like a baseball player would have, where if he refuses to play, there's a big deal. If you go down there and you don't like the job, it's no big deal if you don't stay. I've never done that, but I know many people who have. They decide that this isn't what they thought it would be and they leave. It's a two-way street.

A handful of our informants, however, took the paperwork seriously and argued with agencies about clauses they disliked. Glenn Arthur, for instance, adamantly refused to sign noncompete clauses: "I always go into a contract negotiation and they say, 'Look at this.' I just bracket it and I say, 'Fear and loathing clause—won't sign it.' They squirm and squeal, but they always take it off. The time I did that with The Registry [an agency] they said, 'Well, everyone signs it.' It's like, 'Come on, it's the fear and loathing clause! I know. This is not new to me. Just take it off.' At that point they just sort of go, 'Ahh, he knows the game.' So they come back with a new contract with it crossed out, initialed."

AGENCIES' AGREEMENTS WITH CLIENTS

The contracts that agencies signed with clients were modeled on professional services agreements that made it clear that the client was buying a service from the agency and not from the contractor. The contract identified the contractor as the agency's employee or as the agency's subcontractor in the case of an independent contractor. Lawyers from both organizations scrutinized the contracts to ensure that nothing in them implied that the client was establishing an employment relationship with the contractor.

Agencies cut two types of contracts with clients. With large, established firms that employed many contractors, agencies often signed two-tiered contracts consisting of a "master agreement" and addenda. The master agreement certified the agency as an approved vendor and specified the obligations and commitments that each party would owe the other anytime the agency provided the client with a contractor. As a condition for establishing a master agreement, clients required agencies to show proof of sufficient liability insurance and sometimes proof that they treated contractors fairly and equitably under employment law. When a master agreement was in place, the agency and the client simply signed a separate addendum for each specific deal. The addendum, known as a "work order" or "letter of agreement," referred to the master agreement and then specified the rates, hours, and sometimes the deliverables for a particular deal.

The second type of contract was a standard professional service agreement that was signed separately for each deal. These contracts covered the agency's and the client's obligations to each other as well as the specific terms of the deal. Before signing with a small or unfamiliar firm, agencies ran credit checks to guard against clients that might default and leave the agency liable for the contractor's wages.[19] Client contracts always stipulated the conditions under which the contractor could "convert" to permanent employment. Conversion clauses obligated the client to pay the agency a fee calculated as a percentage of the contract's worth or the contractor's annual salary, prorated to the length of time the contract had been in force. Early in the contract, conversion rates ran as high as 30 percent, declining over time to the point where the fee might be completely waived.

CONTRACTOR-CLIENT AGREEMENTS

To protect themselves even further, some clients required contractors to sign additional agreements. These agreements were intended to reinforce the fact that the client and the contractor were not entering an employment relationship. According to Noah Swetka, Western Phone Company (WPC) asked contractors to sign three additional agreements. The first was a Temporary Worker Acknowledgment that said, in effect, "I do not work for WPC, I work for so-and-so, I am here for this many weeks, but I do not work for WPC." The second was a Confidentiality Agreement, "which basically says they agree to keep our information proprietary and anything they invent remains ours." Finally, contractors were asked to sign a form stating that "they would abide by all EEO [equal employment opportunity] principles and rules." Western Phone Company had once asked contractors to sign a commitment to comply with the company's

---

[19] The fact that agencies were liable even if the client defaulted, motivated some contractors to enter only W-2 deals. The contractors had either experienced or wished to avoid trouble collecting directly from clients.

code of conduct, but no longer did so because the legal department claimed the form made contractors resemble employees. Noah said WPC made compliance with EEO principles explicit because "we had cases of sexual harassment. So we had to do something." These forms were added as riders to the agency's contracts.

In sum, formal agreements were designed not only to specify the terms of employment agreed upon by the parties, but also to put in place a legal framework that protected clients from any attempt by contractors or regulatory agencies to apply employment law to the contracting relationship. In addition to their role as facilitators of market information, staffing firms based their raison d'être on their ability to provide clients with such a legal shield.

CONCLUSION

In this chapter and the last, we have seen how contractors, hiring managers, and staffing agencies advertised their availability; searched for, shaped, and sometimes obfuscated information; encountered and evaluated each other; haggled over terms of employment, including price; protected their interests; and ultimately closed deals. In short, we journeyed into the minutiae of the market for technical contractors. Up close, a market looks quite different than the way it does from the comfortable distance favored by economists and purveyors of business advice. Whereas economists often speak of markets as abstract mechanisms for price setting governed by flows of information and the dynamics of supply and demand, we have seen that the market is also a drama complete with a structure, multiple lines of action, rising tension, and eventual denouement.[20] For contractors, agents, and, to a lesser degree, hiring managers, entering the market for contractors involved more than engaging in organized exchange; it meant becoming involved in a slice, if not a way, of life. To put this slice of a contractor's life into perspective, we need to ask, first, what the drama of market action teaches us about the market's structure.

---

[20] Although economists routinely discuss markets, surprisingly few have attempted to describe what markets are and how they operate. In an important paper that reviews economic and sociological thinking on markets, Swedberg (1994) shows how the concept of market became increasingly abstract and removed from activities of trade. Smelser and Swedberg (1994b) claim that economic discussions of markets seek to predict market outcomes but rarely describe their actual operations. Sociological depictions, on the other hand, typically seek to describe but rarely predict. In this sense, our approach is decidedly sociological.

Two Markets

On close examination, what appeared to be a single market resolved into two, each with its own structure, norms, and scripts. One was the market for direct deals, the other the market for brokered deals. The market for direct deals was a two-party production where contractors and hiring managers encountered each other head-on, assuming the classic roles of a buyer and seller negotiating the terms of a job and a price. To play the direct market game, contractors had to qualify as independents, which meant willingly assuming the legal and practical responsibilities of an independent contractor. Information channeled through networks of professional relationships arranged and fueled encounters between independent contractors and hiring managers. The backdrop of professionalism emphasized reputations, trust, accurate information, and the quality of the services being bought and sold. In combination with the dyadic structure, the professional networks and norms that underwrote the market helped minimize haggling between the parties.

The market for brokered deals, on the other hand, was a triadic affair: between the contractor and the hiring manager moved the agent. Agents served as go-betweens who managed the flow of market information and arranged matches, while seeking to separate contractors from hiring managers until deals were struck, thereby creating the space to maximize their own profits. The market for brokered deals was open to all contractors whether incorporated or not, and it emphasized the quantity and timeliness of information and services. The brokered market's commercial ethos and its three-party structure allowed for greater manipulation of information and more intense haggling, if not outright gaming.

When looking for jobs and skilled professionals respectively, contractors and hiring managers had to decide not just whether to go to the market, but in which of the two markets they would participate. The decision required making informational, administrative, and financial trade-offs. Managers and contractors preferred the market for direct deals because they placed high value on the accuracy of the information they received about each other and on the quality of the match between the person and the job. The problem with the direct market was that professional networks delivered only sporadically. Their operation depended on whom one knew, whom they knew, whether the people they knew had the appropriate skills or information, and whether people with the skills were available. Consequently, when needs were pressing and schedules were tight, contractors and hiring managers turned to the market for brokered deals, where agencies armed with extensive databases could quickly provide large quantities of information on people and jobs.

Turning to this market, however, also meant risking making decisions on information that might be out-of-date, inadequately filtered, potentially overwhelming, and even intentionally misleading.

Going to the market for direct deals meant that managers and contractors had to shoulder more of an administrative burden. This was particularly true for contractors. To find and close direct deals, contractors had to incorporate, keep their own books, market themselves, pay their own taxes, and continually expand, maintain, and activate their own networks. Doing direct deals demanded that clients manage the hiring process and develop procedures that would shield them from the legal trouble of having contractors construed as employees. In the market for brokered deals, staffing agencies relieved both parties of their administrative burden.

At least on the face of it, the market for direct deals was less costly because both parties avoided the agency's markup. Contractors could theoretically recapture some of the agency's markup while clients would incur lower costs. In reality, however, direct deals carried indirect costs for contractors that arose from their informational and administrative demands. Contractors not only had to absorb the costs of incorporation and the time and effort required to manage themselves as businesses, which meant paying higher taxes, but they also had to invest time and effort in creating and maintaining networks. For hiring managers, direct deals were essentially costless beyond the time invested in making the deal. Firms, however, believed that direct deals were more costly to the company because decentralized hiring carried a loss of financial control.

Some contractors chose to operate exclusively in the market for direct deals while many others relied entirely on the brokered market. The former were individuals whose skills were scarce and in high demand, who had substantial reputations in their technical communities, and who had extensive networks. The latter were often contractors who were new to the market, whose skills were widely distributed, whose networks were sparse, or who wished to avoid the hassles of managing their own business. A significant number of contractors operated in both markets, although brokered deals were more common than direct deals. In general, the top management of firms preferred the brokered market, while hiring managers preferred the direct market.

Ultimately, however, institutional pressures favored the brokered market. IRS rulings and other legal ambiguities had created a world in which corporate policy increasingly forced contractors and hiring managers into the brokered market to protect firms from litigation. By the time of our study, even direct deals frequently ended up as pass-throughs in the brokered market. The shift toward brokered deals that began in the late 1980s highlights how the market for technical contracting had become a dual market in a second and more important way. Although it had once been so, the market for contractors was no longer simply an arena where short-term access to technical skills was bought, sold, and brokered. It had also become a market where agencies sold and clients purchased peace of mind, legal protection, and ultimately, an exemption from the obligations as well as the direct and indirect costs of U.S. employment law.

Three-Way Market Dynamics

In chapter 5 we saw that in the market for technical contractors information was scarce, ambiguous, and sometimes invalid. The voids and asymmetries in the distribution of information created a niche for staffing agencies, which did much more than simply cull information, match needs, and broker deals. Agents actively shaped information to their advantage. This meant that in the market for brokered deals, matching contractors to jobs rapidly became a three-way game in which all actors hoped to muster information to their advantage. But as the sociologist Georg Simmel argued nearly a hundred years ago, in a triad the one who can best control the flow of information between the other two or play one off the other becomes the *tertius gaudens*, the "third who benefits."[21] In the negotiations we examined, who achieved the position of the *tertius gaudens* varied, but there was no doubt that staffing agencies had the initial advantage and that agents actively sought to capitalize on that advantage by minimizing contact between contractors and managers and by insisting on the role of go-between.

The triadic structure extended the uncertainties of the information game into deal making and cast a shadow of doubt, if not mistrust, over even the most cordial negotiations. All parties were aware that their partners could position themselves to enhance their own advantage at the others' expense. Contractors and hiring managers were especially suspicious of agents in this regard. The only question was where to draw the line between acceptable and unacceptable self-interest. At the time, the consensus seemed to be that the line was drawn at a markup of 40 percent.

Contractors, clients, and agencies had developed three broad strategies

---

[21] Simmel developed the notion of triadic interactions and the *tertius gaudens* in *Conflict and the Web of Group Affiliations* (1922). More recently, Ronald Burt (1992) has linked the notion of the *tertius gaudens* to ego networks characterized by structural holes. A person's social network is marked by structural holes when he or she has relationships with people who do not have relationships with each other. This is precisely the kind of structure that agents tried to maintain between clients and contractors. Burt has shown that structural holes are correlated with power and career success. He also argues that structural holes are a precondition for successful entrepreneurship.

for containing and even sidestepping triadic dynamics of suspicion and mistrust. Managers and contractors tried to reestablish a presumption of trust by forming relationships with and giving repeat business to agents whom they thought were especially knowledgeable, ethical, and likable. In other words, they brought agents into their personal and professional networks. Clients sought to guard against agencies' excesses by granting a small number of agencies the status of an on-site or approved vendor in return for an agreement to contain margins. Finally, agencies like ITS hoped to limit opportunism by charging lower markups and rewarding their agents on volume.

In addition, each of the three parties employed tactics designed to advance their cause while checking the interests of the others. Hiring managers insisted on evaluating contractors themselves to guard against being hoodwinked by agents and contractors and by using their firm's market power to keep bill rates low. Agents utilized an arsenal of sales strategies to convince hiring managers to accept higher bill rates and to persuade contractors to accept lower wage rates, thereby increasing their own markups. Contractors sought to fight back by gathering information on rates, by simultaneously working with multiple agencies which they could play off one another, by forming alliances with hiring managers when possible, and, if all else failed, by issuing ultimatums.

Market as a Form of Work

Learning how to negotiate the market became a defining characteristic of what it meant to be a contractor. To sustain a career in contracting, contractors had to enter the market to find and close deals several times a year. Moving successfully in and out of the market so frequently meant continually monitoring market trends, cultivating networks and relationships, keeping one's skills up-to-date, and being prepared to market oneself on a moment's notice. In a sense, then, contractors were always in the market: when actually looking for jobs the market was in the foreground; when on the job it remained conspicuous in the background.

Thus, the market was not the soon-to-be-forgotten liminal space between periods of work, as it is for most permanent employees. For contractors, the market *was* work. Professionals have historically seen the need to market themselves as a supporting activity, at best, and, at worst, as an unpleasant necessity at odds with the notion of professionalism. In sharp contrast, being able to manage market dynamics was a central aspect of the contractors' notion of professionalism. In the contractor's world, market expertise complemented technical expertise and only if one possessed both could one anticipate success.

Market expertise implied both knowledge and skill. Professional contractors had to understand how market information was organized, how to operate as an independent, how staffing firms were organized and operated, and what clients and agencies required from the relationship. Market expertise also involved skills: the ability to network and the ability to bargain, sometimes with gloves off.

Living in the market, then, was part of what it meant to adopt a contractor's lifestyle. It was the complement of being on the job and, as such, it set the tone for how contractors experienced employment. Once a deal was closed, contractors entered firms as a purchased commodity. Their status as a commodity, reinforced by the growing preference for brokered deals, placed contractors in an anomalous position in the firm that shaped their experience on the job.

PART III

Life on the Job

KATRINA LABOVSKI, a young technical writer with a degree in English literature, sounded like an existentialist when she described her decision to become a contractor: "I knew that [it] would require some courage and a leap of faith because contracting is, you know, unstable by its nature." The instability of which Katrina spoke went beyond the risk of not being able to find a steady stream of contracts and its potential to devastate her cash flow, although these possibilities concerned her. It went beyond even the uncertainty of not knowing what she would be doing or for whom she would be working from month to month. Katrina seemed to sense a deeper uncertainty that was, in her words, part of contracting's "nature." This uncertainty was tied to the quality of the relationship that she accepted each time she signed a contract and went to work. At Apple, where she had been a permanent employee, Katrina explained, "I was part of a large, well-respected documentation group that was doing a lot of interesting things and shared a vision of the future. As a contractor, I'm temporarily tied to the goals of all these different groups and I have my own personal goals, but less of a sense of, you know, community." This feeling of absence of community permeated all our informants' descriptions of the contractor's life on the job. Like Katrina, many told us that the freedom and autonomy they desired came at a cost: in the companies that employed them, they often felt like "outcasts," "outsiders," or "resident aliens." It was accepting and learning to live with this sense of placelessness that required the "courage" and the "leap of faith" of which Katrina spoke.

Had Katrina been an anthropologist, she might have referred to her sense of contracting's instability as "liminality." Liminality, as Van Gennep (1960) defined it in *Rites of Passage*, his classic study of ritual in primitive society, refers to transitional episodes that serve as the threshold between culturally defined states or stages. Liminality, in this sense, is both a structural and an experiential condition. It occurs when people find themselves temporarily outside the well-defined roles that society ascribes to its members. During such episodes people temporarily lose or suspend their taken-for-granted notions of who they are and how they fit into everyday life.

As the anthropologist Victor Turner (1982) observed, most of us experience liminality only for brief moments or short periods of our lives—as when, for example, we are adult enough to die for our country but still too much of a child to buy alcohol or, as it once was in America, to vote.[1] For contractors, however, as Katrina's practical philosophizing suggests, liminality is a continual condition, indeed a way of life. If traditional employment bestows stable membership in a community of work and a well-defined social identity to go with it, contracting places its practitioners in social limbo: each time they accept a contracting assignment, they enter a social world in which the meaning of their involvement is riddled with ambiguity.[2]

In the next three chapters we explore in detail the ambiguities of everyday life on the job, their sources, and the efforts to resolve them. Chapter 7 documents how clients tried to place limits on contractors' claims to membership by reducing the employment relationship to a simple purchase of a commodity. Chapter 8 illustrates how the practical realities of technical work and the contingencies of project life challenged and undermined the fiction of employment with no social strings attached. Chapter 9 recounts how these conflicting forces shaped contractors' social relationships on the job and how contractors had to carefully navigate between them to create a coherent professional identity.

---

[1] Turner (1982) popularized the term and extended its use beyond Van Gennep's (1960) original focus on ritual events in traditional societies. To do so, he distinguished *liminal* from *liminoid* experiences. The former, he claimed, are found in the rituals of primitive societies, while the latter are metaphoric applications of liminal experiences to modern societies. In his work he identified such phenomena in a wide variety of settings: student life, motorbike gangs, unemployment. Contracting, in our view, clearly belongs to this category.

[2] At least in the United States, people's sense of identity is tied to the work they do. While occupation has long been a source of self-definition (Hughes 1958; Van Maanen and Barley 1984; Barley and Kunda 2001), over the course of the twentieth century employing organizations, rather than occupations, have increasingly provided a context for identity formation. As Kunda (1992:161) points out, many organizations offer their employees a "member role" that "includes explicit, detailed, wide-ranging, and systematically enforced prescriptions for what members in good standing are to think and feel about themselves, their work, and the social arrangements under which it is performed." Employees' social identities are forged as they embrace or distance themselves from the member role offered them. In either case, organizational membership provides an important and stable source of meaning for employees. It is precisely this social anchor that contractors, for better or for worse, lacked.

Chapter 7

CONTRACTORS AS COMMODITIES

"I REALLY DO SEE contractors as a commodity," said Neva Boyd, an IT manager at Chipco, matter-of-factly. "For me, it doesn't matter if it's Person A who's producing the product or Person B who's producing that product. It doesn't really matter, as long as I get the work done." Neva's perspective on the contractors she employed was widely shared by the managers we interviewed. Although managers' reasons for hiring contractors varied, their view of how contractors fit into their company's social system sounded remarkably similar. Like Neva, these managers routinely referred to the contractors they hired as "skill sets," "resources," or "warm bodies." The managers' rhetoric implied that contractors were there for the sole purpose of doing the work and it was perfectly legitimate to equate their employment with the deployment of any other resource necessary for production: they were to be purchased when necessary, used efficiently, and disposed of when no longer useful.

The rhetoric of commodification translated into three broad types of managerial action. First, managers tried to limit their involvement with contractors to directing their task performance. Second, clients delegated all other managerial responsibilities to staffing firms who were the employers-of-record. Finally, clients took symbolic and practical steps to limit contractors' sense of membership in the organization's community of work.

MAINTAINING A TASK ORIENTATION

One of the benefits of viewing contractors as commodities was that commodities did not require extensive management. Rather, managers could limit their interactions with contractors to directing task performance and evaluating the results. Thus, when talking about how they dealt with contractors, most managers articulated what one called a "sink-or-swim" philosophy of management. Managers expected contractors to arrive fully proficient and ready to work, to "hit the ground running." They threw contractors directly into the work and said they had no qualms about demanding that agencies replace contractors who floundered, much like they would return any other defective good. "I don't want to hire someone if I have to coddle them," said Anthony Greener candidly. Randy Bouchet, of Raster, expressed a similar view: "We expect that we're hiring people with a specific skill set. We bring in people that we think can do the job and, if they can't, we don't allow much of a learning curve. If they don't know QA Partner, we don't train them.[1] We just let them go. We had one person who came in, and after about two weeks it was clear that she wasn't cutting it. Within two days I had another contractor."

Contractors knew that this was the score. Our informants repeatedly told us that clients were intolerant of contractors who needed ramp-up time. "You better hit the ground running," Marty Keely advised. "On your second day, if you're not producing, they get rid of you. They don't bring you in to learn, they bring you in to do their work. So there's very little opportunity to get acclimated. You have to be quick on your feet. Hit the ground! Run! And do *not* attach to anything in the company!"

Of course, contractors recognized that it was often impossible to hit the ground running for a variety of practical reasons. "The reality is that there is a learning curve no matter where you work," explained Yolanda Turner. "You don't know where the bathrooms are; you have to know where the servers are, what the printer names are, what maps to what. Nobody ever walks in ready to start working, no matter how smart they are. To shift gears is a real challenge. For some people it may not be, but for me, it is. I take a couple weeks or longer to get myself acclimated." But managers and permanent employers were rarely willing to give contractors that much time to adapt. "They can even be rude and insensitive," Yolanda continued. "They say, 'You don't know this? Are you stupid? You're supposed to know that! Why did we hire you?' Although I've been very angry at times, I've learned to do a lot of posturing." Like Yolanda, most contractors said that it was best to pretend that you had no questions and to learn as quickly as possible.

Because managers expected contractors to have the necessary skills, they assumed that contractors only had to be told about the scope, the requirements, and the constraints of the jobs they were expected to perform before they could put their skills to use. Therefore, when contractors arrived, the hiring manager's first act was to set the parameters of the task and clarify expectations. Rodney Fisher, director of technical services at Chipco, outlined what he told new contractors: "I say, 'Here's the scope of work, what to expect. Here are the individuals with whom you have to work. Here's the training—knowledge transfer—that I expect to take place. These are the team meetings that are going to occur,

---

[1] QA Partner is a software tool for testing the functioning of GUI interfaces and object-oriented programs.

the notes that are going to be published, the documentation that's required, and then disappear in two months when we're satisfied.'"

Knowing that clients expected immediate results, contractors were, if anything, even more adamant than hiring managers about the importance of clarifying expectations at the outset of a contract. Many claimed that managers were often vague and imprecise about what they really expected. "In contract work," Asaf Weiss confided, "you often find there are no specs. Seldom are requirements really well-defined. Instead you find people saying, 'Joe said what we'd really like is this and not that.' At that point you have to say, 'Well, okay. Did Joe write that down? Because what happens if I do this and this isn't what Joe wanted?'"

Informants who had contracted for any length of time discovered that if they did not clarify expectations early, they could easily fall victim to shifting priorities and to definitions of the project's scope that they saw as unreasonable. When that happened, contractors might find themselves being taken advantage of, saddled with the blame for work gone awry, or even fired. "Managing the expectations of the client is probably the most important and most difficult part of the job," Victor Post claimed. "For the longest time, I didn't manage expectations at all," he continued. "I said, 'Okay, what do you need me to do?' And they would say, 'We want the moon,' and I would say, 'Okay, I will go get it.' My attitude was, I am getting paid by the hour and I will do whatever it takes. But that is not sustainable." Doug Hill even advised contractors to specify clearly from whom they would and would not accept orders, because once on the job, contractors found that multiple people tried to assign them tasks:

> Whenever I set up a contract, I establish that I will have one and only one designated contact person. If you don't do this, life is hell. Some guy will come by and ask you to do things, and you don't know if he has any authority. You've got to structure it into your initial agreement. I've been walking through the company, and the chairman of the board has pulled me aside and said, "Hey, you've got to do this and this and this." And I said, "I work for Tom Lowe." And he said, "Do you know who I am?" And I said, "Yes, and as soon as Tom Lowe tells me to do that, I'll do it." You don't always make friends, but you need to do it. And you do it by defining the work relationship from the outset, no matter how hot-to-trot they are in the company. The client should bear the emotional burden of the relationship.

After setting clear expectations, managers tried to confine supervision to "tasking," assigning specific pieces of work, and to providing contractors with feedback that would shape the work as it progressed. In general, managers reported providing this kind of feedback in the course of daily interaction or in team meetings, although in some firms full-time engineers also "tasked" contractors. Hiring managers claimed that they evaluated contractors primarily on output and did not worry too much about how the work was done. Managers asked: Did a program work? Were negotiated deadlines met? Was a piece of software installed correctly? The contractors that we interviewed confirmed that they were usually evaluated on their output and that this was what they found attractive about contracting.

The sink-or-swim philosophy and the focus on task accomplishment meant that clients felt no obligation to help contractors develop, either as experts or as persons. Managers reported that they never offered contractors the kind of "one-on-one" development sessions that they held with permanent employees. Neva Boyd, for example, drew the distinction between how she supervised employees and how she supervised contractors:

> If you have a performance problem with a [full-time] engineer, you've got to protect yourself legally. So you go through a lot of steps to give the engineer every possible chance to succeed. You have a talk with them. Send them e-mail if the problem persists. Have another talk with them and try to agree on specific goals that they can achieve in a short time frame. If things get really bad, you can put them on something called a "performance plan," and after a period of time they have to show concrete progress that's documented in HR. Only then you can begin the process of firing them. With contractors you generally don't do all that. It's pretty clear from the start what the contract is about, so they've already got a list of concrete goals. If it's not working out you'll talk with them, but over a much more compressed period of time. If it doesn't work in weeks, they can be gone.

To make sure that managers could concentrate solely on managing tasks, clients delegated all additional managerial responsibilities for contractors to staffing firms.[2]

DELEGATING MANAGEMENT RESPONSIBILITIES

Delegating the status of employer-of-record to agencies allowed clients to abdicate their responsibility as employers. As employers-of-record, agen-

[2] Of course, clients could not pawn independent contractors off on a staffing agency unless the contractor was on a pass-through. Independent contractors on direct contracts tended to be highly skilled, experienced experts. They tended to have collegial and relatively autonomous relationships and were assumed to need little supervision. Their involvement with the firm resembled a professional-client relationship.

cies assumed the legally required obligations that the clients jettisoned. They filed employment documents, deducted payroll taxes, provided limited benefits, and paid the contractor. However, they rarely went beyond the bare minimum required by law. Agencies were neither qualified nor expected to supervise the contractors' technical performance. They also preferred to distance themselves from personnel management issues not only because such problems were messy, but also because few contractors stayed with an agency long enough to make such involvement worthwhile. In the absence of a long-term relationship, agencies gained little by improving contractors' work habits, skills, or demeanor. Agents made their commissions by filling job orders and keeping contractors working, not by making them happy or by ensuring that their relations with clients were harmonious.

Most contractors reported that once they signed a contract and began work, they had little interaction with recruiters or account managers until the contract was nearly over. At that point an agent might call to see if the contractor anticipated extending the contract or if he or she wanted the agency's help in finding another, but even then, some agencies never called. Although contractors who worked as W-2s were required to provide their agency with weekly or biweekly time cards, most simply faxed their cards to the agency's accounting office and received checks in the mail or through direct deposit.

There were three broad exceptions to this general pattern. First, agents sought out contractors when they believed that the contractor had violated (or was about to violate) the contract in a way that jeopardized the agency's interests or the agent's compensation. Word that a contractor was considering converting to a permanent employee ("going perm"), ending a contract prematurely ("walking"), or violating a "noncompete clause" by contracting with the same client through another agency evoked a response. In these cases agents would call or visit the contractor, explain why the contractor's behavior was unacceptable, and do their best to bring the contractor back into line, sometimes by threatening legal action.

The second exception occurred when a client felt that a contractor's behavior was a problem. Although such cases were rare, when behavioral problems arose clients usually contacted the agency because it was the employer-of-record and because clients were hesitant to act in ways that might suggest they had taken too much responsibility for the contractor. Behavioral problems ranged from habitually showing up late, poor hygiene, and personality clashes to misusing corporate e-mail, using drugs on the job, or exhibiting poor mental health. After hiring managers contacted an agency, events unfolded in one of two ways.

Sometimes agents intervened and tried to resolve the problem, either on their own or in collaboration with the client. In these instances, hiring managers had almost always expressed concern for the contractor's welfare, thereby indicating that they wanted to do more than get rid of the problem by getting rid of the contractor. In these cases, the hiring manager also usually had an ongoing relationship with the agent. Consequently, the agent recognized that resolving the problem would enhance the client's loyalty to the agency and perhaps even help the agency retain the contractor, if the contractor was still deemed an acceptable risk. More commonly, however, clients did not want to treat behavioral problems as human resource problems. Instead, they simply wanted to fire the contractor. In these cases, agents delivered the bad news and then did what was necessary to bring the contract to a close. The agent invariably sided with the client and offered to find a replacement, a process known among agents as "backfilling."

The third exception to agents' tendency to minimize their managerial responsibilities grew out of the idiosyncrasies of certain agencies' strategies and cultures. Contractors acknowledged that a handful of firms deviated from the norm by making special efforts to interact with contractors in the field. Progressive Staffing and Systems Professionals were among these. Progressive Staffing portrayed itself as a staffing agency that cared about the contractor's welfare, a philosophy that reflected its founder's belief that loyalty mattered and loyalty came from treating contractors with respect. To ensure continuing contact with contractors, Progressive Staffing required agents to deliver paychecks in person every Friday. The firm also encouraged agents to give contractors small gifts such as T-shirts and mouse pads and, from time to time, to bring them pizza or take them to lunch. Because agents were partially evaluated on whether they made such contacts, they took the requirement seriously, even though many would have preferred to do otherwise. Thus, Progressive Staffing's agents stood out because they acted more like a concerned employer.

Systems Professionals went even further. Systems Professionals' contractors were, in fact, full-time, salaried employees. Systems Professionals also expected its contractors to stay with the firm for a period of years during which they would place them with a variety of clients. Because Systems Professionals had a more traditional employment relationship with its contractors, it felt obligated to cater to their needs, to teach them new skills, and to help them construct careers. To achieve these objectives, Systems Professionals had created the position of staff manager, a role distinct from account manager and recruiter. Every staff manager had a group of approximately thirty-five contractors. Staff managers cooperated with Systems Professionals' technical services group to assess each contractor's skill level and to develop a plan for enhancing the contractor's skills—a form of career development that entailed thinking about what assignments and training opportunities would build the contractor's expertise. They were required to visit, at regular intervals, every contractor for whom they were responsible. They conducted performance and salary reviews and served as the contractor's primary point of contact with the firm. Most significantly, staff managers were paid to listen to, empathize with, and resolve contractors' "issues."

Systems Professionals' approach to handling the employer's traditional role as a manager of human resources was the proverbial exception that proved the rule. Systems Professionals took an active interest in its contractors' careers and experiences, precisely because they were permanent Systems Professionals employees. Systems Professionals' willingness to be involved with contractors' work lives contrasted sharply with the actions of most other staffing agencies, which took a minimalist approach to managing contractors once the contract began. This meant that, in practice, most agencies took upon themselves only bare-bones "people management" activities and did as little as they could get away with.

By emphasizing tasks and delegating "people management" responsibility to staffing agencies, clients sought to create a managerial system that was consistent with their view of contractors as commodities. The system was designed to allow clients to make use of contractors' skills while allowing contractors no claim to any of the legal or customary rights of membership. To further bolster this view of the contractor's role, clients sought to draw symbolic distinctions between contractors and full-timers. These distinctions amounted to a frontal assault on the trappings of membership.

CREATING OUTSIDERS

Most clients had a number of formal policies designed to set contractors apart from employees. The first and most immediately obvious addressed the sign of identity that was closest to the body: the identity tag. In corporate America, identities are displayed in the form of badges that clip onto clothing or dangle from chains worn around the neck. The badges announce the wearers' names, display their pictures, and proclaim their position in the firm. Corporate IDs usually have colored backgrounds or borders. They allow access to corporate facilities and serve a variety of social purposes, not the least of which is to enable people to position one another in the corporate pecking order. Firms routinely required contractors to wear badges that broadcast their identity as a contractor. Sometimes these badges bore the word "contractor" prominently displayed for all to read, but they were always of a different color or shape than the badges worn by permanent employees. Thus, by simply walking around, contractors continually announced their outsider status.

The badges achieved their purpose. Permanent employees admitted to taking note of the color of a person's badge. In interviews, engineers tried to assure us that color lost its meaning over time, but occasionally permanent employees confessed to altering their behavior on the basis of color, especially when they did not know the contractor personally. Nancy Cato, a software development manager at AC, suggested that the effects were noticeable, but subtle: "You've got people with the blue ID badges and people with the orange badges and people with the yellow badges. So you might smile and wave at the blue badges and not at the yellow badges." One of her more outspoken employees suggested that the ramifications were more far-reaching:

> If you see blue on the back or a blue slip or whatever it is that they have, they're employees. If there's white down here, [*points to his badge*] they're employees. Any other color, all bets are off. I always notice a person's badge. I've been in a position to have to notice. If I say certain things about certain projects and there's a contractor standing there, I run the risk of compromising the project. If it's a contractor that I'm supposed to be working with and I know they've signed a nondisclosure agreement, then it's okay. But if it's a contractor that I don't know or anybody with a different color than white or blue standing around—I just don't talk about it. Cafeterias are very unsafe places these days.

If badges were the most common way of distinguishing contractors from permanent employees, space ran a close second. The quality of one's work space has long signaled status in organizations, and there are few resources that employees guard more zealously than their offices. The top executives of large firms often reside in locations distant from the workforce or on the top floors of buildings where views are better. Lesser executives usually have corner offices or offices with windows and more floor space. First-level managers and the rank and file do without windows and often without walls. The quality of an office's furnishings and the freedom to personalize space also speaks to standing in corporate America. The type of desk at which one works, a chair's upholstery, even the color of the carpet on the floor can be important cues for insiders who know how to read them. Given that space is so significant, it is unsurprising that clients found ways of assigning contractors less desirable space, even amid the mazes of gray, modular cubicles where they housed their engineers and software developers. Like wearing a different colored badge, spatial inequities were meant to signal that contractors were just passing through.

Precisely how clients differentiated contractors spatially varied from firm to firm. Most frequently, clients simply stuffed two or more contractors into a cubicle normally occupied by a single employee. At one site we visited, the contractors were not only required to share cubicles, but most of the cubicles were congregated in a single area separated from the permanent employees by a six-foot partition. The contractors, all software developers, called the partition the "firewall." A contractor invited us behind the firewall to tour his space:

> Sure, come on down. I'll show you. We're way away from the permanents, so I've got to get up and walk over every time I want to see a permanent AC person. They haven't mixed us up. And you'll notice too that the permanent staff all have large, nice desks, but they've got four of us crammed into this area that is smaller than this little office here. So it's pretty tight. I've got a work area that's about three and a half feet. So that just speaks volumes: you're a temporary worker because you don't have any room to put up stuff. Like if you're a perm you probably have your Joe Montana poster up on the wall. I've got no room to put any of that stuff up.

In other firms, contractors were assigned even less desirable spaces, in part, because offices were already overcrowded. Contractors told stories of being assigned to work in laboratories, cafeterias, hallways, and other unlikely places. David Roberts, an experienced nomad who had contracted his way across the country, told us about contracting at General Electric: "My office was the cafeteria because they didn't have any desk space for me, although there was plenty of space. Their area for contractors was full. There were plenty of empty offices for directs. These offices were the same as those where they put contractors, but we weren't allowed to use them. 'Oh no! The contractor area is full!' So I had a locker in the hall and I stayed in the cafeteria. You've heard of hunting and gathering? Well, I had to gather and hunt. I actually had a couple of big bags. I'd gather my stuff and go hunt for a station where somebody was pregnant, gone that day, whatever."

Felix Harden, who had contracted for many years as a technical writer at UNIX Hardware, lived in an arguably worse environment:

> I've always had pretty substandard space at UNIX Hardware. Even now I'm still in this "thing." It was the first-aid room, not an office. When I first came in, there was a cot in there and a big first-aid box fused to the wall. It was right next to the kitchen. So we'd have people running in from the kitchen holding fingers like this [*grabs his index finger*], right above my computer. They finally blocked that [entrance], but still I don't have real work surfaces like most offices.

I've got these real cheap tables. It was just two contractors in this little room for a while and now there's an intern in there. I had it to
myself for a while and that somehow didn't seem right to them, so
they gave me an intern.

Limiting the kinds of events that contractors could attend was the
third way of signaling that contractors did not enjoy the benefits of
membership. Although contractors were usually invited to meetings
that focused on their project, most firms barred them from gatherings,
such as "all hands meetings," where corporate issues were discussed.
At one firm, permanent employees reported that contractors were even
excused from team meetings when the meeting turned away from task-
related issues to matters of corporate policy. Firms frequently excluded contractors from team-building exercises and corporate celebrations, including lunches, retirement parties, and outings. In some
firms, contractors were not allowed to use the corporate health facilities or to ride the bicycles that employees used to travel around the
company's "campus." Unlike full-timers, contractors were rarely given
presents when their project team passed a milestone. Some firms even
had policies against giving contractors T-shirts and other marketing
"collateral."

In addition to identity tags, office space, and rules for participating in
company events, our informants reported a variety of other, more idio-
syncratic methods for marking contractors. They told us of firms that refused to provide contractors with passwords for entering computer systems that were crucial to their assignments. Before contractors could
work, a permanent employee had to log them into the system. Advanced
Computers was widely known for requiring contractors to include the
phrase "non-AC employee" in their voice mail greetings and e-mail sig-
natures.[3] Another firm demanded that contract programmers work the
night shift. Firms that allowed permanent employees to telecommute
sometimes forbade contractors to do so. Conversely, firms that discouraged permanent employees from working from home allowed contractors to telecommute. Computing equipment could also be deployed to
distinguish contractors. Most contractors had access to equipment iden-
tical to that used by permanent employees. But in some cases, contractors were given older models, or they were given computers but no printers. A few contractors even told stories of being allowed to use better
computers than the full-timers used. Several contractors, who had
worked for companies doing defense work, told of having to be escorted

---

[3] Ironically, the practice assisted the sales force of many staffing agencies, who could
now more easily distinguish permanent employees from contractors when cold calling to
prospect for leads.

to the bathroom by armed guards, an indignity from which permanent employees were spared.

CONCLUSION

By attempting to narrow the obligations of management to the rudiments of supervising a task, by delegating other managerial duties to staffing firms, and by drawing symbolic distinctions between contractors and permanent employees, clients seemed to create a tidy class structure. Like resident aliens, contractors coexisted with full-time employees without being full-fledged members of the community; rather, they were viewed as outsiders, who participated in the work but did not belong. This system reinforced the perception that the contractors' presence in the community was based solely on the principle of limited utilitarian exchange. Like the hired guns, to whom contractors so often compared themselves, when their services were needed they were to ride into town, do their work quickly and efficiently, and leave quietly during the night with their saddlebags full of cash.

Although hiring managers, and even contractors, found the imagery of commodification appealing, and many managerial practices and organizational routines supported and reinforced it, there were also practical limits to its applicability. In the midst of the everyday routines and crises of technical work, the distinctions and tightly constructed boundaries between permanent employees and contractors began to blur.

Chapter 8

CONTRACTORS AS EXPERTS

EFFORTS TO MANAGE contractors as if they were commodities originated with and were shaped by senior management. With the help of lawyers, staff, consultants, and the managerial press, top management formulated policies on how to treat contractors that clearly distinguished them from permanent employees. Once these policies were in place, however, senior managers turned their attention elsewhere, leaving implementation to the hiring managers who actually used the contractors' services. Hiring managers, for the most part, shared senior managers' view of contractors as commodities, found the focus on task performance convenient, and accepted the need to enforce distinctions between employees and contractors.

Hiring managers, however, also had projects to manage. The everyday requirements of managing a team populated by both employees and contractors confronted them with problems unforeseen by policy makers and inconsistent with their own rhetoric. These problems were of two types. First, the need to integrate and coordinate the efforts of team members counteracted the distinctions that firms used to signal that contractors were not employees. Second, the specific roles that contractors played on project teams and the unique knowledge they possessed created dependencies that challenged the belief that contractors could be purchased and then cast aside like a spent resource.

INTEGRATION: CREATING TEAM MEMBERS

Because hiring managers were responsible for coordinating the efforts of project teams, they straddled the fault line between contractors and employees. As frontline supervisors, they were saddled with enforcing the distinctions between contractors and full-timers. But they simultaneously had to ensure that both groups meshed well enough for projects to be completed on time.[1] Pressure to integrate contractors into the project team despite their distinct status arose because engineering work is, by

---

[1] In her study of temporary workers in light industrial manufacturing, Vicki Smith (1998) also noted that managers faced a similar dilemma and often chose to integrate temporary workers into work groups on the factory floor.

definition, teamwork. Project managers understood that technical projects were complex and that technical knowledge was so specialized that it was impossible for engineers and software developers to execute discrete parts of projects on their own. Rather, technical work consisted of an endless flow of interactions between those who design the various pieces of a complex technology. The patterning of interactions that was most conducive to successfully completing a project rarely, if ever, conformed to distinctions between those who belonged and those who did not. Thus, any notion that technical professionals could be hired to do isolated pieces of work was largely a fiction.

Although coordination usually went smoothly, at least as smoothly as any technical project can be expected to go, when tensions arose between contractors and employees, it was the hiring manager's job to resolve them. Technical managers were acutely aware of the dilemma they faced. Randy Bouchet articulated the tension:

> Managing and integrating are two separate issues. One is easy; the other is hard. Managing is easy because we give these guys and gals [QA contractors] a very discrete list of things that we want them to do. We work with them to establish a time line, and then we hold them to it. And that makes it pretty easy to manage, right? [*He smiles ironically.*] Integration into the team is a little more problematic because I have to be very careful to not include them in the employee perks sort of stuff that we do. I really try to maintain a clean separation, *at that level*, between the regular employees and the contractor. On the other hand, they have to work closely with the engineering team because they have to ask the right questions to get the job done. They have to interact with their fellow QA peers. So there's an interesting tension there. On the one hand, you really do want them to become members of the team, and on the other hand, from a legal perspective, you have to be careful not to give them stuff that they don't need to have.

James Hambly, manager of a software development group at Advanced Computers, called his predicament "walking a fine line," an idiom that technical managers from a number of companies used to talk about their supervisory "challenges": "You have to have everybody come together to work, act, and think like a team. At the same time you have to tell people, 'Well, you know, you're not all part of the same company.' You have to do things that show clear differentiation between employees and nonemployees. You know, because Microsoft screwed everything up for everybody. So the most difficult thing is trying to create and maintain esprit de corps, at the same time you clearly show differentiations."

As did James, many hiring managers blamed their dilemma on

Microsoft, the Darth Vader of high tech routinely vilified in Silicon Valley firms for a variety of sins. Were it not for the legal consequences of Microsoft's blatant exploitation of contractors, these managers argued, it would not be necessary to insist on such strong distinctions between contractors and employees. Other hiring managers justified the need for distinctions in terms of equity: it was important that employees not feel that the firm was slighting them, especially when contractors were paid more than employees. But most hiring managers felt that the need to make distinctions was counterproductive, if not overblown and petty.

Yet, hiring managers did not blame senior management for creating policies that made their jobs more difficult. Instead, they wrestled with how to soften or circumvent the distinctions so that they did not interfere with a team's ability to get its work done. Some managers felt they should integrate contractors into the group simply because it was the right thing to do. All recognized that integrating contractors into a team was pragmatically necessary for creating an effective work environment. Nancy Cato, a project manager at AC, believed that unless contractors were made to feel part of the team, they might perform well but never "transfer their knowledge" to full-time employees before they left:

> I found that it's important to include contractors and have them be a part of the team, not just have them off coding in a corner somewhere. So, I make sure that I have project team meetings and not just "permanent people meetings" that leave the contractors out in the cold. To me that's really important. To make sure that they adhere to standards and good coding practices, I want to have design specs. I want to have code reviews. I want to have walk-throughs. I want to have learning be transferred over to my permanent people and know that I have a knowledge base that I can go back to after they're gone. That's probably more important than it is with a permanent person. You tend to be able to find permanent people later. Temporary people you lose.

But the gulf between recognizing the importance of integrating contractors into the team and figuring out how to do so was wide. Hiring managers had discovered on their own what social scientists have long known: that making distinctions between people is much easier than softening a distinction once made. Hiring managers spoke of a variety of techniques for making contractors feel welcome and for bridging the distance between contractors and full-timers. Some tried to locate contractors near the permanent engineers. Others said they made a point of stopping by the contractors' cubicles to say hello and to ask if they were having problems. One manager, who felt bad about not being able to invite contractors to lunches and other outings, held impromptu team parties for which she baked cookies and to which she intentionally invited contractors. But among hiring managers who took the need to integrate contractors seriously, the most common ploy was simply to acknowledge the official policies and then circumvent them.

One hiring manager argued that contractors were not allowed to go on outings to restaurants and recreational facilities because firms were not allowed to pay for contractors, lest they be confused with employees. Thus, the manager reasoned, there should be no problem if contractors paid their own way. So the manager routinely encouraged contractors to accompany the team, but told them that they would have "go Dutch." Another hiring manager invited contractors to all meetings, but organized her agenda so that work-related and strategic topics were discussed at different parts of the meeting. She "let contractors leave," as if doing them a favor, when the group came to the latter topics. Others introduced technical topics into meetings to which contractors would typically not be invited in order to justify inviting them. Some, like Rodney Fisher, even chose to ignore the policies altogether:

> Managers of different teams have different philosophies. I invite contractors to all of our staff meetings, generally to all of our team-building events, to all of our off-sites, and all of our Christmas parties. I believe that if you're going to continually use a contractor or a consultant, and they're going to be part of the organization at some level for some amount of time, you want them to feel a sense of ownership and camaraderie with their peers for the time that they're there. And I think that isolating them by saying, "Don't come to the staff meetings, don't come to business meetings, don't come to Great America, don't come to the Christmas party," doesn't help. I never sat back and really assessed whether this contributes to their overall engagement. I just personally think it would, because I think I would like to be treated that way. More of a principle I guess.

In their attempts to integrate contractors, managers received considerable assistance from contractors themselves. Contractors noted that policies of differentiation sometimes made them feel like "members of a lower caste" or "second-class citizens." Yet, most accepted differentiation as a fact of life and understood that hiring contractors placed managers in an ambiguous situation. As Katrina Labovski put it, "The hiring manager is rarely the person imposing these IRS-shy policies. These policies typically exist in large companies. It's the tax department or some risk management group that is behind the policies."

Contractors clearly understood (and were usually pleased) that they were not employees. They knew they were hired for their expertise for a short period of time to accomplish a specific task. They also knew that they were paid more than employees and that this upset the full-timers. The distinctions and formal indignities that firms forced on contractors seemed a small price to pay for higher salaries and immunity from corporate politics. Like Eugene Elliot, many contractors argued that the distinctions were largely symbolic anyway: "It's symbolic that they put you in a small cubicle. I think they want to compensate for the fact that they pay contractors more. The employees can go and say, 'You're paying him more,' but then they say, 'Yeah, but he doesn't have as good working conditions.'"

As long as the inequities didn't interfere with getting the work done, most contractors didn't care about being denied perquisites. Not being given a T-shirt was hardly a significant slight: if contractors needed a T-shirt, they could afford one. Nor did contractors complain about being excluded from meetings. After all, many had become contractors, in part, to avoid such demands. Besides, contractors felt that complaining, even about office space, would violate the "professional" relationship they had with their clients. William Bish, an aerospace engineer who had contracted on and off for over thirty years, explained:

They are caught between a rock and a hard place. If they treat you too much like an employee, you might say, "I'm an employee, where are my benefits?" Of course being professionals they say, "Okay, let's not make the job shoppers feel uptight. Let's not make them feel we are standoffish. So we invite them to the meetings and we go out and drink beers with them." But they have to watch out that we don't become too much like the employees, because then we can go, "Hey! I'm an employee! I go drink with them. I go to meetings with them. I get supervised by the same boss." So, that is part of the paranoia. They have to walk sort of a line, not to look too much like your employer. But you know, if there is a problem you usually go to your supervisor. We are all professional. You walk up and say, "I have a problem here."

In fact, some contractors claimed they felt so sorry for the awkward position in which managers and employees were placed that they went out of their way to make full-timers feel comfortable with the distinctions they had to make. George Mayall, a systems administrator at Chipco, felt this kind of compassion:

For the most part, I was treated the same as everyone else. Every once in a while, there were external activities, like the Chipco picnic or they went to Great America. They couldn't drag contractors along quite as easily or we might have to pay part of our way, which is kind of fair since we're not actually part of the company. They can't let us in completely, but at the same time they sort of want us there because it's supposed to be a team-building exercise. It goes back and forth. There were a few times when they did invite contractors to these events and a few times when they didn't. I think it was just kind of whimsical and depended on how much money they had in the department at the time. There have been a bunch of times when I offered to stay behind because someone has to be here. So I offered to be the one to stick around. Some of the times when I was offering, I think they were trying to decide should they invite me or shouldn't they. Will I be offended if I don't go? So just by offering to stay I think I took off some of the burden of the decision, made things a little bit easier on them.

Dependence

The risk of a becoming dependent on a contractor's knowledge and skill was the second challenge to the policies and practices of commodification. Contractors were usually brought on board to provide expertise that employees lacked, to perform supplementary, but crucial, tasks such as quality assurance, or to fill out an understaffed project team. On occasion, contracting worked roughly the way the rhetoric implied, but only when firms hired individuals with skills that were widely available and when the task was extremely focused and bounded. But even then, treating contractors as commodities was more difficult than it first appeared.

In all cases, contractors assumed responsibility for tasks on whose successful completion the work of others hinged. Moreover, technical work often consisted of subprojects, such as writing a module of code, that were done individually and had their own logic and history of development. Consequently, it was difficult for one technical worker to take over a partially completed task from another. Furthermore, technical work, no matter how routine, always involves a significant amount of contextual knowledge. For example, writing a subroutine, altering the structure of a database, and even testing a software application required developing familiarity with the larger system to which the work contributed. Developing this kind of contextual knowledge took time. Thus, the departure of a contractor, especially before a project ended, meant, at minimum, an unanticipated delay and extra work for employees. In many cases, losing a contractor meant not only losing time, but also knowledge for which there was no ready substitute. For this reason, at least for the duration of a project, clients tended to become reliant even on contractors who worked as temporary full-timers or support technicians.

Toshi Yamamato, a lead engineer at Advanced Computers whose team included several contractors who were working as temporary full-timers consolidating data from legacy databases, remarked: "If our contractors left, it would be devastating. They have so much knowledge! I try to put some of the tasks onto permanent employees. But they have lots to do already. So yeah, if they leave, they leave big holes."

Even the company-specific knowledge that contractors gained when doing relatively mundane work was of value to a firm, and its value increased the longer the contractor was employed. For this reason Monty Kirkman, an IT manager at Chipco, hesitated to hire contractors for jobs that he expected to last more than a few months. When contracts lasted longer, Monty found that his contractors became indispensable: "We don't like contractors to hang around more than nine months, because then we're saying that should be a full-time position. I mean, in nine months they would know too much about the company and it would be too hard to replace them. They will acquire so much knowledge and skill that it will be hard to get somebody else to pick up where they left off."

When firms required the expertise of a developer-consultant or an experienced expert, the odds of dependency increased. Clients could not easily dismiss or replace highly skilled contractors who provided knowledge that permanent employees lacked. Losing a contractor with crucial expertise could bring work to a standstill. Noah Swetka, an IT manager at Western Phone Company, spoke of losing such highly skilled experts. "Frankly," Noah confided, "in many ways contractors are sometimes better than permanent employees, just because they have the right skill set. They're better trained. They are focused on the job because they don't have to worry about anything else. But there's a downside. We're getting in the mode of having them come in and build new things and when the contract is up and they walk out the door, the people who have to maintain it have no idea what the code looks like."

Although the nature of technical work and the role that contractors played created conditions for dependency, the combination of a company's culture and size amplified or dampened the effect, in part because it influenced the type of contractors that the company tended to hire. For instance, Advanced Computers was known for fostering a family-oriented culture among its employees. Consequently, it hesitated to employ contractors in roles that threatened the knowledge and status of full-timers. AC rarely used contract software developers to do more than write code, even when the contractor had prior experience as an architect. Design responsibilities and other prestigious tasks were reserved for employees. As a result, AC's contractors typically worked as support technicians or temporary full-timers. Their work was almost always "scoped" by employees. This reduced the degree to which AC became dependent on it contractors. In fact, at one AC site, contractors referred to themselves as "worker bees" and to their tasks as "pounding nails." Paul Hinton, a contractor at the site, explained his view of AC's approach:

I think the methodology here is that the engineers do more project direction and contractors do most of the programming. I don't say engineers never do the programming, but I think their basic responsibilities are more project oriented and they have access to our skills. So they'll make work assignments to us to do certain levels of programming. We're not responsible for project level activities. At the Money Store, I had a direct project and full responsibility. AC employees do that and we are the worker bees, which is fine. That's what we're hired to do. We do the actual implementation.

In contrast, the way Chipco used contractors encouraged dependency. Chipco had historically made few distinctions between contractors and employees, although managers were beginning to question the practice. Work was allocated to those who had appropriate expertise. Because technology changed so rapidly, this often meant that contractors found themselves doing more interesting and challenging work than full-timers. Sally Hynes, a project manager who oversaw IT development, remarked:

At Chipco if we're going to do a new software installation, if we're going to do an upgrade, if we're going to do anything new, we usually go out and we hire [contractors] to do it, which means that the employees get to do the day-to-day stuff. They get to do the old stuff. They don't get to do the new stuff. And so the complaint is always, "Why do the contractors always get to do the new stuff? Why don't we get to do the new stuff?" We do it partly because of budget reasons. The other thing is, the reason that I brought in an external consulting group to do the upgrade was because there was not much expertise in the group in doing that kind of work. So if I said, "Okay, we're going to do this upgrade," nobody in my group would know what to do. So my thought was I can hire the knowledge.

Managers and employees were acutely aware of their dependency. Hiring managers, who articulated a sink-or-swim philosophy of employment at one point in our discussions, often confessed to dependence at another. To guard against becoming too dependent, one might expect that firms would have attempted to limit contractors' engagements, just as Monty Kirkman suggested they should. But most firms, including Chipco, responded to dependency with precisely the opposite strategy. Rather than dismiss contractors, they extended contracts.

The contractors whom we interviewed explicitly told us that it was commonplace to have a contract renewed several times. In fact, most highly skilled contractors had been in situations where they continued to work while employees were being laid off in significant numbers around them. Bill Smith, a verification engineer who worked for Motorola, was representative: "The pro of contracting is people want you. You know, you're not being abused because they really want you there. They're behind; they need your expertise. The people they have can't do your work. For instance, you know, I'm at Motorola. I had a six-month contract that was up in January, and I'm still there. They're laying off fifteen thousand people, but I'm still there. The reason I'm still there is because they can't find people inside that can do the work I can do."

Independent contractors, who were not subject to the eighteen-month limit that the IRS placed on W-2s, were often renewed many times. In fact, we encountered technical writers, hardware engineers, and software developers who had worked for the same client for over four years. When hiring managers encountered an experienced expert whose skills they respected, they would sometimes retain the contractor even during slack times so that they could deploy the person on upcoming projects. This happened to Richard Stevens, a crack Java developer at UNIX Hardware: "I was working for Aron for a while and he was cognizant of the fact that it's hard to find people. So losing me, even if I didn't have anything to do, would have wasted him a lot of time and effort finding somebody else. So even though our project ended, he was a little more like, you know, 'Hang tight.'" Extremely long periods of service were particularly common among developer-consultants, like Doug Hill, who became fixtures in the firms for whom they worked:

> At Seamax the original contract was for ten days. They were a very small company—had thirty employees. They told me they only had enough money to pay me for ten days. Presidents of that company have come and gone. Department heads have come and gone. The ownership of the company has come and gone. Even the company's name has changed. I'm like the guy at the post office. No matter who gets elected to Congress, I still deliver your mail. In fact, the guy that hired me was VP of their internal operations. He brought me in and told me, "We don't have a lot of money. If you can't do it in ten days, tell me now." A year later he left the company. I was still there. A year after he left, he stopped by, he walked in the door, and when he saw me he said, "What the hell are you doing here?" "Same thing." He's been back twice in the last two years and I've been there both times. They now have eight hundred employees. There're only twenty-four that have been there longer than I have.

Longevity was only one upshot of dependency; autonomy was another. Highly skilled contractors with expertise that clients found crucial repeatedly remarked that hiring managers gave them a surprising amount of freedom and autonomy. Although a contractor's autonomy had a number of sources, one important source was the client's fear that the contractor would depart. Vicky Chenalt, for instance, was a technical writer on contract to UNIX Hardware. At the time we interviewed her, she had been at UNIX Hardware longer than any other member of her work group. She was allowed to work from home, she set her own hours, and she was recently given the task of training newly hired technical writers. Vicky almost felt guilty about the extent of her independence: "They are kind of afraid I'm going to leave and I think that's given me a lot more latitude in the last six or eight months. I mean, I basically show up when I want and tell them what I'm doing and play, and they're happy with it. I guess to a certain extent I'm probably abusing it, but they seem happy with the results."

Dependence had more serious consequences as well. Organizational theorists have long known that organizations not only become dependent on those who possess scarce and important resources, but dependency also confers power, which those in dependent positions resent.[2] Permanent employees in every firm we studied told horror stories designed to underscore the dangers of hiring contractors. In each case, the story recounted the tale of a contractor on whom the firm had unwisely come to depend. At some point in the story, the contractor walks unexpectedly, usually under suspicious circumstances, leaving the full-timers in a lurch. Sara Munzer, a full-time Oracle database developer at Chipco, told the story of a contractor with marital problems.

> He was a great contractor until he started having trouble at home. He lived in Sacramento, came here, and went home on the weekends. Started having trouble with his wife and was getting divorced and it was a disaster. We were just getting ready to go through a release upgrade. Major thing for our group. You plan it for nine months. And about a month before we were doing that, he just quit. "I've got to go back to Sacramento. My wife's leaving me." His child was suicidal. It was like he was gone instantly. We had this really good experience with him and then it was just a disaster. But it taught us something about contractors. Don't rely on them too much. You don't want to put too many eggs in one basket, especially with a contractor.

Experiences such as these had made some managers skittish of using contractors. In fact, some believed that contractors understood just how

[2] The notion that firms or people gain power to the extent that others depend on the resources they provide is a key tenet of Pfeffer and Salancik's (1978) "resource-dependency" theory of power. When others have no substitutes for the resources that a person provides, the person's power increases (Hickson et al. 1971; Hinings et al. 1974).

easily clients could become dependent and that they intentionally sought to foster the dependency. These hiring managers, like Rodney Fisher, felt that firms needed to be on their guard:

> My personal belief, having been in the IT industry for fifteen to twenty years now, is you never want to bring in contractors to work on projects that become core competencies within the organization. When core competencies and knowledge are not shared with the permanent employees, it creates a separation among permanent employees and contractors. Permanent employees get upset when they see that a contractor gets to do something very high level and strategic, that they believe they should have done. One of the biggest problems with contractors is that 80 percent of the time (a) they're not open in sharing their knowledge and information, and (b) there is always a hook for downstream work because it's their livelihood. You must be very careful in setting up your engagements with contractors.

CONCLUSION

The rhetoric of commodificaton sketches an economist's dream world, a spot market unencumbered by sentimentality, social relationships, or extraneous obligations. Contracting, in this widely shared view, was heralded as opening a world in which employment relations were subject only to the naked logic of supply and demand, a world in which doing a task and doing it well was all that mattered. When a firm needed a particular set of skills, it simply went to the market. When the skills were no longer needed, the contractor was dismissed. However, the realities of technical teamwork constantly challenged this image of a depersonalized trade of wages for skill. Managing integration and dependencies required a manager to repersonalize the employment relationship. Thus, while hiring managers struggled to preserve the appearances of clear distinctions between contractors and permanent employees, they also found ways to respond to the undeniable fact that the people with whom one must interact are not easily treated as commodities, whatever the wishes of legal departments and the claims of managerial rhetoric. In practice, then, everyday life on the job for inhabitants of the social world of contracting was permeated by a complex and subtle set of perceptions, beliefs, and feelings. These not only shaped the behaviors and interactions of contractors, managers, and employees, but also provided the backdrop against which contractors negotiated and defined their identity. It is to this underbelly of the myth of commodification that we now turn.

Chapter 9

NAVIGATING BETWEEN RESPECT

AND RESENTMENT

THE GAP BETWEEN managerial rhetoric and corporate policies and the hiring managers' informal practices sent contradictory messages about the contractor's status. On one hand, firms went to great lengths to signal that contractors were outsiders; on the other hand, contractors could become quite integral to the firm's operations. These contradictory messages left contractors to make sense of their status by sifting through the signs and signals they received daily from managers and employees as they went about their work.

The contradictory signals that contractors received were reflected in the stories contractors, managers, and employees told about how full-timers treated the contractors they temporarily admitted into their world. These stories were of two distinct types. The first were tales of respect that told how full-timers valued contractors, both for their technical skills and for their professional demeanor. The second type were tales of resentment. These told the exact opposite story: how full-timers signaled their displeasure with the way contractors performed and their perceptions of the inequities that contracting created.

TALES OF RESPECT

Giving Advice and Receiving Confidence

Although contractors were officially hired to perform specific and sometimes narrow jobs, they frequently found their role expanding, especially in their interactions with hiring managers. Because contractors eschewed organizational politics and because all parties expected them to be highly mobile, contractors claimed that they were able to establish what they called "more honest" relationships with their clients. Tony Rodriguez, a contractor who managed IT projects for government agencies, explained: "One thing I can do as a contract employee that I couldn't do as a full-timer is be honest, straightforward, and up-front. I can say, 'Here are the facts.' I don't have to worry about politics. On the way in, I say, 'I am going to tell you exactly the way I feel about everything. You can

take it or leave it. That is why you hired me, to give you my opinion.'"
Tony claimed that his last boss had actually told him, "You know, you
are the only one who gives me a straight answer. You are the only one
that does not test the winds politically before you give me an answer."
Chris Laube, an IT contractor at Chipco, echoed Tony's sentiments:

> The difference between contractors and employees, I would say, is
> that the contractors generally will say more of what they think is
> right, not what they think their managers want to hear. And I think
> that is very valuable. Unfortunately companies don't seem to foster
> that level of honesty with their employees, because the only way an
> employee can progress is through the corporate hierarchy and if
> they upset their managers they're not going to progress. To the con-
> tractor, it really doesn't matter. You can upset somebody and you
> won't get hired by that person. But it's a very big valley and there's a
> lot of jobs out there. So you can afford to upset people to a certain
> extent. You can't be brutal with them, but you can be honest.

Many hiring managers concurred. They seemed to value contractors,
especially those who were highly skilled, because they spoke their minds.
Like contractors, hiring managers attributed this frankness to the fact
that contractors stood outside the world of corporate politics and organizational careers. Some managers even suggested that the contractors'
status as outsiders made them easier to work with than full-time employees. Monty Kirkman, from Chipco, was one. "Some of the problems we
usually have between people disappear when you hire contractors," he
told us. "Contractors know they're only here for a limited time and the
full-time people know that, too. So there's not that much competition or
friction between them. Contractors tend to be more professional and
they don't take personal sides. Full-time people are always interested in
promotions and reviews and so there is competition, friction, which
doesn't happen with contractors."

Managers sometimes reciprocated this frankness and openness. Developer-consultants and experienced experts often said that managers not
only sought their opinions but also treated them as confidants. These
contractors believed they enjoyed more open relations with managers because managers ironically felt that with outsiders they could share sensitive information that they could not share with employees. Brian Willingham told us that he was, at first, taken aback by his clients' openness,
but gradually came to realize that his clients had no one else to whom
they could complain. He likened his role to that of a therapist:

> I've got one customer—I come in sometimes and she'll just unload
> on me for about three or four minutes, and I go: "Where the heck

did this come from? It's not my fault, you know!" Then it finally dawned on me: she's just got somebody she can unload on. If I unload on somebody in-house, you know, if I talk to my fellow employee, it could come back to haunt me. Contractors, they know what's going on; they can relate to what's going on, so they understand the situation. It's private, personal. It's not going to come back to haunt you, because I'm not going to say, "She's really upset today, and I really think you ought to dump her." It's like a therapist. They treat contractors different than they would a fellow employee. In a lot of the companies I've worked for, I act like a sounding board. They didn't tell you anything about that back in contracting school! A lot of it is letting the customer talk, get it off their chest, and then you can say, "Okay, now that you're feeling better, let's go deal with the problem."

Richard Stevens, who was widely recognized as a guru within UNIX Hardware, also spoke of being treated as a confidant. "I actually have had managers tell me things about politics that they didn't want the employees to know. Like, 'This product is dead. There is no future in this thing you're working on. Don't tell any of the employees. Don't destroy morale here. We don't want to bum them out. But this is the way it's going to be.' They know we're not likely to leave just because the product is dead. We're not thinking of a career, because we don't have a career path. They tell you to get your opinion, to inform you, to keep you abreast of the fact that you may need to look for another job. All those things."

Stevens was even more amazed to discover that his impartiality and reputation as an expert garnered what he thought of as undeserved respect from the full-time software developers with whom he worked:

With people closer to the project, like tech leads, you can even get this opposite reaction, which is really strange. You get people seeking out the contractor's opinion and valuing only the contractor's opinion on certain things. Part of it might be impartiality. Part of it is a respect that is due you because you are here at the bidding of how good your work is, not because you were here for whatever. I was actually a little bit surprised because I've been asked technical questions about things I had no idea about. I knew that the employees who worked on them knew the answer to this stuff, but they sought me out to answer the question. I thought that was really strange. And I didn't mind. It's great. You know, it's their fantasy.

Contractors argued that managers sought their advice and treated them as confidants, precisely because they were independent of the organization's system of control. This seemed particularly obvious to contractors who had first worked for a firm as an employee and who then returned later as a contractor. Kurt Rhodes, however, had worked in Boeing's information systems department for many years as a full-time employee. He left Boeing to become an independent contractor, but soon found himself back at Boeing where he had been working as a contractor for several years at the time of his interview. Rhodes discovered that he enjoyed more respect as a contractor, and he attributed his good fortune entirely to others' perception that he must be an expert if Boeing had taken him back on contract. "The only difference [between being a full-timer and a contractor] is that I get a little more respect," he told us. "They figure, 'If they hired him back as a contractor, he must be good.'"

Going Perm

One of the strongest signals of appreciation and respect for contractors was receiving an offer to join the client's firm as a full-time employee. Most informants who had worked as contractors for any significant period of time had, at one time or another, fielded such an offer. Although contractors found such offers flattering, few accepted. Managers also reported trying to "convert" contractors whose skills and abilities they valued. For example, Nancy Cato recounted how Advanced Computers had gone out of its way to convert an experienced expert to a permanent employee:

> When one of our permanent people who'd been on the team for fifteen years decided to leave and go to another department, Richard became the only person who knew anything. We were at risk of losing the only knowledge we had left, plus he was really just a super programmer. We *begged* him. We actually opened a req, but he wouldn't apply for it. He said he really didn't want to go perm. Another open req came up and we said, "You really, really, really ought to think about doing it." Richard was somebody who we had actually enabled to work at home, which is just about unheard of for a contractor, because he destroyed his knee skiing. He telecommuted for months. We set him up at home with a PC and modem, which security says we're not supposed to do, but he's just so good.

In the end Advanced Computers managed to convince Richard to convert. This was the not the case at Chipco, which also tried to "capture" one of its developer-consultants. Managers and employees at Chipco told us about Gene, a software developer who worked from his home at Lake Tahoe, whom everyone in the IT department held in high regard, not only for his technical skills but for his willingness to share his knowledge with others. Sara Munzer, a permanent employee, remarked: "Gene's been around forever. Anytime you need him he's there. He's really sharp. He encourages people to learn about what he's put in place so that they can support it themselves. He's willing to teach you whatever you want to learn. He comes here about once a month, but he's always available by phone and he works pretty much our hours, plus other hours. I tend to talk to him about something that went wrong with a program that's in place. I might call him for advice on how to solve something because he's very experienced." Chipco had made Gene several offers to come aboard full time, but he consistently refused. Shirley Dancr, the CIO, told us: "We've offered Gene a job three or four times. We'd prefer that he become an employee, but he has refused us. He wants what he's got. He does fantastic work. So every year we keep telling him 'This is your last year,' and then we renew him for another year. So, he'll probably be around longer than me."

Becoming a Lead

Except for Tony Rodriguez who specialized in project management, none of our informants were directly hired into positions with organizational authority. However, a fifth (22 percent) of the contractors we interviewed had, at one time or another, been asked to assume the duties of a "project lead" during the course of a contract. In engineering environments, being a lead means coordinating and integrating the technical efforts of a group of engineers, as well as making decisions about the technical direction of the team's work. Thus, when contractors became leads they acquired authority over permanent employees as well as other contractors.

Aron Murphy, a project manager at UNIX Hardware, explained the logic and the risks behind making a contractor a lead:

> Red [a contractor] was the sharpest guy in the group. We were going to make him a lead engineer. He wasn't made a lead at first, simply because he was a contractor. But it was clear he was a leader in the group. I mean, if he were a full-time employee it would be a no-brainer. So we were thinking, "Okay, we're going to compromise the rules and we're going to go ahead and make him a lead if he agrees to do that." Everybody would have been fine with it. We just acknowledged that he could leave at some time. What's happening is we're putting somebody in a lead position who is a temporary employee, who could leave at a moment's notice. That's risky. I don't think of it as a policy problem or like we're endangering somebody else's job; it's purely a matter of risk to the project from a project

management standpoint. That's how I think of it. But if this guy has been a contractor for four years at UNIX Hardware, chances are he's going to stay here for another fifteen years. So if he's lead material, then make him lead and then let's try and roll him into full-time if we can.

Although in this case the contractor turned the offer down, just being given the offer was a clear message of respect. Stu Davis, a contractor who actually accepted such a position at Scientific Atlanta, explained its significance as a sign of acceptance:

> At Scientific Atlanta, it doesn't matter too much whether you're a contractor or a permanent employee. I mean there's a point at which it matters to the company. There's a certain reluctance to get you involved in some issues if you're a contractor, but working on a daily basis, you're as much a part of the team as full-timers. In fact, they made me a team leader. I've got a couple guys working for me. And Blake [a manager] was starting to get flak about it and he says, "Look. I trust this guy"—he's only known me for two or three weeks—he says, "I trust this guy a lot more than I trust these other two guys I'm saddled with. And I'd rather have him do the team lead role than the other two guys." So, I'm very much a part of the company. Of course, I've been there now a total of three years, but in different parts of the company.

Respect for contractors, in short, came from both managers and employees and derived, for the most part, from the contractors' ability to make technical contributions and handle themselves professionally. It also came, in some cases, from contractors' ability to use their outsider status to their clients' benefit. Contractors were particularly attuned to signals of respect that came from managers. But contractors also had to contend with signs of the second reaction to their presence: a simmering and occasionally explicit resentment.

TALES OF RESENTMENT

If respect was the yin of the contractor's experience on the job, resentment was its yang. Resentment was manifested in two kinds of complaints that contrasted contractors with permanent employees. The first, shared by managers and employees alike, focused on contractors' "lack of commitment" and the performance problems that resulted from this attitude. The second ran deeper and was usually expressed by employees rather than managers. This complaint focused on the perceived inequities between contractors and employees.

Lack of Commitment

If there was one criticism of contractors that was most frequently expressed in our informants' tales, it was the claim that contractors "lacked commitment" or were "not loyal."[1] This criticism reflected deeply ingrained and widespread beliefs about the meaning of the employment relationship. Commitment and loyalty, in this view, were the bedrock of traditional white-collar employment. As long as employees did their best and the firm remained financially sound, employers promised implicitly, and sometimes even explicitly, to provide employees with secure jobs. In return, employees were expected to offer their loyalty to the firm, even to the point of sacrificing their time and outside interests.[2]

For many white-collar workers, the firm became a primary source of identity and an object of emotional attachment. In such a world, few criticisms were more biting than for one's colleagues to say that one was undependable, disloyal, or lacked commitment. Most managers and employees we interviewed still felt it was proper to be committed and loyal to their firms, though their belief system had been strained by the realities of the new economic order. Contractors, in particular, represented a visible, daily challenge to the continued belief in an employment regime based on reciprocal trust and commitment. It is perhaps, therefore, unsurprising that fulltimers articulated a diffuse imagery of contracting that portrayed contractors, however experienced they might be, as self-interested mercenaries who, in a pinch, could not be trusted. Conversely, their commentaries portrayed full-timers as the firm's self-sacrificing, unsung heroes.

Aron Murphy put it this way:

> I don't think of contractors as being very emotionally invested in what they are doing. That's completely unappealing to me. I feel a part of this company. I don't like to say that it defines me, but it is part of who I am. I would like for this company to do well. I'm dis-

---

[1] Scholars have also predicted that contingent workers would exhibit less commitment to their work than do permanent employees. However, some research shows that contingent workers are as committed as or even more committed than full-timers (Pearce 1993; Benson 1998).

[2] *Finding Time*, Perlow's (1997) ethnography of a product development team, provides an illustration of how and why full-time employees equate working long hours with commitment and loyalty.

appointed when it doesn't. More than one contractor has said that to me: "Look, I just want to make it clear. I will do whatever you tell me. I don't need to be happy. I don't really care." Sometimes we've had philosophical conversations about the direction of the company, and the conversation with them will generally end with, "Yeah, I don't really care. I don't care how the company is doing. I'm just hired to do this piece of work and that's all I really want to worry about, and then I'm going home."

Shane Maxwell, a systems administrator at Chipco, was even more explicit:

As an employee you have stock. You don't want there to be any problems. You want the company to keep rolling, keep making money. At one point this guy, Quay, said, "I'll fix this problem," and it was something to do with printing. But it was the kind of thing that you had to check out every three or four hours and clean out some disk space. Well, he went home and neglected to tell anybody about that for a weekend. So the machine crashed. It was our main print server, we lost $40 million in a product that wasn't shipped. And so it's just a little bit of how much you care about your position because you can always leave, go to a different company. You know, go work on a different contract. So I think that's kind of what I'm trying to get out—that attitude. I think contractors are a little bit more lackadaisical, just overall. It can be in their quality of their work, the way they dress, you know, their thoroughness.

Managers and permanent employees supported their claim that contractors were, as a group, undependable and uncommitted by pointing to a constellation of sins that they felt were common among contractors. In all cases, the contractors' behaviors and attitudes were said to jeopardize the interests of the firm and cause more work for permanent employees. One widespread complaint was that contractors did "shoddy work." The essence of the complaint was not that contractors lacked skills. Instead, the issue was how contractors' attitudes shaped the way they applied their skills. Permanent employees seemed to believe that superior technical work demanded an attitude of persistence and long-term responsibility that the structure of contracting did not permit.

Permanent employees argued that because contractors had short time horizons and cared only for their own welfare, they cut corners, put in minimum effort, and sometimes even sacrificed quality. By the time any mistakes were discovered, the offending contractors were long gone and employees were left to rectify the situation. As Helena Miller, a software developer at Advanced Computers, explained, the contractors had no reason to be invested in the long term or the common good:

> They send AC employees to classes on solving problems and how to approach things, so there is a standard that we follow. Contractors don't go through these courses on development and what you need to do quality work. And so, when they approach a problem, the concept is, "Okay, I've got this project to do," and what they are expected to accomplish may not be spec'd out exactly. So they just accomplish a little bit here and there, and the term is up and they say, "Oh, we're done." And then a lot of times the full-time people say, "No it's not done, you haven't done anything." I think the AC employees tend to take it more personally. This is their piece of code and they're going to make sure that it meets the quality standards that AC has. Some of the contractors don't do that. They ask for a lot of money and we've given them a task, but they get the bare minimum done and then when they hand it back, the employee ends up fixing everything and making everything work.

It is perhaps no surprise that permanent employees, who perceived contractors as competitors, voiced such concerns. But managers also leveled similar complaints. Sally Hyncs, a project manager at Chipco, was typical. Sally felt that the contractors' mercenary work ethic sometimes created more work for full-timers, which the full-timers resented. "If you give the work to an employee," she claimed, "the quality is much better because the employee is going to be here for the long haul. But if you give it to a contractor and the contractor knows he has a three-month engagement and he's going to be gone, a lot of times he doesn't care. He doesn't care whether he follows your standards. He doesn't care how he codes the thing, because he's going to be gone. So if he codes it really badly and it's a mess, then he doesn't care because you've paid him. He doesn't have to maintain it and fix it. So that's another reason that you get a little bit of friction between employees and contractors."

Closely related to the claim that contractors' lack of commitment led to substandard work was the widespread complaint that contractors often left without finishing the job they were assigned. In such instances, either another contractor had to be hired or a permanent employee had to complete the task. Because stepping into the middle of an unfinished job often meant puzzling through what the contractor had accomplished, permanent employees argued that little time was saved by hiring the contractor in the first place. Permanent employees and managers almost always illustrated their complaints with a story of a contractor who simply failed to show up for work one day without prior notice. Vic Verma's story was particularly memorable. "One guy was in the middle of a project," Vic claimed. "We thought everything was going fine. One day his coat is over the back of his chair, his coffee is there warm and his monitor is on, but he was gone. He just left everything. He just walked out." The moral of such stories seemed to be that contractors were often so self-interested that one could not count on them to fulfill even the terms of the short-term bargains they struck.

A third observation that managers and employees used to justify the claim that contractors were insufficiently committed was that they were less willing than full-timers to shoulder additional responsibilities. Permanent employees accepted open-ended job descriptions because they were invested in the firm's well-being, because they were evaluated on their willingness to do anything asked of them, and because failing to do so brought peer pressure. Firms relied on the employees' spirit of voluntarism to cover unforeseen circumstances. Contractors, in contrast, felt bound only to perform the tasks for which they were hired. Permanent employees argued that because contractors often interpreted their duties so narrowly, they did not contribute enough to merit their presence. Even managers, like Russell Brown, argued that supervising contractors sometimes demanded too much "hand-holding" because they were insufficiently invested in the firm:

> I wasn't extraordinarily excited about the results I was seeing, mostly because I didn't feel like they were very committed to this project. They were working a good solid forty-hour week, but they were not terribly interested. You know, these are people who aren't familiar with this product, so I'd expect them to come to meetings and ask questions, to volunteer to take on responsibilities. I found that didn't happen very often. When I hire a contractor, particularly these contractors who are fairly highly paid, I expect them to be proactive in terms of finding work, finding things that need to get done. My expectations were that they should be behaving very much like a senior engineer. So part of their job is to figure out what has to get done. And so we are spending a lot of time hand-holding, you know, giving them individual assignments and walking them through how to solve the problems, and that's not the most efficient use of my time.

The complaint that contractors did not shoulder enough responsibility appeared in a variety of guises. In some cases, the complaint was that contractors did not work quickly enough. Fernando Natzel, a software developer at UNIX Hardware, explained how difficult it was to induce an experienced expert on which his team relied to adopt his anxiety about meeting deadlines:

In the New Jersey start-up there were a lot of contractors. I worked with one, a voice specialist. He was very sharp, very bright. But he would just do as little as was necessary and not work as much as we were working. In fact there was another contractor. He was like cranking out computer screens. He had a specific rate in mind, one screen every two days. And since only he knew how to do that stuff, he could pretty much do it at his own pace. He was taking his time about it and the director asked him during a meeting, "Can you do it any faster? We have this deadline coming up, we're behind." And he did not and just kept on. They have no commitment to the company, especially in a start-up.

In short, managers and employees who worked with contractors seemed to share an abiding suspicion that contractors' lack of commitment could ultimately become detrimental to the quality of their technical contribution. But this also is where the views of managers and employees diverged. After considering the disadvantages of employing contractors, managers not only decided to use them, they showed them signs of respect when they performed well and rewarded them handsomely for their services. Employees, on the other hand, saw the respect that managers accorded contractors as grounds for a second complaint: inequity.

Inequity

Complaints about inequity focused on two distinct issues that troubled permanent employees. First, employees complained about the higher wages that contractors were paid. Second, in some cases full-timers resented the opportunities for more interesting technical work that some contractors received.

INEQUITABLE PAY

Of all the complaints and discontents occasioned by the use of contractors, disgruntlement over the contractors' wages was the most commonly voiced. In the world of permanent employment, higher wages have long signaled seniority, greater skill, or greater authority. The association between money and merit lies at the heart of the incentive system that employers have used for decades to motivate employees. In fact, the system has become part of our culture, part of the unwritten psychological contract that we expect employers to honor, an expectation that is particularly strong among white-collar and professional employees. Workers rarely openly resent another person's salary, as long as it seems commensurate with their service, status, or contributions. The problem was that contractors generally had less seniority in the firm than all but the most recently hired employees. Many had no more expertise than the full-timers with whom they worked, and most had no formal authority. By all rights, employees reasoned, contractors should have been paid the same as, and perhaps even less than, permanent employees with similar skills. Yet, managers knew, and permanent employees believed, that contractors were paid significantly more than full-timers. Many managers and all permanent employees felt that this disparity was not justified.[3]

Contractors naturally tried to keep their hourly rates secret, but word inevitably got around. When permanent employees discovered what contractors made, they felt cheated. When given the opportunity to speak, permanent employees voiced outrage at what they saw as a violation of the moral order. A Java programmer at UNIX Hardware told us, "I find it deeply troubling that companies even bring in contractors. They pay them double what we get." Shane Maxwell, a young systems administrator at Chipco, struggled to reestablish the link between pay and merit, but failed to convince himself:

> You always have to pay your dues and show people what you can do and earn respect. But when you can't do the things that you said you could do and you're getting a huge amount of money, a lot more than people who have been here for a while, that creates problems. The person I'm thinking about, not to name names, makes two and a half times what I make and I do two and a half times the work. I can justify it as: I'm young, I've got a year of experience and I've got a lot to learn, and I'm making more money than I ever have before in my life. But it just makes me kind of want to strangle that person because they're just taking up space.

Contractors were well aware that permanent employees resented their wages. Almost every contractor we interviewed told us that wage inequity was an often unspoken point of tension between contractors and full-timers. Roger Garley, a CORBA programmer, remarked:

> I have seen some management types treat contractors as subservient kinds of people. And that's just part of the deal. I think there is some resentment. You know, you've worked in the business for ten years

---

[3] Managers, too, often found the contractors' wages too high for their standards of fairness. These perceptions found expression during the deal-making process. However, because managers were the ones who decided to hire contractors and because they negotiated these wages, they could hardly be expected to complain openly once the contractors had been hired. The wage differentials, however, did make managers more resentful in cases where they felt they were not getting their money's worth.

and here comes this guy off the street who is highly skilled but knows nothing in terms of the business. And so if you're a permanent employee, you tend to wrap your self-worth around your position, your salary, because you're always competing against people. You're always comparing yourself against this other person, how am I doing against him, as you're climbing the corporate ladder. And here comes this guy off the street, and you realize he's on a different ladder. He's way above you for whatever reason. You know it comes down to dollars, stuff like that.

Some contractors even went out of their way to disguise the fact that they were doing well financially. "One thing I learned at Honda," explained Olivia Crum, "was you shouldn't flaunt your wealth. At one point I was driving a Beamer and that created too much envy. So, I went out and bought a Jeep. They were disappointed because they wanted me to buy a Honda, but I didn't like any Hondas. The attitude changed when I drove just a regular car. Since that time, I don't flash my income. And most of the [contractors] that I've met have experienced the same thing. So, you always have more than one car—the car you drive to work and the other car."

Hiring managers also spoke of the troubles wage inequities created for their permanent employees. In fact, jealousies over wages were the most frequent problem that managers cited when asked about the challenges of managing project teams composed of contractors and permanent employees. Nancy Cato, like other managers we interviewed, admitted that permanent employees had left the firm over the issue. The story she recounted mirrored that of every other hiring manager with whom we spoke. When confronted by an employee disgruntled over discrepancies in pay, the manager's only recourse was to point out that contractors paid their own benefits, had less job security, and didn't enjoy the perquisites of membership. If the employee remained unconvinced, the managers could say little else except to suggest that the employee try contracting for himself.

INEQUITABLE OPPORTUNITIES

Although discrepancy in pay was the most frequently mentioned bone of contention, it was not the only inequity that permanent employees resented. Full-time technical employees also disliked the fact that contractors were often hired to do technically more challenging and exciting tasks. Permanent employees felt in such cases that the technical challenges should be theirs, and that contractors, if used at all, should be assigned more routine jobs. They believed that assigning "sexy" work to contractors was an indication that their managers did not believe they were sufficiently skilled. On this point, contractors, like Bruce Wise, were often sympathetic. "Sometimes you will find that permanent employees kind of resent contractors to some degree," Bruce confided. "They see contractors as interlopers. They see them as people who are doing work that they could do, but are not allowed to because management does not have confidence that they could accomplish this, so they get someone from the outside. And to some extent, that is probably true."

Hiring managers recognized that assigning contractors to challenging work was a disincentive and some argued that doing so was a mistake, even if experienced contractors might be able to do the work more quickly. As Neva Boyd explained, a move was afoot at Chipco among lower-level managers to change the policy, but the change had not yet been carried out. "I know that this is a problem right now," Neva confessed. "We have a lot of contractors in-house. The contractors get the sexy, sizzling project work. The full-time employees get the mundane work and they're not happy about it. So what I want to do is shift that, so that I'm bringing in contractors to do more of the mundane, tedious work and then have the full-time staff doing much more of that interesting, cutting-edge type of work."

THE ROOTS OF RESENTMENT

Although resentful managers and employees spoke about everyday affronts, the roots of their resentment seemed to run deeper. The differences between contractors and permanent employees that we have reported were only the tip of an iceberg of change that threatened the institutions of permanent employment. Every manager and technical employee we interviewed was well aware that employment was far less secure than it was a decade earlier. Downsizings and layoffs were commonplace, even among engineers in the Silicon Valley at the height of the technical boom. The presence of contractors was a daily reminder of just how tenuous permanent employment had become and how little employers actually seemed to value their permanent employees' loyalty or the sacrifices they made for the firm's well-being. Although paying contractors more than full-timers was a grievance, the affront was more substantial.

Ironically, contractors were more articulate about the nature of the affront than were permanent employees, perhaps because so many had left permanent employment as a result of their dissatisfaction with the way employers had treated them. Contractors believed that they symbolized the disintegration of traditional employment and that their presence in the workplace posed an implicit threat to the permanent employees' sense of security. Glenn Arthur said:

Oh, employees are resentful. You've heard that one before. Employees are resentful because contractors make a lot of money, have more autonomy, make them feel bad about their own situation. Very seldom is the relationship with an employee not tainted by your status as a contractor. It works out okay with managers, but with peers and associates, there's always a specter. If you're in a place for a long time it starts to fade and they start to see you as their own, but it never advances all the way with most folks. Corporate employees would say: "Oh, you're threatening my job" and it's like, "I am?" It's like, "Well, yeah. They are experimenting with outsourcing my role here. You're here to take away my security. You're essentially the Judas. You're being paid more money than I am to be the experiment for the company to figure out whether or not I'm expendable."

Permanent employees and hiring managers never explicitly drew the connection between the use of contractors and the dismantling of the traditional employment relationship. To do so would have required them to blame their employers, which, for one reason or another, few were willing to do. Nevertheless, at some level, permanent employees understood the broad implications of the contractors' presence and found ways to express their resentment.

EXPRESSIONS OF RESENTMENT

Contractors reported that employees made their feelings known in subtle ways, typically by either ignoring the contractor or by making jokes that revealed underlying tensions. Roger Garley recounted how resentment was expressed at the Advanced Computers site where he worked. "It's not made really clear," Roger replied when asked how employees expressed resentment and jealousy. "There's been joking. You know, 'You make more money than I make, and you're not working as hard as I'm working.' And I say, 'Well yeah, but I could be gone tomorrow and you won't be.' They go off and say, 'I don't like your haircut and good-bye.' It doesn't bother me really all that much. I just know that when I walk in here, I feel like I'm a guest in somebody's house. There are certain things you don't do as a guest. I'm a long-term guest."

Occasionally, however, resentment led employees to behave in ways that intentionally complicated the contractor's job. Asaf Weiss explained how full-timers could make a contractor's life difficult:

On this particular contract, we seem to have a hard time getting information from them, information regarding the system that we're supposed to be testing. We need to have input criteria so that we can test the application. Well, the person I'm supposed to be talking to is not accessible. We're not allowed to talk to them directly. We have to set up scheduled meetings and it can become tedious. It can be very difficult for you to actually perform the job you were hired to do. To some degree they feel like, "Well, you know, these guys are getting at least twenty bucks more than I make an hour. They're doing the same crap. Why should I help them? You do it; you figure it out." A lot of times there seems to be a front put up. It's not that obvious, but when you go to get the information it's not there. So, we're like, "How do we get this information?" "Well, let's see; let me talk to so-and-so, and let me find out what they know and see if we can get it for you." Meantime you've lost a day. Yeah, you're getting paid for that day, but you're running up against a time line here.

In some cases, resentment, and the resistance it spawned, actually erupted in open hostility. David Roberts recounted,

When I worked at HP last year, [I was part of] an integration group, so it all came down through us. There was a guy that I worked with, he was nice to me the first month. I was working through Volt [a staffing firm] at the time. I told them to take me off of per diem because I had moved there after a month. So they said, "Okay, we'll send you a new contract." What do they do? They faxed it to HP! All this stuff is supposed to be real confidential, the rates you're making. So who picks up the thing off the fax machine but the guy that's sitting across from me. So from that point on, he literally won't talk to me. I had to go to the boss and ask him, "Can you please get this guy to talk to me?" So it turns out [the guy gives me] a fifteen-minute slot in the morning and a fifteen-minute slot in the afternoon. I was talking with him every day up to this point. The animosity starts when they see the differential in pay.

FORMING AN IDENTITY

Contractors' experience of life on the job consisted of a never-ending series of mixed messages. On one hand, clients needed their expertise and respected, even sometimes celebrated, their contributions. On the other hand, their presence, regardless of their performance, inevitably engendered suspicion, envy, and resentment. These conflicting messages created a kind of catch-22, a "damned if you do and damned if you don't" situation, that contractors found difficult to resolve. If contractors took responsibility and initiative, then full-timers who worried about job security perceived them as a threat and an object of envy. If they worked by the book, they were condemned for lack of commitment and shoddy work. Contractors sensed this double bind and responded in a variety of ways.[4]

All learned to think of themselves as outsiders; what varied was how they made sense of their experience. Younger and inexperienced contractors usually felt the pain of estrangement. Many wanted to be accepted as legitimate members of the community to which they were temporarily attached and saw the limits placed on their membership as a form of rejection. "I felt like an illegal alien," Brian Pusher confided as he told us about his first contract. "Novidigm, where I had worked before becoming a contractor, was a very small company, less than two hundred employees when I left. Everyone knew everyone else. There was little politics in the organization. I moved from there to here. The work space they gave me was a dump, and the computer was older than everybody else's because I wasn't an employee. Basically, I was given a task and left alone to fend for myself." The experience was so unpleasant that Brian soon took a permanent job to regain a sense of belonging.

Those who remained contractors eventually learned other ways of viewing and managing their status. Adaptation required contractors to resolve three issues. First, contractors had to decide how they would approach their work in an environment where they could never truly become a member. Some chose to take initiative and go beyond the letter of their contract at whatever cost. They adopted the distanced, impartial stance of an expert, ignored the organizational politics, and championed, without compromise, a technical perspective on their work. These contractors understood and accepted that such a stance might ultimately threaten employees, especially when it enhanced their status in the eyes of management. They also understood that taking a strong technical stance could sometimes threaten managers, thereby risking dismissal. The strategy's payoff was that they were more likely to be perceived as competent practitioners and sometimes even "gurus."

Other contractors chose to work by the book. They stuck to the terms of their contract and focused on the specifics of the task they were asked to perform. Regardless of the quality of their performance, contractors who took this stance risked being viewed and condemned as mercenaries. Full-timers often ignored their presence, viewed them as servants, and sometimes used them as scapegoats. Many contractors took a middle position between these extremes depending on the exigencies of the situation, the specifics of the task, and their own preferences and skills.

Whichever stance they took, their outsider status forced contractors to

---

[4] See Kunda and Van Maanen (1999) for an application of Hochschild's (1983) useful notion of emotional labor to the analysis of the impact of a market rather than an organizational orientation on the way professional workers manage their emotions at work.

resolve a second issue: how to present themselves and their work to managers and employees. Some contractors did not care what others thought and staked their reputations entirely on their technical accomplishments. They accepted that when their work was done they would simply move on, possessing both a fatter wallet and more experience, which they hoped to use in landing their next contract. Many contractors recognized, however, that it was to their benefit to build relationships that would allow them to navigate between respect and resentment. Their agenda was simple: they wanted to shape the way managers and employees perceived their contributions.

Contractors did this by sending messages that assured managers and employees that they were the type of person who would work diligently in the client's best interest. For example, several informants told us that the first several weeks of a contract were crucial for framing the client's perceptions. These contractors made a point of initially working longer hours than the contract required and making those hours visible for all to see. They also agreed to participate in meetings that they could easily have avoided and refused to charge the client for the time. In doing so they made a calculated gift, which, at least implicitly, elicited obligations. Once expectations were set, these contractors returned to more normal hours. Other informants reported that they made a point of constantly updating managers on the status of their work until the manager indicated that it was no longer necessary. Contractors also knew that they could curry favor with employees by willingly sharing what they knew, by helping employees anticipate and resolve problems, and by socializing with employees after hours. Ironically, contractors who had chosen contracting, in part, to remove themselves from corporate gamesmanship found themselves back in the impression management business. This, too, they came to regard as part of their occupational expertise.

The third and perhaps most fundamental issue that contractors had to resolve in the process of coming to terms with their outsider status was developing a coherent identity that could account for their experience and guide their actions. The terms that contractors used as they struggled to describe their roles provided clues to the identities they constructed for themselves. These ranged from "guest," "resident alien," and "hired gun" to "troubleshooter," "analyst," "problem solver," and "consultant." Although these terms differed in their various connotations, all pointed to the elements of an identity that was widely shared among our informants, an identity that turned their outsider status and social distance into a professional tool. The imagery of the coolly detached expert created a buffer that allowed contractors to disassociate their sense of self-worth from the cues they received from clients. In fact, by coming to view themselves as detached specialists, contractors were often able to even empathize with and feel superior to the full-timers. They could see that their presence in the workplace violated the promise of traditional employment on which full-timers based their security and sense of worth, and reasoned that one could hardly blame employees for being resentful.

Unlike full-timers doing similar work, contractors learned to disassociate their definition of self from the immediate context of their technical practice. Instead, they came to orient themselves to the larger world of contracting and to reference groups that lay beyond the boundaries of the firms for which they worked. They became, in their own eyes, itinerant experts whose expertise consisted not only of their technical skills but also of their ability to construct honorable and meaningful careers by moving between clients. To sustain the identity of an itinerant expert, contractors had to learn to manage the demands of the contract cycle. This meant learning new ways to manage the resources upon which they constructed their professional identity. It is to the management of these resources that we turn in the final section of the book.

PART IV

Living the Cycle

THE DECISION TO become a contractor and the rhetoric surrounding the lifestyle was often tinged with romanticism. As we saw in chapter 1, this was particularly true in the new media where free agency was heralded as an antidote to the shackles of corporate life and a prescription for individual freedom. Although our informants were hardly revolutionaries, by choosing to contract most set out, like Poor Richard, with the hope of finding the American Dream. They sought not only a fair market value for their skills, but also, as they repeatedly told us, the rewards of autonomy and self-reliance. They longed to escape the oppressive and sometime irrational social demands of the workplace and to wrest control of their time from greedy institutions. They hoped to make their way in the world of technical work by relying on their own wits and resources. To accomplish this, like all professionals, they had at their disposal three types of capital: their time, their skills, and their network of professional relationships.

But once contractors began to treat their time, their skills, and their relationships as capital, the consequences proved less romantic than they initially imagined. As they encountered the realities of the market and the workplace and accepted itinerancy as a permanent condition, they discovered the necessity of adopting a stance toward temporal, human, and social capital that differed considerably from that of professionals practicing in an organizational context. As one of our informants summed up the situation, it was "a whole new ball game."

Learning to survive the contract cycle taught contractors three important lessons. First, more often than not, the distance between having flexibility and enjoying it was vast. Not only was taking time off from work costly, but being free to allocate one's time as one saw fit did not necessarily mean more leisure. Second, like a prize-winning garden, expertise required continual cultivation if clients were going to pay for it. In fact, cultivating human capital was more costly, more risky, and more time consuming than most contractors had appreciated when they were still employees. Finally, contractors discovered that temporal and human capital were not worth much without social capital, the network of relationships that allowed contractors to repeatedly and reliably find work. As a consequence, contractors found themselves embedded in a network of mutual obligations that had all the characteristics of a social system. Apparently, even in the land of individualism, independence required interdependence.

Part 4 explores each of these lessons in depth. Chapter 10 looks at how contractors came to define and evaluate their temporal capital and then allocate it between the various activities that a contracting lifestyle necessitated. Chapter 11 examines what it meant for contractors to take responsibility for their human capital. At issue are how contractors decided which skills were important, how they acquired them, and how they kept them up-to-date. Chapter 12 focuses on social capital. It examines how contractors thought about, constructed, and managed their social networks; how they used their networks to find work; and the significance of these networks for the labor market. Together these chapters offer an in-depth, behind-the-scenes view of what it actually takes to be an itinerant expert, while highlighting the distance between the lives contractors anticipated prior to entering the market and the lives they came to lead.

Chapter 10

TEMPORAL CAPITAL

SINCE THE DAWN of the industrial era, employers and employees have struggled over who shall control how much of a worker's time.[1] Industrialization separated the workplace from the home for the first time in history. The spatial distinction, in turn, created a temporal trade-off between work and the rest of life: hours spent at work were hours not spent at home or play, and vice versa. Sharp boundaries between work and life were drawn first by ringing a bell or sounding a whistle, and later by punching a "time clock." During the nineteenth and early twentieth centuries, management and labor fought sometimes bloody battles, initially over the notion of timed labor itself and then over the length of the workday. By the end of World War II, Americans had institutionalized a temporal détente, of sorts, in both law and accepted practice. For the majority of Americans this meant an eight-hour day, a forty-hour week, and payment for overtime unless the employee was exempt from the Fair Labor Standards Act.[2] Managers and professionals, however, worked much longer hours, not only because they were exempt, but also supposedly because they were "committed professionals," they derived intrinsic satisfaction from their work, and employers granted them greater job security than they granted hourly workers. In addition, the gendered division of labor helped preserve a sense of work-life balance, especially among the middle class. This détente in the battle over time was, however, short-lived.

Sometime during the 1970s middle-class Americans awoke to the idea that they were "overworked" and began to rally around the banner of "flexibility" in search of more control over their time. By then, enough middle-class women had entered the workforce to raise concerns over dual-career families.[3] Men and women in such families found it

---

[1] E. P. Thompson's essay, "Time, Work Discipline, and Industrial Capitalism" (1967), offers an analysis of how industrialization shifted Western culture's notions of time from what he called "task orientation" to "timed labor." Roediger (1989) discusses labor's battles for control over the time that workers owed employers.

[2] For details of the National Labor Relations Act, the Fair Labor Standards Act, and the subsequent transformation in U.S. labor relations, see Gold (1998) and Kochan, Katz, and McKersie (1986).

[3] Research on the temporal demands of full-time employment exploded during the 1980s and 1990s, especially after the publication of Juliet Schor's *The Overworked Amer-*

exceptionally difficult to raise children when both spouses worked forty hours or more a week.[4]

Over the next twenty-five years flexibility escalated into a social and political issue with the call for programs and policies that would make it easier for dual-career couples and single parents to take care of family needs. In response, employers gradually adopted a variety of programs designed to provide employees with options for controlling their work time. These included allowing workers to telecommute, take personal leave, and vary the start and end of their workday. The latter was often called flextime.[5] In 1993 Congress passed the Family and Medical Leave Act, which formally granted American workers the right to take twelve weeks of unpaid leave per year for family and medical emergencies.

Despite the spread of flexibility programs, evidence suggests that few people actually use them. For example, flextime is more common than any other flexibility program. Although a significant majority of all employers (between 60 and 80 percent) report offering the benefit, most recent surveys suggest that little more than a quarter of all eligible employees take advantage of it.[6] The utilization of other flexibility programs is even lower. For instance, recent studies indicate that no more than 6 percent or 7 percent of working Americans telecommute and that less than 0.25 percent of the workforce telecommute full-time.[7]

In short, even under the best of circumstances, permanent employment offers a very limited sort of temporal flexibility. Although many employers allow employees to vary their arrival and departure time and take time off during the course of a day for personal business, most companies still expect employees to work forty or more hours a week. In fact, national data show that Americans report working more hours today

---

ican: The Unexpected Decline of Leisure (1991). The general consensus is that normative and cultural pressures have played a significant role in creating the time famine. Readers interested in the temporal demands of the workplace should see Perrin (1991), Bailyn (1993), Perlow (1997), Hochschild (1989, 1997), and Kunda (1992). Robinson and Godbey (1997) offer an important dissenting view on the thesis of the overworked American.

[4] Historically, women from blue-collar families were more likely to work than women from the middle and upper classes. Although these women undoubtedly struggled to balance work and family, work-family issues did not become a topic for social and political debate until affluent women entered the workforce in large numbers.

[5] On the growth of flexibility programs, see Osterman (1995), McShulskis (1997), Greenwald (1998), and Galinsky and Bond (1998).

[6] McShulskis (1997), Greenwald (1998), and Galinsky and Bond (1998) report data on the percentage of employers offering flextime programs. For data on usage rates of flexibility programs, see Galinsky, Bond, and Friedman (1993), Bond, Galinsky, and Swanberg (1998), Mead et al. (2000), Eaton (2000), Blair-Loy and Wharton (2002), and Golden (2001).

[7] For data on telecommuting, see U.S. Department of Transportation (1993), O'Mahony and Barley (1999), and Mead et al. (2000).

than they did several decades ago.[8] Technical work is especially notorious for demanding long and often unreasonable hours.[9] Thus, contracting seemed to promise technical professionals an opportunity finally to escape temporal tyranny.

THE TEMPORAL PATTERNS OF CONTRACTING

As we saw in chapter 1, the rhetoric of contracting, particularly that of free agency, extols the flexibility and freedom of the contracting lifestyle.[10] On the pages of *Wired* and other popular magazines, contractors are depicted as entrepreneurs who reclaim a portion of their surplus value by directly marketing their skills to employers. Liberated from organizations, contractors can bargain with employers to create the kind of work-life balance they desire. Many articles feature vignettes of contractors who live in exotic locales and work remotely, thereby blending work and everyday life, and once the contract is over, they are free to take well-deserved vacations. The abiding message is that contracting breaks down the artificial separation between work and home and liberates workers from the temporal shackles forged in the industrial era.

At first glance, our informants seemed to concur. Although temporal flexibility was not one of our informants' primary reasons for becoming contractors (they were more likely to seek income and freedom from corporate politics), many claimed they enjoyed more control of their time than they did when they were permanent employees. Over a third (39 percent) told us that flexibility was a significant, but not always anticipated, benefit of contracting.

When talking about flexibility, contractors invariably began by

---

[8] Surveys that ask respondents to estimate the number of hours they work each week consistently show that hours of work have increased (see Schor 1991; Rones, Ilg, and Gardner 1997; Jacobs 1998). However, work diary data tell a different story. Robinson and Godbey's (1997) sophisticated diary studies show that hours spent at work have actually fallen since the 1960s, but that the choppiness of people's workdays has increased (as have hours spent watching TV). Time researchers have yet to conclusively explain why the two methods yield such different results. One account suggests that intermingling family and work duties increases the choppiness of a day and leads people to overestimate the hours they spend at work. Another explanation points to the fact that people are actually spending more time at the workplace even though they may spend part of the day doing other things.

[9] Kidder (1981), Kunda (1992), and Perlow (1997) depict the temporal demands placed on engineers and other technical professionals. In addition to normative pressures felt by workers in other occupations, "gutting it out" is often seen as heroic action in technical cultures.

[10] See Beck (1992), Bridges (1994), Caulkin (1997), Darby (1997), and Pink (1998).

painting a picture of permanent employment as temporal slavery. They assured us that employers tried to extract as much work as possible for the salaries they paid and that as a permanent employee one had little choice but to acquiesce. People who resisted management's greedy demands for their time were passed over for raises, bonuses, and promotions, or worse yet, became fodder for the next downsizing. Never one to mince words, Harry Stevens put it succinctly: "They own your ass!" Roger Garley, a programmer who was contracting at the time for AC, a firm celebrated for its employee-centered culture, explained what it meant to "be owned": "They dump a lot of work on their permanent staff," he told us. "Some of the people on this team are juggling two, three projects, and a lot of them are working a lot of overtime. They're really grinding it out. They're working late and working weekends. You see burnout in some of those people." Bill Smith recounted similar stories of his experience at Motorola: "People actually went in on Fourth of July—the actual Fourth of July! They signed in so people could see they signed in."

Contractors insisted that vacations were a casualty of permanent employment as well. Brenda O'Boyle, who had recently returned to permanent employment after working as a contractor for over a decade, remarked, "What has changed for me is that as a contractor if I decided I wanted to take a month off that would not have been a problem. Now, there is a certain lack of freedom. My husband wants me to take a month off to go on a trip with him. I can't ask for a month off. They would laugh in my face! He is so used to me being a contractor he is like, 'Well why not?' Well, I have to be there, because now I have to accrue my hours of vacation time."

Contractors assured us that they experienced time differently. Unlike "perms," who were confined to one organization and who had no choice but to toe management's temporal line, contractors' lives flowed with the contract cycle. The cycle, our informants claimed, allowed two kinds of "flexibility" unavailable to permanent employees. First, cyclical encounters with the labor market opened the possibility of claiming long stretches of time between contracts for oneself. Contractors who so desired could control the rhythm of their work by spacing their contracts to create time for taking vacations and following avocations. Second, contracting allowed contractors to choose which hours of the day and which days of the week to dedicate to work even when they were on contract.

In short, the contractors' experience of time had a coarse and a fine grain. The contract cycle's coarse grain offered control over the time between contracts, while its fine grain allowed contractors to allocate their time during the course of the contract. Contractors believed that together, contracting's coarse and fine grain afforded them more flexibility than permanent employees enjoyed. But, as T. S. Eliot warned, "Between the idea / And the reality . . . / Falls the Shadow."[11]

The Coarse Grain

Permanent employment, in many ways, shields people from encounters with the labor market. Although an employee may eventually need to find a new employer, looking for work has little bearing on the calculus by which most employees reckon time. In sharp contrast, having to enter the labor market repeatedly to secure new assignments defined the very essence of contracting. It should, therefore, come as no surprise that within these cycles contractors parsed time into periods of employment and unemployment. They did not, however, use these terms to talk about their experience. Instead, they talked about "being on contract" or "having downtime."

"Being on contract" referred to periods when one or more clients compensated the contractor for work. "Downtime"—also called "beach time," "bench time," or "dead time"—referred to the periods between contracts. What distinguished downtime from unemployment was that contractors understood and accepted downtime as inherent to contracting. Most expected to incur downtime sooner or later. As the connotative distinction between "beach" and "bench time" suggests, contractors sometimes viewed downtime as a luxury, a time for pleasure and relaxation, for going to the "beach." At other times, they saw downtime as the equivalent of sitting on the "bench" out of play, waiting to return to the game. Furthermore, downtime did not necessarily mean a period without work. Many contractors strategically used downtime to learn new skills and expand their professional network. The cyclical rhythm of being on contract and having downtime, as well as the contractor's sense of control over both, varied considerably and underwrote his or her perceptions of flexibility.[12]

The contracts our informants signed were written for periods ranging from three to nine months, but contractors recognized that they were often being hired for the length of a project whose completion was almost impossible to predict. Under most circumstances employers renewed contracts until the project was completed or until the contract

[11] T. S. Eliot, "The Hollow Men."

[12] The cyclicality of contracting bears a structural resemblance to the seasonal rhythm of preindustrial work. But while contracting breaks down the linear view of time associated with industrial employment, it differs significantly from a temporality based on diurnal cycles. Specifically, the periodicity of contracting's cycles has considerably greater variance than natural cycles whose recurrence can be predicted in advance.

could no longer be legally renewed.[13] Our data suggest that the average engagement lasted seven months.[14] Variation was determined, in part, by occupation and skill. For example, technical writers and Web page designers tended to have shorter contracts than software developers or system administrators.[15]

Nevertheless, even with extensions, all contracts eventually came to an end. At this point, the contractor faced the possibility of downtime. Every informant we interviewed spoke of downtime as an inherent risk of contracting. A few told us that they found the possibility of downtime stressful, if not downright frightening. These tended to be individuals who were new to contracting, who worried about the economic security of their family, or whose spouses were uncomfortable with the risks of contracting. One was Anna Kapoor, who had recently come to the United States from India to be with her husband. We asked Anna where she "saw herself in a couple of years." She replied: "Two years down the road is too far. I am still thinking, 'Do I have a contract next month?' I stress a lot over whether I will have a job after this. I mean, it is okay to say that the market is good and there is no need to worry. But you do."

Steve Louthan, who had experienced several months of downtime that coincided with his wife being laid off from her job, also worried about downtime. Earlier in his career he had been laid off from a permanent job and was out of work for several months. At the time we interviewed him, he was considering returning to full-time employment because he feared what might happen to his family if he had difficulty maintaining a steady stream of work. As he put it, "Say something turns bad and my contract at Cisco is terminated, so what happens? I have my $860 a month mortgage, my $300 a month car payment, my $300 a month food bill, I don't know what else, you know, utilities, electric, gas, water." Steve ultimately did return to full-time employment.

Most contractors, however, took downtime for granted. While they never scoffed at its possibility, they spoke as if it was a normal event. These contractors were able to normalize downtime because experience

---

[13] Incorporated contractors could renew their contracts indefinitely. However, contractors who worked as employees of staffing agencies faced an eighteen-month limit on contract length, set largely in response to Internal Revenue Service regulations.

[14] We calculated this figure by asking our informants how long they held each contract and by averaging the results. The modal contract was cut for three months and was subject to renewal.

[15] The work of a technical writer could be accurately estimated, and the work of a Web designer was self-contained. In contrast, the work of a software developer interfaced with the work of others and was often subject to change. Because systems administrators were hired to maintain infrastructures, the longer they worked for a client, the more knowledge they acquired and the more indispensable they became.

had taught them that it was rare and that if it occurred, they could generally weather the storm. Julian Stoke was one of those who had come to terms with the possibility of downtime:

> I used to get really nervous. The six months' hiatus [that he once experienced] was really hard on my psyche. I would go into any contract or any job—I had some permanent jobs after that—with fear and trembling. Anytime the boss would say, "Hi," I was afraid I was about to get fired. I still have a tiny bit of that. Since then I have never had more than a two-week gap. I have learned that I can make it. If something happens and there is a larger gap, I know that I will make it work out somehow and second of all, it generally won't be that long.

Some contractors with substantial experience even treated the possibility of downtime cavalierly, characterizing the process of finding a new job as trivial. "Around here," said Jose Martinez of life in the Silicon Valley, "if you have seven years' experience, you can work literally all the time. You can literally finish a contract at noon and start the next one an hour later. Eat lunch and then go to your next one." Most of the contractors we interviewed expected periods of downtime to last no more than a few weeks, and their experience generally supported this stance. Table 10.1 documents the longest duration of unwanted downtime reported by our informants. Roughly a third had experienced no downtime of any duration since becoming contractors. The longest period of unwanted downtime for another quarter of our informants was less than two months.[16]

Nevertheless, downtime was always a possibility, and its negative consequences were always a realistic threat. Consequently, contractors took active steps to protect themselves. Our informants had four general responses to downtime: they sought to endure it, minimize it, schedule it, or embrace it as an unanticipated gift.

---

[16] No data were available for a third of the contractors we interviewed. But this third consisted primarily of individuals who had been contractors for a short period of time, of highly skilled independent consultants, and of contractors who explicitly told us that they used downtime to pursue hobbies and vacations. If one assumes that unwanted downtime was not salient enough for this group of informants to have mentioned it explicitly, then one is left with the conclusion that at least among the contractors we interviewed, unwanted downtime was rare and of relatively short duration. One might argue that downtime lacked salience for many of our informants because we interviewed them at the height of the economic boom of the late 1990s when jobs were plentiful and labor was scarce. Under such conditions, contractors could afford to take a cavalier attitude toward downtime. We suspect that the economy did play a role, especially among younger contractors who had never known bad times. But we also suspect that the contractors' orientation to downtime reflected the fact that many had learned to control downtime, especially those who had been successful contractors for a number of years.

TABLE 10.1
Longest Duration of Unwanted Downtime Reported by Contractors

Longest Duration of Downtime	Number of Contractors	Percentage of Informants
None	22	31.0
Less than a month	9	12.5
1–2 months	9	12.5
3–4 months	6	8.0
5–8 months	3	3.0
Not reported	22	31.0

ENDURING DOWNTIME

If contractors were wary of downtime, it was because it posed a practical problem: how to continue to meet expenses despite a disruption in income. Because contractors framed downtime as a period of negative cash flow, they argued that you could take away its sting if you could cover or reduce your expenses while on the bench. The most common strategy for weathering downtime was to maintain a cash reserve.[17] As Bill Smith put it, when asked to contrast the difference between being a contractor and a full-time employee, "You want my own personal feeling? The difference between being on contract and permanent is the amount of money I have in my savings account." Like Bill, many contractors spoke about the importance of having a savings account earmarked explicitly for when you were on the bench. These funds went by a number of names ranging from "backup money," "a cushion," "a nest," to "fuck you money," which implied the freedom to walk away from a contract gone sour. In general, our informants believed that a stash equivalent to three to six months of income was sufficient.

A second tactic for enduring downtime was to manage expenses carefully. Some contractors told us they tried to avoid debts that they couldn't afford to service without working. These informants saved for major purchases, such as cars and appliances, which they paid in cash to avoid taking out loans. Others, like Olivia Crum, spoke of the importance of resisting the temptation to spend money indiscriminately during periods of downtime even if it seemed like the money was available. Olivia described what happened during her one significant period of downtime: "I went through my savings. A lot of the extra income that I

---

[17] Unlike full-time employees who have been laid off, contractors do not qualify for unemployment.

had earned from being a consultant was quickly dribbled up because I hadn't had a vacation in years. So, you know, you take a vacation. You come back and you fix up the house. You do all these things. Then after a couple of months, you look at your bank account and you say, 'What have I done?' But that was a learning experience that I wouldn't repeat." Asked how she thought things were different, she replied, "I sock more money away and plan my major purchases better."

Although less common than setting aside money and controlling purchases, some contractors resorted to playing what Steve Louthan called "money games" with creditors or the IRS to reduce their financial bur dens during downtime:

> Well, you play money games, you know. You try to save as much as you can, obviously. But with all those bills, I wasn't capable of saving enough. So, you do things like call the credit cards and say, "Hey look, I can't afford to give you more than 15 percent." "I'm sorry, sir, we can't accept less than 30." I said, "Well, then sue me. Sue me, okay?" "Sir, we'll have to take you to court." "Okay, fine, I'll declare bankruptcy, and then you can eat your interest rate and the debt." They reconsider. They say, "Okay, 15 percent will be fine" [*laughs*]. And you structure your W-4 form with nine allowances. The IRS will allow you nine allowances without having to explain them. As a contractor you make sure that you've saved everything that you can possibly save for a tax deduction, because you're going to need it. You will owe a lot in taxes at the end of the year. But that's easier to get through than it is to get through six months when both you and your wife are unemployed.

From the contractor's perspective, being able to endure downtime without hardship was crucial, but it was a second line of defense. Minimizing downtime was preferable.

MINIMIZING DOWNTIME

Many informants reported that they began searching for a new job as soon as the current contract began to wind down. Usually they could anticipate the end of a contract by the terms of the contract itself or by the amount of work that was left to do. Experienced contractors pointed to more subtle social cues that allowed them to anticipate even unscheduled termination. Peyton Nugen, a systems administrator, explained what to look for: "Then one day, there's nothing for you to do. You can feel it coming. At one point the manager is around all the time and is really excited. Then the manager just kind of ignores you. Then you know that you have a couple of weeks left. That's when you know they will fire you. Things start slowing down first, although I usually end before they end."

Informants argued that if they began searching for a new contract two to three weeks before the end of their current contract, they could almost always secure another contract in time to avoid downtime. To increase the odds of finding work in such a short period of time, informants employed a number of tactics. One was to work more or less exclusively with a staffing firm that was committed to keeping its contractors employed. A completely different tactic was to play one agency off the other, especially if one's current agency refused to line up a new job until it was clear that the client would not renew. Mike Rudolph, a systems administrator, described the tactic: "What I've encountered is that when I'm nearing the end of a job, the headhunters want me to stay until the end of the job. Of course, what that means is that I'll be sitting for a couple of weeks without a paycheck. So I have been forced in most cases to switch to a different headhunter at the end of one particular job so that I can get another lined up before I'm just sitting around for a couple of weeks."

Other contractors employed their personal and professional networks to generate opportunities. Still others made use of the Internet, knowing that staffing firms routinely trolled online job listings in search of possible candidates for openings they were trying to fill. This tactic worked particularly well when contractors had skills that were in very high demand, such as the ability to write COBOL during the Y2K scare.

A final tactic for minimizing downtime was to work several contracts simultaneously. Brian Willingham reported having six contracts in play at once. Typically, contractors who held multiple concurrent contracts were software developers and technical writers who worked a significant number of hours from home. These individuals staggered their contracts' end times so that they were never without compensation.

Although no informant explicitly gave a name to the period of time at the end of a contract when they began to search for the next, a useful name for this period might be *bridge time*. With this concept we can outline how contractors who sought to minimize downtime understood the coarse grain of contracting's temporal structure. Minimizers saw downtime as a problem instead of an opportunity. Their objective was to incur no downtime involuntarily. They used bridge time to unite two periods of contract time so that they could, in essence, skip over downtime and ensure continued employment.

SCHEDULING DOWNTIME

A third and less common approach to controlling downtime was to schedule it and use it for one's own purposes. A handful of contractors planned downtime when they wanted to devote a continuous block of time to learning a new technology or skill. They might use this time for taking formal courses or for studying on their own. Others planned downtime as a way of pursuing an avocation. For instance, Bruce Wise sailed with his wife and son on their yacht six months of every year. Charles Eaton contracted for six to eight months and then turned his attention to photography and scuba diving, which took him to Malaysia and other exotic locations. Charles had published several books of underwater photography.

EMBRACING DOWNTIME

A final group of informants embraced downtime as an opportunity for an unplanned vacation or a much-needed break. "It is not uncommon," explained Ray Gregory, a multimedia designer, "to have a couple of weeks off. But that's okay! Part of the reason I like contract work is that you work on something and when you get done, you get to take a break for a while, if you made enough money. It is almost like you can go off on an adventure of some sort." Victor Post, an Oracle database administrator, saw downtime in much the same way:

> Most of [my downtimes] have been planned in that I knew when a contract was coming to an end or, more often, I saw that my contribution was trailing off. So I would tell the client, "I am costing you money and I am really not doing you any good, so why don't we do some documentation and I will hand whatever I am responsible for over to someone else who will be here for a little longer." And then I look at that as a vacation. And that's another reason why the money issue isn't just to buy cool toys. It is so I don't have to work twelve months out of the year.

The strategies of enduring, minimizing, scheduling, and embracing downtime represented different interpretations of the contract cycle. Most informants used one strategy or another. Those who preferred to minimize downtime, despite how cavalierly they might otherwise talk, implicitly saw the contract cycle as a threat. Their notion of control entailed regaining the security of continual employment by lining up the next contract before the current contract ended, in order to pivot quickly from one job to the next. Those who scheduled or embraced saw downtime as an opportunity to live a different lifestyle. For schedulers, downtime was a resource to save or spend as they saw fit. For embracers it was a windfall: they did not associate downtime with failure and accepted its opportunity costs as a fair bargain.

Among our informants, endurers and minimizers outnumbered schedulers and embracers. Seventeen informants said that they routinely scheduled or embraced downtime for breaks, vacations, or hobbies, even though the vast majority of the remainder claimed that the freedom to do so was one of contracting's primary benefits. Almost as many (thirteen) said that they had not taken a vacation for a number of years, while another twenty-three took no more than one or two weeks each year.[18] Jose Martinez described his summer vacation as a single day between contracts spent going on amusement park rides interrupted with cell phone calls to his recruiter. When we asked Teresa Dolan what she did outside work, she responded, "I've been married for eighteen years, and I must say our honeymoon was the last time we took a vacation." Marty Keely told us matter-of-factly: "I can't take time between projects, because that's time that you usually try to market yourself to land your next contract. So you don't get to relax. I remember a seven-year stretch where I took no vacation. It was only after I got married and the pressure came from my wife that I finally took a two-week vacation to go to Hawaii. But that was it and that was a long time ago."

In sum, natural breaks between contracts made it possible for contractors to take time off, but a desire to control the contract cycle led most to avoid doing so. For many, vacations bore a suspicious resemblance to unwanted downtime and its consequences: increased expenses, decreased income, and an uncomfortable sense of insecurity and failure. On this score, contractors seemed to be at least as bound to work as their colleagues who were permanently employed. Interpretations of contracting's rhythm were only one factor that influenced the way contractors used their time. Contracting's fine grain, the organization of hours within a day and days within a week, exerted a less cyclical but more incessant pressure on contractors' temporal choices.

The Fine Grain

Contracts usually specified the number of hours per week that contractors would devote to the job, but they often granted considerable leeway in the choice of which hours to work. Some contractors, like Maria Sanchez, used their flexibility to work nontraditional hours: "Usually the hours are flexible, so there's a feeling of control. Even though you're working at midnight, you're the one who decided you wanted to work at midnight. I know some companies are flexible anyway, but when they know you're consulting, they're usually more open about you being flexible because they just want the job done. They don't care that you're not there eight to five. They just want results."

Other contractors exercised flexibility on a weekly basis. These informants valued the freedom to take a day off and, like Sumantra Kumar,

---

[18] The remaining 50 percent did not spontaneously discuss vacations or the lack of vacations.

some aspired to work four-day weeks. "I have very good relations [with the people at work]," Sumantra told us. "I know these people very well for maybe nine months. So they said, 'If you want to take a Friday off, you can, as long as your work is up-to-date. Next Friday this is what you are supposed to deliver. Do that Thursday and go off, we don't care. You can do forty hours in four days, no problem.'"

Because contractors bore much of the responsibility for deciding when to work and how much to work, they became acutely conscious of how they spent their time. Every hour was a resource, a commodity, or a form of capital, which they could invest in a variety of ways. They could invest hours in doing work directly related to the contract. They could also invest hours in activities that ensured their long-term employability: managing their business, developing new skills, and maintaining their networks. Like most of us, contractors could also choose to invest hours in their families, hobbies, or leisure. The need to make these trade-offs, often on a daily basis, led contractors to develop an accountant's appreciation for the microeconomics of time. They kept track of the hours they worked, carefully distinguishing between "billable" and "nonbillable" hours.

Billable hours were, simply, the number of hours a contractor could charge the client, usually calculated on a weekly basis. Some contractors set annual targets for the total number of billable hours they wanted to work. As Jose Martinez told us, the baseline for contractors he knew was usually a forty-hour week, the standard for a permanent job. Jose himself, however, often worked multiple contracts and billed well above the average, often reaching seventy or eighty hours a week.

Hours worked but not billed were known as "nonbillable" hours. Nonbillable hours were of two types. The first were hours that contractors spent on work related to the contract for which they could not or would not bill. The second were hours spent on tasks that were not directly related to the contract. Informants specifically spoke of the former as "nonbillable hours," and we shall use their term. Because no contractor had an explicit term for the second type of hours, we shall call them *support hours* to signify that contractors typically used such hours to renew their skills and remain professionally viable.

Informants worked nonbillable hours for a number of reasons. Sometimes jobs simply required more time than the contract allowed. Contractors worked these additional hours because they agreed to provide a deliverable by a certain date, because they could not always estimate the amount of time the work required, because they were poor at managing time, or because they wanted to adhere to their own standard of excellence. Nitin Kumar, a software developer, explained why he often worked more hours than he billed: "I end up working more than I charge. Maybe 10 percent more. I usually bill for eight hours a day, but there is so much more you do: you try things, you think. If it doesn't work, you try new things. I guess it averages out to fifty hours a week. Sometimes you need to take an extra week, and often you need to work weekends. You have to meet milestones, show progress. If you haven't, you can't bill."

Contractors also logged nonbillable hours because they wanted to make a good impression on the client. By working more hours than they billed or by attending meetings and engaging in other unpaid activities, contractors hoped to signal a level of dedication that would preclude them from being terminated before they were ready. "I want to make sure that when they are laying off contractors," Tony Rodriguez confided, "I am the last one on the list. So I do a lot of things. Like when I came on board for the first two weeks I probably worked seventy hours a week and billed them for forty. I had been there a week when they noticed that I was there at six in the morning until six at night."

Finally, like professionals everywhere, many of our informants found their work to be engrossing. "It sucks you in," Brenda O'Boyle told us. "It's real exciting. It's just not an eight to five world." Jeff Dorsey explained how he lost himself in his work: "I am kind of obsessive when it comes to this stuff. I can sit there and do this stuff until 2 A.M., wake up, go to work, come back, and do it until 2 A.M. again, you know, for at least a few days straight, because I enjoy it so much when I see all these images coming together on a Web page. It is something you can't really quit. I guess it would be the same as painting or something you really, really enjoy."

In addition to hours worked for clients, contractors invested considerable time in support activities, such as learning new skills and maintaining professional networks.[19] Although downtime could be used for support activities, most contractors found periods of downtime to be too short and unpredictable, and it was often necessary, in any case, to learn while on contract. Staying up-to-date required a significant investment of time, as Anil Rao attested:

I need to know what's going around, what's in demand, what's developing, how the software is changing, how the hardware is changing. It takes a lot of research every day, trying to stay ahead. But it's all worth it. I spend at least an hour a day. Maybe twenty minutes at work and about an hour at home—sometimes even two, three, four hours at home—trying to call people, other agencies, job shops, software, hardware companies. I'll ask questions and talk to them:

[19] Chapters 11 and 12 cover these activities in depth.

how is the software changing and when's the new version coming out?

In addition to acquiring new skills, all contractors devoted time to business activities. Even contractors who worked primarily through staffing firms actively marketed themselves. Marketing activities ranged from maintaining one's network of contacts to developing brochures, attending meetings of users' groups, going to career fairs, talking to recruiters, revising résumés, and posting them on the Web. In addition, contractors who worked from home typically had a considerable amount of computer equipment to maintain and upgrade. Independent contractors and those who were incorporated had the additional burden of maintaining tax records and other bookkeeping chores.

Brian Willingham nicely summarized the amount of time contractors spent in support activities and how these activities inflated the number of hours they worked while decreasing the hours they billed:

> I read an article one time, where "a good consultant should spend 50 percent of their time learning," and that's what I've been doing lately. I'm spending almost 50 percent of my time trying to keep current— reading the trade magazines, going to the meetings and stuff. You figure I spend 10 to 15 percent of my time doing marketing, another 10 to 15 percent of my time doing the housekeeping chores when you've got your own office. Gee, that leaves maybe 15 to 20 percent of the time that's billable. Think about the rate I'd have to charge if I was working only twenty hours a week. Nobody's going to spend $400 an hour for me. I'm not that good. So, how do you juggle all this?

In short, the fine-grained temporal structure of contracting differed considerably from that of permanent employees doing similar work. First, contractors had to balance more kinds of time. In addition to hours of paid work, contractors were obligated to invest substantial time in unbillable and support activities. Second, contractors enjoyed a level of flexibility unavailable to most of their permanent counterparts. Consequently, they confronted the ever-present choice of how to spend every hour. Third, unlike salaried employees, contractors could put a precise value on every hour of the day—their hourly wage. Thus, when choosing how to spend their time, contractors could calculate to the penny the opportunity costs of every unbillable, support, or leisure hour.

Finally, unlike employees whose jobs buffer them from the implications of how they spend each hour of the day, contractors were immediately exposed to the consequences of their choices.[20] The number of

[20] Employees may be evaluated on parameters such as efficiency and time utilization, but these occur on an annual basis and without clear measures other than managerial impressions.

billable hours that contractors worked translated directly into income. Investments in unbillable hours affected the probability that clients would extend their contracts or give them good recommendations. Hours spent in support activities shored up contractors' reputations, skills, and networks, which, in turn, shaped the outcome of their next foray into the labor market. These distinctive aspects of the fine-grained structure of contracting focused contractors on the trade-off between different ways of spending an hour. Generally speaking, contractors approached the trade-off in two ways. One group placed considerable value on family and leisure, while another valued time mainly for its economic potential.

Although the first group took economic criteria into account and valued contracting's high wages, they used its flexibility to set aside time for other purposes, which they also valued. These purposes varied widely. Some contractors sought greater balance between work and family. They spoke about the importance of being available for their children and budgeted their time accordingly. For Richard Stevens, flexibility meant not only choosing which hours to work, but also limiting those hours. "I now am a father. I have two children. And now "job one" for me is managing my time myself. And that means making the income that I need to make in as little time as possible and not working forty hours. So I like to work as little as possible. And I don't think employee situations afford that. I work generally thirty hours a week, but I can work twenty hours some weeks. And I like that." Judy King also valued contracting's flexibility for the freedom it gave her to devote time to her children.

For other contractors, work was a necessary evil, which contracting's flexibility allowed them to minimize. Kent Cox told us candidly why he typically worked only thirty hours a week: "I'm a goof-off. I mean I like the rest of my life. It's very important to me. I've adapted to working less than full-time." Cox used the time he bought for himself to write science fiction, pursue his interests in dance, and hang at the beach. Although he didn't regret his lifestyle, he was fully aware of its cost. "You know," he confided, "every so often I kick myself 'cause if I'd have put in sixty hours a week for the last five years at these rates I'd have at least a house to my name."

A handful of our informants valued both work and leisure, but did not routinely plan for one or the other. Instead, they made temporal decisions spontaneously. Without reneging on their obligations, these contractors worked when they felt like it and took time off when they wanted. Doug Hill expressed this stance:

> I try to maintain some kind of a pattern with clients because it helps them. But at the same time, I shift my schedule to meet my needs. If we're going to have a couple of days of very good weather, and there

are no major conflagrations burning at a client, I'll decide that maybe what I want to do is pack my cameras and get on the road. I'll say, "Hey look, I've got other things going on and instead of me being in on Tuesday and Wednesday, I'm going to be in on Thursday and Friday. I'll see you then unless you have a problem with that." That's what I do usually, 90 percent of the time.

Contractors like Richard, Judy, Kent, and Doug used contracting's flexibility to create temporal rhythms that accommodated their daily needs and values. They seemed to have achieved precisely what free agency promised. Among our informants, however, they were the exceptions.

The temporal logic of contracting tempted most of our informants to maximize their income by working as many hours as possible. As Brian Willingham explained, time became money. "When you're a contractor, all you have is your time," Brian told us. "You can only sell your time—you use it or lose it. You can only sell your time, so you need to maximize it. You need to figure out how to sell the most time! 'Cause when it's gone, it's gone. You can't go back."

The pressure was even more acute on older contractors who sensed that their days of being able to charge high rates were numbered. Asaf Weiss saw it this way: "I was always hoping that if I could earn more money, I could cut down the number of hours. But because the money is good, I find it very difficult to turn it down. I'm gettin' on in age—I'm forty-two now, and I should be thinking about retirement. If I'm ever gonna have any kids and all that other wonderful stuff, I need to have some money in reserve. So, I kind of look at it like, 'Get it while you can.'"

Contractors who equated time with money were acutely aware that every hour they failed to work was lost compensation. Charles Over, a software developer who attributed his divorce to contracting, described the experience of wasting time and feeling money pass through his hands. "The funny thing about contracting is you develop this mentality. I was one of those guys that said, 'I take a day off—I'm losing $800. Oh my gosh!' Or, you know, a holiday comes up and I felt, 'How can I work this holiday?'"

The pressure to work long hours came not only from the contractors' desire to maximize their income. Ironically, like the permanent employees who were their foils, informants reported that they also felt pressure from clients. Although clients did not have formal authority over contractors, market forces nevertheless gave clients considerable clout. The dynamics of development projects created time pressures known in development circles as "crunch time." At these crescendos, managers demanded long hours not only from permanent employees but from contractors as well.[21]

While contractors had no formal obligation to work longer hours than they had contracted to provide, there were good reasons to do so. Some contractors feared termination. "You must satisfy the employer," Nitin Kumar confided. "He is under no obligation to keep you, so you work weekends. There are no boundaries, no times set aside. The family suffers. You take a laptop home, dial in, work from there." Others, like Yolanda Turner, believed that failing to respond to client pressure could harm their reputation and, hence, their ability to find work in the long run:

> Nobody's telling me to do anything. Nobody's saying, "You have to do this. You have to be here at a certain time." But, say it was a real critical part of the project that needed to be done by Monday and I decided, "Oh, I'm not coming in," and I didn't have a really good reason. I mean, I'm still not dinged, but it's just, you know, it's filed in the back of somebody's mind and they'll say, "Well, she's not as dependable as we thought she would be."

A number of informants reported that equating time with money was so ingrained that they could no longer enjoy leisure. Julian Stoke described taking time off in the middle of the day to chaperone a group of girls from his church around San Francisco's Fisherman's Wharf. When the girls misbehaved, he began to begrudge them his time: "They were really terrible. They spread out in all directions and I ended up with the other chaperone, just the two of us walking around. I was counting those dollars going off. I was really upset about that." He summed up his experience by admitting that for contractors "there is a huge temptation to work every hour of the day." Doug Hill, who worked for several clients simultaneously, made it abundantly clear that time was his most valuable resource: "You can do a lot of things to me: you can call me names; you can throw rocks at me; you can shoot at me, and I won't care. Waste my time and I'll drive over you in the parking lot."

In short, many contractors were constantly concerned with the opportunity costs they would incur if they took advantage of contracting's temporal flexibility. As a result, many felt guilty about taking time off, even

---

[21] Crunch time and crises are endemic to engineering and software development. Crises figure prominently in ethnographies of high-tech work (Kidder 1981; Kunda 1992; Perlow 1997). Gersick's research (1988, 1989) suggests that crunch time may reflect a general tendency in how groups respond to deadlines. Gersick found that most groups wait until deadlines loom before exerting a concerted effort to complete a task. Allen's (1977) data on high-performing and low-performing R&D teams suggest that low-performing teams are particularly prone to late stage crises.

when they were on vacation. Marty Keely detailed the experience of doing such a cost-benefit analysis: "[Contracting] is like being a stockbroker. It's not about the fact that you made a million dollars today on your portfolio, it's about the fact that you left $200,000 on the table. If you didn't sell today and waited until tomorrow, or sold earlier, you could have made that 200,000. So this is the lingering thought in your head as a fund manager. The same thing is true in [contracting]. Time becomes money. When time becomes money, management of that time becomes a critical asset. You tend to take a lot less vacation."

When contractors used an economic metric as the sole measure of time, they often discounted the worth of other activities whose economic value was difficult to calculate. This was especially true for leisure. When we asked Olivia Crum about her life outside work she responded: "What life? I mean I work three weekends out of the month. I work most holidays. I've put in an average of twelve hours a day for the last four years. So the demands are just as great or greater [than permanent employment]. I work overtime because I want the extra money." When contractors billed seventy or eighty hours a week, they simply had little time left with which they could be flexible.

THE RHETORIC AND REALITY OF FLEXIBILITY

Our story points to an intriguing discrepancy between what contractors say and what they do. On one hand, our informants almost universally claimed that they were free to allocate their time as they desired. On the other hand, with a few notable exceptions, most contractors minimized downtime, worked long hours, and took little time for themselves. Carmella Diaz, a multimedia designer who regularly juggled a number of contracts simultaneously, articulated this discrepancy in the course of an interview. Before our eyes she seemed to discover that she was not as flexible as she thought.

> The greatest benefit for me is having a flexible time schedule, although here at SGI, I have to come in every day—which is perfectly fine, because it's just for a certain period of time. [*Interviewer: So why is the flexibility so important to you? Are there things you do outside work?*] Actually I think I work more now because I work until late at night. I work weekends, and—I mentioned to you I was on vacation. That was my first vacation in two years.

Table 10.2 makes clear that, like Carmella, the majority of our informants had less flexibility than they claimed. The table cross-classifies contractors by whether they achieved coarse- and fine-grained flexibility.

TABLE 10.2
Percentage of Contractors Who Achieved Coarse- and Fine-Grained Flexibility

	Coarse-Grained							
	Yes		No		Not Specified		Total	
Fine-Grained								
Yes	10%	(7)	1%	(1)	1%	(1)	13%	(9)
No	10	(7)	46	(33)	15	(11)	72	(51)
Not specified	4	(3)	3	(2)	8	(6)	15	(11)
Total	24	(17)	51	(36)	24	(17)	100	(71)

We classified contractors who used downtime as an opportunity to pursue avocations or long vacations as having achieved coarse-grained flexibility. We classified contractors who worked less than thirty hours a week or who varied their daily or weekly schedules to accommodate family and personal interests as having fine-grained flexibility. As table 10.2 indicates, nearly half of our informants (46 percent) experienced neither. Of the two, coarse-grained flexibility was apparently easier to achieve (24 percent) than was fined-grained flexibility (13 percent). Only 10 percent of our informants reported having both.[22]

To make sense of this discrepancy we must consider what contractors meant by "flexibility." When contractors spoke of having greater flexibility, what they seemed to be saying was that they felt as if they, not the employer, were in charge of their time. It was this subjective sense of freedom that they valued. Thus, having flexibility had less to do with how contractors actually spent their time than with their belief that their choices were voluntary. Maria Sanchez, for example, made it clear that she was willing to work every bit as hard as any permanent employee, just as long as she felt she had the choice:

[22] Although these data seem to suggest that there is something about contracting that leads contractors to work long hours, an alternative explanation might be that contractors work more hours because they are more likely to have family responsibilities. Although we do not have the data to compare contractors and full-timers directly, under this line of reasoning we would expect that contractors would have had less flexibility if they were married and had children. Among our informants this was not the case. We tested to see if there were statistically significant differences between contractors who had either type of flexibility and those who had none. Gender, marital status, and the presence of children did not distinguish our informants, although gender and marital status approached statistical significance and we would expect them to become significant in a larger, randomly selected sample of contractors.

[*Interviewer: Do you work a lot of weekends?*] It's cyclical. Like the time line I'm looking at for my project that I'm going to consult on, there's going to be a crunch, I would say, the first two weeks of September. And then maybe the two weeks before Thanksgiving. You know, there's some times where you brace yourself and say, "Okay, this is where you're going to kill yourself." I mean, as long as you can plan it out and psyche yourself into the fact you're going to be working long hours this time versus being told you have to work long tomorrow. I mean, at least you're the one planning out when you're going to kill yourself.

One might argue that contractors chose to work long hours and failed to take advantage of their temporal freedom because they were greedy. The lure of money was indeed strong for some of the contractors we interviewed. But to blame avarice for the fact that contractors made little use of the flexibility they claimed to value so highly would be to interpret too narrowly what our contractors were struggling to communicate. Even those informants who spoke about how difficult it was to forfeit money were telling us less about greed than about the meaning that time had acquired after they made the transition into contracting.

Accepting the discipline of the market made contractors acutely aware of the value of their time and of their personal responsibility for its efficient deployment. Contractors learned, in short, to treat their time as a form of capital and regularly made calculated decisions about its allocation and use. It is this consciousness of investment that the popular press downplays when glorifying contracting's flexible lifestyle. As we have seen, some contractors did indeed take advantage of contracting's flexibility, just as the promoters of free agency predicted: they took long vacations, pursued time-consuming avocations, and devoted more time to their friends and family. Doing so, however, meant that they had consciously chosen to invest their temporal capital outside the market. But most contractors chose otherwise. To survive in the market and maintain their status as itinerant experts, they believed they had to put their temporal capital to work.

There were two ways contractors put their temporal capital to work. One has been the topic of this chapter: liquidating it for profit by transforming temporal capital into billable hours. The other was to invest it for greater returns in the future. Investing meant transforming time either into human capital by sinking time into activities that maintained, enhanced, and built their skills, or into social capital by spending time cultivating relationships that would allow them to find the next contract. Without investing time, contractors might wake up one day to find that their time had no value at all.

Chapter 11

BUILDING AND MAINTAINING HUMAN CAPITAL

THE DANGER OF OBSOLESCENCE

Brian Willingham had a theory of technological obsolescence that would have made a labor economist proud. He claimed that the value of knowing a programming language or application was a concave function of time that, in the end, crashed suddenly. When a language or application first attracts attention, Brian claimed, those who can write the code or use the application can demand high wages because their skill is rare. But as the technology becomes popular and more people become skilled in its use, wages decline. Wages decline even further when users begin to migrate to the technology's successor. At some point, however, wages begin to increase again because firms that have decided to stick with the older technology have difficulty finding experts to maintain it. Eventually, when there are no legacy systems left, demand for the skill completely ceases and it becomes worthless. Brian explained:

> I could still be programming COBOL on HP3000 computers and making a nice, comfortable living. I figure that's my ace in the hole, that or FoxPro. For a long time there was this standing joke that there were three RPG programmers left in the world—this is an old programming language—and they all worked for Standard Oil up in Richmond. Standard had this old RPG system that they didn't want to replace, but that needed maintenance. So, they were charging like, $500 an hour or something and Standard Oil was willing to pay 'cause it was cheaper than having to junk the whole thing and rebuild it from scratch. So that's your retirement fund [*laughs*]. What happens is you'll have a technology that's very popular; everybody wants it, so there's a lot of demand for it. Then, a new technology comes along and replaces it. So all of a sudden, the demand drops way off, but there's still plenty of people who know how to do that technology so the price goes way down [*traces two curves in the air*]. And then you go far enough out in the curve, nobody cares about that technology anymore, so nobody's learning it anymore, like COBOL. Nobody learns COBOL anymore. All of a sudden, demand is there. All of a sudden the price starts going back up. The way it works is: when you're ready to stop learning, you can still make money right on into retirement.

The trick, however, was timing the slide into retirement just right. Otherwise, the decision to stop learning would be economic suicide. As Brian put it, "At some point, though, all of the RPG stuff is going to go away, and then what do you do? I'm sure that the RPG programs don't exist anymore up at Standard Oil." Tony Rodriguez, a contractor in Montana who specialized in program management, offered a more Californian image of the dynamics of obsolescence and learning. "It's just like surfing," he mused. "You go in, you crash, and you swim back out against the waves. Then, you get to come back in. It's not like rafting where you just get on the river and ride."

Although most contractors were less analytic than Brian and less poetic than Tony, all were aware that their fortunes tracked the life cycles of technologies and that these, in turn, drove the need to learn. "Staying on the curve," "riding the next curve," and "getting up the learning curve" were common images, as if contractors were lay labor economists who appreciated the idea of a diffusion curve and its implications for wages and learning. Although we interviewed a few older contractors who had chosen to mine their experience with legacy technologies, most were still committed to remaining on the cutting edge. They believed that unless they did so, their wages would fall, and that it would become harder and harder to find jobs even if they were willing to become a "bottom-feeder," to work for low rates doing tasks that no one else wanted to do.

Avoiding obsolescence meant that contractors not only had to sharpen their skills incrementally, but from time to time they also had to "remake themselves" by learning an entirely new technology or technique. Experienced contractors, like Roger Garley, estimated that a remake was required about every five years, given the pace of change in high technology. "I think about obsolescence a lot," Roger said seriously, "because when you're a contractor, they could suddenly decide they don't need any C++ UNIX Sybase and I'm out of a job. So you always have to be looking over the horizon. What's the next good technology and what do you want to be doing? I've been doing this now for almost fifteen years, and I've gone through I don't know how many languages. It seems like about every five years you have to remake yourself."

At the time we did our interviews, the Internet was escalating the pace of change and creating a sense of urgency about retooling, especially among software developers. Brian Willingham, who graduated from college in 1976, echoed the sentiments of most contractors:

Everything I learned in college has been obsoleted now four times over. I've had to relearn my trade four times and it's become much harder over the last few years. Used to be, every couple of years, computers would have a new, faster processor or whatever. Programming tools stayed fairly constant. They'd come out with a new revision of the same old programming product. Now, the Internet has just changed everybody's time frame. You're now talking, like dog years: Internet years. The tools that I'm using now—none of them existed two years ago. Most of the programming concepts I use didn't exist three or four years ago. All of a sudden, the rapid evolution that happened in hardware, we're now seeing happen with software. Especially last year, people were like, "I can't take it anymore: I can't learn Java and Web and IP and object-oriented programming—all this stuff—all at once." We had all these new technologies all coming in all at the same time.

One could argue that all technical professionals, regardless of whether they work as permanent employees or contractors, face the same problem. After all, obsolescence is primarily a function of the rate of change in a particular field. Thus, holding a person's field and willingness to learn constant, the rate of change should affect all practitioners similarly. Such an argument has merit, but it overlooks the possibility that employment relationships can shield individuals from or expose them to the effects of technological change. As we discussed in chapter 7, clients expected contractors to "hit the ground running," to walk into a job with all the skills necessary for the job. We also learned that firms often hired contractors to acquire skills and knowledge that permanent employees lacked. Contractors concluded that if they did not keep pace with technology, clients would turn back to their permanent employees because they were less expensive.

Whether right or wrong, our informants clearly believed that they had to worry more about obsolescence and learning than did permanent employees. When asked to contrast contracting with permanent employment, Olivia Crum noted, with some disdain, that employees were less motivated to keep current: "One of the mistakes that employees make is that they get stagnant. They get comfortable because, you know, they aren't going anywhere. Whereas a consultant has to look at, 'Okay, I'm in business for myself, so I have to keep my skill level up.' You know, 'I have to find out what the latest and greatest curve is so that I can be on it.'"

Contractors argued that employees could afford to be sanguine about keeping up-to-date because firms were more forgiving when they went stale. Firms not only offered full-timers opportunities to learn new techniques and technologies, but employees could draw on the skills of their entire group to compensate for their own waning knowledge. In contrast, contractors believed they were on their own. Contractors claimed, with some justification, that hiring managers did not assess a full-timer's skills as fastidiously as they did a contractor's skills and that clients would consider contractors obsolete more quickly than an employee with equivalent knowledge. When asked how quickly she found her skills becoming obsolete, Kathy Jacobs, a software developer with degrees from Wellesley and Stanford, reckoned the degradation of her employability in months, even though she felt that the gap between what employers wanted and what she knew was not all that difficult to bridge:

[*Interviewer: You find that your skills become obsolete quickly?*] Very quickly! Let me see. How many months? I don't know, but it's very quickly. Because when they hire you, they don't want to train you, they want you to know the exact things right away. If you worked with one database, it is not such a big jump to work with another. You know, to go from Informix to Oracle is not such a big deal. But most of the time, they want you to know Oracle and the latest stuff right then. So, yeah, you can become obsolete. You know, your salary will go down, which is actually what's happening to me. My salary's been going down for the last five years [*laughs and traces a negative slope in the air*], because I've been working thirty hours a week and I'm not putting enough effort into keeping myself really marketable. They'd rather hire someone with just a couple years' experience who knows the latest stuff than someone who has been doing it for a long time but who does not have the exact set of tools.

Contractors were also quick to note that permanently employed engineers have the option of moving into management when they tire of keeping up with technological change. Indeed, study after study shows that about a third of all engineers choose a managerial path sometime within the first ten years of their career.[1] Contractors who wished to remain contractors had no such option. When they tired of staying current, they either focused on a legacy technology or began to think about returning to full-time employment precisely because they saw permanent employment and a shift into management as a way of slowing down. Steve Louthan, a technical writer who was considering returning to permanent employment when we interviewed him, remarked: "The competition is getting a little stiffer because the application packages that a writer needs to know are getting more complicated, more complex, more work-intensive. And so, you do have to keep up with it, without a doubt. At forty-five I'm getting a little tired of playing that rat race game, which

[1] For studies of engineers' careers, see Ritti (1971), Bailyn (1980), Katz and Tushman (1981), Bailyn and Lynch (1983), and Rynes, Tolbert, and Strausser (1988).

is why I'm at Cisco. Cisco wants to bring me on board direct, and I would just as soon focus on the network engineering side of technology and also focus on working my way into a management position, rather than continue this contracting thing."

None of the contractors we interviewed had thought explicitly about the need to stay current before they became contractors. The majority were professionals who did so as a matter of course, simply because learning about technology was "fun." But after making the transition, all quickly realized that what was once just fun had become a necessity: being able to offer skills that were in demand was essential if they wanted to continue contracting. We routinely asked our informants what advice they would give someone who was considering becoming a contractor. Advice on staying current was only surpassed by the admonition that would-be contractors should face up to whether they were ready to handle the possibility of downtime. "Find what's hot out there and go learn it," counseled Peyton Nugen. "For me it's NT. For a programmer, it's Java. Java is taking over everything. With wires, it's Cisco. Before you jump and leave the cushion, you have to prepare yourself because you can rely on the security of a company as an employee, but as a contractor you have to rely on your skills."

THE RISKS OF LEARNING

Experienced contractors warned that making choices about what to learn was risky; it meant betting on the future. If they bet poorly, they would be unable to control their downtime and their families would bear the cost. Choosing was risky for several reasons. First, there were always competing technologies: different programming languages, different applications that accomplished similar tasks, even different hardware protocols and architectures. In vibrant fields with expanding alternatives and no standard, it was even difficult to know what criteria to use for making a choice. Contractors spoke of being overwhelmed by options. Yet, unlike permanent employees, they had to make commitments without the assistance or backing of an organization that could absorb the cost of a bad choice. Longtime contractors like Doug Hill knew that even a dominant paradigm carried no guarantees:

I hit my e-mail twice a day just to stay up with the newsgroups on what's coming out. My God, any one of those things is almost a career commitment! You think there are 30 of them today. Tomorrow there'll be 35 and 135 a year from now. I think just knowing what to study is complicated. You know, it's easy to be a Monday-morning quarterback, to look back and say, "This technology's going to make it and this technology's not going to make it." Right now everybody is all upset about Windows 95/98 [because of the Microsoft antitrust suit and the emergence of Linux]. Something could happen. I've spent a lot of time becoming Microsoft-certified and so on and so forth. What if something really were to happen? A technological change could come through. You become an overnight dinosaur. That is a real danger.

Deciding to invest in a technology that soon became outmoded was a scenario that troubled contractors. Another was investing time and money in a technology only to find out that it was incapable of doing what its promoters claimed. "You can end up blowing off time learning a technology," explained Brian Willingham. "I spent the last three months screwing around with a technology that would have allowed me to take my FoxPro programming and do it on the Web. It was software that would allow a person using a Web browser to send a request to the server, and the server would go to FoxPro and process the request. Unfortunately, the company that made it—it was run by a friend of mine—had only one major client. So he really didn't fix all of the problems. It's not ready for prime time. I tried to do a project using this technology and it hasn't worked out. Now I am just putting in time, because I can't charge them for the time I spend getting the project back to the same level of functionality it was at when we started."

Too little friction in the supply and demand for labor was another source of risk. Contractors who made wise choices, in the sense that they decided to learn technologies that proved popular, often saw their wages quickly decline as other contractors flocked to the technology. Under such circumstances maintaining income often required learning yet another technology. The more quickly the bandwagon moved, the less time the contractor had to recoup his or her investment. Tony Rodriguez considered this the real downside of "surfing":

I know a lot of contractors that are always trying to ride the wave. They're always reading the papers, trying to figure out what technology is the latest and greatest. They're really chasing fires to some extent because they're always trying to predict, "How can I keep my billable rate up?" When I first started the project in Missouri, we were trying to hire a process modeler. That was when this process modeling stuff was really mysterious. People were getting 200, $250 an hour to come in and do process modeling. It was just amazing but people didn't know how to do it. So they were getting incredible amounts of money. One of the guys we tried to hire was getting $200 an hour; two years later I could have hired him for $65. I mean he called me trying to get a job at $65 an hour. And that is the problem. Most of the guys who are trying to get on the curve barely get there and then, they have to ask what is the next thing?

At minimum, making a poor bet cost contractors time that they might have spent elsewhere. Sometimes bad bets meant throwing real money away, as well. Olivia Crum had recently swallowed such a loss. "During my downtime I took a course on Power Builder," she told us, "but I couldn't get anybody to give me a shot at using it and it cost me $1,200 to take that course." Some contractors actually avoided seeking the kind of training they desired for fear of losing large sums of money. Yolanda Turner wanted to move into systems administration, but had delayed for just such a reason. "There's so much out there to learn and so many directions you can go in," she sighed. "I want to get with a consulting firm and have them send me on projects. But I've been reluctant to spend any money on NT training or Novell training because there's so much to learn and then it keeps changing. What you might pay $9,000 for may be outdated in another couple of years and you have to go on to something else."

Even when contractors made sound choices, the direct and indirect costs of keeping current were significant. Staying current led contractors to invest significant sums in equipment and software that they used at home to develop and maintain their skills. Anil Rao claimed that he spent roughly half his annual income on new equipment each year. Migrating to a new skill set might also require contractors to reduce their rates, since some employers were unwilling to pay high rates to contractors who had not already proven their skills at another client's expense. Teresa Dolan remarked, "Learning new skills has been hard for me. When I moved from the legacy skills to the newer, more popular skills, I had to lower my rate because I was coming in as a neophyte as opposed to someone who had several years of project experience and good references. Mostly customers want references of real projects as opposed to something that I did at home. So learning new skills as a contractor is a challenge."

Yet despite the significant cost of remaining up-to-date, the cost of not doing so was greater. The trick was to choose well and keep learning. Given the importance of staying marketable, it should come as no surprise that contractors had theories and strategies for targeting skills and technologies that would maximize employability while minimizing risk. Remaining up-to-date entailed three distinct but entwined activities that shaped contracting's lifestyle: scanning for new developments, choosing technologies on which to focus, and developing acumen with those technologies.

Strategies for Remaining Current

Scanning

Discussions of learning and skill development in academia, business, and education often assume that learners somehow already know what's worth learning. The assumption is convenient because it allows discussants to focus on ways of knowing and styles of learning and to debate how best to access or design delivery systems. In everyday life, often the hardest part of learning is knowing what there is to know and, within the set of possibilities, what is actually worth knowing. Technical contractors were well aware of this prior problem. They perceived their worlds as awash in information. Not only did they need to monitor developments in their own field, but they also needed to stay abreast of developments in other fields, because these often had implications for their own. Furthermore, information about new technologies, capabilities, and trends rarely came in well-digested formats, and even when it did, the digesting had to be taken with more than a grain of salt. Clues about what technologies were worth learning and what skills were worth developing were scattered, inconsistent, ambiguous, and often shrouded in marketing hyperbole. Dealing with the plethora of information demanded constant vigilance: a continual processing and sorting of data on trends and developments that we call "scanning."

The purpose of scanning was to gain awareness of new technologies, the fate of existing technologies, evidence of emerging trends, and clues about the fortunes of firms. Scanning was not particularly difficult to do. It entailed little more than reading, talking, and then thinking about and investigating further what one had read and heard. But scanning took a considerable amount of time. Although we did not directly assess the hours that contractors devoted to scanning, our sense was that scanning accounted for most of the hours that contractors devoted to staying current. In fact, scanning was what most contractors seemed to have in mind when they talked about "staying up-to-date."

Tools for scanning were simple enough. Most contractors would agree with Ashish Goshal's list. When asked how he stayed up-to-date, Goshal, a designer of databases, remarked, "If I had to put them in order, then I would say my colleagues first, and then, second, the Internet, and the third is magazines." In contrast to the engineers that other investigators have studied, contractors were readers.[2] Many subscribed to a variety of

---

[2] Allen (1977) showed that compared with scientists, engineers read very little. This was because most permanently employed engineers relied on a smaller group of engineers whom Allen called gatekeepers. Gatekeepers kept up with the literature and became sources of knowledge for their organizations.

magazines and journals ranging from popular technical magazines like *PC Week* and *Byte* to specialty journals like *EE Times* or *Embedded Systems Journal*. Books were of secondary importance for scanning, but figured more prominently once contractors decided to focus on a specific technology or skill.

Contractors were also talkers. Contractors spent considerable time chatting with colleagues on the job or via e-mail. By talking they learned what was "hot," how other professionals evaluated new developments, and why people preferred some technologies rather than others. Out of the stream of discourse emerged an awareness of what some contractors called "the buzz," a term that denoted a kind of excitement as well as an apparent (but sometimes fickle) consensus about where a technology or field was headed. At the time we collected our data, the buzz among software developers centered, among other things, on Java, C++, and accessing databases via Web browsers. References to these technologies appeared in most of our interviews with developers. In the multimedia community, specialists seemed concerned with how long Macromedia might dominate the field.

The Internet was a particularly important source of information for contractors. The World Wide Web was densely populated with sites devoted to technical tools and techniques. Most software and hardware companies maintained Web sites that provided not only information on product specifications but also troubleshooting guides, helplines, software patches, technical documentation, and the opportunity to download demonstration programs. Many contractors belonged to Usenet groups and bulletin boards, where they could post technical questions and search for solutions to problems.[3]

Some contractors scanned broadly, monitoring a range of information sources. Others adopted a more focused approach to monitoring information. Doug Hill's strategy was to concentrate on key vendors whose activities he knew would affect his practice as a database designer and systems analyst:

> [*Talking about reading news groups*] Primarily, I subscribe to almost anything that Microsoft sends out, because even when Microsoft is wrong, I will find out who's bumping into them. That will trigger where I should look [*laughs*]. When they're right they're right.

---

[3] The Web also offered sites that provided contractors with information on trends in contracting. Representative sites included Contract Employment Daily (www.cedaily.com), The Computer Consultant's Message Board (www.realrates.com/bbs/), and High Tech Careers (www.hightechcareers.com). These sites published articles on such practical issues as how to think about taxes or negotiate with staffing agencies, as well as salary trends broken down by region and occupation. See chapter 5.

When they're wrong, it's a clue as to what is right. I do a lot of what Microsoft does. I pay attention to Lotus. I peruse certain key words. Whenever I hear about a new processor, anything Intel does . . . Intel's the vortex. I basically have pruned Apple from my list.

Contractors spoke of scanning as if it were a natural activity that was seamlessly integrated into their daily activities. As Hernando Galvez put it, "I live and breathe this stuff, so I'm on top of the technology before it's released." Contractors said they surfed the Web for technical information during lulls at client sites. They read technical magazines while commuting or at home for relaxation after dinner. Accessing Web sites and monitoring Usenet groups was, for many, a form of entertainment that sometimes kept them awake until the small hours of the morning. At work, conversations among technical workers almost always came around to technical developments, issues, and trends. Stu Davis gave us a sense of the scope of scanning as an ongoing activity and how contractors used various sources to cross-reference information and expand their awareness:

I look on the Internet, of course. You know, object-oriented stuff is real big right now and I've done some of that. I've got about a half dozen magazine subscriptions I want to start, stuff like *Electronics, EE Times,* and *Embedded Systems Journal.* I used to do a lot more reading than I do now—like, *C User's Journal, C++ User's Journal.* But, gosh, the Internet is such a great information tool. I hear about all kinds of new stuff like RUMBA.[4] So I'll go to Rational Systems, Rational Rose.[5] I'll go look at their products. Object Time up in Canada, see what that's all about. Some of these companies have demos you can download. They'll have manuals and lots of information there. And I talk to the guys that I work for and with. "Well, why do you do it this way? Why do you write the code this way?" And "Why do you use this particular set of programming conventions?" "Well, we find that this gives us the best maintainability or the tightest code" or whatever, and I file all these things away in my mind so I can pull them out later on and use them.

Choosing Skills

Scanning prepared contractors to choose which technologies to learn, once the time came to make a choice. In general, contractors chose to

---

[4] RUMBA is software that allows users to access databases residing on a host server from a Web browser.

[5] All firms mentioned in this passage were software vendors.

delve more deeply into a technology when the "buzz" became over-whelming, when it became clear that the market was shifting or that a new technology was becoming "hot." For many contractors, wages and the time it took to get the next job were barometers that signaled the ap-propriate time for change. In response to a question about what he meant by "monitoring the market," Ray Gregory replied, "Well, on the real practical level it is how many months do I go without getting any work. It is sort of like that. But it is also paying attention to the buzz. As long as I can come up with another assignment within a few days after I am done with an assignment, I feel there is some life left in my little niche."

When contractors sensed their niche was growing smaller, they began to feel an urgency to move on and faced the question of which technolo-gies and skills to learn. In cases of incremental change, such as the release of a new version of an application or operating system, the choice and the learning process were relatively easy. Trends that implied "remaking oneself" required more thought. Our informants articulated four broad strategies for choosing which skills to develop next.

BETTING ON A CORE TECHNOLOGY

One strategy was to identify a core technology that seemed technically and economically stable. Stability had several sources. Some technologies appeared to be stable because they were infrastructural: they were plat-forms on which numerous other technologies depended. Operating sys-tems are a good example. Bob Howard, a systems administrator who had specialized in NT-based networks, was considering migrating to UNIX not only because it was more ingrained in the local market, but because he thought UNIX would adapt more readily to changing requirements.

Contractors also deemed tools to be relatively stable when they were central to an industry or community of practice.[6] Contractors reasoned that technical communities were less likely to abandon tools that were the "workhorses" of daily practice. It was for this reason that Ray Greg-ory had decided to place his bets on Macromedia Director, a high-level tool for developing multimedia products:

Macromedia has a fairly significant reputation and a significant per-centage of the industry that it is focused on. I think there will always be something like CD-ROMs that people will be using for corporate

---

[6] "Community of practice" is a term coined by Lave and Wenger (1990) to refer to a group of people who cluster around a task, technology, or line of work. Members of a com-munity of practice train each other and exchange information on how to do things.

presentations or marketing tools or training or kiosks. It has an advantage over building a project in something like C++, because you have a huge head start on the environment. Macromedia Director is like a programming environment. So you have a means of whipping out a product in three months instead of taking a year. That continues to be a key point in a lot of the companies I have worked with. Multicom, for example, bragged about all the different tools that they used. Almost all of their stuff was done in Director, but they did not mention Director once in their prospectus. They bragged about their C++ and their PEARL and all these other technologies because they are sexy, but Director is the workhorse in their particular niche.

Newer technologies gained a kind of stability when they were the basis on which a significant proportion of an organization's operations rested. Because shifting away from such technologies would cost organizations a considerable amount of money, contractors reasoned that most users would retain the technology even when offered alternatives. Oracle, SAP, and Peoplesoft were examples of such systems at the time we did our research. Each of these technologies were all-encompassing, integrated IT systems to which firms were entrusting their various databases. Applications programmers and data developers argued that learning these systems was a solid bet for maintaining employability for a number of years.

HEDGING THE BET

A second strategy was in some ways the converse of the first. Instead of focusing on one relatively stable technology, some contractors hedged their bets by learning several interrelated technologies and tools. Contractors who adopted a hedging strategy tended to work in fields that were less settled. Their work was less specialized and of broader scope. Hence, they had to respond to broader trends. Brian Willingham was a good example. The small businesses that he served had begun to migrate from workstations on a local area network to Internet-based architectures and applications. Since no integrated tools had emerged for accomplishing the range of tasks his clients were asking him to do, Brian found that he had to learn an array of new tools, technologies, and techniques. Nor could he predict which, if any, would stand the test of time:

> Right now, there's been a lot on Internet servers, anything to do with Internet, HTML, database programming. This is where I've been putting a lot of energy lately: learning new tools, dealing with the fact that I can no longer just use one tool to solve all my problems. I'm gonna have to learn four or five tools because the industry is very immature at this point. We're still trying to figure out how you do this. Once you figure out how to do it, you can build a nice inte-

grated tool set that does everything you want. FoxPro for Windows–based programming was wonderful 'cause it was a database, it was the display up on the screen, it was our programming logic, and it was an all-in-one, nice, neat package. Here I've got HTML editors. I've got server software. I've got database software. I've got three different types of mediating software to grab this stuff out of the database and turn it into HTML. I've got operating systems and firewalls. Do I want to do it all? Do I want to try to concentrate on one part? How do I take all this complexity and crystallize it so when I talk to my customer I can say, "Yeah, here's what I need to do. Here's what you need to do." Right now, I'm putting a lot of investment into the Internet and Internet technology because I think that's going to be where it's going to be at. And we shall see. And if not, they've still got the COBOL programmer jobs up in the city [*laughs*].

FOLLOWING THE MONEY

Contractors who sought a core technology or hedged their bets did so by examining trends in technology to determine what to learn next. They hoped to make an investment that would ensure their ability to control downtime for a period of five to ten years. Other contractors had shorter time horizons and chose to learn skills to maximize short-term income. Like Olivia Crum, contractors who took this approach chose the technologies they would learn based on information about wage rates: they followed the money. When asked how she decided what to learn, Olivia replied, "You try to find out which one's paying the most money." She went on to describe how she learned where the money was: "One trade magazine I subscribe to is a contractor magazine. *Contract Professional* is the name of it. It's all about the consulting industry. One of their features is trying to highlight, you know, the lucrative new areas. It also tries to give you hints on trying to be a career contractor and consultant." Typically, contractors who followed the money made smaller technological jumps. For example, they moved from one programming language to another or from one database application to another, rather than jumping from one occupational community (say quality analysis) to another (like database programming or systems administration).

STICKING TO A FUNCTIONAL AREA

Finally some contractors sought to ward off obsolescence by committing themselves not to a technology or tool, but to a functional area or type of application. For instance, some programmers and database developers chose to specialize in financial, human resource, or manufacturing applications. Hardware engineers and embedded systems engineers also tended to remain with areas of application, such as guidance systems or telecommunications. Tony Rodriguez laid out the general logic from the perspective of a programmer. He advised new contractors:

> Don't fall into: "I have to learn this. I have to learn that. Visual Basic, I need it." You know, programming languages are always going to change. If you want to get into the contract world, pick a good business area like taxes or welfare or child support. Because your knowledge will transition, will transcend all of the technology waves. Because when they bring in designers and analysts, it is the same basic concepts.

Developing Acumen

Having decided to develop expertise in a new technology or area of practice, contractors faced the problem of acquiring knowledge and experience. Although, as we showed in chapter 10, contractors used periods of downtime to learn new skills, few consciously incurred downtime for this purpose. Most felt they needed to acquire new knowledge and skills while continuing to work, otherwise their income would suffer. Developing acumen was, therefore, something that contractors typically felt they had to do in addition to working, as part of their work, or, most commonly, both.

Our informants reported using a variety of strategies for learning new skills. They took classes at community colleges and universities and attended training programs sponsored by vendors. Some joined local users' groups. Several had even founded such groups. Others took advantage of vendor-sponsored certification programs and sought credentials such as Microsoft Certified Systems Engineer. Formal training, coursework, degrees, and certifications, however, played a relatively small role in most contractors' quest to acquire skills. By and large, contractors preferred to teach themselves.

Almost every contractor we interviewed talked about purchasing and reading technical books and manuals. Contractors also turned to the Internet for more focused knowledge. On the Web they found not only documentation and tutorials but also other technical professionals who were willing to answer questions when they encountered a problem they did not understand. Victor Post relied heavily on the Internet and on a local users' group. "Oracle maintains forms on their Web site, and that has turned out to be a gold mine of information," Victor explained. "I also use Usenet. There are four newsgroups that I subscribe to. If I have a question, I will post it there. I get some good answers from Australians. Oracle in itself is a subculture of computer technology. I belong to a users' group here south of Puget Sound, the Puget Sound Oracle Users' Group. And there is some good information to be had from the users' group. Most of the people I see as hangers on, they are just there to sponge up whatever they can from other people, but there are some creative people who go there as well."

Reading and talking about technology, however, were insufficient for learning new skills. Technical knowledge ultimately involves doing: writing programs, fixing machines, producing Web pages, or designing chips. Learning to do requires practice. Without practice, contractors could not really claim they had acquired skills. Because doing was so central to technical knowing, most contractors purchased software and hardware to experiment on their own. In fact, nearly a third of our informants maintained computer labs in their homes, which, many noted with pleasure, were tax deductible. Home labs were particularly common among software developers, but systems administrators and even technical writers reported having a significant amount of computer equipment, which they used not only for work and play but also to learn new technologies and skills.

Young, single contractors often shared houses with other contractors. Because the housemates had similar interests and owned their own technologies, their homes became technology centers where work, learning, and recreation fused. Bob Howard remarked:

> With the two roommates that I have, I think we have six computers right now—all different operating systems, different types of hardware setups. We have a DSL line—a dedicated line—it's on all the time. So we have our own little mini-network. And we just set things up and we play with it. We break it and sort of learn just by doing. When I actually set myself down to try and learn, it's not for a certain contract that I'm on, it's for what I want to be doing. Right now I'm studying UNIX. I just have basic level knowledge of it and I'd like to learn more. I'd like to have a contract where I could get my hands into it, but I'm not going to have that unless I can show Systems Professionals that I know this amount right there, just a quantified amount and I'm able to pass a technical review or whatever test that they give me.

Vicky Chenalt and Felix Harden, a technical writer and programmer who were married to each other, told us that building a computer lab was a key criterion for choosing the house they bought. They chose a house with a bedroom large enough to hold five computers and various peripherals. They installed a DSL line and networked the entire home.

Several contractors even went so far as to become beta testers for vendors so they could acquire hands-on knowledge of new technologies before the technologies were released, thereby ensuring that they were always on the cutting edge. Charles Eaton, for example, had met and developed a friendship with a Microsoft representative. He convinced his friend to give him a copy of Access, Microsoft's database program, before it was released. Consequently, Charles knew how to work with Access before it was sold to the public. Since then, Microsoft had provided him with advance copies of all subsequent versions of the software. Hernando Galvez had developed a similar relationship with IBM. He saw partnering with vendors and doing pilot projects as a primary strategy for building new skills and learning new technologies:

> I select pilot projects that I know are going to give me the experience to develop proficiency in a certain technology, and I do these pilot projects at cost or at no cost. I target specific technologies. I'll give you an example. There's one coming up right now. There's a database engine called S-Space. And it's built on another technology they call a PO-1 engine. So, what I'm doing right now is, I am aggressively pursuing this package in terms of getting experience and some level of certification with this package. What I'll do is I'll get myself into a training program. I'll acquire the actual software. I'll try to see if they have any kind of partner programs with the company. And I'll try to get involved in a partner program. I'm a partner in development for IBM in something that they developed called NQ Series. NQ Series is middleware, but it's important to me because at the time that I was becoming a partner for IBM, I was anticipating getting a contract from Republic National Bank for doing a QA on what they called their Pipeline Project, which was based on this NQ Series software. So several months before, I began acquiring knowledge with this product and experience, so that when the time came, I knew who the players were, I knew where the resources were, and I had intimate knowledge of what the software actually did.

Although buying hardware and software, maintaining a home computer lab, and serving as a beta site were useful strategies for gaining hands-on knowledge, these strategies had limitations. For example, it was impractical, if not impossible, to learn some technologies outside of the workplace. This was an important limitation for hardware designers and for quality assurance technicians, whose work required considerable infrastructure. Although technical writers had little need for elaborate technical support, they too found it difficult to write documentation outside the context of an ongoing project. Furthermore, many employers were unwilling to accept "home learning" as a substitute for "prior experience." Consequently, the contractors' most common strategy for developing acumen with new technologies was to land contracts that would allow them to learn on the job.

Having targeted a new technology, contractors sought to secure contracts that allowed them to develop hands-on experience. Contractors preferred this approach because it meant that they would, in effect, be paid to learn the skills they desired. The trick was to find work that pushed the contractor's envelope of knowledge without requiring skills that were so far beyond his or her level of understanding that failure was preordained. For lack of a better term, we shall call such contracts "stretchwork."[7]

Contractors clearly evaluated contracts according to the job's potential to extend their skills in desired directions. In fact, some informants implied that a willingness to take on work for which one was not completely prepared was what ultimately separated those who succeeded from those who failed at contracting. Glenn Arthur subscribed to this philosophy:

> You know it's funny; people come to me and ask me if they could get into contracting. For instance, a friend of my wife called me the other night and said, "Well, I'm thinking about getting into contracting." He had been doing conversion routines for news data and that's all he wanted to do. He was like, "Well, I'm really looking for a shop that is doing conversion routines on news data. I work for Knight Ridder and I'd like to do more of that." It's like, "Well, what are the tools that you use?" "Well, we use some C++." "Well, you could clearly get work as a C++ contractor but, you know, you might have to let go of this conversion routine specialty." He's like, "Well no, it's what I do best." He's not going to make it as a contractor. You've got to have this kind of attitude: "I'm a contractor, there's nothing I can't understand. You think that's complicated, give it to me. I'll simplify this in three days." You have to have that. You can't expect to be led into something and have things explained to you. You have to get out your M16, throw in a grenade, and run in screaming and firing.

Contractors generally sought stretchwork via one of two paths. The more conservative of the two was to take a contract that required skills which the contractor already possessed, but which also demanded her to work with a technology that she wanted to learn and did not know. By "piggybacking" off existing skills, contractors "built their résumés" gradually, minimized the risk of failure, and controlled downtime without having to "bluff their way into a job." Brian Willingham preferred this approach:

---

[7] We are grateful to Siobhan O'Mahony for developing the notion of stretchwork.

You get contracts that keep stretching you. I know C programming, but I don't know the Web, so I'll get a project that requires C programming on the Web. I know C, so I will stretch a little bit, I'll start learning web stuff. Okay, I know C and the Web, now I'll get something where I'm working with [inaudible]. And you constantly pick up projects. So, the customer's effectively paying for your learning. The customer pays one way or the other anyway, because otherwise you charge outrageous rates to cover the time that you're learning, and all the downtime.

Peyton Nugen also preferred to piggyback his way to new skills. To extend his expertise, Peyton took a contract in a firm that made extensive use of Lotus Notes, an application with which he was not proficient. Peyton claimed that by simply working with Lotus as an NT administrator, he learned 30 percent of what he needed to know about the application. He claimed to have increased his knowledge of Lotus to 60 percent by reading manuals at home after work. Then, by experimenting with what he had read while on the job, he claimed his understanding of Lotus rose to 90 percent. Peyton's next contract was as an expert in Lotus Notes.

A more risky strategy was to jump headfirst into a contract that required skills that the contractor did not yet possess. These contractors prepared by learning just enough about the technology—key terms and ideas, for example—to "talk their way into" the job. The strategy demanded that contractors possess considerable confidence in their ability to learn and a willingness to do whatever it took to deliver and to avoid the impression that they didn't really know what they were doing. Failure to disguise one's ignorance could result in being fired. Steve Louthan's move into writing UNIX documentation exemplifies the approach:

When they laid me off, I said to my friend, who was also my agent, "What have you got out there that is UNIX and systems administration?" He said, "Well, you've never done it before." I said, "Owen, I can write anything. You get me the interview. Give me two weeks up front. I'll buy the books. I'll read them cover to cover. Open the door; I'll close the sale." So, he said, "Okay, we're aiming our guns at Stratus. That's where you want to be. They're doing UNIX systems administration on a quadruply-redundant hardware platform." I bought two books: *The C Programming Language Handbook* and the *UNIX Systems Administration Handbook*. I read them both, cover to cover, twice. I flew through that interview with ease, because to me, you know, one operating system is similar to another. I had already become extremely familiar with DEC's VMS operating system and that is extraordinarily complex. It takes a twenty-five by twenty-five room with bookcases halfway up the wall to house all the books that describe DEC's VMS operating system. And so, I figured, how hard can UNIX be? I learned the basic rudiments of C and I learned how to speak UNIX. I went for the interview, I was already an accomplished writer at that point; I knew how to structure a manual. That wasn't an issue. The issue was the technical side of it. I had to convince the manager that I knew UNIX and I knew C. And he was experienced at it. Well, I did convince him, and he hired me.

Julian Stoke had also "bluffed his way into" contracts on several occasions: "I am a real fast learner. The company I worked for in Richmond for a year was using a protocol called Borland Delphi. It had come out early in the year in beta. Later that year I talked the company into hiring me even though I didn't have any experience. Hardly anybody had experience. But I had gotten a copy of the beta version and did everything I could with it at home. I could tell him all these different things I would do with it and how to do it. The technology I am using now, which is called Visual Age, is an IBM platform for developing programs. I did the same thing. I got a copy and worked with it at home. I have had two contracts where that was the requirement. I could not point to anything in my résumé that said I have done it for two years, so I had to talk my way into it. I was able to do that by using key words, general concepts about how the thing works."

Although most contractors agreed that it was not unreasonable to seek contracts that required skills that one did not yet possess, they disagreed about how this could be done ethically. Some, like Julian and Steve, saw no problem in bluffing, as long as one was willing to do what was necessary to deliver. Others felt that at the very least, it was incumbent on contractors to tell employers that they didn't have all the skills necessary, but that they could learn the skills quickly enough. If the employers then offered the contract, they had been forewarned. A minority went so far as to argue that it was unfair to charge an employer full rates if one were using the job to learn a new set of skills. Carmella Diaz subscribed to this philosophy:

> United Defense wanted me to use Authorware, but I'm more fluent with Director. Both Authorware and Director are products of Macromedia. I was insisting on using Director, but they insisted on Authorware. I had no idea how to use it. They want you to know it from day one, but I did inform the client that I was more fluent with the other software package, but they had a preference. And since I'd done two previous projects with them, I guess they felt they could trust me. I told them it would take me twice the amount of time, so

I'd just divide the hours. Let's say it took me twenty hours to learn chapter 1, I'll just charge them eight, nine hours, I mean not the whole twenty hours. Actually they even told me that they were worried I probably wasn't billing them for all the hours.

Ultimately, then, the contractor's objective in finding jobs was not simply to avoid downtime but to fashion a continual stream of learning opportunities that would enable her to acquire skills that would keep her in demand. The success of a contractor's career was, therefore, partially measured by the degree to which the stream of contracts took her into more vibrant areas of technology, broadened her résumé, and made her more easily employable without the need to devote periods of time to retooling. Contractors knew that pursuing a string of contracts that did not eventually stretch one's skill base ultimately meant that one would find oneself without work or doing unexciting work that paid little. Doug Hill warned, "I think the good contractors have always recognized that you need to keep yourself flexible and open. But it is possible to wind up doing small things. You know, the same pigeonholing can happen to you as a contractor. If you fail to educate yourself, you not only now have all of the entrepreneurial risks, but you have the same drawbacks as an employee."

Conclusion

Building and maintaining the human capital that enabled contractors to avoid obsolescence and stay in control of downtime demanded a significant investment of time and energy. Although contractors preferred to learn new skills on the job, most devoted significant periods of their own time to scanning and more focused learning. Hence, developing human capital became an ongoing activity that shaped contractors' lives. Not only did they spend significant amounts of uncompensated time maintaining, extending, and enhancing their expertise, but many also altered the contours of their living space and their leisure activities to optimize their ability to learn.

In short, contractors epitomized the rhetoric of continual learning. Learning became a central life activity that blurred the boundary between work and everyday life. Contractors found themselves in a situation where they had to keep learning to stay viable. Everyday activities— reading, talking, and Web surfing—became inextricably tied to work. Much the same thing happened to their social relationships.

Chapter 12

BUILDING AND MAINTAINING SOCIAL CAPITAL

ALTHOUGH CONTINUALLY augmenting one's human capital was necessary for ensuring steady employment, by itself it was insufficient. Our informants universally agreed that without social capital, they could not make optimal use of their human capital. Even contractors at the cutting edge of their occupation required access to information about clients who needed their services at the precise moment that they needed a job. Otherwise contractors could not squeeze downtime out of the cycle by moving directly from one contract into another. In theory, contractors could acquire timely information at arm's length from databanks and agents and, as we have seen, our informants did often turn to agencies and online databases for assistance. But as we also saw in chapter 5, contractors claimed that the managers, agents, permanent employees, and other contractors with whom they had personal relationships were more reliable for quickly locating and securing work.

Thus, when our informants needed a job, most turned to their networks as well as to agencies. Almost every contractor we interviewed spoke spontaneously about the importance of building, maintaining, and using networks of friends, acquaintances, and colleagues to find jobs and control downtime. Through these relationships contractors acquired three critical resources: referrals, references, and technical information.

Because referrals and references were so critical for finding jobs, contractors claimed that networks brought "job security." By job security contractors did not mean what most of us mean when we use the term: the ability to retain a job over time despite the ups and downs of the economy. Instead, contractors defined job security as the ease of finding the next job. In the corporate world it has become fashionable to call this kind of security "employability." Contractors, however, never used this term, and for good reason.[1] Discussions of employability almost always tell people that they need to maintain their human capital to remain marketable. For contractors, job security was about social capital, and in terms of social capital, contractors believed they had more "job security" than permanent employees. Although employees might be equally skilled,

---

[1] None of our informants ever used the term "employability." In fact, only one used the word "employable" and on that occasion, he was talking about the importance of keeping one's skills up-to-date.

contractors professed to have better developed networks. Jose Martinez spoke for most of the contractors we interviewed:

> [Permanent employees] think they have job security. They don't. In fact, they have practically no job security, especially in California where you can be fired whenever the company likes. Job security is the ability to get a job. [Permanent employees] don't have job security because they don't have the networks. They can't call someone and get a job tomorrow morning. They think they have job security, but it's on paper. Real job security is when you have a network of managers and recruiters where you simply call them and say, "Okay, my contract finished," and they say, "Great, I can place you somewhere tomorrow morning." That's where you have real job security; you're able to get a job. The reality is the staff person has no connections to a next job. They don't have social relationships.

We do not have the kind of data that would allow us to depict with precision the formal structure of the contractors' networks or to compare their networks systematically with the networks of employees. Consequently, we cannot prove or disprove Jose's claim. But we can use concepts drawn from network analysis to specify the contractors' perceptions of their networks more precisely and to explain how contractors believed their networks differed from those of permanent employees. This, in turn, helps us understand why contractors believed that their networks enabled them to control downtime and how building and maintaining networks shaped their lifestyle.

To understand how contractors thought about social capital requires us to unpack Jose's claim that employees "don't have social relationships." Taken literally, the claim is false. Not only do employees have social relationships but, as anyone who has worked full-time knows, coworkers develop deep, multifaceted, and long-lasting bonds. So, when Jose and other contractors claimed that employees lacked relationships, they did not really mean that employees lacked social capital or that they had no networks. Instead, contractors resorted to such hyperbole as they struggled to articulate how important networks had become to their lives and how their relationships seemed to differ from those they had as permanent employees.

Three attributes of social capital were especially salient for contractors. First was the *reach* of their relationships—the size and diversity of their networks. Second was their sense that *reputation* was the currency of social capital. Third was *reciprocity*, which lubricated the machinery of networking. Contractors spoke as if reach, reputation, and reciprocity were associated with different properties or sectors of their networks. Reach was a matter of the network's composition (who comprised their networks), the network's range (the number of organizations to which their networks gave them access), and a particular pattern of ties that network analysts call "structural holes." Reputation was tied to the contractors' sense that they participated in a "small world" defined along occupational lines. Finally, although reciprocity marked many of a contractor's relationships, it figured most prominently in the repeated exchanges that occurred among the individuals who formed what we shall call a contractor's "referral clique."

REACH

Our informants claimed that their networks extended further than the networks of permanent employees. Greater reach meant access to information about jobs from a wider set of sources. Although reach certainly increased as contractors made more acquaintances, our informants understood that the size of their networks was not all that mattered. More important were the composition and range of the network: the types of actors with whom they had relationships and the number of different settings in which these actors were located.

Composition

Jose spoke to the importance of composition when he told us that contractors' networks were "triangular," that they included not only other contractors but managers and agents as well. In contrast, he argued, most permanent employees confined their relationships to immediate supervisors and coworkers, who were usually employees as well. According to Jose, full-timers tended not to build relationships with contractors and with other managers, even within their own firms, and they avoided getting to know recruiters altogether. Consequently, when employees were laid off, they were handicapped: they had access neither to people who had jobs nor to people who knew about jobs. Without this kind of social capital, Jose explained, even cutting-edge skills could not guarantee that a person could secure work rapidly enough to avoid downtime:

> Engineers are so bad at getting jobs! They have a résumé, they have a skill set, they think, "Okay, cool!" They think that if you have these skills and you match, you will get a job. They don't understand that you have to socialize with the manager. You have to have lunch with people. You have to cooperate with people. And when they get fired, they don't understand why they got fired. They don't understand recruiters. They don't like recruiters because they think

they're sharks or something. So they won't talk to recruiters and when they don't have a job, they don't know whom to call. The recruiter doesn't know who they are. The recruiter, he gets a résumé. "I don't know who this person is. I've never dealt with him before, I don't know if he's okay or not. On paper he looks good, but I don't know who he is." So the engineers have this huge problem, even though they can look really good on paper.

Although other contractors did not use "triangular" (or any other term) to refer to the diversity of their relationships, their commentaries on how they found specific jobs generally confirmed Jose's observation on the composition of contractors' networks. Contractors worked with a large number of managers, recruiters, and other contractors over the course of their careers. Although they eventually lost contact with many of these people, most stayed in contact with those with whom they had some affinity. Many of our informants told us of hiring managers who had hired them repeatedly and who had also helped them find work in other firms. Judy King, for example, had just started working for a manager for whom she had already contracted twice: "At Hal Computers I found out on a Tuesday that they decided they were going to let me go. They did not have work that they could transfer me to. They were getting their funding cut. I sent out résumés both to managers that I knew and to agencies that I know. By Friday I had another job with another manager that I had worked for off and on. This is going to be the third time that I worked with her."

Although most contractors spoke cynically about recruiters in general, about half of our informants also had ongoing relationships with one or two recruiters with whom they communicated regularly and through whom they had found work on numerous occasions. All but the newest contractors knew other contractors, and most had found work through such contacts.

Range

Range, or the diversity of locales into which a network stretched, was even more important for managing downtime than the network's composition. Each new job immersed contractors in new relationships. They almost always worked alongside contractors and employees whom they had not previously known. With each job they also usually met a new hiring manager and, more often than not, encountered new recruiters and account managers. Thus, as contractors gained experience, their networks began to span a growing number of firms, agencies, industries, and occupational communities. In fact, long-term contractors spoke of networks that crossed states and sometimes countries. This was particularly true of "nomads" or "road warriors" like David Roberts: "I was living in Syracuse, working for General Electric. I was there for a year and a half or so. Then a friend of mine down in St. Louis that I'd met at Bell Aerospace in Niagara Falls called me up. He says, 'Hey, we got this good project down here in St. Louis.' That's where I met a guy that was a manager whom I worked for later on a 1099. And I dragged a bunch of buddies on up on 1099s."

Contractors argued that because employees moved less frequently, their range of contacts was more restricted. Employees were tied primarily to coworkers in the firms where they currently worked and perhaps where they had worked in the past. The longer the employee remained with one employer, the more restricted his or her network's range became. Stu Davis expressed the idea as follows:

> I feel that contractors theoretically should have more job security than the permanents. Contractors have more contacts because they're in and out of places. They have contacts through former employers, through agencies, and through other contractors. Whereas employees, their contacts are with other employees and with former bosses. They're much more limited in their contact base. So, if I was laid off the project at the end of tomorrow and I absolutely had to have something, I could find a job that day if I was willing to work for, say, only $45 an hour. I could start with no problem.

Aside from the contractors' own tendency to cycle through a large number of work settings, two additional dynamics enhanced their network's range. First, the agents, managers, and contractors with whom the contractor had relationships generally knew other managers, contractors, and agents whom the contractor did not know. To the degree that a contractor's contacts were willing to mobilize their own contacts to assist the contractor, they effectively extended his or her network into more settings. Such "two-step" or indirect referrals were common. Contractors who were already on contract and, hence, out of play, routinely told recruiters and hiring managers about other contractors who might be able to do the work. Second, the contractor's contacts were themselves highly mobile. As Vicky Chenalt put it, "People cycle." As a contractor's contacts moved from firm to firm, they extended the contractor's reach into an expanding array of agencies, companies, and technical communities.

Jose Martinez's and Stu Davis's theory of how the networks of contractors and permanent employees differ and why contractors' networks offer more security is consistent with Ronald Burt's research on networks rich in "structural holes."[2] According to Burt, structural holes arise when

---

[2] See Burt (1992).

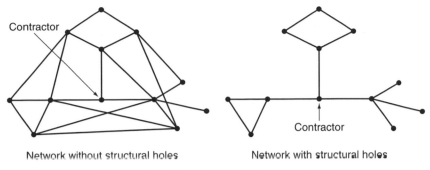

Network without structural holes   Network with structural holes

Fig. 12.1. Personal Networks with and without Structural Holes

we have relationships with two or more people who do not have even indirect ties with each other. Pragmatically, this means that each of our contacts is more likely to provide us with unique information because each is tied to different people. In contrast, networks lack structural holes when we know people who, in turn, know each other. In such cases information tends to circulate within the network, so that each contact is likely to provide us with the same information. In other words, networks marked by structural holes offer access to more opportunities than do networks with few structural holes. Figure 12.1 depicts the difference between the two kinds of networks.

Jose and Stu seemed to be arguing that employees primarily know people who know each other. Consequently, their contacts tend to be aware of the same set of opportunities. In contrast, contractors tend to know more people who have fewer direct and indirect ties among themselves and, hence, offer a wider range of information. Burt and other researchers have shown empirically what the contractors instinctively knew: structural holes are associated with greater career advancement and access to more entrepreneurial opportunities.[3]

REPUTATION AND OCCUPATIONAL CIRCLES

Although the reach of a contractor's network dramatically improved the odds of timely access to information about jobs, reach alone was insufficient for securing referrals and references. In addition, people who knew about jobs had to be motivated to share their knowledge of opportunities with the contractor. Even agents who were reputedly indiscriminant

---

[3] See Burt (1992, 1997, 2001), Podolny and Baron (1997), and Mehra, Kilduff, and Brass (2001) on the utility of networks with structural holes.

about placing "warm bodies" had an incentive to refer contractors whom they knew to be both skilled and reliable. Doing so increased the odds that clients would bring repeat business to the agency. Contractors, employees, and hiring managers had even more incentive to be selective: they would have to work with and rely on the contractor. Moreover, contractors lost credibility with clients when they recommended other contractors who proved incapable or unreliable. Consequently, contractors soon learned that in contracting circles, reputation was the currency of social capital. As Hernando Galvez put it, "You are your work."

Differences in reputation determined which contractors would receive referrals and recommendations and which would not. "Reputation is important," Brian Willingham warned, "and if you do a bad job on a project, you'll stop getting calls." Glenn Arthur made the point more dramatically:

> There seem to be these conversations at companies that I've never heard, but I am sure they go on. It's like, "These damn contractors, they don't do shit. You hire them and they don't get anything done and they don't do things to spec and they lip off. You get these kids who are just cowboys and they think they can do everything. I'm just pissed off. I've never had a good contractor." And someone says, "Well, you know, we hired a contractor to do a spec for our Web server and he was pretty good." "Okay, who was that? Got a number?" And that's how people come to us. You know, we don't always do great things, but it seems competence in this business is starting to be an increasingly rare commodity.

As we saw in chapters 5 and 6, agents and hiring managers routinely asked contractors not only to suggest other contractors for openings, but also to provide recommendations for contractors who were already under consideration for specific positions. Experienced informants were willing to be honest if they did not feel another contractor was worthy of recommendation. In explaining why they would do so, Marty Keely pointed to the second attribute of their networks that was salient for contractors: the sense that they moved in "small worlds."

> I was at a project at DHL systems, the package shipment company. We were hiring someone and a résumé came on board. I had worked with this guy and he was a reject from another project I was on. I was very vocal. I said, "This Pedro guy, I've worked with him. In fact the company got rid of him. I don't trust the résumé. Now if you want to bring him in, that's your business." They never brought him in. Now you may say, "Wow, that was immoral of you to pass judgment on others," but the point is, this is a small circle. If I said I

know this guy and he came on board and did a bad job, it would reflect on me.

The image of a small world, or what we shall call a "network of practice," emerged repeatedly in our interviews. Sociologists of work and occupations have long recognized that the members of an occupation or specialty know of and interact with other members of their occupation who work in other organizations. For instance, cardiac surgeons know other cardiac surgeons who practice not only in their own hospitals and local communities, but also in hospitals and communities throughout the country and, in some instances, the world. Sociologists refer to these social collectives as occupational communities. The problem with the notion of an occupational community is precisely that it assumes that all members of the community are members of the same occupation. Lave and Wenger coined the term "community of practice" to overcome the idea that common membership in a recognizable occupation was the defining characteristic of the social collectives in which practitioners participate and within which occupational expertise and knowledge circulate. The notion of a community of practice rightly focused attention on the idea that a type of practice is an important nexus of organizing, but this concept is also limited in that it assumes face-to-face interaction among people who are locally situated. To adequately portray how knowledge and expertise are organized requires a concept that recognizes that a type of work may involve members of multiple occupations who may or may not know each other but who do similar work, who are indirectly linked to each other, and who participate in a social system that facilitates the flow of work-related knowledge and information.

It was to address these issues that Brown and Duguid proposed the notion of a "network of practice." They wrote:

> We prefer to think of these loose epistemic groups as "networks." . . . Reflecting what binds these networks together and enables knowledge to flow within them, we call these extended epistemic networks "networks of practice." Practice creates the common substrate. With the term network, we also want to suggest that relations among network members are significantly looser than those within a community of practice . . . most of the people within such a network will never know, know of, or come across one another. And yet, they are capable of sharing a great deal of knowledge.[4]

"Network of practice" seems to capture what contractors had in mind when they talked about being part of a "small world."

[4] Brown and Duguid (2001, 205).

Experienced contractors claimed that after a time, they began to encounter the same individuals as they moved from contract to contract. Repeated encounters were defined largely along occupational lines. These encounters traced out a cluster of contractors, permanent employees, and hiring managers who were involved in the same or closely related specialties. Structurally speaking, contractors portrayed such circles as social groups extending beyond their own personal contacts, although their personal networks intersected with the circle's membership. Contractors did not necessarily know all the members of the circle, and many of those whom they did know were simply acquaintances. Nevertheless, as Marty Keely explained, it was within these circles that reputations were minted and circulated:

> You may think there are a lot of people working in this industry and that the chance of running into a familiar face is very slim. Well actually, it's quite the other way around. The odds are very high that you will run into the same people within two years. It's a very small world, a very small community of people who end up doing the same kind of work over and over again. People tend to specialize. So you find yourself in the same circle. This is why it's more important not to burn bridges and to do quality work, because you find yourself in the same circle over and over again. I mean, I go to a new project and we're hiring. I see résumés of guys I worked with. It's that incestuous [*laughs*].

Judy King offered a similar perspective. "Remember we're in a little microcosm," Judy advised. "We're specialized here. It might not be this way if I were someplace else. Although most friends of mine who have worked in [places] like New York say it's similar in the big cities. It's difficult not to run across the same people, and it's difficult not to know who's good and who's not. I would say in this area, reputation is far better than anything else you can possibly bring to the table."

In fact, experienced contractors believed that if one's reputation within a network of practitioners—one's social capital—was sufficiently strong, it could overcome the lack of specific skills. Kent Cox remarked: "My career has been not so much getting hired to do the same thing, but getting hired by people I know who can't find someone they need to fill a particular niche, so they hire someone they think can learn to do it." Stu Davis also testified to the power of reputation:

> I mentioned my buddy James Green, the guy from Motion Electronics. I knew he was working as a permanent employee at a company doing point of sale systems. We'd had some conversations. I knew he wanted to hire me, but didn't know if he could afford me. I had

an interview in October at a company up in North Carolina, but I was too expensive for them. The recruiting agent for that company told me, "Man, I just talked to your friend, James, who you gave as a reference. Boy, he must really like you. He said some real glowing things about you. The first thing he said was, 'Oh no! I wanted to hire Stu for my project.'" Well, I called up James and said, "James, I don't know if you all have a need for anybody, but I'm available." James says, "Great. Come on in. We want to talk to you." So, I did. Sat down and he says, "We've got his point of sale system running on an NCR platform running PC DOS. We gotta port it to an IBM platform running MS DOS. We'd like you to do it for us. Down the road we want to go to a Windows NT platform." I said, "Great, I'd love to. I've got a question for you. Are you guys aware that I know nothing at all about Windows NT?" "Oh yeah, we know that." "Okay, are you also aware that I know very little about DOS and nothing at all about point of sales systems?" "Oh yeah, we know that." I said, "Well, here's my rate. It's gonna cost you." And they go "Gulp. Ahhh . . . Well, when can you start?" I said, "Well, let's see. Its 2:30 now. I could be back here by 4:00 and ready to go." I had worked with these guys before on this project for Robert Shaw Controls. They knew me. They knew how I worked. They knew the kind of code that I wrote, the work ethic, and all this, and that's why they wanted me. And I know because they told me that in those words.

RECIPROCITY AND REFERRAL CLIQUES

If reputation was the currency of social capital, then reciprocity was the lubricant that enabled referrals to flow more smoothly. As contractors told stories of how they found work, reciprocity—the exchange of favors and resources—emerged in a variety of guises. Hiring managers offered work to contractors whom they knew and, in return, contractors did favors for hiring managers that went beyond the terms of their contract. They might work additional hours without charge, provide advice on hiring other contractors, or share tools to which the client did not have access. Although contractors' relationships with recruiters were usually fleeting and purely economic, when contractors developed ongoing relationships with recruiters, reciprocity emerged. In return for repeated referrals, contractors gave recruiters the names of potential leads, they shared information on the firms where they worked, and they taught recruiters technology and terminology. Agents, in turn, sometimes paid contractors bonuses for referring contractors whom the agent subsequently placed. Often these were lump sum payments, but sometimes the contractor received an hourly margin. Olivia Crum told us of such an exchange: "They needed a new person, so I pulled in a consultant friend of mine who had converted to an employee at TRW. Now he starts next week at Nissan working for Ernst and Young with me. So the agency is going to pay me a dollar an hour for every hour that he works. I asked them, 'For how long?' They said, 'As long as he's there.'"

The most frequent form of reciprocity, however, occurred among contractors themselves: the mutual exchange of referrals. When contractors landed a contract they often discovered that the client had need for additional help. This gave contractors an opportunity to "pull in" other contractors whom they knew. "Pulling in" another contractor involved convincing a hiring manager to employ a colleague who was in need of work and for the quality of whose work one was personally willing to vouch. Most experienced contractors had been "pulled into" a job one or more times by contractors who were already working for a client. Conversely, many had returned such favors. Although contractors might occasionally extend referrals to or receive referrals from any contractor in their network, repeated exchanges of referrals were usually confined to a handful of individuals who formed what we call the contractor's referral clique.[5]

Most experienced contractors told us that they had developed close personal and professional relationships with a small number of other contractors—typically five to ten people. With these individuals, friendship, loyalty, and professional relations merged. As Peyton Nugen put it, "You go out together. You tell each other things. They call you up if they have a question on a subject they need to know." Contractors were fairly selective about the people with whom they formed such associations. Peyton continued, "You build this network out of those that can help you, out of the ones you like, that are on the same level. For example, there are a lot of C programmers at HP, but a C programmer has nothing in common with me."

Members of a referral clique served as each other's technical advisors and were committed to helping each other find work. Often members of such cliques practiced complementary specialties, so that when one person landed a contract he or she was able to bring in other members of the group. Brian Willingham explained:

> I have friends who are consultants, and we'll pass work back and forth to each other. "I don't have time for this project," or "I'm not qualified." You know, it's not my area of expertise, but I know

[5] By a clique, network analysts mean a group of people whose ties with each other are denser than their ties to people outside the group. For various ways of defining cliques, see Wasserman and Faust (1994).

somebody who does. So, I'll just say, "Here it is, go have fun with it." I've got projects that way too, like the one that I'm working on at GT Mart. I'm bringing in Bob as a consultant. He knows more about Sequel Server than I do, so I'm going to let him handle that part of the project. In my circle, it's not like, "Gee, they're my customers," and, "I don't want to let you [know] any of my trade secrets." It's more like, "There's plenty of work out there." It's not like we're desperate for customers at this point. It's more like part support group, part professional organization, part "Gee, at least we have some friends in our life 'cause we're working so many hours."

Most of the work that passed through referral cliques was hit or miss. Members referred work to other members as opportunities arose. But this was not always the case. For instance, small companies that were looking to ramp up quickly often made strategic use of a contractor's referral clique to staff projects. They hired a contractor and then relied on the contractor's referrals to staff other positions. Some contractors, like Jose Martinez, actively sought such opportunities. Jose explained:

Here [in the Silicon Valley] it's totally normal to do a start-up. A group of guys will come up with an idea, they'll approach a couple VCs and propose the project. The VCs throw the money into it. The recruiters come in and they staff the place with the top guns, contractors with ten years' experience. They know how to set up the whole office. Literally within two days you have a company. They come in, they know how to create things, they bring all the software with them. We carry our $7,000 laptops with us, with all of our software, all of our programs, and all our scripts already installed. We jack it into the network, and within two days we're all working together. A lot of us know each other from previous projects. I can come into a company and then simply call friends of mine and bring them in. We've all worked together, we all know each other really well, so we move around from company to company. I work literally at a new company almost every month. And it goes really well like that.

In sum, contractors had redefined job security to mean the ability to find their next job. In this sense they believed that they had more job security than permanent employees. They thought their networks were better structured for acquiring information about and landing jobs for three reasons. First, like employees, contractors had strong reciprocal ties with a small number of friends. But whereas employees had close relations with coworkers in the same organization, contractors had strong ties with a handful of contractors who formed a referral clique that exchanged technical information and job opportunities. The contractors' friends were not only committed to helping each other find work, they could deliver because their access to clients gave them access to jobs. Second, as contractors moved around they became aware that they were part of a loosely bound "network of practice," an occupational circle comprising people who did similar or complementary work. Members of these circles knew each other's reputations for expertise, and if a contractor's reputation was solid, members of the circle would vouch for and even refer the contractor to clients and agents. Finally, as contractors moved from job to job and as the agents, contractors, and hiring managers whom they knew also circulated, the contractors' networks were constantly expanding into new organizations, agencies, and industries. Thus, unlike permanent employees, contractors' networks covered more ground.

The overall image is one in which contractors were embedded in a network of relations organized in concentric regions. As depicted in figure 12.2, the central region of the contractor's network is composed of members of his or her referral clique. Here relations are strong and dense: all members of the clique are tied to one another. The second region consists of people who do similar or complementary types of work: the contractor's occupational circle or network of practice. Relations among the members of the network of practice are less dense. Finally, in the outermost region are hiring managers, contractors, and agents who are not members of the same network of practice but to whom the contractor turns for information on jobs. Relations among these individuals are even less dense.

Figure 12.2 is a representation of the social world in which contractors practiced. This world was where contractors lived large portions of their professional lives and from which they derived the social capital that activated and animated their human capital. These relations comprised the safety net that allowed contractors to put their skills to work and minimize downtime. Building and maintaining such social capital required enough time, effort, and energy that it became central to the contracting lifestyle.

NETWORKING: BUILDING AND MAINTAINING NETWORKS

Although contractors' networks emerged, in part, as a by-product of their movement from contract to contract, networks also required explicit attention. Simply meeting someone was usually insufficient for establishing a relationship, and relationships atrophied if they were not renewed. Thus contractors not only "worked *through* their networks" in

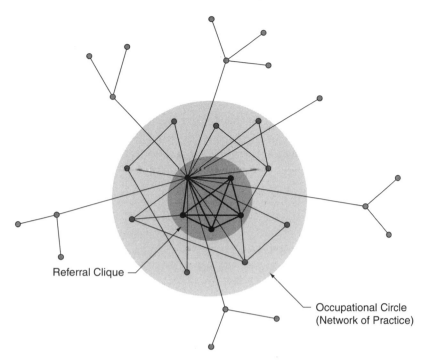

Referral Clique

Occupational Circle
(Network of Practice)

Fig. 12.2. A Hypothetical Contractor's Network

the sense that work often came through the people they knew, but they also had to "work *on* their networks" in the sense of cultivating and husbanding relationships that might generate jobs.[6]

Most contractors did not enter contracting with networks that were sufficiently well developed to provide the kind of job security that they desired. When leaving permanent employment, contractors were hampered by the fact that most of their relationships centered on the firm they were leaving. They had not yet developed a reputation within a network of practice and their networks had few structural holes. Cultivating such a network took time and was a source of concern for most new contractors. Katrina Labovski explained how difficult it was to find her first

---

[6] Bonnie Nardi, an anthropologist who has studied work practices among technical workers and entrepreneurs in the Silicon Valley, used the term "Net-Working" to refer to the activities and strategies by which people build and maintain contacts. Her intention was to emphasize that networking is not simply a matter of meeting people, as the popular idiom implies. Instead, it is a form of work aimed at building the social infrastructure that enables one to practice one's craft. See Nardi, Whittaker, and Schwarz (1999) and Schwarz, Nardi, and Whittaker (1999).

contract, after being laid off from Apple Computers, because of her lack
of contacts:

> I looked very, very hard. My approach from the beginning was, "I
> think I really want to be independent. I don't want to work through
> recruiters." So, I would call companies that I wanted to work for
> and tell them about myself. I spent a lot of time on the phone, and
> people were kind of sending my résumé out—that sort of thing. And
> nothing was happening. You know, it takes some time. People
> would tell me, "Oh, in a few weeks we might have something." So,
> I started talking to other contractors who were doing better than me
> and one of them said, "You know, when I was first starting out, I
> worked with recruiters, because these people's full-time job is to
> look for work." So, I did talk with some recruiters as well [*with a
> sneer*]. And nothing happened as a result of that either. I did my best
> networking. I contacted everyone that I knew who was a staffer or
> contractor or whatever to find out if there was anything that I could
> do. And that's the kind of stuff that kept me busy for those two
> months until I finally got my first contract.

Because contractors' networks were occupationally centered, even experienced contractors could find themselves without adequate social capital if they decided to switch fields. For example, after spending years as
a circuit designer, Brenda O'Boyle decided to move into quality assurance, the field in which her husband also worked. On making the shift,
she discovered that her contacts were no longer useful because they centered on integrated circuits. "Prior to getting into this end of the business, I had an extensive network in the IC business," Brenda lamented.
"That was the biggest shock to me when I decided to give that up. I was
like, "Oh my God, I don't know anybody!" I know people my husband
knows, but those aren't people who know me—who know my work—so
they certainly couldn't recommend me." Brenda estimated that it took
her over a year to build a new network.

Lacking contacts, most novices and experienced contractors who
shifted fields turned to staffing agencies to locate their first jobs. Once
they began to land contracts, meet people, and establish relationships,
they gradually became less reliant on agencies, although most continued
to use them. Although few of the contractors we encountered consciously
made networking a primary form of activity (in fact, some went to great
lengths to assure us that they were not "networkers"), the majority were
aware of the need to form and cultivate professional contacts. Contractors exhibited an array of philosophies and strategies for doing so.

One small group of contractors approached networking as a calculated activity. These individuals had explicit strategies for meeting people whom they could fold into their network of contacts. Several informants had joined professional societies and users' groups as a way of making contacts that could lead to referrals. Two had actually started a users' group, partially for this reason. Another admitted that she sometimes contacted agencies and interviewed for jobs which she had no intention of taking, simply to meet agents and hiring managers. Stu Davis even replied to job announcements, just to keep his name in circulation: "I get notifications [about jobs] from *CE Weekly*. Occasionally one will be pretty interesting and I'll respond to it. Even if I'm not actively looking, I'll respond just to be sure they know that I'm alive. You know, 'Hey, this guy may not be available now, but we're keeping him in mind for something down the road.'"

We encountered another small group of contractors who claimed they abhorred building relationships expressly for enhancing their careers. These individuals talked about the phoniness of "networking" or "gladhanding" and the fleeting nature of relationships among contractors. Herman Jay, for example, who described himself as a "wanderer" and who worked primarily through staffing agencies, remarked:

> Job shop contacts are about as tenuous as job shop jobs. When I was with Oracle we had a very nice group that worked well together and we would go out for a beer. Everyone said, "Oh, let's stay in touch." I made sure that everyone had my e-mail, and for a while I corresponded with several of them. Then one guy finally got a job. I didn't hear from him. I thought maybe he hadn't got my e-mail. I sent him another. He wrote back, "Gee, it is really nice to hear from you. I am real busy but I will write back as soon as I can." Never heard from him again.

By and large, however, most contractors lay somewhere in between. They were aware that networking was important, and they devoted time to developing and maintaining relationships, but they portrayed their activities as simply a part of everyday life. When we asked contractors how they built contacts, three responses predominated. The most frequent focused on "doing good work." If contractors performed well and reliably, they would naturally develop the kind of reputation necessary for garnering referrals. Hernando Galvez's comment was typical:

> I think the most important part is that you have to continue to do good work. And if you're not doing the work yourself, then whoever's working for you has to be doing good work. And really, that's what you build your reputation on. And if your job is providing a service to a customer, then 50 percent of it may be the quality of the

work the person does. But the other 50 percent of it is how you service your customer. In other words, how do you react to their needs? How do you react to situations? And that's really what it comes down to. For me, getting business is about always making sure that you have a referral source. And you can't have a referral source if you're not doing a good job.

Contractors also talked about the importance of helping others as a way of developing relationships that would mature into contacts. "That is where networking has worked really nicely for me," Jeff Dorsey told us as he explained the importance of giving and receiving help. "If I don't know how to do this, or I don't have an answer, I can call one of my buddies at Microsoft who might know, because they have been focusing on this. Or if I need a tool I will say, 'Do you have anything that does this?' and they will be like, 'Oh yeah, we have that. I will send it to you in an e-mail.' I think the most important thing in the industry is that it really pays off to help people. I know that I would not have gotten into the industry if it had not been for a few people helping me dial in my résumé and introducing me to other people who gave me informal interviews. And I am totally thankful. On my Web site, I have this huge thank-you page to these people."

Most important, however, for building networks was developing friendships and bonds of trust that provided the footing for sustaining relationships into the future. Judy King explained:

> One of the things that I do when I get a job is bond with the people that are there, so that when we go forward I know that I can depend on them and they know they can depend on me. And it's difficult to cut those bonds. On the other hand, e-mail and the fact that the Valley is so small makes it not so difficult. I have friends that I've been e-mailing for fifteen or twenty years. There's one friend that I was working with in TRW in '96. We have lunch or breakfast once a month. I have lunch with another woman, my ex-boss at Sun, a couple of times a month and so forth. So I stay in contact with people through e-mail, just so I don't lose those bonds. I mean it's useful because I can always push on those relationships if I need them at some point. But they are also relationships. They are people I've met and worked with. We went through a lot. We sat up all night, did all-nighters, whatever it was we needed to do in order to get the project done, so the relationship remains.

Once contacts were established with agents, hiring managers, and other contractors, contractors spoke of spending time maintaining the relationships. Although we encountered no contractors who admitted to using contact management databases or tickler files as tools for systematically maintaining contacts, a number of informants said they knew other contractors who did. Judy King had found jobs through a friend who cultivated such a database. "I have a friend, Jonathan," Judy told us, "who actually has this huge e-mail list of agencies, friends, headhunters—a couple hundred names. He sends out messages to the list if he wants to contact people when he is looking for a job. And he reverses that. Whenever he gets a call from somebody saying, 'Gee are you available?' he says, 'No, but you should try this person.' I found a couple of jobs through Jonathan."

Although most contractors were not as systematic as Judy's friend, in the course of interviews contractors frequently mentioned that they kept a list of people whom they routinely called when they needed work. Most informants also told us that they actively attempted to stay in touch with key people in their network even when they didn't need work. They spoke of periodically phoning or sending e-mail to contractors, hiring managers, and employees whom they had met on previous jobs. Contractors also spoke of arranging to have lunch or a drink with members of their network as a way of "keeping in touch." The number of contacts that contractors actively tried to maintain ranged from ten to fifty people. Frequency of contact also varied. Contractors might speak weekly, if not daily, to members of their referral clique, especially if they were collaborating on contracts. They might contact other individuals every three to six months, "just to say, 'Hi, how's it going?'"

Our impression is that most of our informants devoted a considerable amount of time to maintaining relationships, although we did not systematically ask them for estimates of the time they devoted to cultivating contacts. Lunches and breakfasts typically take a minimum of an hour. Phone calls made with the intention of renewing friendships also take chunks of time. It was not uncommon for contractors who consciously sought to maintain their networks to spend more than an hour a day in such activity. Anil Rao claimed that he spent an hour or more every day networking with friends and contacts.

The important point is that contractors not only spent a considerable amount of time building and maintaining their social capital, but that such activities became deeply entwined with their everyday lives. Although some contractors claimed they kept their professional and social networks separate, many found that friendship and professional ties overlapped to such a degree that the nature of the relationships became difficult to distinguish. Jeff Dorsey explained the ambiguity in response to a question about how he built his networks:

My buddy Jerry, for instance, worked at Magnolia when I worked there. The only reason I got to be good friends with him and his wife is because we all like mountain biking. Then we started snowboarding together. We just became really good friends and he was sick of Magnolia and I'm like, "Well, you know a lot about computers, why don't you get into the software industry?" So, I would go over there and show him a few things and tell him this is what they look for, study this kind of stuff. And then it was just a matter of me going to my boss and saying I have this guy, he does not have any professional experience, but he is a really good friend of mine, he knows his stuff, and he learns stuff really quickly. It's just a matter of pushing for your friends. It's the same thing you would do for any of your friends. It's nothing extraordinary. And in turn he has turned around and helped some of his friends get into the software industry too.

Relationships among the members of a referral clique were especially likely to meld work and friendship. Glenn Arthur joined with friends he had made when working as a permanent employee for a now defunct knowledge engineering firm to start Expert Support, a collective that actually functioned as a staffing firm. Interestingly, Glenn explicitly viewed his friendships with these contractors as a form of capital:

Here's a clear instance where trust in the relationship and friendship adds value. I think generally you just can't quantify the economic benefit of having a network of people who trust each other and want to do right by each other. That was something we happened to have. That was the capital. I mean my stock options from Tech-Knowledge didn't mean much. I made a little money 'cause I sold some of them early. Made about seventeen grand. Big deal. When we all left TechKnowledge, I don't think any of us knew at the time, but I think what we were doing was leaving with whatever capital we had. The only real capital we had to call our own was the relationship we had among the engineering group and we made that work. I mean that was the capital with which Expert Support was built and that continues to supply leverage for all of us in Expert Support. I think that if we hadn't had the experience at TechKnowledge, never in a million years would I enter into that relationship with a bunch of strangers.

We met several contractors who were married to each other and a number of contractors who shared a home with other contractors. A few other contractors told us that they socialized frequently with contractors. The majority of our informants, however, had a social life that was separate from their work relationships. Nevertheless, almost every contractor we interviewed told us that he or she had found one or more jobs with the help of people they referred to as "friends."

For some contractors, the realization that they relied on friends to find work evoked an uncomfortable ambivalence. Hernando Galvez, for instance, was adamant that we understand that he did not approach his relationships instrumentally, an attitude that he associated with "networking." Instead, contacting friends in his search for jobs was an extension of his relationship with them:

> I have never—as part of engaging in some networking activity or attending some function—made a contact that I would say I was able to successfully engage in business with. I don't have an active marketing effort. I don't try to make believe I have one. But let's say I'm gonna be out of work in March. So what's going to happen? Well, probably around December, I go through my little list of people that I have, you know, maybe forty to fifty people. But I don't keep a tickler file. I know people who do that. Like they'll keep a tickler file and, "Oh, yeah. My computer's telling me I should call this guy because I haven't spoken to him in thirty days." I don't do that. I sort of sense when it's time to call someone. It's just like a friend you haven't seen in a while. You know, it's time to call this guy up I haven't spoken with and find out what's going on with him, right? You pick up the phone and you call this person and say, "Hey, how you doing? It's been a while. Hey, how you been?" And you have a little conversation and meet for lunch. You do something like that and then that's it. I mean, so you get some information. I'm not actively building intelligence. I keep in touch with people. I don't go out of my way.

Hernando's ambivalence points to an irony that haunted the importance contractors came to place on building and maintaining social networks. As we saw in chapter 3, many contractors claimed they left permanent employment because they disliked how the social and political dynamics of organizational life interfered with what they thought of as a more rational approach to technical decision making. Contracting seemed to offer our informants an opportunity to separate the political from the technical, the social from the pragmatic. As contractors, they believed they could focus entirely on the task and be rewarded for doing so. In short, our informants entered contracting with a dream of separating the social and technical aspects of work. Ironically, however, contractors soon found that the exigencies of contracting demanded that they weave social and task dynamics back together to find work. In this sense relationships proved to be even more important for our informants than they had been when they were permanent employees.

But there was a crucial difference. The social relationships which contractors had found distasteful as permanent employees were typically power relationships marked by conflict and competition. The social relationships in which contractors became so deeply entwined were symmetrical and marked by reciprocity. Contractors found jobs for each other in a kind of potlatch system. Hernando's ambivalence about the instrumentality of networking is, therefore, less of an inconsistency than it first appears. Contractors were not adverse to the interpenetration of social and work relations. In fact, they had learned that social capital enabled them to take advantage of human capital. What they disliked was the sense that they were unable to engage in a form of reciprocal exchange. When people were unable or unwilling to reciprocate, networking became equivalent to using people.

Being a contractor ultimately required paying careful attention to one's temporal, human, and social capital. The three were integrally entwined. Temporal capital had to be used to build social and human capital. Human capital was mobilized by social capital. Social capital, in turn, provided access to jobs and to advice networks that enhanced human capital. Becoming a contractor meant adapting one's lifestyle to the realization that self-reliance meant accepting a form of professionalism in which the practitioner was his or her own safety net. Work, therefore, not only expanded, but the ability to draw a firm line between one's professional and one's other selves blurred. Ultimately, then, contracting brought its practitioners not only a new lifestyle but also a new identity: that of the itinerant professional.

Chapter 13

ITINERANT PROFESSIONALS
IN A KNOWLEDGE ECONOMY

OVER THE COURSE of this book we've journeyed through the everyday lives of technical workers who have chosen to live beyond the boundary of traditional employment as itinerant experts. These men and women consciously rejected the familiar pains and comforts of organizational life for the freedom and accompanying risks of the marketplace. As a group they partook of a way of life, a culture of work, which challenges the prevailing theories and entrenched practices of employment. Yet, contracting is poorly understood, and efforts to explain its emergence and significance have suffered from an excess of ideology and a dearth of data. Our journey was designed, in the manner of traditional ethnography, to produce a detailed, balanced, and accurate depiction of how contractors structured and interpreted their experience and how the lives they led were different from the ones they left behind.

Our objective, however, was to produce more than a mere ethnography, because contracting is more than a mere fragment in the rich mosaic of American working life. Ultimately, contracting is a manifestation of the groundswell of change that, by all accounts, is shaking the foundations of work and employment in the United States. By closely studying contractors' everyday lives, we gain a strategic vantage point for viewing, evaluating, and, perhaps, even shaping these changes. As we immersed ourselves in the mundane and sometimes esoteric details of our contractors' lives, we tried to keep the bigger picture close at hand. It is to this larger picture that we now turn. We first summarize the details of what we think we have learned about technical contracting to provide the foundation for our claims. We then show how the everyday lives and practices of contractors speak to the broader context of the American industrial landscape. Specifically, we argue that contracting directs our attention to a resurgence of occupational organizing in the wake of bureaucracy's retreat and the free market's advance. We end by suggesting what a renewed appreciation for occupational dynamics could mean for individuals, firms, and public policy.

ITINERANT EXPERTS: THE CONTRACTING LIFE

We began our journey by immersing ourselves in the practical realities of the market for technical contractors: a complex social world marked by a sea of information that contractors had to periodically navigate to find their next job. Here we met the cast of characters that populate the contractors' world and shape its dynamics: sales-oriented account managers and recruiters hungry for the next deal; hassled project managers in need of quick access to expertise; watchful executives and human resource managers who guard the bureaucratic and legal cultures of client organizations; and other contractors who, at different times, might be competitors vying for the same jobs or collegial sources of support and market information. We also visited various scenes, both virtual and real, where market transactions and encounters unfolded: the bustling back rooms of staffing agencies; on-site and long-distance job interviews; information-rich Web sites; users' groups; and the mazes of cubicles where high-tech work is done. The contractors whose lives we followed tacked back and forth between these characters and scenes to emerge from the market, time after time, with a deal in hand.

Successfully navigating the market for technical expertise required considerable effort and skill. Making deals in the market, newcomers soon learned, was more like haggling in a bazaar than shopping at a suburban mall. Indeed, the novice's first impression was of a confusing and often overwhelming abundance of opportunities and information of unknown quality, all of which clamored for attention. It was a bazaar, however, without clear spatial and temporal boundaries. Contractors discovered that with a Web browser they could enter the market day and night. In fact, persistent and occasionally unscrupulous hawkers of market information regularly beat a path to their telephones and computer screens without invitation. As in all bazaars, beneath the seemingly chaotic hubbub of deal making was more order than first met the eye. Contractors, to survive, quickly became adept at playing an information game—learning to gather, order, disseminate, interpret, select, and use information about jobs, skills, rates, and clients. They built networks of other contractors, agents, and hiring managers to locate, filter, distribute, and validate the information. To complement and extend their networks, many turned to staffing agencies. These agencies, eager to cash in on the market for contractors, specialized in gathering, filtering, and disseminating market information for others. For a price, they offered contractors the functional equivalent of a ready-made network. Together networks and agents, when skillfully deployed, produced steady streams of leads and opportunities.

Finding job opportunities, however, was but the first step in making a deal. To close deals contractors also had to engage in complex, three-way bargaining with hiring managers and agents. This process exposed contractors to an unexpected reality: bargaining was more than just haggling over rates that maximized income. Contractors discovered that they also had to negotiate the very definition of their skills. To the surprise of newcomers and the consternation of those who regard skills as stable and testable abilities, definitions of "technical skills" were never clear-cut. There was always a gap between what contractors believed they could do, what they said they could do, and what the clients claimed they wanted. To land a job, contractors had to identify and bridge this gap.

Thus, in the course of finding a job, contractors packaged their expertise and experience, sold their potential to learn, redefined requirements and deliverables, drew on their networks to generate recommendations, and, if necessary, bluffed their way into jobs. They also discovered that clients did not enter the market simply to find technical expertise, although most clients believed that this was what they were doing. Hiring managers also wanted to purchase peace of mind and an exemption from the hassles of managing permanent employees. Savvy contractors knew they had to sell these less tangible "products," and many did so explicitly. Contractors, therefore, periodically subjected not only the value of their skills but also their occupational identities to tough bargaining and the discipline of the market.

From the churning marketplace we followed our itinerant experts into the relative calm of the job. Even here, however, there was considerable drama beneath the rational veneer of technical work. Although a contractor's position in the client organization was usually well enough defined in legal terms, how he or she actually fit into the social fabric of organizational life was problematic. Because everyday life in most firms was still governed, to a great extent, by traditional notions of employment, the people with whom contractors worked struggled with conflicting images of the contractor's rightful place and the mixed feelings these generated. To make the most of the contractor's skills, hiring managers discovered they had to integrate the contractor into the flow of activities and the network of relationships. In fact, managers sometimes gave contractors opportunities that were closed to employees or tried to recruit contractors into permanent positions. At the same time, managers also overtly distinguished between contractors and full-timers to reassure themselves, their employees, and corporate watchdogs that contractors could make no claims on the prerogatives of membership. When the need arose, managers also benefited from the comparative ease with which contractors could be dismissed. Employees were similarly torn between the use they made of contractors' expertise, the friendships they established with contractors, and their envy of the contractors' skills, rates, and apparent freedom. For employees, contractors often became symbols of the tenuousness of all employment in today's economy. The contractors' role in the companies where they found temporary respite from the market was, therefore, rife with ambiguity.

This inherent ambiguity was the defining feature of the contractors' experience on the job. Contractors knew that no matter how appreciated, accepted, and integrated they became, they were still outsiders. Firms repeatedly drove this fact home in countless symbolic ways, from the color of the contractors' badges to the size and location of their office space. For some, the sense of being a second-class citizen was a constant source of anxiety, dissatisfaction, and irritation. Others took it in stride, or even found the distance that it created comforting. But one way or another, all contractors had to learn to live with their liminality. To do so, they carved out roles for themselves, ranging from "gurus" and "trusted confidants" to "hired guns" and "warm bodies" purchased solely for their "skill sets." These roles allowed contractors to rationalize their status and resolve the practical dilemmas of life on the job. Ultimately, however, their status as outsiders was more than a symbolic issue: all contractors knew that sooner or later they would have to return to the market in search of another job.

Thus, the itinerant expert's life was characterized by a distinct temporal rhythm, a repetitive cycle of moving from the market to a job and, then, back to the market. Contractors who wished to maximize their income had to learn to manage this cycle by continually honing and reinventing their technical skills—their human capital—with an eye to technology's potential trajectory and sensitivity to the waxing and waning of technical fads. Investing in human capital was not only costly in terms of time and money; it was risky. Contractors might choose a promising path only to find that the market had gone elsewhere, leaving them to absorb the costs of obsolete skills and orphaned technologies. It was the contractors' willingness to assume full responsibility for accumulating and managing their human capital that distinguished them from technical workers who preferred permanent employment.

Although continually investing in technical skills was necessary for successfully finding jobs and avoiding downtime, by itself technical knowledge was insufficient for having a lucrative career as a contractor. Contractors also required social skills and social capital. Even the most valued expertise was useless unless the contractor could repeatedly rise above the clamor of the market, often on short notice, to attract the attention of hiring managers. This required developing networks of contacts that could channel information, generate leads, and vouch for the contractor in a timely and convincing way. It also required expanding one's notion of skill to include finesse at networking, bargaining, and interviewing. Together social skills and social contacts complemented and enhanced the value of contractors' human capital.

Thus, even if contractors were not fully aware of the significance of their choice, by choosing the life of an itinerant expert, they crossed the divide between employer and employee. The technical work they performed hardly differed from what they had done before, but their relationship to their work changed dramatically. They were no longer salaried professionals viewed by firms as "human resources" to be acquired, maintained, nurtured, and profitably deployed. Rather, they became commodities to be bought, used, and discarded as any other resource. Nor did contractors see themselves as human resources. They came to view themselves as independent owners of their own human capital, as entrepreneurs who relied on their own skills to navigate between success and failure. This change of orientation had far-reaching consequences for how contractors' lives unfolded. By demanding the independence of a capitalist, contractors also incurred its risks. With independence came the need for self-reliance.

THE AMBIGUITIES OF SELF-RELIANCE

During their more optimistic moments, contractors thought they had come close to achieving the American dream. Even after accounting for the cost of purchasing their own benefits, most believed they were making more money than they could have made as full-time employees. Many even claimed that their future was now more secure, because they were continually employable, or at least more easily employable than laid-off employees with similar qualifications. Nearly all of our informants told us that contracting had released them from the social constraints of organizational life. They no longer had to conform to the whims of managers who once controlled their fate, and within reason they could speak their minds while focusing more exclusively on the technical aspects of their work.

But there were caveats to this rosy picture. Like many Americans who have aspired to self-reliance over the years, our itinerant experts found that independence came with strings attached. Reaping the benefits of itinerancy meant facing the constraints of a market, an institution from which contractors had been previously shielded. Like all capitalists who examine their books closely, contractors discovered the gap between revenues and profits: each dollar came with hidden costs that few fully appreciated when they entered contracting. Although our informants recognized that they would have to pay their own taxes and provide their own benefits, most initially underestimated how much time and money this involved. Eventually, most contractors learned to manage these costs. But there were costs that almost no one anticipated: the costs of developing and maintaining human and social capital. Traditionally, these were costs borne by employers and were largely invisible to employees. When taking these costs into account, contractors discovered that to be successful capitalists, they had to set aside profits for reinvestment.

Like capitalists, contractors also learned that they could not entirely offset the costs of doing business by simply raising their rates. At some point, the only path to greater profit was to utilize their capital more efficiently: to work longer hours. Thus, contractors' initial expectations about flexibility proved to be naïve. On the face of it, they did have more control over their time than employees. They could negotiate clearly defined temporal expectations at the beginning of every contract, and they could choose to allocate their hours between work and leisure as they saw fit. They were not subject to employers' demands for "commitment" and "dedication," which sapped the permanently employed professionals' time. Thus, some contractors were able to take long vacations, pursue time-consuming avocations, and juggle hours to fit the needs of their friends and family.

But time also became the contractor's most fungible resource, which they learned to measure in hours, rather than weeks, days, or months. Contractors could choose to spend their hours on compensated work, in which case the hours were "billable." Alternately, they could devote hours to building human or social capital or to business matters, such as calculating their taxes. In these cases, their hours were "nonbillable," even though hours so spent remained crucial for maintaining long-term employability. Finally, contractors could allocate hours to leisure and other nonwork activities. But the catch was that any hour spent one way could not be spent in another. Consequently, contractors developed a hypersensitivity to the opportunity costs of time. Faced with making explicit trade-offs between income and leisure and having to cover the costs of their independence, many contractors chose not only to work long hours but also to spend additional time each day investing in their social and human capital. In fact, some discovered that they could not enjoy leisure time without a lingering awareness of its costs. As a result, many contractors exercised their flexibility by working long hours and forgoing vacations for years at a time. Ironically, the market's constraints on time often seemed to penetrate further into their lives than did the demands of the greediest organization or the most intrusive boss.

Contractors had hoped to enter a world in which the "objective" market for hard skills would obviate the need for interpersonal gamesmanship. By and large, contractors got what they wanted: they had distanced themselves from the politics, incompetence, and inequities of organizational life, which they had found so oppressive when they were employees. But over time, they discovered that the market was also a social institution. Contractors could not repeatedly locate jobs, close deals, and survive on the job unless they embedded themselves in networks of communication and obligation that were in their own way just as "political" as the corporations they had left behind. Although they were no longer imprisoned in an "iron cage of bureaucracy," they found themselves suspended in webs of dependency that were no less constraining.[1] Thus, free agency and self-reliance did not mean freedom from social constraints or absence of reliance on others; it simply meant that the contractors' social dependencies had changed context.

At the outset of our journey we contrasted free agency's and institutionalism's images of contracting. At first glance, one might conclude that a modified version of free agency's somewhat utopian depiction of contracting fits the contractors' experience better than the institutionalists' darker portrait. Most contractors did find contracting to be a form of liberation. They perceived themselves to have more control over their destiny and to be economically better off than they had been as employees. They sometimes even called themselves "free agents," and they experienced few of the difficulties that the institutionalists fear they might. Contractors had greater bargaining power than lower-skilled temporary workers and rarely felt as if they had been forced into contracting involuntarily. All claimed that they could return to permanent employment whenever they desired. Although contractors came into conflict with staffing agencies, most had learned to bargain with agencies, play them off each other, and make alliances when doing so was to their benefit. Experienced contractors even had the option of doing without staffing firms, and many exercised their option by incorporating and doing direct deals. Thus, the institutionalists' concerns about contingent labor seem inappropriate for highly skilled contingent work.

This conclusion, however, requires qualification. As ethnographers we opted for depth rather than breadth. As a result we cannot claim that our sample represents all technical contractors. Although we believe we have portrayed our informants' experience accurately, we cannot speak for technical workers who tried contracting and then returned to permanent work. We also cannot speak to the experience of contractors on H1B

---

[1] Max Weber (1968/1922) argued that the ethos of rationality, epitomized by bureaucratic forms of organizing, had become so integral to Western culture that there was no escape from its "iron cage." Ellul's (1964) critique of a technologically driven society rests on similar assumptions about the inevitability of society's march toward greater rationality and efficiency in all realms of life.

visas or to members of occupational groups that we have not studied.[2] Most important, like most social science, our research is historically situated. We did our fieldwork during one of the tightest labor markets in U.S. history. To give a full account of contracting, one would need to know what happened to contractors and to contracting after the collapse of the "new economy." Did the contractors' belief in the security of human and social capital survive the crash, as advocates of free agency might contend? Were contractors the first to bear the brunt of the recession, as the institutionalists might argue? How did the changing conditions affect those committed to a contracting lifestyle? Although we provide commentary on this situation in the epilogue, researchers must ultimately answer these questions empirically to fully resolve the debate between the institutional and free agency perspectives.

If the only issues were which perspective most adequately describes the contractors' lifestyle and how that lifestyle fares with the ups and downs in the economy, then these caveats would end our story. But beneath free agency's and institutionalism's conflicting interpretations of the contractors' experience lie larger concerns. At issue is whether notions of markets and organizations are sufficient for conceptualizing the underlying logic of employing itinerant experts.

ITINERANT EXPERTS AND THE SOCIAL ORDER

Free agency's and institutionalism's conflicting images of contingent work carry assumptions about the social context in which work should occur. The rhetoric of free agency rests on implicit faith in the efficiency of free markets and casts doubt on any efforts to regulate economic activity. Because advocates of free agency assume that the greater social good will emerge from the free play of the market's invisible hand, they have no need to question what type of social system contingent labor markets

---

[2] H1B visas are issued to foreign nationals who enter the United States explicitly for the purpose of working. H1Bs are typically granted to people who possess skills that are scarce in the U.S. labor market. During the 1990s a significant number of technical workers, especially Indian programmers, were brought to the United States to work as contractors. A worker must be must be sponsored by an American employer to be granted an H1B. Many technical contractors were sponsored by staffing agencies that specialized in bringing foreign workers into the United States. The agencies either marketed the contractors directly to clients or provided them to other staffing agencies, in what were known as "third-party" deals. The use of H1B contractors was a contentious political issue. Opponents claimed that they were undermining the wages of Americans, while proponents argued that H1Bs were necessary for meeting the demands of a tight labor market. Although the issue received considerable attention in the press, significant research on the problem has yet to be published.

might create. Their answer, in fact, is a forgone conclusion: if unhindered, exchange among self-interested actors will create a labor market in which information flows freely and rewards distribute themselves in proportion to the demand for workers' efforts, skills, and initiative.

In sharp contrast, institutionalists do not believe that markets are independent of other social forces. Rather, markets are embedded in and shaped by legal, social, cultural, and historical processes. These processes inject power and privilege into markets, which make it impossible to achieve equitable and frictionless exchange by market principles alone. If fair exchange is the goal, societies also require institutions that limit opportunism, facilitate the flow of information, and enable the formation of human capital. Thus, institutionalists argue that the market cannot and should not be trusted to ensure social welfare. Instead, organizations such as governments, corporations, unions, and trade associations must monitor and curtail the range of possible outcomes.

Historically, the institutional perspective underwrote the New Deal, which made permanent employment the cornerstone of the American system of social welfare. The New Deal's image was one of reciprocal obligations between employees and employers backed up by a system of countervailing powers among unions, firms, and governmental agencies. Institutionalists have levied their critique of contingent labor from this perspective. They argue that contingent employment will undermine the system that currently promote security, provide benefits, and ensure the equitable distribution of income. Consequently, they have sought either to shore up existing institutional arrangements or to propose new types of organizations that will ensure security in a postindustrial economy.

At first glance, free agency and institutionalism seem to offer diametrically opposed images of social order. Proponents of free agency promote the market as an antidote to the inefficiencies of a bureaucratic society. Institutionalists promote bureaucratic and regulatory constraints as remedies for the social ills of free markets. When reduced to these terms, the conflict between these two positions is part of a long-standing, familiar, and ultimately ideological debate that can never be resolved on empirical grounds. Cast in these terms, our data could be employed by either camp. Promoters of free agency could point to the benefits of contracting as proof of their claims, while institutionalists could claim that the experience of high-end contractors in no way nullifies their critique of contingent labor and, if anything, provides evidence for growing wage disparities produced by unregulated markets. If we were to accept institutionalism's and free agency's terms of debate, all we could do would be to take sides on ideological grounds, call for more research, or argue for some kind of middle ground. We believe, however, that our story serves the debate in a radically different way: it allows us to reframe the debate by altering its terms.

The conflict between advocates of free agency and the institutionalists rests on the assumption that any economic order can be described on a continuum of organizational forms ranging between markets and hierarchies. In fact, the field of organizational economics, which is based largely on the theory of transaction costs, makes the debate's underlying distinction an explicit point of analysis.[3] The debate over contingent work is, therefore, usually framed as a decision about which point on the continuum is economically, if not morally, superior. But this framing limits both perspectives' ability to acknowledge and conceptualize social orders that may be structured along different dimensions. We contend that making sense of contract labor markets requires considering at least a third dimension—occupational forms of organizing.

Although occupational forms of organizing were once more prevalent than either markets or hierarchies, advanced industrialization, which shaped the economic history of the early twentieth century, undercut occupational institutions and processes and marginalized the role of occupations in social theories of industrial society.[4] In fact, occupational organization was for many years treated as a special case, relevant only for addressing the market power of high-status professions such as medicine and law.[5] However, our story of contracting and how contractors organize their lives has the flavor of occupational organizing. Contractors' efforts to forge a unique kind of professional practice point to incipient patterns of occupational association and to proto-institutions organized along occupational lines. To better understand the significance of these emerging patterns of association, we first need to consider traditional forms of professional practice.

[3] The literature on transaction cost analysis as an underpinning for organizational structure has burgeoned since the 1980s. Oliver Williamson (1975) triggered this school of thought with his book, *Markets and Hierarchies*. Although transaction cost theories of organizational structure are quite nuanced, they grow out of an attempt to explain when an organization will provide a good or service for itself rather than purchase the good or service in the market.

[4] For an account of how the study of work and occupations disappeared from organization studies, see Barley and Kunda (2001).

[5] Contemporary sociologists view professions as occupations that have successfully secured jurisdiction over a line of work. Professionalization is typically associated with an occupation's possession of an esoteric body of knowledge, state-mandated licensing, formal training programs, and professional associations that create barriers to entry and a basis for defending their jurisdiction from the expansionist tendencies of other occupations. Johnson (1972), Freidson (1973), Larson (1977), and Abbott (1988) are key texts in the vast literature on professions and professionals.

Professionals and Professionalization

Historically, professions have been organized in three ways: what occupational sociologists call free professions, professional firms, and corporate professions. Each mode of organizing offers a solution to three problems that every professional practitioner faces: how to maintain expertise, how to build client relationships, and how to ensure long-term economic security. Free professionalism is the oldest mode of professional practice and is associated most closely with medicine and law. Doctors and lawyers of the nineteenth and early twentieth centuries, who served individual clients in a local community, were prototypical free professionals. They acquired their skills and knowledge through schooling or apprenticeships supervised by other practitioners. Once certified by members of their profession, they chose a location where they could practice their craft without stiff competition. Because free professionals thrived in an era when their field's knowledge grew relatively slowly, when many of the problems that professionals solved were routine, and when most clients could not evaluate the quality of a professional's practice, remaining sufficiently up-to-date was within the grasp of most practitioners.

Finding clients was relatively easy for free professionals because they provided services that just about everyone needed at one time or another. The inevitability of illness and legal needs also guaranteed long-term economic security, as long as local competition remained light. Doctors and lawyers were well enough compensated to accumulate sufficient wealth to provide for long-term security. Professional associations further protected the free professional's future on legal grounds. Barriers to entry and professional norms encouraged informal geographical monopolies and discouraged aggressive marketing. Nevertheless, individual practitioners still faced what amounted to a free market for their services. Competitors could move into communities and vie for clients, and clients were free to choose between different providers using whatever criteria they valued. In fact, such competition, in combination with increasing specialization, gave rise to the second form of professional organizing, the professional firm.

Professional firms are formal organizations composed primarily of practitioners of the same craft. Law firms, medical practices, architectural firms, accountancies, and engineering consultancies are examples. During the twentieth century, practitioners began forming such firms for a number of reasons. First, professional firms allowed practitioners to specialize, which, in turn, allowed them to offer a wider range of services than any single individual could offer. Second, professional firms brought economies of scale: sharing physical and human capital enabled groups of professionals to handle more clients at lower marginal costs. Finally, professional firms allowed some practitioners (partners) to extract rents from the work of others, thereby allowing the first group to extend their potential income beyond what was possible for a professional in solo practice.

Professional firms brought together a critical mass of practitioners, often representing different age cohorts and specialties, who could pool their expertise to jointly foster professional development. Professional firms also allowed a hierarchical division of labor in which higher status members could focus on finding clients, while practitioners with less status specialized in providing services, thereby enlarging the firm's client base. Hierarchical differentiation not only increased the partners' wealth, it offered younger practitioners the security of salaried employment and a stepping-stone to their own practice. Because professional firms included a number of specialties, they encouraged the practice of joint referrals, which ensured the flow of clients. In sum, the emergence of the professional firm populated the market for professional services with competing firms, thereby aligning professional markets with markets for other goods and services.

Corporate professionalism is the third traditional mode of organizing professional practice. Corporate professionals are practitioners who work as salaried employees of firms staffed by a variety of occupations and who are often supervised by managers who are not members of their profession. This mode of organizing was tied to the rise of industrial corporations, especially those in the chemical and electronics industries, which made extensive use of technical and scientific knowledge. In fact, engineers, software developers, and technicians have rarely, if ever, practiced as free professionals or as members of professional firms.[6] Although corporate professionalism is typically associated with technical workers, it has recently become more common among members of other professions including lawyers and accountants.[7]

By accepting the role of corporate professionals, practitioners found ready-made solutions to the problems that all professionals must resolve. Because they worked for a single firm and received a salary, they had no need to concern themselves with marketing their services or competing

---

[6] The primary exception is civil engineering. Civil engineers must be licensed to practice, and a significant percentage of their work takes place in structural engineering firms. Perrucci (1971), Ritti (1971), Zussman (1985), Whalley (1986), and Meiksins and Smith (1993) provide useful discussions of the social organization of engineering in the United States and other industrial nations.

[7] Although sociologists have yet to pay much attention to the phenomenon, during the latter half of the twentieth century, management itself appears to have begun to spin off specialties, such as marketing and finance, which have many of the attributes of professions.

for clients. Furthermore, as employees, corporate professionals received a full range of benefits. Because firms historically shielded their professionals from layoffs, corporate professionals could, until recently, also expect long-term job security. The costs of maintaining the corporate professional's expertise were borne by the employer, who paid for advanced training and membership in professional associations. In fact, employers often encouraged and rewarded service to the profession and, at least in the case of R&D labs, provided a fully developed occupational community with many of the trappings of a university or a government lab.

Despite these comforts, corporate professionals are more likely than other professionals to experience tension between the norms of professional work and the requirements of the context in which they practice.[8] Technical values and professional aspirations sometimes clash with corporate goals of efficiency and profits, producing what technical professionals disdainfully refer to as "politics." As we have seen, it was precisely such tensions, and the dissatisfactions they produced, that led many of our informants to seek alternatives to corporate professionalism.

The Professionalism of the Itinerant Expert

One option that our informants fantasized about, and at least twelve had tried, was to become an entrepreneur by founding a professional service firm or a technical start-up. Yet, all but one who tried eventually failed. They failed, in part, because they lacked the capital (if not the skills) necessary for running a business. The odds were also stacked against them from the very beginning. Most new businesses die young, independent of their founders' skills.[9] Thus, for the majority of our informants, contracting was the only route out of corporate professionalism.

Becoming a contractor meant setting aside traditional models of professionalism. As a result, our informants found themselves without ready-made solutions for resolving a professional's practical problems. As they encountered these problems in their daily work, they had to invent their own solutions or adopt solutions widely practiced by other contractors. As they did so, they began to forge what can be viewed as a

[8] Sociologists have written about the tensions experienced by professionals in corporations since the late 1950s when the topic generated a small cottage industry of research. Most of the research focused on engineers. Key books and papers in this tradition include Kornhauser (1962), Scott (1965), Peltz and Andrews (1966), Miller (1967), Perrucci and Gerstl (1969a, 1969b), Engel (1970), Raelin (1985), and Von Glinow (1988).

[9] The dynamics of births and deaths among populations of organizations has received considerable empirical attention in the last two decades, spawning a school of organizational theory known as population ecology. See Hannan and Freeman (1988) for a comprehensive treatment of the tenets of population ecology.

new form of professionalism, which combines elements of traditional modes of practice with entirely new approaches. We shall call this mode of practice itinerant professionalism.

Like free professionals, technical contractors worked as solo practitioners and, in most cases, arranged for their own benefits. They drew on their professional networks for referrals and recommendations and took responsibility for their own professional development. Like members of professional firms, contractors frequently worked for one organization, a staffing agency, but offered their services to another. Like corporate professionals, they practiced inside organizations, often as members of a team whose work was subject to management's direction. But unlike free professionals and members of professional firms, technical contractors rarely had ongoing relationships with clients and were not paid on a fee-for-service basis. Nor were they salaried like corporate professionals or members of professional service firms.

Itinerancy led contractors to different solutions to the problems of finding clients, maintaining expertise, and ensuring long-term security. Unlike other professionals, they found clients by augmenting their networks with the services of staffing agencies. In fact, some relied exclusively on agencies. These contractors were well aware that using an agency conflicted with traditional images of professionalism. They resented submitting themselves to members of a sales culture and allowing nonprofessionals to make a substantial profit on their services. But since using a staffing agency was often a necessity, contractors resolved their dissonance by incorporating agencies into their model of professional practice: being savvy in one's dealings with agents was a form of expertise.

Contractors generally developed and maintained their technical expertise much like any other professional: they took classes, joined professional associations, consulted other professionals, and educated themselves. But compared with professionals who practiced in other contexts, the contractors' skills were subject to more frequent evaluation in the marketplace and they enjoyed fewer protections against obsolescence. Contractors' efforts to stay up-to-date were consequently more sustained, intense, and ongoing. Moreover, unlike most other professionals who distinguish between apprentices and full-fledged practitioners, contractors blurred the distinction between newcomers and veterans.[10] Regardless of experience, they thought of (and presented) themselves as continual learners. They saw jobs as opportunities for learning and sought to arrange contracts into sequences that enabled them to acquire

[10] The blurring of the distinction between newcomers and old-timers may reflect the fact that so many of the contractors we encountered worked in software development and IT-related occupations. These areas of practice change so quickly that newly minted graduates are likely to have more cutting-edge skills than do practitioners with years of experience.

and practice new skills. Thus, under itinerant professionalism, work itself became a credentialing process.

Itinerant professionalism also hinged on a radically different solution to the problem of security. Security always entails guaranteeing one's continued employability, which, in turn, can rest on a variety of foundations. Although all professionals must rely on the enduring value of their expertise, traditional models of professionalism bolster security in other ways. The free professional's well-being rests partially on his or her reputation in a community and partially on the fact that clients have recurring needs about which they have little expertise. Corporate professionals and members of professional firms rely for security on their continued affiliation with, and the goodwill of, their employers. Contractors had recourse to neither safety net because of their transitory relationships with clients and agencies. Their security as itinerant professionals rested entirely on their ability to network and to maintain skills that others would buy.

In short, our informants' mode of practice had the trappings of a distinct form of professionalism, and contractors themselves seemed to experience their practice as unique and coherent. They exhibited what sociologists call consciousness of kind as well as consciousness of difference: setting aside technical specialty, contractors believed that they had more in common with each other than they did with professionals who did similar work under other models of professionalism.[11] Informants repeatedly told us that their permanently employed counterparts had little understanding of their brand of practice or of the problems and opportunities they faced. More important, even though clients occasionally tried to tempt contractors back into corporate professionalism, most were unwilling to return. Thus, despite itinerant professionalism's problems and challenges, our informants overwhelmingly preferred it to corporate professionalism.

Nevertheless, itinerant professionalism had a significant Achilles' heel, especially for members of technical occupations. Historically, technical occupations have lacked strong institutional supports to underwrite their

[11] To identify with a group, one must perceive oneself to be similar to other members along whatever dimensions are phenomenologically relevant to the group, but one must also perceive oneself to be different from individuals who are not members. Discussing the concept of community, Weber (1968/1922: 42–43) insisted that consciousness of kind occurs only in conjunction with consciousness of difference: "A common language, which arises from a similarity of tradition through the family and the surrounding social environment, facilitates mutual understanding . . . but, taken by itself, it is not sufficient to constitute a communal relationship . . . it is only with the emergence of a consciousness of difference from third persons who speak a different language that the fact that two persons speak the same language and, in that respect, share a common situation, can lead them to a feeling of community and to modes of social organization consciously based on the sharing."

professionalism. By institutional supports we mean organized systems and communities that foster occupational identities and that assist in creating, storing, and disseminating substantive knowledge. Most professions have occupational associations, training programs, conferences, journals, and accreditation procedures that support all members of the occupation regardless of their mode of practice. But when compared with medicine, law, and accounting, the institutions of technical occupations have long been weak.

For example, with the exception of civil engineering, engineering societies never acquired exclusive legal rights to control entry, training, or licensing.[12] More important, they have no procedures for evaluating and sanctioning professional performance. Even engineering journals play a less important role in disseminating technical knowledge than do the journals of other professions, in part because engineering is an oral culture.[13] The relative weakness of engineering's professional institutions is rooted in the fact that other than civil engineering, most technical occupations developed as corporate professions. In fact, during the 1920s engineering leaders, such as Frederick Taylor, sought to gain control of the engineering societies in the hope of transforming electrical and especially mechanical engineering into free professions modeled on law and medicine. Employers blocked these engineers from developing full-fledged professional institutions by gaining control of their professional associations and ousting the reformers.[14]

For this reason, technical occupations have long relied on corporate employers for institutional support. Firms have been particularly important in funding technical schools and have played active roles in technical societies. They have also served as important repositories of expertise, largely because technical knowledge is often proprietary and application-specific. Beyond the initial degree required for practice, most advanced technical training occurs on the job within firms. Alvin Gouldner would have called engineers and technicians "local" professionals. Unlike "cos-

---

[12] For instance, even though the Accreditation Board for Engineering and Technology (ABET) certifies engineering programs, certification is not necessary for a school or department to train engineers, and firms appear quite willing to hire graduates of non-ABET-certified programs. In software development the situation is even less structured. Large numbers of software developers have never taken courses in programming or computer science. What matters in software development is whether one can write code and how elegantly one can write it.

[13] Thomas Allen (1977) showed that engineers rarely rely on written materials, aside from textbooks and engineering reports. Instead, they prefer to acquire technical knowledge through conversation. For this reason, Allen argued, those engineers who do read—engineers whom he called "technical gatekeepers"—were particularly important in R&D labs.

[14] Layton (1971) documents the short-lived "revolt of the engineers."

mopolitan" professionals who are involved in national and international networks of practice, local professionals orient primarily to their employer and their occupational networks are composed primarily of fellow employees.[15]

Consequently, even though technical professionals may gain independence when they become contractors, they lose access to corporate professionalism's supports. This loss is crucial. Practitioners require contact with other members of their occupational community to function as technical professionals. This is because technical knowledge typically emerges unevenly across a community of practitioners as different members encounter problems and devise solutions.[16] Without involvement in an occupational community, practitioners lack access to these developments. Nontechnical issues of practice, such as finding work, also usually require collective solutions. To fill the institutional vacuum, our contractors had begun to build occupational communities conducive to itinerant professionalism, often with the help of sophisticated communication technologies.

Community building was usually spontaneous and informal, driven less by conscious design than by contractors' efforts to solve immediate problems. We observed contractors forming and participating in networks that offered both technical and nontechnical support. Some of these communities involved face-to-face interaction, but many others were "virtual": they existed primarily on the Internet and were organized around bulletin boards, chat rooms, and Usenet groups. These forms of communication offered much more than recreation, though they served that purpose too. They were important channels for exchanging market information and technical tips. We also observed more formal efforts to organize contractors along occupational lines. Some of our informants had taken responsibility for founding and managing users' groups. Others had founded partnerships and occupational collectives that enabled group practice. Entrepreneurs had begun to cater to the contractors' need for occupational communities by publishing journals and magazines, such as *Contract Professional*, which addressed issues that contractors repeatedly faced. Other entrepreneurs had founded Web-based employment services, such as DICE, Monsterboard, and Contract Employment Weekly, and affinity groups, such as Working Today and the Professional Association of Contract Employees (PACE), which provided

[15] Gouldner (1957–1958) adopted the terms from Merton (1957). Goldner and Ritti (1967), Kronus (1976), Goldberg (1976), and Jauch, Glueck, and Osborn (1978) have studied the implications of the cosmopolitan-local dichotomy among technical professionals.

[16] For how knowledge emerges and is communicated within occupational communities and communities of practice, see Van Maanen and Barley (1984), Orr (1997), and Wenger (1998).

contractors with group insurance plans and discounts on the tools of the trade.[17]

Even certain staffing agencies functioned as fledgling occupational institutions. Some agencies had begun to experiment with forms of organization that resembled contractor collectives. Systems Professionals, which provided its contractors with opportunities for serious technical training and served as a nexus for organizing the occupational community of UNIX systems administrators, was one example. Another was Expert Solutions, which explicitly operated as a cooperative. In addition to finding work for its members, Expert Solutions minimized markups, offered group benefit plans, and had developed a system for spreading income so that no member experienced unpaid periods of downtime.[18]

These proto-institutions were a far cry from the more entrenched institutions of traditional modes of professionalism. By comparison they were incipient, loose, and decentralized. They lacked a well-developed professional ideology, an accepted theory of practice, and a formal mandate to legitimize their status as institutions. Nevertheless we contend that these arrangements, however weak, represent important steps toward institutionalizing itinerant professionalism as a stable and coherent mode of practice. Thus, the emergence of itinerant professionalism as an identifiable trend provides a platform not only for conceptualizing the structure of postindustrial labor markets, but also for formulating policies that can shape these developments in useful directions.

The Occupational Dimension

In recent years social scientists have struggled to formulate images of postindustrial organizing. Analysts have offered many intriguing suggestions about how firms are changing and markets are being transformed. Yet, most analyses are handicapped precisely by the assumption that a postindustrial order can be adequately described in term of markets, firms, or some combination of the two. There can be no doubt that firms and markets will play crucial roles in a postindustrial economy and that they are likely to take forms that differ from the past. There is already

[17] Working Today is a nonprofit affinity and advocacy group founded by Sara Horowitz in 1995. Working Today serves contractors and other contingent workers in New York City. It offers contractors health insurance, portable pensions, and other benefits. More information on Working Today can be found at www.workingtoday.org. PACE is organized by James R. Zeigler, who also publishes the extremely useful online book, *The Contract Employees' Handbook*. Information on PACE and the handbook can be found at www.ce-handbook.com.

[18] Expert Solutions is located in Mountain View, California. We interviewed the founders as part of our research.

evidence, however, that thinking solely in terms of firms and markets constrains our ability to perceive, understand, and shape the evolving *system* of work and employment.

The evidence comes from three sources: studies that point to the collapse of bureaucracies and boundaries of firms, research that shows the increasing importance of occupational forms of organizing, and studies that document the role that regional, national, and even global networks play in stimulating economic performance. We believe the dynamics of technical contracting and the emergence of itinerant professionalism offer a clue to how these disparate insights about the changing industrial structure can be integrated into a coherent image. To see how this is possible, we need to briefly review the three strands of evidence.

The Collapse of Bureaucracy

The collapse of bureaucracy and the blurring of the boundaries of firms is the most widely acknowledged change associated with the shift to a postindustrial economy. Analysts have employed a variety of terms and metaphors to capture the development and the forms of organizing that are emerging in its wake: virtual organizations, shamrock organizations, network organizations, boundaryless organizations, and lean structures are but a partial list.[19] Although these attempts to characterize new forms of organizing differ in important ways, most analysts agree on four underlying trends.

The first is the trend toward "flatter," "leaner" organizations. Since the mid-1980s corporations have systematically reduced the number of middle managers they employ, often eliminating entire layers of hierarchy, thus shortening firms' chains of command.[20] Second, corporations have shifted to "outsourcing" goods, skills, and services that they once provided for themselves. Outsourcing means that firms now turn more frequently to other firms not only for janitorial and food services, but also for manufacturing subassemblies, maintaining information technologies, developing software, and acquiring other professional services. Delayering and outsourcing reduce headcount by compacting an organization along its vertical and horizontal axes respectively. Combined, these trends reverse the industrial era's strategy of making firms self-sufficient through vertical and horizontal integration.[21]

---

[19] These terms are to be found respectively in Byrne (1993), Handy (1989), Powell (1990), Arthur and Rousseau (1996), and Womack, Jones, and Roos (1990).

[20] See American Management Association (1996).

[21] Vertical integration refers to acquiring firms and resources so that the acquirer owns all steps of a manufacturing process from raw materials to the distribution of finished goods. Strictly speaking, horizontal integration refers to acquiring competitors in the same industry. But the term is also sometimes used to refer to acquiring firms in unrelated industries.

As firms become less self-sufficient, their boundaries become more permeable because lean firms must, by definition, acquire more resources externally. Ties to other organizations, therefore, become more critical. Although firms can certainly purchase supplies, skills, knowledge, and other resources on the open market, price and availability are easier to coordinate and control when buyers, suppliers, and collaborators enter into long-term relationships governed by contracts and reciprocal trust. Most analysts agree that forming and managing strategic alliances constitutes a third trend in postindustrial organizing. Researchers have conclusively shown that strategic alliances have become increasingly common over the last two decades.[22] These alliances include marketing, supply, manufacturing, licensing, and research and development agreements between two or more firms. Strategic alliances embed organizations in evolving networks of relationships, which place a premium on managing efficient flows along supply chains.[23]

Finally, more and more organizations are turning to project teams as a model for organizing productive activities. Unlike functions or divisions, projects have limited life spans and rely on temporary concentrations of resources and personnel that can be jettisoned or redeployed when the project ends. Although high-technology firms have long organized themselves this way, project structures have gained popularity in industries as diverse as banking, health care, advertising, insurance, and education. As we saw in chapter 2, project structures and an increasing willingness to outsource partially account for firms' expanding use of contractors.

Occupational Forms of Organizing

Although less widely discussed, the occupational structure of society has also changed significantly over the last four decades.[24] In 1950, 40 percent of all Americans were directly employed in the production of goods either as craftspersons or as operatives and laborers.[25] By 1998, employment in these occupational groups had fallen to 24 percent, mainly at the

[22] The research literature on strategic alliances constitutes a significant percentage of contemporary research on corporate strategy. The prominence of strategic alliances has given rise to network images of how industries are organized.

[23] Supply chain analysis refers to methods for optimizing flows of resources, goods, and services from suppliers to manufacturers and, then, on to distributors. Information technology is critical to the management of supply chains. Supply chain analysis has attracted much recent attention in operations research and industrial engineering.

[24] For detailed analyses of the changing occupational structure in the United States and other industrial nations, see Block (1990), Szafran (1996), Barley (1996), and Hecker (2001).

[25] The percentage of employed Americans for 1950 and 1998 are drawn respectively from table 1 in Barley (1996) and table 1 in Braddock (1999).

expense of semiskilled and unskilled workers. Although the proportion of the labor force engaged in craftwork declined slightly from 14 percent to 11 percent, the proportion of Americans employed as operatives and laborers was halved, falling from 26 percent in 1960 to 13 percent in 1998.

The demise of blue-collar work has been offset by tremendous growth in the white-collar labor force. Employment in managerial, service, sales, clerical, professional, and technical occupations rose from 47 percent in 1950 to 72 percent in 1998. Although the increase in white-collar work is hardly news, several details of the shift are poorly appreciated. Analysts often suggest that an expansion of clerical and service jobs has largely offset the decline in manufacturing. Consequently one frequently hears that the American economy is being transformed into a service economy marked by low-paid jobs in fast-food franchises and clerical sweatshops.[26] Occupational data do not support such claims. Clerical employment peaked in 1970 at 18 percent of the labor force and has subsequently declined by a percentage point. Even more problematic for the claim that America is becoming a service economy are data on employment in low-skilled service work. Lower-skilled service jobs now account for 16 percent of the workforce, but service employment has grown by only four percentage points since 1960, when it accounted for 12 percent. Nor do managerial and sales work account for most of the increase in white-collar work. Today 1.5 percent and 4 percent more Americans work respectively as managers and salespersons than in 1950. The largest expansion in white-collar employment has occurred among professional and technical occupations. Since 1950, professional and technical employment more than doubled, growing from 8 percent to 18 percent of the workforce. In fact, by 1991, professional and technical workers had become the largest occupational sector, surpassing even clerical workers and operatives. The Bureau of Labor Statistics currently estimates that by 2010, one in five Americans will be a professional or a technician.[27]

If employment in craft, professional, and technical work is a rough index of the relative importance of occupationally organized work, then census data clearly indicate that occupational forms of organizing are becoming more prominent. Figure 13.1 summarizes the shift toward occupational organizing. It plots the ratio of horizontally (or occupationally) to vertically (or hierarchically) organized sectors of the labor force since 1900. The ratio's denominator tracks the vertical sector as the percentage of Americans employed in managerial, sales, operative, and clerical

[26] This thesis is articulated by Bluestone and Harrison (1982), Aronowitz and DeFazio (1994), and Ritzer (1998).

[27] This estimate comes from Hecker (2001).

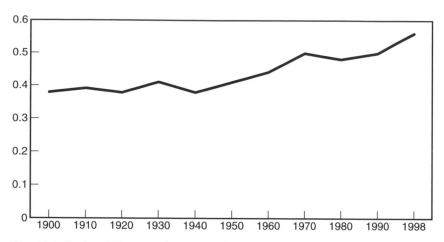

Fig. 13.1. Ratio of Horizontal to Vertical Occupational Sectors in the United States: 1900–1998

jobs. The numerator represents occupationally organized work, the percentage of the labor force employed in craft, professional, and technical work. Between 1900 and 1998 the ratio grew from 0.38 to 0.56. Not only has most of the shift occurred since 1950, but the rate of the shift to occupationally organized work increased in the 1990s.

Networks and Economic Vitality

A third strand of evidence in the literature on postindustrial organizing points to the importance of social networks to the vitality of economic regions. Relevant social networks may be based on occupational and professional ties, expertise in related technologies, involvement with an industry, exchange between suppliers and customers, physical proximity, ethnic identity, social class, and even friendship. Social and economic historians have long recognized that familial, religious, ethnic, and political ties were crucial to preindustrial commerce. In a careful analysis of social networks in medieval Florence, John Padgett showed that commerce in Italian city-states pivoted on business alliances formed among friends, family, and political allies. Which ties mattered in Florence depended, in large part, on which period of the city's history one is discussing.[28] For our purposes, the important point is that as one era's defining pattern of

[28] For Padgett's insightful work on the economy and social networks of Renaissance Florence, see Padgett and Ansell (1993), Padgett and McLean (2002, forthcoming), and Padgett (2001).

relationships gave way to another, the rules and the types of organizations that supported trade and finance in Florence also changed.

Although interpersonal relationships have always played more of a role in modern commerce than economists, and even sociologists, acknowledge, most analysts agree that the spread of bureaucracy relegated social ties to secondary status as a guarantor of trust in transactions.[29] Indeed, the defining characteristic of bureaucratic organizing was the replacement of patrimony's arbitrariness with specified rules and procedures for taking action and rewarding performance.[30] As economic transactions increasingly occurred between organizations headed by professional managers instead of entrepreneurs and owners, legally binding contracts increasingly overshadowed social ties as the basis for agreement, trust, and exchange.[31]

The Second Industrial Divide, Michael Piore's and Charles Sabel's influential treatise on the decline of mass manufacturing and the rise of flexible production, argued that a combination of craft production and flexible technology would become increasingly important, at least in some sectors of postindustrial commerce. In making their case, Piore and Sabel drew attention to the distributed networks of Northern Italy's industrial districts and the New York garment industry, where groups of small manufacturers were able to quickly produce high-quality goods in small lots for burgeoning boutique markets. These firms tended to be geographically clustered and to be bound not only by business alliances but also by informal social relationships and cultural ties. Skeptics doubted Piore and Sabel's thesis, in part, because the manufacturing of clothing did not seem relevant to a high-technology economy. A more important critique, from our perspective, is that Piore and Sabel seemed to assume that a permanently employed and organizationally embedded labor force would be responsible for craft-based production. In short, they did not take the distinction between occupation and organization to its logical conclusion.

Annalee Saxenian has shown that Piore and Sabel's argument becomes

---

[29] Mark Granovetter (1973, 1974, 1985) has been particularly influential in arguing for the importance of understanding how social relationships underwrite market transactions. This perspective has been central to the emergence of the new field of economic sociology (see Smelser and Swedberg 1994a).

[30] For Weber (1968/1922) bureaucracy was an advance over traditional forms of organizing. Bureaucracy drove out the inequities of patrimonial systems, creating more predictable and rational societies and opening opportunities based on merit. Those who view bureaucracy as inherently problematic would do well to consider what life was like prior to bureaucracy's emergence as a dominant organizational form.

[31] James Coleman (1974, 1990) has written extensively on the role that the law played in defining the concept of the corporation as an actor, hence laying the legal groundwork for an organizational society.

more relevant to the American high-technology sector when analysts take the mobility of skilled workers into account. In *Regional Advantage*, Saxenian compared the social structure and business practices of the Silicon Valley with those of Boston's Route 128, the center of the "Massachusetts Miracle" of the 1960s and 1970s. Whereas the economic vitality of Route 128 stalled in the late 1980s and early 1990s, the Silicon Valley was able to rejuvenate itself. Saxenian argued that the Valley's economic vitality rested on networks of interpersonal relationships that spanned firms and linked investors, entrepreneurs, and technical professionals. On Route 128, managers and technical professionals tended to remain with a single firm and competitors resisted collaboration. Technical professionals in the Valley, however, collaborated across firms and moved frequently from one organization to another in search of better salaries and greater challenges. Saxenian argued that the Silicon Valley benefited from these more dynamic networks because they facilitated the flow of expertise and capital within the region. More recently, Saxenian has shown that dense, fluid interpersonal ties between globally mobile Indian and Taiwanese entrepreneurs in the Silicon Valley have fed the development of India and Taiwan's high-tech economies and have linked those economies to the economy of the Bay Area.[32]

Taken together, the trend toward outsourcing, the increasing importance of occupational forms of organizing, and the mounting evidence that social capital and interfirm mobility are vital to vibrant high-technology industries, provide a backdrop for interpreting the emergence of itinerant professionalism. Viewed from this perspective, the spread of technical contracting seems to be more than a simple manifestation of the free market's resurgence. Nor does technical contracting seem to represent merely the failure of existing labor institutions to protect workers from exploitation. Instead, technical contracting and the itinerant professionalism it fosters may actually represent an incipient economic form, which for lack of a better term we shall call a "matrixed economy."

Our image of a matrixed economy draws inspiration from the "matrix" form of organizing that aerospace firms pioneered in the 1950s and that has subsequently diffused across most high-technology industries from semiconductors, computers, and software to biotechnology and pharmaceuticals.[33] Figure 13.2 displays a typical project matrix or overlay. In a matrix structure, technical professionals are typically assigned to functional areas. In aerospace, functional areas include propulsion, guidance, and power systems. In software development, functions might en-

---

[32] See Saxenian and Hsu (2000) and Saxenian and Li (forthcoming).

[33] Galbraith (1971), Davis and Lawrence (1977), Allen (1986), and Katz and Allen (1985) discuss the concept, benefits, and pitfalls of matrix organizations.

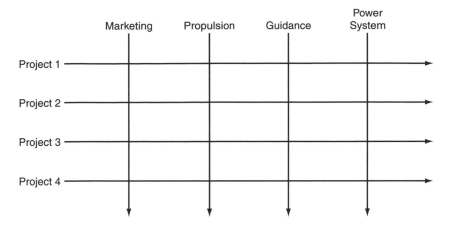

Fig. 13.2. Project Matrix

compass device drivers, interface design, and so on. Like a discipline, an occupational community, or a community of practice, functional areas are concentrations of specialized expertise. Functional managers are responsible for recruiting, training, evaluating, and developing professionals and for developing, codifying, and maintaining the company's body of expertise.

To do their actual work, however, technical employees are assigned to one or more separately managed projects that cut across functions for limited periods of time. While on the project, technical experts collaborate with members of other specialties to produce a working product or component. A project manager, responsible for coordinating the project, directs the experts' work on the project, while a functional manager usually allocates the experts' time to different projects and evaluates and rewards his or her performance. Once a project is finished, experts return, literally or metaphorically, to their functions until they are reassigned. Thus, in a matrix, technical experts are jointly managed by both functional and project managers. Ideally, a project matrix enables engineers to remain up-to-date in their field (function) while simultaneously orienting themselves to the specific needs of a project.[34] In other words, a matrix is formed by temporary intersections of occupations and tasks.

[34] Of course, organizational life rarely conforms to ideal depictions. Like other engineering-based solutions to organizational problems, the matrix is more elegant on paper than in practice. In a matrix, joint control and ambiguity of authority and responsibility invariably produce conflict and politics. These may be managed to a firm's advantage, but they also produce frustrations that lead some technical professionals to seek alternatives to corporate employment.

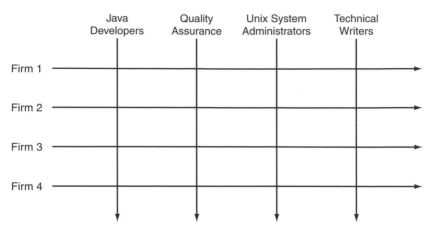

Fig. 13.3. Matrix Economy

With the emergence of itinerant professionalism, extending the logic of a project matrix from a firm to a high-tech economy is relatively straight-forward, entailing only a step up in level of analysis. As figure 13.3 illustrates, in a matrixed economy firms are equivalent to projects, and occupational communities or communities of practice are equivalent to functions. Staffing agencies and networks of practitioners allocate itinerant experts for a limited period of time to firms, whose projects become temporary loci of practice. While "assigned" to a firm, the itinerant professional collaborates with other specialists, who may be employees, contractors, or both, to complete a specific task that usually involves developing a product or delivering a service. Subsequently, the itinerant expert "returns," however briefly, to the community of practice until networks and agencies are activated and the contractor moves to another firm.

Thus, in a matrixed economy, firms become the loci for a set of projects, and occupations become the nexus for accumulating, developing, and disseminating knowledge. Firms access occupational knowledge through temporary employment relationships. The occupational needs of the itinerant professional—learning and maintaining professional expertise, finding clients, and ensuring long-term economic security—are handled *outside* firms through a combination of individual initiative, professional associations, occupational networks, and for-profit ventures.

All this means that a matrixed economy cannot operate without some form of occupational organizing, even if it is no more fully developed than loose and overlapping networks of practice. It should also be easier for a matrixed economy to develop when occupational specialists and the firms that require their services are geographically clustered. Clustering reduces the costs of mobility and increases the odds that members of a specialty will develop ties to each other. Thus, one would expect to find more developed matrixed economies in large cities and in high-tech enclaves like the Silicon Valley, Austin, Boston, Raleigh-Durham, Tel-Aviv, and Bangalor. However, as our data suggest and Saxenian's research shows, when itinerant experts are willing to travel long distances, matrix logic can extend beyond regions to entire countries and even around the globe. Thus, of the two conditions that facilitate matrix dynamics, occupational forms of organizing appear more essential than geographical proximity.

In sum, we see contract labor markets as evidence of the larger trend toward occupational forms of organizing in a postindustrial economy. The importance of the occupational dimension undermines the view that contracting represents a shift to free agency in a free market. Although market dynamics are involved, the market for itinerant expertise is not free, in the traditional sense of the term, because it cannot operate successfully without the support of occupational structures and the informational services currently offered by staffing agencies and professional networks. Likewise, recognizing the importance of occupational dynamics underscores why it would be a mistake to heed uncritically any call to resolve the imperfections of the market for high-tech contractors by returning to the organizationally based institutions of the past. Doing so would be tantamount to reinforcing corporate professionalism, which, as we have seen, truncates the networks of practice that facilitate the flow of technical expertise by favoring the firm's power over that of the practitioner.

Nevertheless, like the institutionalists we believe that structural supports are required to resolve a number of problems that plague contract labor markets. For example, left alone, the market is unlikely to rectify contractors' inadequate access to health insurance and retirement plans. The market is also unlikely to create significant pressure for altering the laws and administrative rulings that have unwittingly advantaged staffing agencies by forcing large numbers of contractors to work through agencies. Nor is the market likely to facilitate the maturation of occupational institutions that would assist contractors in developing skills, social capital, and other resources. Resolving these issues will require new institutions tailored to the exigencies of itinerant professionalism and the logic of a matrixed economy.

SUPPORTING ITINERANT PROFESSIONALISM

Benefits

The American system of social welfare remains closely tied to the cultural and legal institutions of permanent employment. Since the New

Deal, most Americans have acquired health insurance and pension plans through their employers. Employers not only negotiate with insurance carriers for lower group rates, but large employers usually subsidize insurance and contribute directly to pension plans. As we saw in chapter 2, one of the reasons that firms have turned to contractors is to avoid paying benefits, payroll taxes, and other expenses of employment. Although it is certainly possible for contractors to purchase their own health insurance, rates for individuals for the same level of protection are usually higher than for members of group plans. Aside from investing in an individual retirement account (IRA), contractors are also largely precluded from tax advantaged retirement plans unless they incorporate, join a professional association that offers a 401k plan, or tie themselves to a staffing agency long enough to qualify for a 401k.[35]

Research has consistently shown that low-skilled temporary workers are less likely than full-time employees to have retirement accounts and health insurance.[36] Our data suggest that much the same was true for the contractors we interviewed, although the problem was more severe for pension plans than for health insurance. Table 13.1 indicates that of the informants for whom we had data, 45 percent had no pension plan. Another 20 percent contributed only to an IRA. Twelve percent contributed to a 401k plan through an agency, and another 10 percent had a Keogh or SEP-IRA. In short, the majority of our informants had little in the way of savings earmarked for retirement. The lack was particularly common among younger contractors. By contrast, as table 13.2 shows, only a small percentage of our informants did without health insurance (12 percent). Forty-three percent purchased their own insurance, although many were quick to note that their coverage was not as extensive as it had been when they were employees. Employed spouses covered another 19 percent of our informants. Seven percent had been permanently employed

---

[35] Retirement options for contractors are complex. Here we only outline the main options. Any working American can set up a traditional or Roth individual retirement account. Contributions are limited to no more than $3,500 per year, and interest or dividends accumulate tax-free until retirement. The amount that can be contributed to an IRA decreases as income rises. Legally recognized self-employed contractors can establish a Keogh plan, which allows contributions of up to $35,000 per year or 25 percent of income, whichever is less. Incorporated contractors can also set up a simplified employee pension (SEP) IRA, and then contribute to the plan as their own employer. 401k plans require that the contractor be an employee of a firm that acts as an employer. In short, employment law requires contractors to either incorporate or work for a firm before they can accrue significant retirement savings that carry tax advantages.

[36] Spalter-Roth et al. (1997) and Hipple and Stewart (1996) examine benefits among temporary workers using data from the Current Population Survey.

TABLE 13.1
Our Informants' Retirement Accounts

Source	Number	Percentage
None	22	45
IRA	10	20
401k	6	12
SEP	4	8
Keogh	1	2
Permanent employment	6	12
Unknown	22	

recently enough to still qualify for COBRA benefits.[37] The remaining 19 percent found insurance through staffing agencies or elsewhere.

Although staffing agencies have increasingly begun offering pension plans and health insurance as a way of attracting contractors, most require that individuals work for the agency for six to eighteen months before they qualify for coverage. Because the average contract lasts from three to nine months and because contractors rarely work for the same agency sequentially, few contractors ever qualify for the agencies' plans. Thus, the tendency for contractors, especially younger contractors, to be

TABLE 13.2
Our Informants' Sources of Health Insurance

Source	Number	Percentage
None	7	12
Self	25	43
Spouse	11	19
COBRA	4	7
Staffing agency	3	5
Canadian government	1	2
Bank	1	2
Permanent employment	6	10
Unknown	13	

[37] The Consolidated Omnibus Budget Reconciliation Act of 1985 allows employees who resign or who are terminated to continue to purchase, as individuals, the health insurance provided by their former employer for a period of eighteen months after separation. The law was designed to allow workers and their families access to health insurance between jobs. Consequently, COBRA benefits are a stopgap option for people who become career contractors.

underinsured and to forgo retirement accounts entirely represents a significant long-term problem, not only for the contractors themselves but for society as well. Establishing portable pension and health care plans that would follow contractors from job to job, modeled perhaps on education's TIAA-CREF (a portable pension plan for education), would largely eliminate the benefit problem. One can imagine a system that would require agencies to contribute to these plans whenever an agency served as a contractor's employer-of-record regardless of the length of the contract. Another approach would be to change employment law to allow affinity groups and professional associations to provide contractors with group rates and continual coverage. Although professional associations can and do offer group health insurance, at present only employers can offer tax advantaged pension funds.

Removing the Staffing Industry's Legal Advantage

As we discussed in chapter 1, during the 1980s the Internal Revenue Service increased its scrutiny of how firms used independent contractors because it suspected that firms were using contractors to avoid paying payroll taxes. Although the IRS's actions were reasonable with respect to tax evasion, its greater regulatory scrutiny unintentionally created a windfall for staffing agencies. To avoid being found in violation of employment and tax law, firms increasingly mandated that contractors establish an employer-of-record relationship with an agency. Although such policies protect firms and reduce the incidence of tax evasion, they ensure a market for agencies whose markups increase the client's cost of employing contractors while also potentially reducing contractors' wage rates.

By brokering information and assuming the legal duties of employers-of-record, agencies clearly offer an important service to contractors as well as to clients. Moreover, without their involvement, the contract labor market would be less viable and perhaps even less vibrant. Thus, the issue is not whether staffing agencies are useful, but rather whether it is efficient to allow agencies to maximize their markups while also offering contractors minimal benefits as employers. The current system essentially supports a significant transfer of funds from the pockets of clients and contractors to the coffers of staffing agencies. Moreover, as we have seen, the size of an agency's markup varies widely. Large firms can protect themselves by entering into on-site and preferred vendor agreements. But small firms and contractors have few options for resisting unreasonable markups, aside from shopping for agencies that take smaller markups. Many agencies resist such shopping by treating their markups as confidential information.

The staffing industry's unintended legal advantage could be addressed in a variety of ways. The government could choose to regulate markups, but such an approach would not only be unpopular in the current economic climate, but also unnecessary. Another approach would be for the IRS and Congress to reexamine the implications of current laws and administrative rulings regarding independent contractors and incorporation. It does not seem impossible to devise tax laws that would protect against tax evasion without making it unnecessarily risky for firms to hire independents or costly for contractors to incorporate.

Yet another approach would be to encourage professional associations and affinity groups to serve as employers-of-record. The Professional Association of Contract Employees (PACE) provides a model. PACE, an affinity group, operates ProTrac, which provides pass-through employer-of-record services for contractors. Contractors become ProTrac employees, known as "division managers." For a markup of 5 percent, ProTrac not only provides payroll and tax services, but also offers contractors access to a variety of benefits, including group health insurance and 401k plans. Although ProTrac is structured as a "for-profit" affinity group, existing professional associations and even professional unions could assume a similar role.

Facilitating Occupational Institutions

We have seen that professional networks and users' groups are crucial to a matrixed economy's operation. Encouraging such groups to form and organize, as nonprofit occupational associations, would assist contractors in a variety of ways. In addition to offering health care and pension funds, such organizations could also contract with service providers to offer contractors discounts on training programs, materials, equipment, and supplies. Occupational associations could also assist with designing curricula and Web sites to assist contractors in finding jobs and keeping their skills up-to-date. Given the speed at which technologies change, it would be difficult for occupational associations to offer extensive curricula and courses. However, one can imagine occupational associations organizing a network of practitioners and users' groups that could respond more facilely to technical developments. By negotiating alliances with community colleges and vendors, occupational associations could also offer members discounted access to certification programs.

One model for such associations is the Free Agent Forum, an online affinity group for contractors, established by John Frederico in 2001. In return for a membership fee, the Free Agent Forum offers affiliates access to job postings, organizes technically oriented networks of practice, and offers discounts on tools and supplies. Free Agent Forum, however, caters to a variety of occupational groups. The Graphic Artists Guild, a craft union for illustrators, Web designers, and other visual media occupations, is more focused. The guild sponsors workshops and classes for members as well as career assistance and job postings. Labor unions and professional societies could play an important role in forming occupational associations, if both were willing to embrace a philosophy of encouraging organizing by craft or specialty, respectively. Historically, unions and professional societies have sought to aggregate across occupational groups. Although reasonable in a world of permanent employment, the pressure for cross-occupational collectives is less suited for the structure of highly skilled contract labor markets.

Encouraging the formation of occupational associations would be of considerable benefit to clients. As we have seen, ensuring that contractors have the skills they claim to have is one of the most significant problems facing hiring managers. Because membership in an occupational association is based on the possession of skills and expertise, occupational associations would be better positioned than most staffing agencies to assess and certify the skills of their members. In fact, certification could well be a revenue-generating service for professional associations. Occupational associations could offer rigorous skill verification for clients who use the association to locate contractors.

Having pushed our generalizations from the everyday realities of itinerant experts to their limit, and perhaps beyond, our journey is done. Our hope is that our ethnographic descriptions of contracting and the realities they expose have contributed empirical grounding to the debate over contingent labor, in particular, and, more generally, to the debate over the changing nature of work and employment at the turn of the century. At a very minimum, we believe our study has illustrated why studies of work have much to contribute to scholarly and practical efforts to address and shape the world of employment that we are wittingly and unwittingly engaged in making for ourselves and our children.

EPILOGUE

WHEN WE LEFT the field in 1999, our informants, along with the rest of the economy, were riding high on the crest of the greatest period of economic growth in modern history. All economic indicators were rosy. The New York Stock Exchange and NASDAQ were reaching new highs on an almost daily basis. Unemployment in Santa Clara County, the epicenter of Silicon Valley, stood at 2.9 percent, a historic low.[1] Venture capital flowed like water and young people with and without technical training were flocking to start ups, many of them Internet related dot-coms. Engineers and IT professionals in the Silicon Valley and other major technical centers could leave a job in the morning and, by many accounts, start another by the next day. In fact, technical talent in the United States was so scarce that the federal government had recently lifted the ceiling on H1B visas to satisfy industry's seemingly insatiable demand for technical expertise.

By November 2001, when the National Bureau of Economic Research officially proclaimed the economy to be in a recession, the world of high technology had taken a 180-degree turn. Venture capital was drying up, the stock market was in a free fall, dot-comers were holding "pink-slip parties," and the technology giants were laying off employees in droves. By July 2002 unemployment in Santa Clara County had risen to 8.6 percent, over two percentage points higher than California's unemployment rate (6.7 percent). The mood of boundless optimism had sunk into tortured pessimism. Those who had flocked to the Bay Area in the late 1990s found their stock options worthless, their jobs disappearing, and the promise of quick wealth nearly as groundless as the hopes of the forty-niners who came to California searching for gold 150 years earlier. The mood was similar everywhere high tech mattered.

As one might expect, contractors and the staffing industry suffered along with everyone else. Between the fourth quarter of 2000 and the first quarter of 2002, employment in the staffing industry fell by 28 percent.[2] During the same period, contractors' wages fell by as much

---

[1] Data on unemployment in California and Santa Clara County were retrieved from databases accessible online from the U.S. Department of Labor, Bureau of Labor Statistics: http://data.bls.gov.

[2] Berchem (2003). Data on the high-tech segment of the staffing industry are unavailable. Thus we use data on the staffing industry as a proxy.

as 20 percent.[3] Nearly half of the firms responding to a survey administered in 2001 by Mercer Human Resource Consulting claimed that they had reduced the number of contractors they employed.[4] Cisco, for instance, laid off more than half of its four thousand contractors.[5]

On the basis of such data, some might argue, as did a recent article in the *Wall Street Journal*, that contracting was an artifact of an unusually tight labor market and that after the bubble had burst, contracting became less consequential for the economy.[6] If this were true, the story we have told should be read, at best, as a history of a bygone era. But we believe it is not. Although contractors, like permanent employees, have surely experienced the ups and the downs of the economy, available evidence suggests that contracting remains (and is likely to continue to be) an important economic phenomenon.

It is important to note that the boom of the late 1990s did not create the trend toward using technical contractors. Contracting existed in the 1960s, grew throughout the 1980s, and picked up steam in the early 1990s before the Internet became available and dot-coms were conceived. Moreover, according to a recent survey conducted by Kelly Services, the proportion of the labor force working contingently was actually 6 percent larger in 2002 than it was in 1998.[7] This could only be true if more permanent workers than contractors were dismissed. Evidence also suggests that employment in the staffing industry is recuperating, while permanent employment remains plateaued. Between March 2002 and March 2003, placements by staffing firms increased by 10 percent and the number of agency employees grew by 11.7 percent.[8] Although some estimates indicate that 25 percent of high-tech contractors were still out of work in 2003, this must be balanced against data that indicate that nearly 20 percent of all IT jobs, both permanent and temporary, were lost since the recession began.[9] Perhaps most tellingly, even as the recession bottomed out in 2002, employment of contingent workers remained twice what it was in 1991.[10] In short, contracting seems here to stay.

Our informants' experience concurs. In January 2003 we tracked down as many of our original informants as possible to determine what

[3] Kelly (2003).
[4] Berry and Van De Voort (2002).
[5] Thurm (2003).
[6] Thurm (2003).
[7] Berchem (2003). Staffing Associations tend to overcount contingent workers; however in the absence of BLS data, the ASA's data are the best that are available.
[8] Berchem (2003).
[9] Gilpin (2003).
[10] Berchem (2003, fig. 1).

had happened since we last talked to them. We were able to reach thirteen by phone or e-mail and found sufficient data for ten more on the Web.[11] Of these twenty-three informants, 65 percent were still contracting, 30 percent had taken permanent positions, and one had left employment entirely to raise a family. Three of the seven contractors who went perm told us at the time of our original interviews that they intended to do so. These individuals left contracting before the downturn started. Those informants who continued to contract universally said that contracts had become more scarce, that rates had fallen, and that they had experienced longer periods of downtime than they reported several years earlier. Yet, many also noted that the worst seemed to be over and that business was now improving.

In sum, it seems reasonable to conclude that some of the details of our study belong to a bygone era. In particular, contractors' wages are now lower, jobs are more scarce, and downtime is more common. However, analogous claims could be made for full-time employment. Thus, contracting's structural position relative to permanent employment does not seem to have changed drastically, if at all, and the essence of our analysis still appears valid. The emergence of itinerant professionalism and its significance for a knowledge economy is as relevant today as it was three years ago. Structural change simply occurs more gradually than the fluctuations of business cycles. It is a mistake to conflate the two.

[11] We had telephone and e-mail addresses for only thirty of our informants.

REFERENCES

Abbott, Andrew. 1988. *The System of Professions: An Essay on the Division of Expert Labor*. Chicago: University of Chicago Press.

Abraham, Katharine G. 1988. "Flexible Staffing Arrangements and Employers' Short-Term Adjustment Strategies." In *Employment, Unemployment, and Labour Utilization*, pp. 288–311. Ed. Robert A. Hart. London: Unwin Hyman.

Abraham, Katharine G., and S. K. Taylor. 1996. "Firms' Use of Outside Contractors: Theory and Evidence." *Journal of Labor Economics* 14: 394–424.

Allen, Thomas J. 1986. "Organizational Structure, Information Technology, and R&D Productivity." *IEEE Transactions on Engineering Management* 33: 212–17.

———. 1977. *Managing the Flow of Innovation*. Cambridge: MIT Press.

American Management Association. 2000. "Need for Talent and Flexibility, Not Cost Savings, Drives Hiring of Contingent Workers." http://www.amanet.org/press/research/talnt718.htm (accessed January 2001).

———. 1996. *1996 AMA Survey on Downsizing, Job Elimination, and Job Creation*. New York: American Management Association.

Applebaum, Herbert. 1992. *The Concept of Work: Ancient, Medieval, and Modern*. Albany, NY: State University of New York Press.

Aronowitz, Stanley, and William DeFazio. 1994. *The Jobless Future: Sci-Tech and the Dogma of Work*. Minneapolis: University of Minnesota Press.

Arthur, Michael B., and Denise M. Rousseau. 1996. *The Boundaryless Career: A New Employment Principle for a New Organizational Era*. New York: Oxford University Press.

Bailyn, Lotte. 1993. *Breaking the Mold: Men, Women, and Time in the New Corporate World*. New York: Mac Millan.

———. 1985. "Autonomy in the Industrial R&D Lab." *Human Resource Management* 24: 129–46.

———. 1982. "Resolving Contradictions in Technical Careers." *Technology Review*, October: 40–47.

———. 1980. *Living with Technology: Issues at Mid-Career*. Cambridge: MIT Press.

Bailyn, Lotte, and John T. Lynch. 1983. "Engineering as a Life-Long Career: Its Meaning, Its Satisfactions, Its Difficulties." *Journal of Occupational Behavior* 4: 263–83.

Banigin, William. 1998. "Visa Program, High-Tech Workers Exploited, Critics Say." *Washington Post*, July 26, sec. 1, p. 1.

Barker, Kathleen. 1998. "Toiling for Piece-Rates and Accumulating Deficits:

Contingent Work in Higher Education." In *Contingent Work: American Employment in Transition*, pp. 195–220. Ed. Kathleen Barker and Kathleen Christensen. Ithaca, NY: ILR Press.

Barker, Kathleen, and Kathleen Christensen. 1998. "Controversy and Challenges Raised by Contingent Work Arrangements." In *Contingent Work: American Employment in Transition*, pp. 1–20. Ed. Kathleen Barker and Kathleen Christensen. Ithaca, NY: ILR Press.

Barley, Stephen R. 1996. *The New World of Work*. London: British North-American Research Committee.

———. 1983. "Semiotics and the Study of Occupational and Organizational Culture." *Administrative Science Quarterly* 28: 393–413.

Barley, Stephen R., and Gideon Kunda. 2001. "Bringing Work Back In." *Organization Science* 12: 75–94.

Barley, Stephen R., and Gideon Kunda. 1992. "Design and Devotion: Surges of Rational and Normative Ideologies of Control in Managerial Discourse." *Administrative Science Quarterly* 37: 363–99.

Baron, James N., and William T. Bielby. 1984. "The Organization of Work in a Segmented Economy." *American Sociological Review* 49: 454–73.

Batt, Rosemary, Susan Christopherson, Sara Horowitz, Ellen Neises, Ned Rightor, and Danielle Van Jaarsveld. 2001. "Net Working: Worklife in a Project Based Industry." Working paper, Economic Policy Institute, Washington, DC.

Beck, Nuala. 1992. *Shifting Gears: Thriving in the New Economy*. Toronto: Harper Collins.

Belous, Richard. S. 1989. *The Contingent Economy: The Growth of the Temporary, Part-Time, and Subcontracted Workforce*. Washington, DC: National Planning Association.

Bendix, Reinhard. 1956. *Work and Authority in Industry: Ideologies of Management in the Course of Industrialization*. New York: Harper and Row.

Benner, Chris. 1996. "Shock Absorbers in the Flexible Economy: The Rise of Contingent Employment in the Silicon Valley." San Jose, CA: Working Partnerships, USA.

Benson, John. 1998. Dual Commitment: Contract Workers in Australian Manufacturing Enterprises. *Journal of Management Studies* 35: 355–77.

Berchem, Steven P. 2003. *ASA's Annual Economic Analysis of the Staffing Industry*. American Staffing Association. http://staffingtoday.net (accessed September 4, 2003).

Berger, Suzanne, and Michael J. Piore. 1980. *Dualism and Discontinuity in Industrial Societies*. New York: Cambridge University Press.

Berry, Diane M., and David M. Van De Voort. 2002. "IT Contractors in a Weakened Economy." *IT Contractor Magazine*. http://certmag.com (accessed September 2, 2003).

Black, Dominique S., and Richard C. Andreini. 1997. *The Information Elite: The Future of the Independent Information Technology Consultant*. Redwood Shores, CA: Information Technology Specialists.

Blair-Loy, Mary, and Amy Wharton. 2002. "Employees' Use of Family-Responsive Policies and the Workplace Social Context." *Social Forces* 80: 813–45.

Block, Fred. 1990. *Postindustrial Possibilities: A Critique of Economic Discourse*. Berkeley: University of California Press.

Bluestone, Barry, and Bennett Harrison. 1982. *The Deindustrialization of America*. New York: Basic Books.

Bond, J. T., E. Galinsky, and J. E. Swanberg. 1998. *The 1997 National Study of the Changing Workforce*. New York: Families and Work Institute.

Bradach, Jeffrey L. 1997. "Flexibility: The New Social Contract between Individuals and Firms." Working paper, Harvard Business School, Boston, MA.

Braddock, Douglas. 1999. "Occupational Employment Projections to 2008." *Labor Review* 122: 51–77.

Bridges, William. 1995. "A Nation of Owners." *INC* 17: 89–91.

———. 1994. *Job Shift: How to Prosper in a Workplace without Jobs*. Reading, MA: Addison-Wesley.

Brown, John S., and Paul Duguid. 2001. "Knowledge and Organization: A Social-Practice Perspective." *Organization Science* 12(2): 198–213.

Bureau of Labor Statistics. 1998. Employee Tenure in 1998. http://stats.bls.gov/news.release/tenure.toc.htm (accessed December 2001).

Burt, Ronald S. 2001. "The Social Capital of Structural Holes." In *New Directions in Economic Sociology*. Ed. Mauro F. Guillen. New York: Russell Sage Foundation.

———. 1997. "The Contingent Value of Social Capital." *Administrative Science Quarterly* 42: 339–65.

———. 1992. *Structural Holes*. Cambridge: Harvard University Press.

Byrne, John A. 1993. "The Virtual Corporation." *BusinessWeek*, October 18: 66–72.

Cappelli, Peter. 1999. *The New Deal at Work: Managing the Market Driven Workforce*. Boston, MA: Harvard Business School Press.

Cappelli, Peter, Laurie Bassi, Harry Katz, David Knoke, Paul Osterman, and Michael Useem. 1997. *Change at Work*. New York: Oxford University Press.

Carlin, John. 1997. "You Really Can Do It Your Way." *London Independent*, November 30, p. 23.

Carnevale, Anthony P., Lynn A. Jennings, and James M. Eisenmann. 1998. "Contingent Workers and Employment Law." In *Contingent Work: American Employment in Transition*, pp. 281–305. Ed. Kathleen Barker and Kathleen Christensen. Ithaca, NY: ILR Press.

Carre, Francoise J., and Pamela Joshi. 1997. "Building Stability for Transient Workforces: Exploring the Possibilities of Intermediary Institutions Helping Workers Cope with Labor Market Instability." Cambridge, MA: Radcliffe College.

Caulkin, Simon. 1997. "Skills, Not Loyalty, Now Are Key If You Want Job Security." *San Francisco Sunday Examiner and Chronicle*, September 7, sec. 4, p. 2.

Christensen, Kathleen. 1998. "Countervailing Human Resource Trends in Family-Sensitive Firms." In *Contingent Work: American Employment in Transition*, pp. 103–26. Ed. Kathleen Barker and Kathleen Christensen. Ithaca, NY: ILR Press.

Cialdini, Robert B. 1984. *Influence: The Psychology of Persuasion.* New York: Quill.

Clinton, Angela. 1997. "Flexible Labor: Restructuring the American Workforce." *Monthly Labor Review* 120: 3–27.

Coase, Ronald. 1937. "The Nature of the Firm." *Econometrica* 4: 386–405.

Cohany, Sharon R. 1998. "Workers in Alternative Employment Arrangements: A Second Look." *Monthly Labor Review* 121: 3–21.

———. 1996. "Workers in Alternative Employment Arrangements." *Monthly Labor Review* 119: 31–45.

Cohany, Sharon R., Steven F. Hipple, Thomas J. Nardone, Anne E. Polivka, and Jay C. Stewart. 1998. "Counting the Workers: Results of a First Survey." In *Contingent Work: American Employment Relations in Transition*, pp. 41–68. Ed. Kathleen Barker and Kathleen Christensen. Ithaca, NY: ILR Press.

Cohen, Yinon, and Yitchak Haberfeld. 1993. "Temporary Help Service Workers: Employment Characteristics and Wage Determinants." *Industrial Relations* 32: 272–87.

Coleman, James S. 1990. *Foundations of Social Theory.* Cambridge: Harvard University Press.

———. 1974. *Power and the Structure of Society.* New York: W. W. Norton.

Conklin, Harold C. 1955. "Hanunoo Color Categories." *Southwestern Journal of Anthropology* 11: 339–44.

Darby, Joseph B. 1997. "The Ultimate Contractor: Lessons from a Parallel Universe." *Contract Professional* 2: 27–32.

Davis, Stanley M., and Paul R. Lawrence. 1977. *Matrix.* Reading, MA: Addison-Wesley.

Davis-Blake, Allison, and Brian Uzzi. 1993. "Determinants of Employment Externalization: A Study of Temporary Workers and Independent Contractors." *Administrative Science Quarterly* 38: 195–223.

Diebold, Francis, David Neumark, and Daniel Polsky. 1997. "Job Stability in the United States." *Journal of Labor Economics* 15: 206–33.

Dillon, Rodger L. 1987. *The Changing Labor Market: Contingent Workers and the Self-Employed in California.* Sacramento, CA: Senate Office of Research.

Eaton, Susan. 2000. "Work and Family Integration in the Biotechnology Industry: Implications for Employers and Firms." Ph.D. diss., Sloan School of Management, MIT, Cambridge, Massachusetts.

Ellul, Jacques. 1964. *The Technological Society.* New York: Vintage.

Engel, Gloria. 1970. "Professional Autonomy and Bureaucratic Organization." *Administrative Science Quarterly* 15: 12–21.

Everett, John O., Roxanne M. Spindle, and Thomas Turman. 1995. "Employee or Independent Contractor: A Determination with Far-Reaching Consequences." *Accounting Horizons* 9: 1–12.

Farber, Harry S. 1977. "The Changing Face of Job Loss in the United States: 1981–1995." In *Brookings Papers on Economic Activity: Microeconomics*, pp. 55–142. Washington DC: Brookings Institution.

Fox, John C. 1997. *Is That Worker an Independent Contractor or Your Employee?* Washington, DC: National Employment Law Institute.

Frake, Charles O. 1981. "The Diagnosis of Disease among the Subanum of Mindanao." *American Anthropologist* 63: 113–32.

———. 1969. "The Ethnographic Study of Cognitive Systems." In *Cognitive Anthropology*, pp. 28–41. Ed. Stephen A. Tyler. New York: Holt.

Freidson, Eliot. 1973. "Professions and the Occupational Principle." In *Professions and Their Prospects*, pp. 19–37. Ed. Eliot Freidson. Beverly Hills, CA: Sage.

Galbraith, Jay R. 1971. "Matrix Organization Design." *Business Horizons*, February: 29–40.

Galinsky, E., and J. T. Bond. 1998. *The 1998 Business Work-Life Study: A Sourcebook*. New York: Families and Work Institute.

Galinsky, E., J. T. Bond, and D. E. Friedman. 1993. *National Study of the Changing Workforce*. New York: Families and Work Institute.

Geertz, Clifford. 1978. "The Bazaar Economy: Information and Search in Peasant Marketing." *American Economic Review* 68: 28–32.

———. 1963. *Peddlers and Princes: Social Change and Modernization in Two Indonesian Towns*. Chicago: University of Chicago Press.

Gersick, Connie J. 1989. "Marking Time: Predictable Transitions in Task Groups." *Academy of Management Journal* 32: 274–309.

———. 1988. "Time and Transition in Work Teams: Toward a New Model of Group Development." *Academy of Management Journal* 31: 9–41.

Gilpin, Kenneth N. 2003. "Temporary Workers: A Barometer of Recovery." *New York Times*. http://NYTimes.com (accessed September 2, 2003).

Gimpel, Jean. 1980. *The Cathedral Builders*. New York: Harper and Row.

Goffman, Erving. 1983. "The Interaction Order." *American Sociological Review* 48: 1–17.

———. 1967. *Interaction Ritual: Essays on Face-to-Face Behavior*. Garden City, NY: Doubleday.

———. 1961. *Encounters*. Indianapolis, IN: Bobbs-Merrill.

———. 1959. *The Presentation of Self in Everyday Life*. Garden City, NY: Doubleday.

Gold, Michael. 1998. *An Introduction to Labor Law*. Ithaca, NY: ILR Press.

Goldberg, Albert I. 1976. "The Relevance of Cosmopolitan/Local Orientations to Professional Values and Behavior." *Sociology of Work and Occupations* 3: 331–54.

Golden, Laura. 2001. "Flexible Work Schedules: Which Workers Get Them?" *American Behavioral Scientist* 44: 1157–78.

Goldner, Fred H., and Richard R. Ritti. 1967. "Professionalization as Career Immobility." *American Journal of Sociology* 72: 489–501.

Gouldner, Alvin W. 1957–1958. "Cosmopolitans and Locals: Toward an Analysis of Latent Social Roles—II." *Administrative Science Quarterly* 2: 444–77.

Granovetter, Mark S. 1985. "Economic Action and Social Structure: The Problem of Embeddedness." *American Journal of Sociology* 91: 481–510.

———. 1974. *Getting a Job: A Study of Contacts and Careers*. Cambridge: Harvard University Press.

———. 1973. "The Strength of Weak Ties." *American Journal of Sociology* 78: 1360–79.

Granovetter, Mark S., and Richard Swedberg, eds. 2001. *The Sociology of Economic Life*. Boulder, CO: Westview Press.

Greenwald, Joel. 1998. "Employers Warming Up to Flexible Schedules." *Business Insurance* 32: 3–6.

Hakim, C. 1990. "Core and Periphery in Employers' Workforce Strategies: Evidence from the 1987 ELUS Survey." *Work, Employment, and Society* 4: 157–88.

Handy, Charles. 1989. *The Age of Unreason*. Cambridge: Harvard University Press.

Hannan, Michael T., and John H. Freeman. 1988. *Organizational Ecology*. Cambridge: Harvard University Press.

Harrison, Bennett, and Mary E. Kelley. 2001. "Occupational Employment Projections to 2010." *Monthly Labor Review* 124: 57–84.

———. 1993. "Outsourcing and the Search for 'Flexibility'." *Work, Employment, and Society* 7: 213–35.

Heckscher, Charles. 1995. *White-Collar Blues*. New York: Basic Books.

Henson, Kevin D. 1996. *Just a Temp*. Philadelphia, PA: Temple University Press.

Hickson, David J., C. R. Hinings, C. A. Lee, R. E. Schneck, and J. M. Pennings. 1971. "A Strategic Contingencies Theory of Interorganizational Power." *Administrative Science Quarterly* 16: 216–29.

Hinings, C. R., David J. Hickson, J. M. Pennings, and R. E. Schneck. 1974. "Structural Conditions of Intraorganizational Power." *Administrative Science Quarterly* 19: 22–44.

Hipple, Steven F. 2001. "Contingent Work in the Late 1990s." *Monthly Labor Review* 124: 3–27.

Hipple, Steven F., and Jay Stewart. 1996. "Earnings and Benefits of Workers in Alternative Work Arrangements." *Monthly Labor Review* 119: 46–54.

Hochschild, Arlie R. 1997. *The Time Bind: When Work Becomes Home and Home Becomes Work*. New York: Metropolitan Books.

———. 1989. *The Second Shift*. New York: Avon.

———. 1983. *The Managed Heart*. Berkeley: University of California Press.

Houseman, Susan N. 1997. "Temporary, Part-Time, and Contract Employment in the United States: A Report on the W. E. Upjohn Institute's Employer Survey on Flexible Staffing Policies." Research report, W. E. Upjohn Institute for Employment Research, Kalamazoo, MI.

Houseman, Susan N., and Anne E. Polivka. 1999. "The Implications of Flexible Staffing Arrangements for Job Stability." Working paper 99-056, W. E. Upjohn Institute for Employment Research, Kalamazoo, MI.

Hughes, Everett C. 1958. *Men and Their Work*. Glencoe, IL: Free Press.

Jacobs, Jerry A. 1998. "Measuring Time at Work: Are Self-Reports Accurate?" *Monthly Labor Review* 121: 42–53.

Jauch, Lawrence R., William G. Glueck, and Richard N. Osborn. 1978. "Organizational Loyalty, Professional Commitment, and Academic Research Productivity." *Academy of Management Journal* 21: 84–92.

Jenero, Kenneth A., and Mark A. Spognardi. 1995. "Temporary Employment Relationships: Review of the Joint Employer Doctrine under the NLRA." *Employee Relations* 21: 127–38.

Johnson, T. J. 1972. *Professions and Power.* London: Macmillan.

Jurik, Nancy J. 1998. "Getting Away and Getting By: The Experiences of Self-Employed Homeworkers." *Work and Occupations* 25: 7–35.

Kalleberg, Arne L., David Knoke, Peter V. Marsden, and Joel L. Spaeth. 1996. *Organizations in America: Analyzing Their Structures and Human Resource Practices.* Thousand Oaks, CA: Sage.

Kalleberg, Arne L., Edith Rasell, Ken Hudson, David Webster, Barbara F. Reskin, Cassirer Naoi, and Eileen Appelbaum. 1997. *Nonstandard Work, Substandard Jobs: Flexible Work Arrangements in the U.S.* Washington, DC: Economic Policy Institute.

Kalleberg, Arne L., Barbara F. Reskin, and Ken Hudson. 2000. "Bad Jobs in America: Standard and Nonstandard Employment Relations and Job Quality in the United States." *American Sociological Review* 65: 256–79.

Kalleberg, Arne L., and Jeremy Reynolds. 1988. "Externalizing Employment: Flexible Staffing Arrangements in U.S. Organizations." Paper presented at the Society for the Advancement of Socioeconomics, Vienna, Austria, July.

Kalleberg, Arne L., and Kathryn Schmidt. 1996. "Contingent Employment in Organizations." In *Organizations in America: Analyzing Their Structures and Human Resource Practices,* pp. 253–75. Ed. Arne L. Kalleberg, David Knoke, Peter V. Marsden, and Joel L. Spaeth. Thousand Oaks, CA: Sage.

Katz, Ralph, and Thomas J. Allen. 1985. "Project Performance and the Locus of Influence in the R&D Matrix." *Academy of Management Journal* 1: 67–87.

Katz, Ralph, and Michael L. Tushman. 1981. "An Investigation into the Managerial Roles and Career Paths of Gatekeepers and Project Supervisors in a Major R&D Facility." *R&D Management* 11: 103–10.

Kelly, Matt. January 2003. "The Talent Economy." http://Talenteconomymag.com (accessed September 2, 2003).

Kidder, Tracy. 1981. *Soul of a New Machine.* Boston: Little, Brown.

Knoop, Douglas, and G. P. Jones. 1967. *The Medieval Mason: An Economic History of English Stone Building in the Later Middle Ages and Modern Times.* New York: Barnes and Noble.

Kochan, Thomas A., Harry C. Katz, and Robert B. McKersie. 1986. *The Transformation of American Industrial Relations.* New York: Basic Books.

Kornhauser, William. 1962. *Scientists in Industry: Conflict and Accommodation.* Berkeley: University of California Press.

Kronus, Carol L. 1976. "Occupational versus Organizational Influences on Reference Group Identification." *Sociology of Work and Occupations* 3: 303–30.

Kunda, Gideon. 1992. *Engineering Culture: Control and Commitment in a High Tech Corporation.* Philadelphia, PA: Temple University Press.

Kunda, G., and J. Van Maanen. 1999. "Changing Scripts at Work: Managers and Professionals." *Annals of the American Academy of Political and Social Sciences,* 561: 64–80.

Larson, Magali S. 1977. *The Rise of Professionalism: A Sociological Analysis.* Berkeley: University of California Press.

Lave, Jean, and Etienne Wenger. 1990. *Situated Learning: Legitimate Peripheral Participation.* New York: Cambridge University Press.

Layton, Edwin. 1971. *The Revolt of the Engineers: Social Responsibility and the*

American Engineering Profession. Baltimore, MD: Johns Hopkins University Press.

Mangum, Garth, Donald Mayall, and Kristin Nelson. 1985. "The Temporary Help Industry: A Response to the Dual Internal Labor Market." *Industrial and Labor Relations Review* 88: 599–611.

Martella, Maureen. 1991. *Just a Temp: Expectations and Experiences of Women Clerical Temporary Workers.* Washington, DC: U.S. Department of Labor, Women's Bureau.

Matusik, Sharon F., and Charles W. L. Hill. 1998. "The Utilization of Contingent Work: Knowledge Creation and Competitive Advantage." *Academy of Management Review* 23: 680–97.

McAllister, Jean. 1998. "Sisyphus at Work in the Warehouse: Temporary Employment in Greenville, South Carolina." In *Contingent Work: American Employment in Transition,* pp. 221–42. Ed. Kathleen Barker and Kathleen Christensen. Ithaca, NY: ILR Press.

McGovern, Marion, and Dennis Russell. 2001. *The New Brand of Expertise: How Independent Contractors, Free Agents, and Interim Managers Are Transforming the World of Work.* Woburn, MA: Butterworth-Heinemann.

McShulskis, E. 1997. "Work and Family Benefits Increasingly Popular?" *HR Magazine* 42: 26–29.

Mead, Rebecca J., Shannon McConville, Paula Harmer, Michael Lubin, Andrea Tinsley, Julie Chang, and June McMahon. 2000. *The Struggle to Juggle Work and Family.* Los Angeles: Center for Labor Research and Education, School of Public Policy and Social Research, UCLA.

Mehra, Ajay, Martin Kilduff, and Daniel J. Brass. 2001. "The Social Networks of High and Low Self-Monitors: Implications for Workplace Performance." *Administrative Science Quarterly* 46: 121–46.

Meiksins, Peter F., and Chris Smith. 1993. "Organizing Engineering Work: A Comparative Analysis." *Work and Occupations* 29: 123–46.

Merton, Robert K. 1957. *Social Theory and Social Structure.* New York: Free Press.

Messinger, Sheldon L., Harold S. Sampson, and Robert D. Towne. 1962. "Life as Theater: Some Notes on the Dramaturgic Approach to Social Reality." *Sociometry* 25: 98–110.

Miller, G. A. 1967. "Professionals in Bureaucracy." *American Sociological Review* 32: 755–68.

Moore, Thomas S. 1996. *The Disposable Work Force.* New York: Aldine.

Muhl, Charles J. 2002. "What Is an Employee? The Answer Depends on the Federal Law." *Monthly Labor Review* 125: 3–11.

Nardi, Bonnie A., Steve Whittaker, and Heinrich Schwarz. 1999. "A Networker's Work Is Never Done: Joint Work in Intentional Networks." AT&T Labs, Menlo Park, CA.

National Research Council. 1999. *The Changing Nature of Work: Implications for Occupational Analysis.* Washington: DC: National Academy Press.

New York Times. 1996. *Special Report: The Downsizing of America.* New York: Times Books.

Newman, Katherine. 1989. *Falling from Grace: The Experience of Downward Mobility in the American Middle Class.* New York: Vintage.

Nollen, Stanley D., and Helen Axel. 1998. "Benefits and Costs to Employers." In *Contingent Work: American Employment in Transition*, pp. 126–43. Ed. Kathleen Barker and Kathleen Christensen. Ithaca, NY: ILR Press.

O'Mahony, Siobhan, and Stephen R. Barley. 1999. "Do Digital Telecommunications Affect Work and Organization? The State of Our Knowledge." In *Research in Organization Behavior*, vol. 21, pp. 125–62. Ed. Barry Staw and Robert Sutton. Greenwich, CT: JAI Press.

Orr, Julian E. 1997. *Talking about Machines: An Ethnography of a Modern Job*. Ithaca, NY: ILR Press.

Osterman, Paul. 1999. *Securing Prosperity: The American Labor Market: How It Has Changed and What to Do About It*. Princeton, NJ: Princeton University Press.

———. 1996. *Broken Ladders: Managerial Careers in the New Economy*. New York: Oxford University Press.

———. 1995. "Work/Family Programs and the Employment Relationship." *Administrative Science Quarterly* 40: 681–700.

———. 1988. *Employment Futures: Reorganization, Dislocation, and Public Policy*. New York: Oxford University Press.

———. 1984. *Internal Labor Markets*. Cambridge: MIT Press.

Osterman, Paul, Thomas A. Kochan, Richard M. Locke, and Michael J. Piore. 2001. *Working in America: Blueprint for the New Labor Market*. Cambridge: MIT Press.

Padgett, John F. 2001. "Organizational Genesis, Identity, and Control: The Transformation of Banking in Renaissance Florence." In *Markets and Networks*. Ed. Alessandra Cassella and Rauch James. New York: Russell Sage Foundation.

Padgett, John F., and Christopher K. Ansell. 1993. "Robust Action and the Rise of the Medici: 1400–1434." *American Journal of Sociology* 98: 1259–1319.

Padgett, John F., and Paul McLean. 2002. "Economic and Social Exchange in Renaissance Florence." Santa Fe Institute working paper 02-07-032.

———. Forthcoming. "Obligation, Risk, and Opportunity in the Renaissance Economy." In *The U.S. Economy in Historical Context*. Ed. Frank Dobbin. New York: Russell Sage Foundation.

Parker, Robert E. 1994. *Flesh Peddlers and Warm Bodies: The Temporary Help Industry and Its Workers*. New Brunswick, NJ: Rutgers University Press.

Pearce, J. L. 1993. Toward an Organizational Behavior of Contract Laborers: Their Psychological Involvement and Effects on Employee Co-workers. *Academy of Management Journal* 36: 1082–96.

Pelz, Donald C., and Frank M. Andrews. 1966. *Scientists in Organizations: Productive Climates for Research and Development*. New York: Wiley.

Perlow, Leslie. 1997. *Finding Time*. Ithaca, NY: ILR Press.

Perrin, Constance. 1991. "The Moral Fabric of the Office: Panopticon Discourse and Schedule Flexibilities." In *Research in the Sociology of Organizations*, pp. 241–68. Ed. Pamela Tolbert and Stephen R. Barley. Greenwich, CT: JAI Press.

Perrucci, Robert. 1971. "Engineering: Professional Servant of Power." *American Behavioral Scientist* 14: 492–505.

Perrucci, Robert, and Joel E. Gerstl. 1969a. *Engineers and the Social System*. New York: Wiley.

———. 1969b. *Profession without Community*. New York: Random House.

Pfeffer, Jeffrey, and James N. Baron. 1988. "Taking the Workers Back Out: Recent Trends in the Structuring of Employment." In *Research in Organizational Behavior*, vol. 10, pp. 257–303. Ed. Barry Staw and Lawrence Cummings. Greenwich, CT: JAI Press.

Pfeffer, Jeffrey, and Gerald R. Salancik. 1978. *The External Control of Organizations: A Resource Dependence Perspective*. New York: Harper and Row.

Pink, Daniel H. 2001. *Free Agent Nation: How America's New Independent Workers Are Transforming the Way We Live*. New York: Warner Business Books.

———. 1998. "Free Agent Nation." *Fast Company*, December/January: 131–47.

Pink, Daniel H., and Michael Warsaw. 1997. "The Free Agent Declaration of Independence." *Fast Company* 12: 182.

Piore, Michael J., and Charles F. Sabel. 1984. *The Second Industrial Divide: Possibilities for Prosperity*. New York: Basic Books.

Podolny, Joel M., and James N Baron. 1997. "Resources and Relationships: Social Networks and Mobility in the Workplace." *American Sociological Review* 62: 673–93.

Polivka, Anne E. 1996a. "Contingent and Alternative Work Arrangements Defined." *Monthly Labor Review* 119: 3–9.

———. 1996b. "A Profile of Contingent Workers." *Monthly Labor Review* 119: 10–21.

Powell, Walter W. 1990. "Neither Market nor Hierarchy: Network Forms of Organization." In *Research in Organizational Behavior*, vol. 12, pp. 295–335. Ed. Barry M. Staw and Larry L. Cummings. Greenwich, CT: JAI Press.

Raelin, Joseph A. 1985. *The Clash of Cultures: Managers and Professionals*. Cambridge: Harvard University Press.

Reinhold, Barbara B. 2001. *Free to Succeed: Designing the Life You Want in the Free Agent Economy*. New York: Plume.

Rifkin, Jeremy. 1995. *The End of Work*. New York: Putnam.

Ritti, Richard. R. 1971. *The Engineer in the Industrial Corporation*. New York: Columbia University Press.

Ritzer, George. 1998. *The McDonaldization of Society: An Investigation into the Changing Character of Contemporary Social Life*. Thousand Oaks, CA: Pine Forge Press.

Robinson, John P., and Geoffrey Godbey. 1997. *Time for Life: The Surprising Ways Americans Use Their Time*. University Park: Pennsylvania State University Press.

Roediger, David R. 1989. *Our Own Time: A History of American Labour and the Working Day*. New York: Greenwood.

Rogers, Jackie K. 1995. "Just a Temp: Experience and Structure of Alienation in Temporary Clerical Employment." *Work and Occupation* 22: 137–66.

———. 2000. *Temps: The Many Faces of the Changing Workplace*. Ithaca, NY: Cornell University Press.

Rones, Philip L., Randy E. Ilg, and Jennifer M. Gardner. 1997. "Trends in Hours of Work Since the Mid-1970s." *Monthly Labor Review* 120: 3–14.

Rousseau, Denise. 1995. *Psychological Contracts in Organizations*. Thousand Oaks, CA: Sage.

Rousseau, Denise, and R. J. Anton. 1991. "Fairness and Obligations in Termination Decisions: The Role of Contributions, Promises, and Performance." *Journal of Organizational Behavior* 12: 287–99.

Rubin, B. 1996. *Shifts in the Social Contract: Understanding Change in American Society.* Thousand Oaks, CA: Pine Forge Press.

Rynes, Sara L., Pamela S. Tolbert, and Pamela G. Strausser. 1988. "Aspirations to Manage: A Comparison of Engineering Students and Working Engineers." *Journal of Vocational Behavior* 32: 239–53.

Saxenian, Annalee. 1994. *Regional Advantage: Culture and Competition in Silicon Valley and Route 128.* Cambridge: Harvard University Press.

Saxenian, Annalee, and Jinn-Yuh Hsu. 2000. "The Silicon Valley-Hsinchu Connection: Technical Communities and Industrial Upgrading." Unpublished paper, Department of Urban Planning, University of California, Berkeley.

Saxenian, Annalee, and Wendy Li. Forthcoming. "Bay-to-Bay Strategic Alliances: Network Linkages between Taiwan and U.S. Venture Capital Industries." *International Journal of Technology Management.*

Schor, Juliet B. 1991. *The Overworked American: The Unexpected Decline of Leisure.* New York: Basic Books.

Schwarz, Heinrich, Bonnie A. Nardi, and Steve Whittaker. 1999. "The Hidden Work in Virtual Work." AT&T Labs, Menlo Park, CA.

Scott, W. R. 1965. "Reactions to Supervision in a Heteronomous Professional Organization." *Administrative Science Quarterly* 10: 65–81.

Simmel, Georg. 1922. *Conflict and the Web of Group Affiliations.* New York: Free Press.

Smelser, Neil J., and Richard Swedberg, eds. 1994a. *The Handbook of Economic Sociology.* Princeton, NJ: Princeton University Press.

———. 1994b. "The Sociological Perspective on the Economy." In *The Handbook of Economic Sociology,* pp. 3–26. Ed. Neil J. Smelser and Richard Swedberg. Princeton, NJ: Princeton University Press.

Smith, Vicki. 2001. *Crossing the Great Divide: Worker Risk and Opportunity in the New Economy.* Ithaca, NY: Cornell University Press.

———. 1998. "The Fractured World of the Temporary Worker: Power, Participation, and Fragmentation in the Contemporary Workplace." *Social Problems* 45: 1–20.

Spalter-Roth, Roberta, and Heidi I. Hartmann. 1998. "Gauging the Consequences for Gender Relations, Pay Equity, and the Public Purse." In *Contingent Work: American Employment in Transition,* pp. 69–102. Ed. Kathleen Barker and Kathleen Christensen. Ithaca, NY: ILR Press.

Spalter-Roth, Roberta M., Arne L. Kalleberg, Edith Rasell, Naomi Cassirer, Barbara F. Reskin, Ken Hudson, David Webster, Eileen Appelbaum, and Betty F. Dooley. 1997. *Managing Work and Family: Nonstandard Work Arrangements among Managers and Professionals.* Washington, DC: Economic Policy Institute.

Spradley, James P. 1979. *The Ethnographic Interview.* New York: Holt, Rinehart, and Winston.

Staffing Industry Report. 1997. *Staffing Industry Report* (Los Altos, CA), 8, p. 6.

Swedberg, Richard. 1994. "Markets as Social Structures." In *The Handbook of*

Economic Sociology, pp. 255–82. Ed. Neil J. Smelser and Richard Swedberg. Princeton, NJ: Princeton University Press.

Szafran, Robert F. 1996. "The Effect of Occupational Growth on Labor Force Task Characteristics." *Work and Occupations* 23: 54–86.

Thompson, E. P. 1967. "Time, Work Discipline, and Industrial Capitalism." *Past and Present* 38: 56–97.

Thurm, Scott. 2003. "Techie-for-Hire's Struggles Illustrate Free Agents' Plight." *New York Times*, April 23, p. A1.

Turner, Victor. 1982. *From Ritual to Theater: The Human Seriousness of Play*. New York: PAJ Publications.

U.S. Department of Commerce, Bureau of the Census. 1997. *Statistical Abstract of the United States: 1996*. Washington, DC: U.S. Government Printing Office.

U.S. Department of Transportation. 1993. *Transportation Implications of Telecommuting*. Washington, DC: U.S. Government Printing Office.

Van Gennep, A. 1960. *Rites of Passage*. Chicago: University of Chicago Press.

Van Maanen, John, and Stephen R. Barley. 1984. "Occupational Communities: Culture and Control in Organizations." In *Research in Organizational Behavior*, vol. 6, pp. 287–365. Ed. Barry M. Staw and Larry L. Cummings. Greenwich, CT: JAI Press.

Von Glinow, Mary A. 1988. *The New Professionals: Managing Today's High Tech Employees*. Cambridge, MA: Ballinger.

Von Hippel, Eric. 1994. "'Sticky Information' and the Locus of Problem Solving: Implications for Innovation." *Management Science* 40: 429–39.

———. 1989. "New Product Ideas from Lead Users." *Research Management* 32: 24–27.

———. 1978. "Successful Industrial Products from Customer Ideas." *Journal of Marketing*: 39–49.

Wasserman, Stanley, and Katherine Faust. 1994. *Social Network Analysis: Methods and Applications*. Cambridge: Cambridge University Press.

Weber, Max. 1968/1922. *Economy and Society*. Berkeley: University of California Press.

Wenger, Etienne. 1998. *Communities of Practice: Learning, Meaning, and Identity*. Cambridge: Cambridge University Press.

Whalley, Peter. 1986. *The Social Production of Technical Work*. Albany, NY: State University of New York Press.

Williamson, Oliver E. 1975. *Markets and Hierarchies: Analysis and Antitrust Implications*. New York: Free Press.

Wilshire, Bruce. 1982. "The Dramaturgical Model of Behavior: Its Strengths and Weaknesses." *Symbolic Interaction* 5: 287–98.

Womack, James P., Daniel T. Jones, and Daniel Roos. 1990. *The Machine That Changed the World: The Story of Lean Production*. Cambridge: MIT.

Zeigler, James R. 2001. *The Contract Employee's Handbook*. Pleasant Hill, CA: Professional Association of Contract Employees.

Zussman, Robert. 1985. *Mechanics of the Middle Class*. Berkeley: University of California Press.

Appendix

CAST OF CHARACTERS

Contractors

Name	Age	Years Worked	Years Contracting	Gender	Married	Occupation
Arthur, Glenn	37	14	10	M	Y	Software developer
Bayliss, Tom	mid-30s	14	10	M	Y	IT specialist
Bish, William	62	44	19	M	Y	Aerospace engineer
Cartier, Deborah	33	10	2	F	N	Software developer
Chenalt, Vicky	NA	NA	NA	F	NA	Technical writer
Cousteau, Les	35	9	1	M	Y	Machine tool programmer
Cox, Kent	36	13	8	M	N	Software developer
Crum, Olivia	48	24	8	F	Y	Software developer
Davis, Stu	45	22	8	M	Y	Embedded systems engineer
Diaz, Carmella	30s	9	7	F	Y	Multimedia developer
Dolan, Teresa	early 40s	18	12	F	Y	Software developer
Dorsey, Jeff	27	8	4	M	N	Quality assurance/ Web design
Eaton, Charles	46	25	5	M	N	Software developer
Elliot, Eugene	NA	NA	NA	M	NA	Software developer
Fitzgerald, Mary Jo	30	5	2	F	N	IT specialist
Galvez, Hernando	mid-40s	22	17	M	Y	Software developer
Garley, Roger	NA	NA	NA	NA	NA	Software developer
Goshal, Ashish	36	9	5	M	Y	Database designer
Gregory, Ray	mid-40s	28	5	M	N	Multimedia developer
Gupta, Sushil	37	12	4	M	Y	Software developer
Harden, Felix	NA	NA	NA	NA	NA	Software developer
Hawkins, Peter	25	3	3	M	N	Systems administrator
Hill, Doug	50s	32	21	M	Y	Database designer
Hinton, Paul	NA	NA	NA	NA	NA	Software developer
Howard, Bob	24	2	1	M	N	Systems administrator
Jacobs, Kathy	34	13	6	F	N	Software developer
Jay, Herman	68	25	13	M	Y	Quality assurance
Juarez, Jose	58	25	5	M	NA	Systems administrator
Kapoor, Anna	28	4	4	F	NA	Software developer
Keely, Marty	37	NA	5	M	Y	Software developer
King, Judy	46	23	7	F	NA	Software developer
Knight, Donald	51	24	2	M	Y	Chip designer
Kumar, Nitin	38	15	13	M	Y	Software developer
Kumar, Sumantra	38	12	1	M	Y	Software developer
Labovski, Katrina	28	6	1	F	NA	Technical writer
Laube, Christopher	NA	NA	NA	NA	NA	IT specialist
Louthan, Steve	45	22	7	M	Y	Technical writer
Martinez, Jose	50s	15	8	M	N	Technical writer

Contractors (*Continued*)

Name	Age	Years Worked	Years Contracting	Gender	Married	Occupation
May, James	35	10	3	M	Y	Systems administrator
Mayall, George	NA	NA	NA	NA	NA	Software developer
Morris, Jerry	23	2	2	M	N	Systems administrator
Muller, Sam	62	28	8	M	Y	Technical writer
Negley, John	46	20	7	M	Y	Systems administrator
Nugen, Peyton	33	12	5	M	N	IT specialist
O'Boyle, Brenda	56	26	12	F	Y	Quality assurance
Over, Charles	NA	NA	NA	M	NA	Software developer
Perry, Mary	32	10	1	F	N	Technical writer
Post, Victor	36	10	8	M	Y	Database designer
Pusher, Brian	26	3	1	M	N	Software developer
Rao, Anil	38	15	8	M	Y	Mechanical design engineer
Revell, Kip	NA	NA	NA	M	NA	Software developer
Rhodes, Kurt	40	18	1	M	Y	Software developer
Ritter, Paula	53	22	19	F	N	Technical writer
Roberts, David	NA	NA	NA	NA	NA	Software developer
Rodriguez, Tony	mid-40s	24	16	M	Y	Project manager
Ross, David	26	4	2	M	N	Systems administrator
Rudolph, Mike	48	19	6	M	Y	IT specialist
Sanchez, Maria	late 30s	16	4	F	N	Marketing consultant
Smith, Bill	late 40s	25	4	M	Y	Verification engineer
Stevens, Richard	40	17	7	M	Y	Software developer
Stoke, Julian	50	23	10	M	Y	Software developer
Strother, John	50	26	1	M	Y	Chip designer
Swartz, Tony	NA	NA	NA	M	NA	Project manager
Turner, Yolanda	52	22	6	F	N	IT specialist
Tyler, Fred	60	34	12	M	Y	Software developer
Watts, Jane	30s	4	4	F	Y	Quality assurance
Weiss, Asaf	42	23	9	M	Y	Quality assurance
Willingham, Brian	mid-50s	24	10	M	N	Software developer
Wise, Bruce	51	29	2	M	Y	Network engineer
Zuckerman, Erik	53	30	7	M	N	IT specialist

Note: NA indicates missing data.

Managers and Permanent Employees

Name	Role	Firm
Bouchet, Randy	Manager	Raster
Boyd, Neva	Manager	Chipco
Brown, Russell	Manager	UNIX Systems
Cato, Nancy	Manager	Advanced Computers
Chen, Susan	HR manager	Logicunits
Cummings, Micky	VP research	Webworm

Managers and Permanent Employees (*Continued*)

Name	Role	Firm
Daner, Shirley	CIO	Chipco
Ellison, Edward	Manager	Savant
Fisher, Rodney	Manager	Chipco
Greener, Anthony	Manager	Codetech
Hambly, James	Manager	Advanced Computers
Hume, Terry	Manager	Advanced Computers
Hynes, Sally	Manager	Chipco
Kirkman, Monty	Manager	Chipco
Larson, Tony	Manager	Groove Technology
Lawyer, Donna	Manager	Chipco
Litkin, Joseph	CEO	Vision Software
Maxwell, Shane	Employee	Chipco
Miller, Helena	Employee	Advanced Computers
Munzer, Sara	Employee	Chipco
Murphy, Aron	Manager	UNIX Systems
Natzel, Fernando	Employee	UNIX Systems
Schmidt, Matt	Manager	Videonet
Smith, Neal	Manager	Vision Software
Swetka, Noah	Manager	Western Phone Company
Yamamato, Toshi	Employee	Advanced Computers

Agency Personnel

Name	Role	Agency
Ahl, Scott	Recruiter	Progressive Staffing
Atkins, Louis	Recruiter	Progressive Staffing
Bach, Lea	Recruiter	Progressive Staffing
Bailey, Erin	Trainer	Progressive Staffing
Brickert, Connie	Recruiter	Progressive Staffing
Cline, Linda	Recruiter	Information Technology Specialists
Close, Benjamin	Recruiter	Information Technology Specialists
Cochran, Julie	Recruiter	Progressive Staffing
Davey, Wayne	Recruiter	Progressive Staffing
Devlin, Karen	Account manager	Progressive Staffing
Fitler, Carol	Recruiter	Progressive Staffing
Head, Orrin	Account manager	Progressive Staffing
Heathcote, John	Account manager	Progressive Staffing
Hill, Miranda	Account manager	Progressive Staffing
Josling, Kevin	Recruiter	Progressive Staffing
Judd, Diana	Trainer	Progressive Staffing
Larsen, Charles	Account manager	Information Technology Specialists

Agency Personnel (*Continued*)

Name	Role	Agency
Lucha, Cynthia	Recruiter	Progressive Staffing
McGuirk, Rebecca	Recruiter	Progressive Staffing
Pacek, Barbara	Account manager	Progressive Staffing
Papper, Lynn	Marketing	Information Technology Specialists
Parish, Anne	CEO	Progressive Staffing
Racine, Maria	VP	Progressive Staffing
Robinson, Leo	VP	Progressive Staffing
Schaff, Nathan	VP	Progressive Staffing
Sunberg, Marc	CEO	Information Technology Specialists
Troxell, Mary	Account manager	Progressive Staffing
Van Leer, Paul	President	Systems Professionals
Wegman, Andrew	Account manager	Progressive Staffing

INDEX